C000132556

OCR
Religious Studies
for AS

Peter Cole
Richard Gray
Consultant: Michael Wilcockson

HODDER
EDUCATION
AN HACHETTE UK COMPANY

Dedication

For Nicola, Jack, Ethan, Elizabeth and Anna Gray

Acknowledgements

There are many people we have to thank. First of all, we are indebted to the very patient, encouraging and inspiring Rob Bircher who has managed us through some very busy periods and tight deadlines. Thanks go to Garth Ratcliffe, who has spent many a long evening correcting and suggesting improvements to the text. Thanks to Paul and Katie Cobb for their positive responses to early ideas and proofs of the text in the sections on Buddhism. Thanks to our colleagues at work and also special thanks to our consultant, Michael Wilcockson from OCR, for his sharp insight and honest comments on many drafts. Finally, the roles of Margaret Gray and June Rowley in supporting the Gray family throughout the whole project can never be overestimated – your love and support has been immense!

The Publishers would like to thank the following for permission to reproduce copyright material:
Photo credits:
p.18 Heritage Image Partnership; **p.20** *t* Getty Images, *b* Getty Images; **p.52** Aquarius Collection; **p.71** *tl* Corbis, *tr* Corbis, *bl* R C James, *br* SPL/Fred Espenak; **p.93** PA Photos; **p.96** both Heritage Image Partnership; **p.102** SPL/CERN; **p.104** Corbis; **p.126** Richard Gray; **p.131** Corbis; **p.135** SPL/K Seddon & T Evans; **p.139** both Corbis; **p.171** Getty Images; **p.199** Corbis; **p.202** SPL/MASA; **p.213** Alamy/Look Die Bildagentur der Fotografen; **p.214** Corbis; **p.240** Ian Britton; **p.241** Corbis; **p.245** Alamy/Rough Guides; **p.247** Alamy/Jon Arnold Images; **p.257** Getty Images; **p.276** Corbis; **p.279** Corbis; **p.285** Richard Gray; **p.297** Corbis; **p.300** Heritage Image Partnership; **p.306** Heritage Image Partnership; **p.320** Heritage Image Partnership; **p.326** Heritage Image Partnership; **p.327** Alamy/James; **p.345** Corbis; **p.347** Corbis; **p.352** Corbis; **p.356** Circa Photo Library

b = bottom,   *c* = centre,   *l* = left,   *r* = right,   *t* = top

Every effort has been made to trace all copyright holders, but if any have been inadvertently overlooked the Publishers will be pleased to make the necessary arrangements at the first opportunity.

Although every effort has been made to ensure that website addresses are correct at time of going to press, Hodder Education cannot be held responsible for the content of any website mentioned in this book. It is sometimes possible to find a relocated web page by typing in the address of the home page for a website in the URL window of your browser.

Hachette Livre UK's policy is to use papers that are natural, renewable and recyclable products and made from wood grown in sustainable forests. The logging and manufacturing processes are expected to conform to the environmental regulations of the country of origin.

Orders: please contact Bookpoint Ltd, 130 Milton Park, Abingdon, Oxon OX14 4SB.
Telephone: (44) 01235 827720. Fax: (44) 01235 400454. Lines are open 9.00–5.00, Monday to Saturday, with a 24-hour message answering service. Visit our website at www.hoddereducation.co.uk

© Peter Cole, Richard Gray 2008

First published in 2008 by
Hodder Education,
An Hachette Uk Company
338 Euston Road
London NW1 3BH

Impression number   5 4 3 2
Year   2012 2011 2010 2009

All rights reserved. Apart from any use permitted under UK copyright law, no part of this publication may be reproduced or transmitted in any form or by any means, electronic or mechanical, including photocopying and recording, or held within any information storage and retrieval system, without permission in writing from the publisher or under licence from the Copyright Licensing Agency Limited. Further details of such licences (for reprographic reproduction) may be obtained from the Copyright Licensing Agency Limited, Saffron House, 6–10 Kirby Street, London EC1N 8TS.

Cover photo © Design Pics/Imagestate
Illustrations by Ken Vail Graphic Design
Typeset in Bembo 11pt by Ken Vail Graphic Design, Cambridge www.kvgd.com
Index by Indexing Specialists (UK) Ltd
Printed in Italy

A catalogue record for this title is available from the British Library

ISBN: 978 0340 95781 3

CONTENTS

Introduction

The aim and approach of the book

- This is a book for teachers and students of religious studies (RS).
- It is a source book of information and is a key tool for completing the AS course.
- The approach is skills-based and focuses on how to develop the key areas of expertise outlined by the OCR specification.
- The content covers the core nature of the AS-level course, including the specification details, the assessment objectives, the levels of attainment and how each of these interacts with the others.
- This book is a complete AS-level package.

In addition, it has been written with two specific aims in mind.

- The course content required by the specification is sharply focused and delivers all the essential facts and relevant material without compromising on quality.

- The focus is always on using the book to develop the examination skills required for success and to encourage an 'assessment for learning' approach.

In covering the most popular aspects of the OCR specification, the book offers a range of curriculum areas. Although only two key areas (units) are studied for examination purposes, this may appeal for the following reasons.

- Some schools may want to offer more than one combination of topics, for example, because they have several groups and more than one teacher.
- Diversity may be offered within a small group, creating more individualised study.
- It may give RS teachers the confidence to extend their specialism, given the nature of the comprehensive support offered by the book, for example, to deliver a topic they have not done before.
- In the light of a synoptic element at A2 ('… candidates are asked to show their understanding of the connections between their chosen areas of study and other specified aspects of human experience …') and the new QCA-driven emphasis on stretch and challenge, it may be advantageous to dip into related elements from other units for general synoptic work, or to provide distinct and discernible extension activities for students who are more able.
- It is interesting to compare the units and further consolidate skills.

How this book aids success at AS level

The difficulties at AS level

The basic problem with AS-level examinations is that many students do not apply what they know effectively. Students can be well instructed in the topics covered, but may not understand the precise demands of the skills specified in the assessment objectives. They have the *what* (the content) but not the *how* (application to a specific focus or question). For example, in the case of AO1 and 'select and demonstrate', the facts are often there in a student's answer but the way in which they are presented does not demonstrate clear knowledge and understanding.

This book uses the BCE and CE date system:

- BCE stands for Before the Common Era and is the equivalent of BC
- CE stands for the Common Era and is the equivalent of AD.

Examiners' reports always indicate that the problem is not *what* the students know but *how* they are answering the questions. Essentially, it is about students 'using and applying their knowledge' to demonstrate the necessary understanding through 'application and analysis of that knowledge'.

This is even more likely to be the case with AO2. There are currently very few books offering organised AO2 material. The ideas of 'problems with …' or 'criticisms of …' are sometimes presented either as questions throughout a text or as a section at the end. Thus, what might require an AO2 response is reduced to an AO1 list of views rather than requiring a questioning approach, demonstrating a process of reasoning. The unfortunate result is that responses do not always reflect students' actual knowledge and understanding.

The problems become self-perpetuating because many resources have been purely content-based. This means there is a risk that students who depend on such resources will be trained and encouraged to reiterate the facts, with little appreciation of the context or application of the assessment objectives.

More recently, text books have started to use tasks or suggestions for work. However, it is still often left to the individual teacher to bridge the gap between knowledge and skills by designing a course that effectively rewrites the content and integrates a focus on skills. Even here, there is a risk of the assessment objectives being separated from the factual knowledge rather than being integral to the learning process. The assessment criteria should not be bolt-on, add-on or out of the blue tasks at the end; instead, they should be driving the learning throughout the course.

The solution: a skills-based approach

All teachers know that the solution is to focus on skills. The problem is how to achieve this in the classroom. How do teachers help students build up their knowledge base while simultaneously training them to develop the skills expected? This is not a new problem.

The approach of this book is to integrate skills with the content. It takes a holistic approach towards assessment objectives and content; it advocates learning the content, not in isolation but in relation to the skills and assessment objectives. To reiterate, this book is intended as a skills-based resource.

Questions at AS level are separated into AO1 and AO2 and this is supported within the book, with a clear AO2 section within every unit. This book is grounded firmly in *Assessment for Learning* (AfL) principles.

What is assessment for learning?

Assessment for learning involves:

- effective planning of teaching and learning
- focus on how students learn
- learner motivation
- emphasis on progress and achievement rather than failure
- a shared understanding of the criteria by which students are assessed.

> **❝ KEY QUOTE ❞**
>
> **Much of what teachers and learners do in classrooms can be described as assessment. That is, tasks and questions prompt learners to demonstrate their knowledge, understanding and skills. What learners say and do is then observed and interpreted, and judgements are made about how learning can be improved. These assessment processes are an essential part of everyday classroom practice and involve both teachers and learners in reflection, dialogue and decision-making.**
>
> **(Qualifications and Curriculum Alliance QCA)**

Effective assessment for learning occurs all the time in the classroom. This book, then, adopts this approach, using features that effectively promote and relate to AfL principles in the following ways.

QCA AfL principles	Related features in this book
sharing learning goals with students	• Reflection and assessment sections that serve to consolidate • AO clearly stated, together with levels of response (see end of this section) • Sharp focus on the precise materials to be selected and evaluated at the start of each section • Examination tips that focus on AOs • Outcomes for tasks related to AOs • Exemplar answers, materials clearly related to levels of response, descriptors
helping students know and recognise the standards to aim for	• Clear and regular reminders throughout the book • Levels of response and descriptors used to measure activities, for example, in planning answers and reviewing answers • Examination tips that remind students of specific skills in the AOs
providing feedback that helps students to identify how to improve	• Reflection and assessment activities to promote this • Use of the suggested template for effective feedback between teachers and students • Use of the template in self-assessment • Peer assessment activities and self-assessment
believing that every student can improve in comparison with previous achievements	• The reflection and assessment tasks are deliberately progressive and refined to see a clearly staged improvement and development in performance • Clear targets on written feedback grid
both the teacher and students reviewing and reflecting on students' performance and progress	• Clear reflection and assessment sections at the end of each part of the unit of study • Feedback grid that also encourages discussion (research demonstrates that oral feedback is most effective)
students learning self-assessment techniques to discover areas in which they need to improve	• Use of feedback grid • Activities that test gaps in learning and provide students with ownership of their work • Suggestions for further or independent tasks and further consolidation of learning
motivation and self-esteem, crucial for effective learning and progress, can be increased by effective assessment techniques	• Focus on celebrating achievement and recognising strengths to build upon • A constant and constructive emphasis on how to improve the quality of answers and meeting the high standards set by AS

Assessment for learning involves using assessment in the classroom to raise students' achievement. It is based on the idea that students will improve most if they understand the aim of their learning, where they are in relation to this aim and how they can achieve the aim (or close the gap in their knowledge).

(QCA)

How to use this book

Assessment for
learning develops
learners' capacity for
self-assessment so
that they can become
reflective and self-
managing.

(QCA)

The features

Students need to be informed and guided in order to plan their learning. They should
be given opportunities to:

- pinpoint their own strengths and be clear about how to develop through the levels
  of attainment
- be clear and constructive about their own weaknesses and how these might be
  addressed in relation to the levels of attainment
- improve their work through reflection, redrafting and dialogue with peers and
  teachers.

The features of this book directly relate to and indicate the skills developed in relation
to the assessment objectives and, more specifically, to the levels of attainment.

Icon	Feature	Skills developed
	Key words	AO1 selection of key terms, understanding correct terminology
" "	Key quotes	AO1 selection of appropriate and relevant material
	Key ideas	AO1 selection and presentation to demonstrate understanding
	Key people, profiles, dates	AO1 contextual information to support AO1 understanding
?	Key questions	AO2 encouraging dialogue, argument, questioning, debate
EXAM TIP	Exam tips	AO1 and AO2 specific focus on individual skills within these objectives, for example, selecting appropriate material and using evidence, correct terminology
TASK	Tasks	AO1 and AO2, interacting and engaging with the specification content, recognising a variety of learning styles to consolidate learning and to stretch and challenge
	Pictures with related tasks	Stimulus for further research, independent thinking to stretch and challenge and further contextualise AO1 material and AO2 issues
	Summary diagrams	To visualise learning and encourage the use of thought-process diagrams in summarising key points and questions as a basis for planning examination answers
	Reflection and assessment	A consolidation of specification content and a focused practice of both AO1 and AO2 skills incorporating specific examination-style tasks
	Suggestions for further activities incorporating AfL principles for improvement	A specific focus on activities that encourage the use of peer and self-assessment for the purpose of effective feedback

The division between AO1 and AO2

As highlighted earlier, in relation to AO2, each topic in the book has a separate section to exemplify the examination question. The inference is that, at AS level, AO2 is dealt with separately from AO1. However, it would be dangerous to think of it in isolation. It is clearly linked to aspects of the AO1, almost an extension of the 'learning from ...' aspect at KS3 and KS4.

The presentation of AO2 material in the book is in keeping with the examination format. A benefit of this approach is that it can assist with the critical analysis of topics. In many books this aspect is either not available or it is not organised sufficiently clearly for the student to recognise.

To see how this works in practice, consider each unit and topic area. Sometimes the two parts of AO1 may be linked in the evaluation as, for example, in Unit 4, *Buddhism*, Topic 1, Part 3. Alternatively, the AO2 may be focused on a preceding part, as with Unit 1, *The philosophy of religion*, Topic 4, Part 3. In the latter case, this is because the two AO1 parts are not linked; however, there is scope for further development of another part for AO2. Indeed, readers may want to go straight to the AO2 section that is relevant to the AO1 material.

Nonetheless, it is important that – right from the start of the course – students are made familiar with the format of an examination paper and the holistic nature of a question with its composite AO1 and AO2. A discussion of assessment weighting is also vital. Once again, the weighting at AS level is reflected by the book's format, AO2 being substantially less represented than AO1.

Feedback and dialogue

In terms of AfL, the dialogue that is deemed essential to enable students to make progress is called feedback by QCA. A strong feature of this book is the wealth of opportunities for students to practise the skills required for examination success. In this they are supported by feedback, analysis and comparison, targeting areas for development in relation to the AOs and levels of attainment. Such a process, however, needs to be effective and not simply mechanical.

Further, QCA indicates that the characteristics of effective feedback include these features.

- It confirms that students are on the right track – it is positive and constructive.
- It stimulates correction or improvement of a piece of work.
- It acts as scaffolding, providing students with support in using their knowledge.
- It offers regular and constructive comment on progress over a number of attempts.
- It is oral as well as written.
- It develops in students the skills to ask for help.

If this is achieved, then '... a culture of success is promoted in which every student can make achievements by building on their previous performance.'

The following ideas may help in using feedback.

- Peer assessment can be effective because students can clarify their own ideas while marking other students' work.
- Once students understand how to assess their current knowledge, and the gaps in it, they will have a clearer idea of how they can help themselves to progress.

> **KEY QUOTE**
> Research has shown that students will achieve more if they are fully engaged in their own learning process. This means that if students know what they need to learn and why, and then actively assess their understanding, gaps in their own knowledge and areas they need to work on, they will achieve more than if they sit passively in a classroom working through exercises with no real comprehension either of the learning intention of the exercise or of why it might be important.
>
> (QCA)

- Teachers and students can set targets relating to specific goals tailored to the level descriptors and assessment objectives. The students will then be empowered to guide their own learning, with the teacher providing support and guidance.
- Student analysis of work that both does and does not meet the assessment criteria can help them to understand what was required from a task and to determine the next steps they might need to take to improve the quality of that work.
- Looking at different styles of writing and answering questions can also help students understand the different approaches they could have taken to the task.

In using this approach to feedback it is useful to have some kind of support in the form of consistent procedure. The grid below is intended to provide this. When applying and using the following grid as scaffolding, students will need to:

- reflect on their own work
- be encouraged to admit problems without risk to self-esteem
- be given time to work problems out.

Feedback grid or scaffolding

Specification area – unit and part	Unit 4, *Buddhism*, Topic 1, Part 1, The historical, sociological, economic and religious background
Question	'Examine …' (AO1), 'Discuss …' (AO2) (See Part 1C.)
General comments on the answer – what was achieved	Teacher feedback
Strengths	Refer to general descriptors from levels of response
Level awarded and reasons (AO1) and/or (AO2)	Refer to specific aspects of the level descriptors
Areas for development – identifying any learning gaps in knowledge, understanding or evaluation	Refer to specific aspects of the level descriptors (usually taken from the levels above, or aspects of that same level awarded, that need development)
Target for improvement (agreed in discussion with teacher, peer or through self-reflection)	A focused and achievable target to enable improvement. Refer to the above areas of development and indicate three ways, with examples, in which this can be achieved
Overall mark out of 25 (AO1) and out of 10 (AO2) Estimated grade	

The structure of the book

This book is divided into units, each of which covers a complete AS unit from the OCR AS religious studies Specification, such as *The philosophy of religion* or *Buddhism*. You will be studying two units to make up your AS. Each unit in the book is sub-divided into topics that always follow a particular pattern; the final part of each topic or part-topic takes the form of an evaluation, to be completed either alongside the previous parts or separately, at the end of the topic.

The checklists you will need

This section is a vital point of reference throughout the course. It is the tool by which everything is measured. Reference will be made to assessment objectives (AO1 and AO2) throughout and to the levels of attainment. Students will need to refer to the following descriptors at regular intervals.

Assessment objectives

AO1 Demonstrate knowledge and understanding

Select, and demonstrate clearly, relevant knowledge and understanding through the use of evidence, examples and correct language and terminology appropriate to the course of study.

AO2 Analysis, evaluation and application

Evaluate critically and justify a point of view through the use of evidence and reasoned argument.

Levels of attainment

Band	Mark	AO1
0	0	Absent or no relevant materials
1	1–5	Almost completely ignores the question • little relevant material • some concepts inaccurate • shows little knowledge of technical terms Communication: often unclear or disorganised
2	6–10	Focuses on the general topic rather than directly on the question • knowledge limited and partially accurate • limited understanding • selection often inappropriate • limited use of technical terms Communication: some clarity and organisation
3	11–15	Satisfactory attempt to address the question • some accurate knowledge • appropriate understanding • some successful selection of material • some accurate use of technical terms Communication: some clarity and organisation
4	16–20	A good attempt to address the question • accurate knowledge • good understanding • good selection of material • technical terms mostly accurate Communication: generally clear and organised
5	21–25	An excellent attempt to address the question, showing understanding and engagement with the material • very high level of ability to select and deploy relevant information • accurate use of technical terms Communication: answer is well constructed and organised

Band	Mark	AO2
0	0	Absent or no argument
1	1–2	Very little argument or justification of viewpoint • little or no successful analysis Communication: often unclear or disorganised
2	3–4	An attempt to sustain an argument and justify a viewpoint • some analysis, but not successful • views asserted but not successfully justified Communication: some clarity and organisation
3	5–6	The argument is sustained and justified • some successful analysis which may be implicit Communication: some clarity and organisation
4	7–8	A good attempt at using evidence to sustain an argument • some successful and clear analysis • might put more than one point of view Communication: generally clear and organised
5	9–10	An excellent attempt which uses a range of evidence to sustain an argument • comprehends the demands of the question • shows understanding and critical analysis of different viewpoints Communication: answer is well constructed and organised

Summary of *Knowledge and understanding* and *Skills* expected by OCR (Specification page 5)

Candidates should acquire knowledge and understanding of:

- the key concepts within the chosen area(s) of study (for example, religious beliefs, teachings, doctrines, principles, ideas and theories) and how these are expressed in texts, writings and/or practices
- the contribution of significant people, traditions or movements to the area(s) studied
- religious language and terminology
- major issues and questions arising from the chosen area(s) of study
- the relationship between the chosen area(s) of study and other specified aspects of human experience

and develop the following skills:

- recall, select and deploy specified knowledge
- identify, investigate and analyse questions and issues arising from the course of study
- use appropriate language and terminology in context
- interpret and evaluate religious concepts, issues, ideas, the relevance of arguments and the views of scholars
- communicate, using reasoned arguments substantiated by evidence
- develop the skill of making connections between the area(s) of study chosen and other specified aspects of human experience.

Part 1

Plato

What am I required to study?

- The Analogy of the Cave (*The Republic* VII: 514A–521B)
- The concept of the Forms
- The Form of the Good

This means I am expected to know about:

- the Analogy of the Cave
- what might be represented in the Analogy of the Cave by the prisoners, the shadows, the cave itself, the outside world, the Sun, the journey out of the cave and the return of the prisoners
- what Plato meant by forms
- the concept of ideals
- the relation between the Form of the Good and the other Forms.

You are not expected to have first-hand knowledge of the text of Plato's *The Republic* but it is important that you focus on the particular aspects referred to in the topic, as listed above. It would be helpful to write your notes under the headings listed in 'This means I am expected to know about', as it is from these areas that the exam questions will be derived.

Remember that your studies will include elements of the *two* basic assessment objectives of:

- Knowledge and Understanding (AO1)
- Evaluation (AO2).

See pages 7–8 in the Introduction to remind yourself of these objectives.

The evaluation material is set out in Part 3 of this topic (page 22) and can be studied either alongside the AO1 material as you work through this topic, or as a discrete topic.

1 The Analogy of the Cave

a) Ancient Greek philosophy

Traditionally, it is generally accepted that the first philosopher was Thales (sixth century BCE). Ancient Greek philosophy covers the period from Thales to CE500 and includes philosophers such as **Socrates**, Plato and Aristotle. Such ancient philosophers laid much of the groundwork for later philosophical debates, especially in **epistemology**, **logic**, ethics and political philosophy. In addition, they developed method in philosophical argument and debate.

KEY PERSON

Socrates (470–399BCE**)** Athenian philosopher, teacher of Plato

KEY WORDS

Epistemology a branch of philosophy concerned with the nature, sources and limits of knowledge
Logic a branch of philosophy that is concerned with the process of reasoning

9

KEY WORD

Platonism the teachings of Plato and his followers

KEY IDEA

The perfect society will occur only when philosophers are made kings.

❝ KEY QUOTE ❞

Perfect society will occur only when … 'philosophers become kings in this world, or until those we now call kings and rulers really and truly become philosophers …'

(*The Republic* 473d)

EXAM TIP

If the question asks you to *explain what the cave analogy illustrates*, then allude to the story rather than spend two pages graphically retelling it. This demonstrates selection and understanding through the use of examples. (AO1)

 KEY PROFILE: PLATO (427–347BCE)

Plato came from a wealthy Athenian family. As a young man, he was strongly influenced by Socrates. When Socrates was condemned to death and executed in 399BCE, Plato left Athens in disgust and possibly in fear of his own life. In 387BCE he returned to Athens and founded the Academy, the first university.

Most of Plato's writings are in dialogue form, although he himself never appears as the speaker. As a result, it is not clear what exactly Plato's own views were. However, the two major theories that make up **Platonism** are the *Theories of the Forms* (see page 13) and the *Immortality of the soul*.

b) The Republic

The Republic is considered by many to be Plato's greatest work. Written in approximately 380–370BCE, it addresses the two questions: 'What is justice?' and 'Is it always better to be just than unjust?' By defining what justice is within the context of an ideal city-state (republic), Plato claims that he is making it easier to understand the nature of justice for the individual person.

For Plato, the key to achieving this ideal city was to have wise rulers who would make decisions for the entire city. Such rulers (guardians) would need to be philosophers, competent to judge between what merely seems to be the case and what really is the case. Plato held that the perfect society will occur only when kings become philosophers or philosophers are made kings.

Plato then discusses what education is necessary for such leaders, as philosophers are made, not born. The goal of this education was knowledge of the Good, and it is in this discussion that the analogy of the cave and the concept of the Forms occur.

c) The story of the cave

The account of the cave analogy is told at the beginning of Chapter VII of *The Republic* (514a–517a).

Plato describes an underground chamber or cave, with a long entrance open to the daylight. A group of prisoners have spent their entire life in this cave. They are chained in such a way that they cannot move their heads and so they stare at a wall all day. Behind the prisoners is a large fire, and between the fire and the prisoners is a raised walkway. Along the walkway various vessels, statues and figures of animals are carried. The objects cast shadows on the wall in front of the prisoners. When one of the object-carriers speaks, an echo against the wall causes the prisoners to believe that the words come from the shadows.

Since the prisoners see only shadows of objects, they would assume that the shadows they see were the real things, the whole truth. Plato suggests that they might engage in some game of remembering the order in which the shadows pass by. A certain amount of honour and glory would then be won for those best able to remember the order or the sequence of the shadows and so make good guesses about which object would appear next.

Suppose a prisoner is released and compelled to turn round. The fire would blind him and the shapes passing would appear less real than their shadows. If he is then dragged out of the cave into the sunlight, he would be so dazzled that he wouldn't be able to see anything at first. As his eyes grew accustomed to the light he would begin to appreciate the full variety of the world. Later, he would be able to look directly at the Sun and finally learn that it provided the seasons, controlled everything in the visible world and is, in some way, the cause of all the things he has seen.

Suppose now that the freed prisoner returns to the cave to persuade the other prisoners that there is another, more real world than that which they have seen. It is likely that the prisoners will not be convinced. This is especially true as the former prisoner is not able to identify the shadows as well as the other prisoners. This is because his eyes have not readjusted to the dim light of the cave. The conclusion the other prisoners would draw would be that the upper world had ruined his sight and that escape out of the cave was not worth even attempting. Indeed, if anyone tried to release them and take them up, they might attempt to kill him.

d) The interpretation of the cave story

The story of the cave is seen as an **allegory** – a story with two meanings, one literal and the other symbolic. In Section 517b of *The Republic*, Plato explains that the story represents the upward progress of the mind from illusion, represented by the tied prisoner in the cave, to finally looking at the Sun, the vision of what is responsible for all that is good and valuable.

In the cave, the prisoners see only shadows but think they are real. This is the stage of unreliable opinions. When the prisoner is freed he sees the fire and has belief that the objects that caused the shadows are all that is real. However the objects are only representations of what is real.

The prisoner who leaves the cave comes to see objects more real than those inside the cave and then he has understanding. Then he can become acquainted with the **Forms** (see page 13). We have innate knowledge of the Forms. This knowledge can be developed by rational thought and reasoning, such as mathematical logic.

The final stage is when the prisoner turns to the Sun and grasps the **Form of the Good**. He has come to see that humankind accesses reality, not through their senses but through intellect. Therefore there is an upward move from the visible and physical realm to the intelligible realm.

When those who have seen the truth return to persuade others, they are threatened. The prisoners prefer their world and reject what they are being told.

In summary, the story of the cave is about the questioning of the very nature of reality. It is by means of intellect rather than experience that true reality – expressed in terms of the Forms – is grasped.

e) Other possible interpretations

The cave story has been the source of much speculation regarding possible interpretation of the symbols. Two areas for emphasis are described here.

i) The process of enlightenment
The story symbolises the stages of enlightenment through which we have to go if we are to become philosophers.

❝ KEY QUOTE ❞

And so in every way they would believe that the shadows of the objects we mentioned were the whole truth.

(*The Republic* 515c)

TASK

Draw your own picture of the cave and mark on it all the features referred to in the story. Objective To help recall and understanding of the cave analogy

KEY WORDS

Allegory narrative in which objects, persons and actions are equated with meanings that lie outside the narrative itself

Form an abstract property or quality; it is not just an idea, but exists independently in a different mode of existence (Plato's *Theory of Forms* is also called the *Theory of Ideas* or *Ideals*.)

Form of the Good that which is responsible for whatever is right and valuable in anything

KEY QUOTE

… you won't go
far wrong if you
connect the ascent
into the upper world
and the sight of the
objects there with
the upward progress
of the mind into the
intelligible region.

(*The Republic* 517b)

KEY IDEA

What we see by sight
are mere imitations of
the true reality.

TASK

Find out about the trial
and death of Socrates
and explain why some
might think Plato was
referring to it in the
story of the cave.
Objectives To
understand the context
of the influence of Plato
and Socrates
To develop
understanding of the
cave analogy

KEY QUOTE

And we say that
the particulars are
objects of sight but
not of intelligence,
while the forms
are the objects of
intelligence but not
of sight.

(*The Republic* 507b)

At first we see just the shadows on the wall. When we move and see the light of the fire we are dazzled by it and can't see anything properly. This represents the puzzlement we experience as we begin philosophical questioning.

As we become used to the light we realise that our former view of reality was not accurate. We pursue our questioning in what Plato describes as a steep and rough journey out of the cave. At first, we are so dazzled by the Sun that we cannot see anything. However, as our eyes become accustomed to the world outside the cave, the more we are able to perceive. This symbolises our growing ability to see the real world and make true observations of it.

Our philosophical enlightenment comes as we realise that the Sun is the true source – as we gain true knowledge.

We are aware that our earlier understanding of the world is wrong but when we go back to tell the others they threaten to kill us because they are afraid of philosophical enlightenment. Later, in *The Republic*, Plato sets out the type of study that the philosopher should undertake. It must be that which will provoke the mind to thought. Plato argues that mathematics has this characteristic and lists such areas as arithmetic and geometry. 'It compels the mind to use pure thought in order to get at the truth.' The final stage is when the eye can look at the Sun itself. This requires the exercise of pure thought that involves rational argument, critical of assumptions, such as the processes of mathematics. The aim is to grasp what each thing is in itself (the Form) and ultimately to apprehend the Form of the Good.

As presented in *The Republic*, the analogy of the cave illustrates why philosophers must rule. They will be the ones who know goodness, for to know goodness itself one must grasp the Form of the Good.

ii) The two worlds

This focus is on the differences between the visible or physical realm and the intelligible realm. The visible world is represented by the cave in which there is illusion and belief. The outside of the cave represents the intelligible realm of true knowledge of reality, where reasoning and intellect lead to recognition of basic Forms and the Form of the Good.

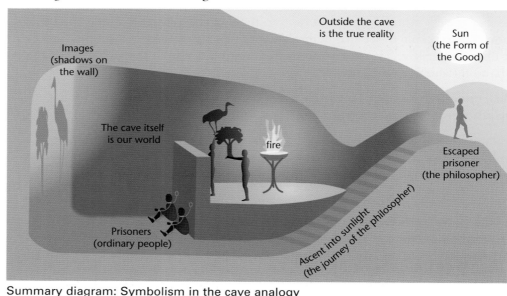

Summary diagram: Symbolism in the cave analogy

2 The concept and theory of the Forms

a) What Plato meant by Forms

Consider the following example. Dogs come in all sorts of shape, size and breed. Nevertheless, we are able to point out particular features of a dog. This means that they must have something in common for us to recognise them and classify them into the same group, called dogs.

Though it is easy for us to recognise and point to an example of a dog, it is not clear what we might point to if we wanted to identify the general term 'dog'. This general term seems to be referring to something different and it is this that Plato called the Form.

Hence all dogs share something of the Form of dog. He taught that the objects and items in our world are but shadows or images or reflections of the Forms.

Another way of thinking about a Form is to take any property of an object, separate it from that object and consider it by itself. At that moment you will be contemplating a Form.

Consider, for example, a page of this book. It has many properties such as rectangularity, whiteness or weight. Together its properties make up this page. A Form is just one of these properties and it exists by itself, apart from space and time. Rectangularity is pure rectangularity, and the rectangularity of the page is just a shadow or image of that pure Form of rectangularity.

In *The Republic*, Plato discussed beauty as an example. His claim was that a Form of beauty exists separately, both from our ideas about beauty and from beautiful objects or people. These ideas or concepts about beauty, and actual beautiful objects, are shadows of beauty. Behind them lies an unseen reality that is **transcendent**, pure, unchanging, eternal and ultimately real – not images or copies. This he calls the Form of beauty.

b) The relationship between Forms and things in our world

Plato claimed that there are degrees of reality. The Forms (sometimes also referred to as Ideas or Ideals) are those which are most real, or ultimately real. They have the characteristics of being unchanging, eternal and pure. These exist in another realm of fully real things. These Forms exist independently of whether there are things in our world that have that property. The Form of beauty would exist whether or not we had ideas or concepts of beauty or whether or nor actual beautiful objects existed in our world.

In contrast, the objects that we see, things in the world, are subject to change; they occur in time and have imperfections. These are but copies, images or shadows of the Forms. However, the Forms are not affected by them. So if this page were destroyed, the Form of rectangularity would be unaffected.

3 The Form of the Good

a) The hierarchy of Forms

In the **Platonic** Theory of Forms, there is a **hierarchy** of Forms. In *The Republic*, Plato states that the highest Form and the most important thing to learn about is the Form of the Good. He makes it fundamental to all real explanation and hence all understanding. However, he admits that he does not know what the Good is, but instead uses analogy to point out its nature. For instance, in the story of the cave, it is the Sun that is analogous to the Form of the Good. Just as the fire gives sight of the visible objects (shadows) in this world, so the Sun (Form of the Good) gives sight to the real world of Forms, in that it provides order and intelligibility to allow us to *know* objects rather than just see them.

---

66 KEY QUOTES 99

… those who have eyes for … beautiful things and just acts … but unable … to see beauty itself and justice itself, … have opinions, but cannot be said to know any of the things they hold opinions about.
(*The Republic* 479e)

… those whose hearts are fixed on the true being of each thing are to be called philosophers …
(*The Republic* 480)

EXAM TIP

Use an illustration to explain Plato's Theory of the Forms. Make sure you draw out how the Forms relate to our visible world of objects. This clearly demonstrates relevant knowledge and understanding through the use of examples. (AO1)

TASK

Choose an object in this world and identify some of the Forms that Plato would have argued it showed.
Objective To develop understanding of the difference between Forms and the actual visible object

---

KEY WORDS

Transcendent having existence outside the Universe
Platonic relating to Plato or his teachings
Hierarchy arranged in a graded order

13

❝ ▐ KEY QUOTES ▌ ❞

… the highest form of knowledge is knowledge of the form of the good, from which things that are just and so on derive (borrow) their usefulness and value.

(The Republic 505a)

The good, then, is the end of all endeavour, the object on which every heart is set …

(The Republic 505e)

All Forms flow down from the Form of the Good, though how they are connected is not made clear. However, using the same analogy again, it seems that just as the Sun provides the energy for nourishment and growth, so the Form of the Good provides order and structure which is the source of the existence of all things.

b) *Knowledge of the Forms*

According to Plato, only the Forms are objects of knowledge, so only the person accepting that there are Forms has knowledge and is a true philosopher. What stands in our way of knowledge is the misconception that the visible world is reality because this assumes that knowledge is based on our senses.

However, the Theory of the Forms makes it clear that it is our mind, not our eyes, that recognises Goodness. To know Goodness itself, it is necessary to grasp the unchanging Form. That is why the guardians or rulers in Plato's *The Republic* have to be philosophers. Otherwise they will not know justice, which comes from knowing the Form of the Good. Indeed this is what all morality is based upon.

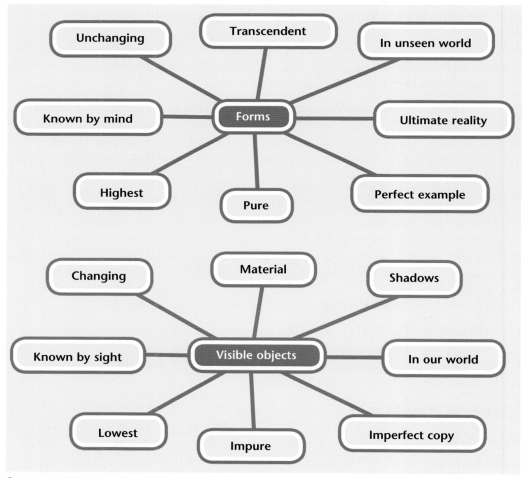

Summary diagram: The differences between the Forms and the visible objects

Reflection and assessment AO1

It is vital to bring together the information that has been covered so far and recognise how it can be transformed into effective examination-style revision and answers. The best way to do this is to ask the question: 'How am I going to be assessed on this information?'

The first way is through assessment objective 1 (AO1). For this objective you need to be able to 'select and clearly demonstrate the relevant knowledge and understanding through the use of evidence, examples and correct language and terminology'.

Use the writing frame provided below to answer this question.

What is meant by the Platonic term 'Forms'?   (25 marks)

As you work through each unit in this book, you will find that the amount of support in these sections will gradually be reduced, in order to encourage the development of your independence and the honing of your AO1 skills.

Key points

- Use the correct *technical language* to refer to Forms.
- Always give an *example* of the term.
- Relate the example to the meaning so that it shows *understanding* of the meaning.

Writing frame

> Plato in his cave analogy likened objects that we see in this world to ...
>
> He chose this analogy because ...
>
> He also argued that there existed another realm that contained Forms.
>
> A Form has the characteristics of ...
>
> To illustrate what is meant by a Form, consider beauty as an example. Plato claimed a Form of beauty existed separately from ...
>
> Behind them lies an unseen reality that is ...
>
> By 'The Form of the Good', Plato meant ...
>
> A true philosopher is someone who ...

An understanding of the concept of Forms is required when discussing the cave analogy and interpretation. The best way to explain the term is to use an example as an illustration. However be aware that you must explain the illustration rather then leave it to the examiner to work it out. The characteristics of the two realms (visible/unseen) then naturally follow.

Suggestion for further application of skills

Construct your own writing frame for the question:

Explain Plato's Analogy of the Cave.   (25 marks)

Part 2

Aristotle

What am I required to study?

- Ideas about cause and purpose in relation to God (*Metaphysics Book 12*)

This means I am expected to know about:

- Aristotle's understanding of material, formal, efficient and final cause
- Aristotle's concept of the Prime Mover.

You are not expected to have first-hand knowledge of any of the texts by Aristotle but it is important that you focus on the particular aspects referred to in the topic, as listed above. It would be helpful to write your notes under the headings listed in 'This means I am expected to know about', as it is from these areas that the exam questions will be derived.

Remember that your studies will include elements of the *two* basic assessment objectives of:
- Knowledge and Understanding (AO1)
- Evaluation (AO2).

See pages 7–8 in the Introduction to remind yourself of these objectives.

The evaluation material is set out in Part 3 of this topic (page 22) and can be studied either alongside the AO1 material as you work through this topic, or as a discrete topic.

1 Aristotle's philosophy

Before examining Aristotle's views about cause and purpose (from his book, *Metaphysics*), it would be helpful to investigate his ideas about matter and to see how this challenged Plato's views. One of the problems faced by ancient philosophy was that of permanence and change. If everything changed, nothing could be permanent. If something was permanent, it could not change. Aristotle recognised that there must be something that remains the same, and yet is also subject to variation. These two things, according to Aristotle, are **matter** and form.

a) Matter and Form

As we have seen in Part 1 (page 12), Plato argued for a dual nature of the Universe with the visible world of shadows and the real world of Forms. In contrast, Aristotle argued that the natural world was the real world.

KEY WORDS

Metaphysics literally 'after physics', Aristotle's book, *Metaphysics*, examines the question: 'What is being?', seeking to explain the ultimate nature of being

Matter that of which something is made

He thought the forms were not separated from things but present in them. Matter is the substance of which a thing is made, while a form is what makes a thing what it is. Unlike Plato, he claimed that matter and form cannot exist separately, but are related. Take, for example, a wooden chair. The matter, wood, is always determined by form, in this case, chair. Indeed a wooden chair has two forms – chair and wood.

b) Potential and actual

Aristotle also made a distinction between the potential and the actual. For example, a girl is a potential woman. Hence a woman can be an actual woman or a potential woman – a baby girl. The actuality is already present in the potentiality. Again, using the illustration of the woman, the woman is present in the baby girl. The baby is a potential woman but an actual girl. Aristotle thus concluded that the same entity has an actual being and the potential being of another entity.

 KEY PROFILE: ARISTOTLE (384–322BCE)

Aristotle, the son of a court physician, was a Macedonian but migrated to Athens when he was 17 to join Plato's Academy. He remained there for the next 20 years. During that time, Macedonia grew in power and Athens reluctantly agreed to accept the Macedonian king as ruler. When Plato died, Aristotle was not appointed as head of the Academy, so he moved to the region that is now known as Turkey. Later the Macedonian king invited Aristotle to be tutor to his son, the future Alexander the Great.

During the period when Alexander was conquering Asia, Aristotle moved back to Athens and established his own school in the Lyceum. He built up a vast library and made many of the lectures freely open to the public. When Alexander the Great died, Aristotle felt it was unsafe to remain in Athens because of anti-Macedonian feeling, so he fled to a Greek island and left behind all his writings, which were mostly in note form.

2 Cause

a) The four causes

Aristotle reasoned that there were four causes:

- the **material cause** – what the object is made of, for example, a statue could be made of bronze, although the bronze in itself does not make the statue what it is
- the **formal cause** – what determines the object and makes it to be what it is, for example, some idea or plan that the sculptor has in mind when working the bronze that leads to the statue being fashioned
- the **efficient cause** – what makes the thing that is caused, for example, the fashioning of the bronze by the artist
- the **final cause** – why it has been made, its purpose, for example, the purpose of making the statue may have been to commemorate a heroic event.

 KEY IDEAS

Aristotle challenged Plato's Theory of Forms because:

- Forms do not explain changes of things since they are not causes of movement in the physical objects of sensation
- Forms do not explain how we can have knowledge of particular things since, according to Plato, Forms place knowledge outside particular things.

 KEY IDEA

Every object has four causes. The first two are *matter* and *form*. The second two are about change – matter taking on (or losing) form.

TASK

Identify the four causes, using the example of a wooden chair.
Objective Checking and reinforcing understanding of the four causes

KEY IDEA

The final cause is the function that the object performs.

TASK

Research the painting, *The School of Athens*. Find out which philosophers are represented and what the artist shows about those philosophers.
Objective to develop understanding of ancient Greek philosophy

b) The meaning of cause

When Aristotle uses the word that is translated as cause it is misleading to think of it in terms of the usual meaning, as in cause and effect. It is more related to the idea of reason.

The first two causes tell how the object is at a given moment, rather than why it has come to be formed in the way that it has. Hence the first two causes are matter and form.

The last two causes tell how the object came to be the way it is. They are about change, which involves matter taking on or losing form.

c) Causes in natural objects

These four causes are clearly identified in manufactured objects, but what about natural objects such as a goldfish? The final cause of a goldfish is not obvious. Aristotle argued that the final causes of natural objects are internal to those objects. By definition, the final cause in such cases is whatever results from the development of that object. In general, this means the final cause is equivalent to the form the object achieves. The final cause of a goldfish is to be a goldfish.

3 Purpose

a) Final cause and function

In the last section it was argued that the final cause of a non-living object such as a statue must have been in the mind of the artist. It exists potentially and then is imposed on the bronze, thus making the statue.

The case of living objects is different. Aristotle sees the final cause in terms of the function the object or organism performs. In the case of a goldfish, then its function is what fish of that kind typically do: swim and reproduce. Such things as bodily organs are also seen in this way, so that the final cause of the ear is the function that it performs: to be an organ of hearing.

The School of Athens, Raphael

b) Purpose and teleology

Teleology is concerned with the final end or purpose of something. Whilst it is certainly true that Aristotle argued that there are ends in nature, he was not claiming that nature has a purpose. Rather, he was identifying the characteristics and behaviour of such objects. Objects in nature seemed to be driven by a striving or direction towards a goal. They seemed to be trying to obtain a certain form proper to them, and their actions are all directed towards this goal. The matter of each kind of object has the potential for achieving a form proper to the object. It is this that Aristotle refers to as an end or goal, or *telos* in Greek. This purpose, achieving what it is good to achieve, may be either unconscious or deliberate. Aristotle thought the teleological goal for humankind was to live a life of a certain nature – to be reasoning creatures.

4 Aristotle's philosophy and God

In his book, *Metaphysics 12*, Aristotle discusses his understanding of God and identifies some aspects of God, as discussed below.

a) Unmoved Prime Mover

There are two ways in which something may be classed as a mover. Either it may itself be moving, or it may be the cause of moving something else. God cannot be moving since he would then be in a state of change. Hence God is seen as the one who causes movement driven by desire and love.

God's life is a perpetual activity of pure thought. The outer heavens and planets are moved by a desire to imitate God's eternal activity, although not consciously. Indeed, all life reflects that activity which is a process of birth, growth and reproduction, in order that life may be maintained forever.

Within this context, the **Prime Mover** is generally understood to be the principal and most dependable entity, sustaining his plans and actions, rather than the first to exist in time. God is prime in the sense that all movement or change ultimately depends on him. Aristotle did not believe the Universe had a beginning.

b) Pure actuality

When potentiality is realised, it becomes actuality. God never changes, nor does he have the potential to change. Hence, he is pure actuality. The movements of nature are inspired by the things of nature being drawn towards him.

c) Immaterial

God who is pure actuality cannot be matter, since matter is merely potential. He must be **immaterial**, the perfect form. Being immaterial, God cannot create movement by physical means, but creates movement by drawing things to himself, which is the reason why everything else in the Universe moves.

d) Not creator

The idea of the unmoved mover explains all things, since without him there would be neither active nor passive change. However, he did not create the world. In Aristotle's time it was thought that matter had always existed.

KEY WORD

Teleology the study of the Universe in terms of ends or final causes

KEY QUOTE

Nature does nothing without purpose, or uselessly.

(Aristotle, *Politics*)

KEY WORD

Prime Mover the self-moved being that causes all motion

TASK

Find out about Aristotle's view of the movements of the stars and planets.
What did this show him about God, the Prime Mover?
Objective to understand the nature and role of the Prime Mover

KEY WORD

Immaterial that which is not formed of matter

KEY QUOTE

It must be of itself that the divine thought thinks (since it is the most excellent of things), and its thinking is a thinking about thinking.

(*Metaphysics Book XII*)

KEY WORD

Disinterested having no stake in something

EXAM TIP

Use technical words where appropriate: for instance, 'form', 'efficient cause', 'teleology'.
This demonstrates correct language and terminology appropriate to the course of study. (AO1)

---

e) Disinterested

The activity of the unmoved mover is self-contained. He can think only of the most excellent, namely himself, and so does not act in the world. It follows that he does not possess any awareness of the world, but is **disinterested**.

He is incapable of physical action and is engaged only in thought.

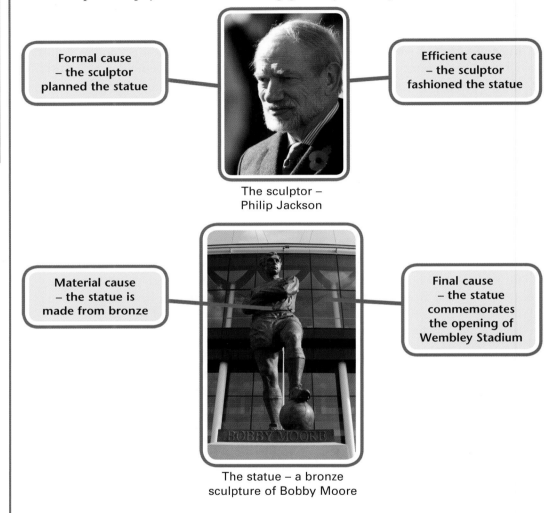

Formal cause – the sculptor planned the statue

Efficient cause – the sculptor fashioned the statue

The sculptor – Philip Jackson

Material cause – the statue is made from bronze

Final cause – the statue commemorates the opening of Wembley Stadium

The statue – a bronze sculpture of Bobby Moore

Summary diagram: The four causes

Reflection and assessment AO1

It is vital to bring together the information that has been covered so far and recognise how it can be transformed into effective examination-style revision and answers. The best way to do this is to ask the question: 'How am I going to be assessed on this information?'
Look back to pages 7–8 in the Introduction to review the level descriptors for AO1. There is a description of the character and features for each level. The exam is marked with reference to these levels.

Look at the following sample answer – a response to the question:

Explain Aristotle's teachings on the Prime Mover. (25 marks)

Biographical material is not relevant to the question asked, and therefore should not be included.

Aristotle, the son of a court physician, was a Macedonian but migrated to Athens, when he was 17, to join Plato's Academy. He remained there for the next 20 years.

The question asked about the need of Prime Mover – therefore first identify a need that Prime Mover then addresses.

Aristotle argued for the existence of a prime mover that accounts for all movement in the world. Moreover, he argued that the prime mover is itself unmoved. This is related to the idea of causes. Nature is caused to move to achieve its potentiality. Everything in nature has a potential that is actualised. The Prime Mover is pure actuality and therefore does not have any potentiality. The Prime Mover is the 'primum mobile'. It is the Prime Mover that explains why objects in nature move. Hence to account for movement there must be something not moving, otherwise it would just go back and back for ever, like dominoes falling. There must be something that is not moving. That is the Prime Mover.

The idea of causes needs to be explained.

Explain by means of an example.

Need to explain what this is and its relevance to the question.

Clear focus here addresses the question but needs developing further.

Explain the example and how it illustrates the need of the Prime Mover.

So what does it score?

In the exam the answer will be marked according to levels (see page 7 in the Introduction). Certainly there is knowledge and understanding shown. The candidate clearly has an understanding of the main reason why the Prime Mover is necessary in Aristotle's philosophy. This demands that it is at least a level 2. However, it is very limited in its explanation and selection of relevant material. Although there is no negative marking in AS level, the first paragraph is irrelevant and so the candidate has penalised themselves and limited the time spent on answering the question set. It does not qualify as a good attempt to address the question (level 4). However, there is a clear attempt to answer the question and it therefore scores lower level 3.

Suggestion for further application of skills

Look at an essay that you have recently completed.

1 Underline in green what could have been omitted or is repeated.
2 Underline in blue any evaluation words.
3 Underline in red key phrases.
4 Identify strengths and weaknesses.
5 Identify how the essay could be improved.

TASK

Using this structure, now write a level 4 answer.

Objective To be able to 'select and demonstrate clearly relevant knowledge' (AO1 descriptor) and working towards a 'good selection of material' (level 4 descriptor)

Part 3

A critical analysis of the issues

What are the issues that I am expected to consider and to analyse critically?

■ Issues arising from, and significance of, Plato's philosophy

■ Issues arising from, and significance of, Aristotle's philosophy

1 Issues arising from Plato's philosophy

a) Problems of interpreting the Analogy of the Cave

The traditional understanding has been that the story is about the questioning of the very nature of reality. It is a picture of the journey of the philosopher who sees beyond the mere shadows of this world. However, look back to page 11 to remind yourself of some alternative interpretations of the story.

Even if we take the traditional interpretation, there are different levels of understanding of some of the features. The cave represents the general condition of 'people like us'. However, the human condition is not a social vacuum and there are people in the cave manipulating the prisoners. This implies false education and a society interested only in the superficial.

Plato sees enlightenment in terms of the intellectual and impersonal, rather than self-knowledge. Escaping the cave offers no personal interest or fulfilment. Indeed in the story, the prisoner is forced to turn round by someone else. The knowledge of the Forms seems theoretical and of little practical use in living.

However, it may be argued that the soul is satisfied by contemplating the eternal Forms, and clear reasoning makes for good practical judgements.

The danger of interpreting analogies is that the original point may be quite simple; it may not be Plato's intention that every small part of the story contains some deep or significant meaning. Every analogy breaks down somewhere and Plato would have known that.

b) Problems arising from the theory of the Forms

Look back to page 13 to remind yourself how Plato sees a Form – as something totally separate, perfect, unchangeable and indivisible. In contrast, the things of the visible world, our everyday world, are imperfect, changeable copies of the Forms. In Part 1 of this topic we considered the example of dogs and how the Form is that which is common to all dogs – dogginess. How can the Form of dog be in each individual dog while remaining indivisible?

? KEY QUESTIONS

● **What did Plato intend to illustrate by the Analogy of the Cave?**

● **Is there any value in escaping the cave?**

TASK

Draw a grid listing the similarities and differences between Plato's and Aristotle's theories of Forms.
Objective Clarification of the fact that there are two views about matter in ancient Greek philosophy

How does the perfect ideal intermingle with its imperfect copy? Putting it another way: the properties that the Forms have of being eternal, unchanging, transcendent, … are all incompatible with material objects. In what sense can there be dogginess without there being a dog? It was this separation between the two worlds of Forms and our world that made Aristotle regard Plato's theory as unnecessary.

However, we do recognise varieties of dogs without being able to say precisely what they share in common, so maybe there is some concept that underlies dogginess.

A second problem is one of limits. Of how many particular things in the world can it be said that there is a Form? Accepting there is a Form for dog, is there also a Form for every single animal and creature? Would there even be a Form for death? It could be argued that things such as death or imperfections are absences, for example, absence of life, so do not have Forms.

Some have argued that because the Forms are not located in our Universe of space and time, we cannot have a concept of them. All our ideas are from sense, but experience and the concept of Forms is not open to that.

One response is to argue that souls are born possessing a concept of Forms. Before birth the souls were in close contact with the Forms in the Platonic heaven. Hence, through recollection, these souls can be reminded of these concepts.

Plato himself identified a possible problem with Forms. If a Form of Good is required to explain why we find some things just, then is there another Form required to explain Good? Indeed, this argument could just go on and on.

In response, it could be said that Good represents perfection in terms of justice and therefore there can be nothing else beyond that.

A major criticism of the idea of Forms has been the charge that the theory has no evidence to support it. However, the reply might be that Forms are not physical matter and therefore not open to empirical testing. It is by thinking as a philosopher that the truth of Forms is seen.

c) The significance of Plato's philosophy

Many see Plato as the person who invented and first practised philosophy in its traditional sense. He analysed concepts and addressed the issue of the structure or nature of reality. Not surprisingly, he has influenced many subsequent thinkers.

In particular, he influenced Judaeo-Christian thought. The idea that there is a perfect realm beyond this world has influenced our understanding of God. Christian theology includes the idea that God is, and God's **attributes** are, unchanging. This has made popular the idea of a division between the physical realm, usually equated with sin, ignorance and a lack of true spiritual insight, and the non-physical realm, a place of perfection, truth, and somewhere God dwells.

? KEY QUESTIONS

- What is the connection between the Forms and the object in the visible world?
- How many Forms are there?
- Are there Forms of things such as death?
- Is it possible to have a concept of Forms?
- What is the evidence that Forms exist?

❝ KEY QUOTE ❞

In response to being asked to discuss the Good: 'I'm afraid that I won't be up to it and that I'll disgrace myself and look ridiculous by trying.' (Plato in *The Republic* 506b–e)

EXAM TIP

Beware of confusing the ideas of Plato with those of Aristotle. Always read through your answer to check for any errors. Accurate knowledge is required to demonstrate the justification of a point of view through the use of evidence. (AO2)

KEY WORD

Attribute a property, quality or feature belonging to a person or thing

2 Issues arising from Aristotle's philosophy

a) Problems of the theory of the four causes

The material cause seems to be assumed and so there can be no new knowledge of the material, for example, what it is and how it operates.

Aristotle's views about the final cause seem to be at odds with modern science.

b) Problems with the concept of Prime Mover

Newton's First Law states that a particle would tend to stay at rest *or* continue to move at a constant velocity if no external force were applied to it. Hence it is as natural for a body to move at a constant velocity as it is for a body to be at rest. Many argue that this removes the need of a Prime Mover.

A more traditional objection to the Prime Mover is the problem of what moved the Prime Mover. To claim that the Prime Mover is unique, and is the one thing that does not require something to act on it, raises the question of why other similar unmoved movers should not exist.

However, it might be said that this unmoved mover is not another in the series of movers but something totally different. For further discussion see the section on the cosmological argument on page 56.

In his book, *Metaphysics*, Aristotle implies that he thought there was more than one unmoved mover. He suggests that the total number of all the movers was equal to the number of separate movements, which was thought to be as many as 55.

c) Significance of Aristotle's philosophy

Aristotle greatly influenced the thinking of such people as Thomas Aquinas. These thinkers blended Aristotelian philosophy with Christian thought. Much of Aristotle's philosophy can be seen in the Five Ways of Aquinas (see page 57).

Following Aristotle, many philosophers have considered the workings of nature as involving the operation of a guiding hand.

3 Possible conclusions

In assessing Plato's or Aristotle's philosophy, it is important to reflect upon the arguments above and arrive at some appropriate conclusion. It may be that you accept none of those listed here, or just one of them, or you may have a different conclusion that is not listed. However, what is important is the way that you have arrived at your conclusion – the reasoning process.

Here are some possible conclusions that you could draw.

a) Plato's philosophy

1   The interpretation of the cave analogy is straightforward. It is the traditional interpretation.

2   The interpretation of the cave analogy is complex. There are different layers of interpretation.

? KEY QUESTION

Is there any need for a prime mover?

" KEY QUOTE "

Chaucer describes his student as being happy by having:
'At his bedded hed
Twenty books clothed
in blake or red,
Of Aristotle and his
philosophie …'

3 The interpretation of the cave analogy is not clear. It may not be the intention of Plato that every small part of the story contains some deep or significant meaning. In other words, every analogy breaks down somewhere.

4 The theory of Forms has no value. It has too many problems.

5 The theory of Forms has problems but they are not insurmountable.

6 Plato's philosophy is significant. It has influenced Judaeo–Christian thought.

7 Plato's philosophy is of limited significance. It is now outdated.

8 Plato's philosophy is of no significance. It is wrong and misleading.

b) Aristotle's philosophy

1 The concept of Prime Mover has no value. It has too many problems.

2 The concept of Prime Mover has problems but they are not insurmountable.

3 The Prime Mover is God.

4 Aristotle's philosophy is significant. It has influenced Aquinas.

5 Aristotle's philosophy is of limited significance. It is now outdated.

6 Aristotle's philosophy is of no significance. It is wrong and misleading.

> ### EXAM TIP
>
> If you are asked to assess a view, do not merely give your opinion. Opinions that are unjustified do not qualify as evaluation. They are merely an expression of a personal view. Evaluation must give evidence of a reasoning process.
> Avoiding mere statements of opinion demonstrates justifying a point of view through the use of reasoned argument. (AO2)

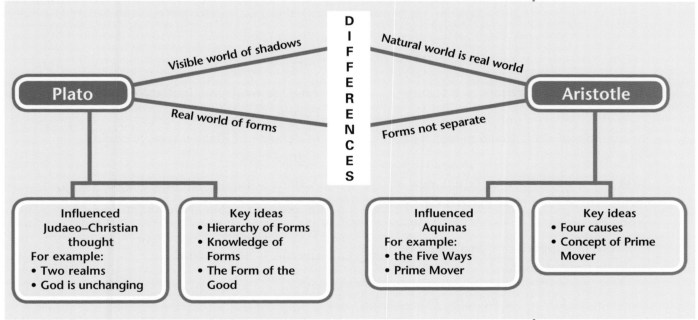

Summary diagram: Philosophies of Plato and Aristotle

Reflection and assessment AO2

Earlier in this topic we considered the assessment objective AO1 focused on knowledge and understanding. The second way of being assessed is through assessment objective AO2. For this objective we need to be able to 'sustain a critical line of argument and justify a point of view'.

Use the writing frame provided to answer the question below.

Critically assess Plato's concept of Forms. (10 marks)

As you work through each unit in this book, you will find that the amount of support in these sections will gradually be reduced, in order to encourage the development of your independence and the honing of your AO2 skills.

Key points

- Always point out the *case in support* of the concept and the *case against* the concept.
- Always *respond to* and *assess* each point as you proceed through the answer so you show critical analysis.
- *Avoid* just listing points.
- *Always use juxtaposition* and *integrate* the views so you show *engagement*.
- Keep relating the material back to the *focus* of the discussion.
- Always give a clear weighing up leading to an *appropriate conclusion*, even if the conclusion is that both sides are equal.
- Remember that the case against can include better *alternatives* as well as *weaknesses* of the case in support.

Writing frame

Plato's concept of Forms is a theory about ...

An example of what Plato meant by a Form is ...

Aristotle argued for a different view of Forms. He argued that Plato's view was wrong because ...

However, in support of Plato's view it could be argued that ...

Another weakness in Plato's theory of Forms is ...

In defence of Plato's view, it could be argued that ...

A third criticism of Plato's theory is ...

In answer to this criticism, it could be argued that ...

Overall, it seems that ...

Although quite basic, this writing frame does focus on critical analysis. It is better to deal with three or four criticisms in some detail, than to compile a longer list with very brief comment. It is important also to make clear in what way your criticism challenges the argument or view.

Suggestion for further application of skills

Construct your own writing frame for the question:

Critically assess Aristotle's concept of the Prime Mover. (10 marks)

Part 1

The concept of God as Creator

What am I required to study?
- The concept of God as Creator

This means I am expected to know about:
- the concept of creation *ex nihilo*
- the way the Bible presents God as involved with his creation
- the imagery of God as a craftsman
- the concepts of omnipotence, omniscience and omnipresence.

You will be expected to have an understanding of the concept of God as Creator, as interpreted by the Judaeo-Christian tradition. This is based on the Bible and some awareness of key biblical texts is necessary. It would be helpful to write your notes under the headings listed in 'This means that I am expected to know about', as it is from these areas that the exam questions will be derived.

Remember that your studies will include elements of the *two* basic assessment objectives of:

- Knowledge and Understanding (AO1)
- Evaluation (AO2).

See pages 7–8 in the Introduction to remind yourself of these objectives.

The evaluation material is set out in Part 3 of this topic (page 36) and can be studied either alongside the AO1 material, as you work through this topic, or as a discrete topic.

1 God as the Creator

a) Created out of nothing (ex nihilo)

God's creation of the world refers to the entire Universe, including the creation of an unseen, spiritual realm. In addition to animals and human beings, God created spiritual beings such as angels. Because God created everything out of nothing, it implies that God created space and matter, as there was a time when the Universe did not exist. Hence creation is not co-eternal with God.

b) Created by the word of God

Both the Jewish Scriptures (the Old Testament) and the New Testament state that the mode of creation was 'by the word of God'. This relates to the sovereign commands of God. In Genesis, the Spirit of God is also referred to in the work of creation. He is pictured giving life to God's creation (see Job 33: 4). The New Testament also emphasises the role of Jesus, who is described as the one through whom creation came about (John 1: 3).

KEY WORD

Ex nihilo Latin phrase meaning 'out of nothing' – God did not use any previously existing materials when he created the Universe

❝ KEY QUOTES ❞

In the beginning God created the heavens and the Earth.
(Genesis 1: 1)

The God who made the world and everything in it.
(Acts 17: 24)

And God said…
(Genesis 1: 3)

… the Universe was formed at God's Command.
(Hebrews 11: 3)

The Bible states that God created the Universe out of nothing (*ex nihilo*).

This is the implication in Genesis 1: 1 and Acts 17: 24.

KEY IDEA

When God began to create the Universe, time began. Before that, there was no time, at least not in the sense of a succession of moments.

" KEY QUOTE "

... and worshipped
and served created
things rather than the
Creator ...

(Romans 1: 25)

TASK

Read Isaiah 40: 6–31
and identify in the
passage the aspects of
God as Creator that are
referred to.
Objective To understand
and distinguish between
the various aspects of
God as Creator

" KEY QUOTE "

The Lord God formed
the man from the
dust of the ground
and breathed into his
nostrils the breath of
life ...

(Genesis 2: 7)

EXAM TIP

If you are asked about
God as Creator do not just
narrate the creation story
in Genesis. You need to
draw out from the account
what we learn about the
creator, or what it reveals
about God's nature.
This demonstrates
relevant knowledge and
understanding through
the use of evidence and
examples. (AO1)

c) Creation is distinct from God but dependent on God

The Creator is separate and distinct from that which he creates. That is why the prophets in the Bible, for example, spoke against idols and images. People were accused of worshipping the created rather than the Creator.

Despite being portrayed as separate from creation, God is also depicted as being involved with this world. Indeed, the Universe is continually dependent on God for its existence and functioning. In Acts 17, in his speech to the Athenians, Paul links these two ideas of transcendence (independent of creation) and immanence (remaining close to creation):

> **The God who made the world ... is not served by human hands, as if he needed anything, because he himself gives all men life and breath and everything else.**
>
> *(Acts 17: 24–25)*

d) Special creation of human beings

Genesis teaches that God created Adam and Eve in a special, personal way. This suggests that, although human beings may be like animals in some respects, they are also significantly different since they are created in God's image and are appointed to rule over the rest of creation.

e) Creation was very good

In the account in Genesis, at the end of each stage of creation it is stated that God saw what he had done was 'good'. Genesis 1: 31 concludes: 'God saw all that he had made, and it was very good.' Even though sin entered the world, the material creation is still seen as good.

f) Creation is purposeful

The Old Testament makes clear that human beings were created for God's glory (Isaiah 43: 7), as were the heavens (Psalm 19: 1–2). God did not need the Universe in the sense that without it he would have been in some way incomplete. Rather, he freely chose to create it. The creation shows God's attributes, including love. God wanted to share something of himself.

2 The nature of God

The creation shows us something about the nature of God.

a) God's authority

The Creator has authority over the creation. The creation does not belong to human beings and we hold the world in trust for God. Therefore, we are stewards rather than owners of the world.

b) God as craftsman

The Bible contains various descriptions of the process of the creation of the world, portraying God as a craftsman or expert builder. For instance, Psalm 8: 3 refers to 'the work of God's fingers' and 'the moon and the stars that God has set in place'. In a similar way, Psalm 147: 8–9 describes God covering the sky with clouds to supply the Earth with rain, which will make grass grow so that cattle have food.

One of the most vivid portrayals of God as a craftsman is in the book of Job.

Where were you when I laid the Earth's foundation?
Tell me, if you understand.
Who marked off its dimensions? Surely you know!
Who stretched a measuring line across it?
On what were its footings set,
Or who laid its cornerstone …

(Job 38: 4–6)

Chapters 38–41 describe the marvels of creation and forms God's answer to Job.

One weakness in such imagery is the implication that creation was from pre-existent matter, like a sculptor using material that already existed. Hence some have preferred the image of God as artist. Again, this conveys the idea of personal expression in the creation but also implies the concept of creation from nothing. This approach of seeing creation as God's self-expression supports the idea of **natural theology**.

c) God is involved with his creation

Unlike the disinterested Prime Mover of Aristotle's philosophy, the Judaeo-Christian view is of a God who is involved and very interested with his creation. For instance, Psalm 102 refers to God looking down from his sanctuary on high and viewing Earth. He heard the groans of the prisoners and released them (Psalm 102: 19–20). Indeed, the whole of the Bible is about God's dealings with human beings. The New Testament in particular claims to show God's love for the world by sending his Son, Jesus, to live and die on Earth so that anyone who believes in him will have eternal life (John 3: 16).

d) God is omnipotent

Omnipotent means all-powerful. The Bible often refers to the power and might of God and claims that God's power is not limited to what he has done. Psalm 115: 3 claims that '… he does whatever he pleases.'

However, there are some things that God cannot do. For instance, God cannot will or do anything that would deny his own character. Hence, God's omnipotence is sometimes defined in terms of God's ability to do 'all his holy will'. God's exercise of power over his creation is also called God's sovereignty.

Philosophers do not generally regard the idea that God cannot do the logically impossible, for example, make a square circle or perform acts that are inconsistent with his nature, as a limitation of his power. God not doing the logically impossible can be seen as a reflection of his nature, since it would mean he would do something contrary to reason.

e) God is omniscient

Omniscience is the ability to know everything. Support for the view that God is omniscient can be found in Biblical texts such as Job 28: 24, '… and he sees everything under the heavens.' Philosophers sometimes refer to God knowing 'all things actual'. This means all things that exist and all things that happen. Psalm 139 is a good example of a declaration of such knowledge.

If God is omniscient it means that he never learns anything new, for if he did then he would not have been omniscient before that time.

❝ KEY QUOTES ❞

The heavens declare the glory of God; the skies proclaim the work of his hands.

(Psalm 19: 1)

You made us for yourself, and our hearts are restless until they find their rest in you.

(Augustine)

TASK

To which aspects of God as Creator does each of the quotes below refer?
Genesis 8: 22; Job 38: 33–37; Psalm 24: 1–2, 115: 16; Isaiah 46: 9–10; Jeremiah 10: 12–16; John 1: 3; Colossians 1: 16–17; 1 Timothy 4: 4
Objective To develop understanding of the nature of God and to identify various aspects of God as Creator

KEY WORDS

Natural theology establishing truths about God through human reason rather than revelation
God's omniscience God knows all things, actual and possible

TASK

Read 1 Samuel 23: 1–12. How does this illustrate God's omniscience of all things possible?
Objective To understand the meaning of omniscience

KEY WORDS

God's omnipresence
there is nowhere free
from God's presence
Pantheism the idea
that the whole of the
Universe is identical
to God or is, in some
way, an expression of
his nature

66 KEY QUOTE 99

... if we are faithless,
he remains faithful –
for he cannot deny
himself.

(2 Timothy 2: 13,
RSV)

EXAM TIP

If you use a quotation then
make sure you explain
its relevance and how it
contributes to the answer.
Quotations should exemplify,
clarify or offer evidence. They
should not just repeat what
has already been stated.
This demonstrates relevant
understanding through use of
evidence and examples. (AO1)

TASK

In groups, discuss the
problems that arise
from views about
eternity and God's
timelessness.
Do you think Boethius'
illustrations help?
Objective To
understand problems
relating to God's nature

f) God is omnipresent

Omnipresence means that God is unlimited with respect to space. Just as Psalm 139 presents a good example of God's omniscience, so it provides a good example of God's omnipresence.

Where can I flee from your presence?
If I go up to the heavens you are there;
If I make my bed in the depths, you are there.

(Psalm 139: 7–8)

Thus there is nowhere in the entire Universe where one can flee from God's presence. This is clearly not the same as **pantheism**, which teaches that God is everything.

God created the material world and therefore it could be argued that, before that moment, there was no space. Yet God existed. This suggests that the way in which God relates to space is not the same as the way that we relate to space.

KEY PROFILE: BOETHIUS (CE480–526)

Boethius was a famous poet, philosopher and politician. One of his major contributions was his concept of eternity. He was accused of treason and, while awaiting execution, wrote a book, *The Consolation of Philosophy*, based on his realisation that God's providence governs all things for the ultimate good, including even the future. He saw eternity as 'the complete possession all at once of illimitable life'. Eternity is not human time stretched out in both directions, but rather a vantage point from which all of time can be seen. Boethius likened God's view to seeing 'all things as though from the highest peak of the world'. Another illustration Boethius used was that of a circle in which the centre point represents eternity and the circumference time.

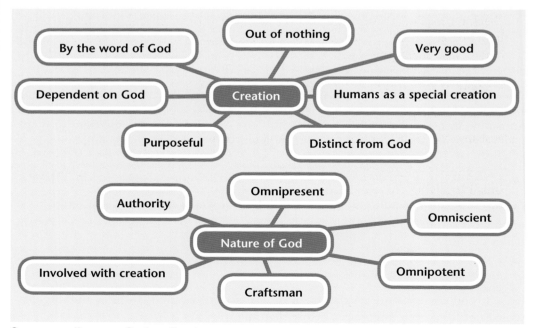

Summary diagram: God as Creator

Reflection and assessment AO1

It is vital to bring together the information that has been covered so far and recognise how it can be transformed into effective examination-style revision and answers. The best way to do this is to ask the question: 'How am I going to be assessed on this information?'

Look back to page 7 in the Introduction to review the level descriptors for AO1. There is a description of the character and features for each level. The exam is marked with reference to levels.

Look at the following sample level 2 answer – a response to the question:

Explain what the creation reveals about the nature of God.   (25 marks)

> The creation account of the Universe is written in the Bible, in Genesis. It shows that God created the world. There are two accounts. One shows the general creation and one shows the creation of humans. All that God creates is said to be 'good'. First, he created light then the sky. After creating land he produced vegetation and the sun, moon and stars. On the fifth day he created animals and then finally humans as the pinnacle of his creation. On the seventh day he rested. Many people think that the seven days of creation is not a literal seven days but seven periods. Others argue that it is literal and evolution is wrong. It shows God creating from nothing. He is purposeful as it was a deliberate creation rather than an accident. It also shows his power to be able to do such a great act. He is almighty and all powerful.
>
> The Psalms are good examples showing God's nature in creation. For example 'He does whatever he pleases'. Christians believe Jesus shows God's love for the world.

Check for material that is irrelevant or material that is not explained. The answer should be organised in a sequential way so the reader follows a clear line of thought and development.

Suggestion for further application of skills

Produce a spider diagram for the following question:

Explain what creation reveals about God as a craftsman.   (25 marks)

Your spider diagram will need to break down the essay title into its component parts, identifying the relevant material required in each part.

TASK
What makes this a level 2 answer? **Identify ways in which you could improve this answer.** **Now write your own answer to the same question at level 4–5.** Objective To develop awareness of the level descriptors and the characteristics of a good answer

31

Part 2

The goodness of God

What am I required to study?
- The goodness of God

This means I am expected to know about:
- God as the one who is morally perfect
- God as the source of human ethics
- the concept of God as law-giver
- the concept of God as judge.

You are expected to have an understanding of the concept of the goodness of God, as interpreted by the Judaeo-Christian tradition. This is based on the Bible and some awareness of key biblical texts is necessary. It would be helpful to write your notes using the headings listed under 'This means I am expected to know about', as it is from these areas that the exam questions will be derived.

Remember that your studies will include elements of the *two* basic assessment objectives of:

- Knowledge and Understanding (AO1)
- Evaluation (AO2).

See pages 7–8 in the Introduction to remind yourself of these objectives.

The evaluation material is set out in Part 3 of this topic (page 36) and can be studied either alongside the AO1 material, as you work through this topic, or as a discrete topic.

1 God as moral agent

As was seen in Part 1 (page 28), the act of creation itself is seen as evidence of **God's goodness**. However, the Judaeo-Christian approach goes further than that and describes God himself as good. Psalm 119: 68 acknowledges this when it says of God: 'You are good, and what you do is good.'

a) God's goodness

The concept of goodness is difficult to define. The meaning of good comprises the ideas of being worthy of approval and of obligation, or that which ought to be done. Hence, to say that God is good is to acknowledge that whatever God approves is good. God is seen as the final standard of good. His character exhibits the highest standard of goodness. He acts consistently with that character, so that what he does is always worthy of approval (good). God's goodness is something that can be relied on by his people. For instance, in Jeremiah 32: 40, God says: 'I will make an everlasting covenant with them: I will never stop doing good to them.'

KEY WORD

God's goodness all that God is and does is worthy of approval

❝ KEY QUOTES ❞

The Lord is good.
(Psalm 100: 5)

No one is good – except God alone.
(Mark 10: 18)

A faithful God who does no wrong, Upright and just is he.
(Deuteronomy 32: 4)

One aspect of goodness is love. For Christians, God's love is demonstrated by God coming into the world as Jesus and dying by crucifixion, so that sin could be forgiven.

b) God as the one who is morally perfect

This idea is similar to that of God's goodness but perhaps focuses more on the idea of holiness. God's holiness means that he is separated from sin. God's nature is always to be moral and never to sin. Leviticus 19: 2 makes clear that God's holiness is the pattern for his people to imitate.

You shall be holy; for I the Lord your God am holy.

(Leviticus 19: 2)

c) God as the source of human ethics

The Judaeo-Christian view is that morality is grounded in the nature of God himself. He is the source and standard of all that is good. It therefore follows that acts are morally good or bad on the basis of God's will or commands. Moral obligation comprises obeying God's commands. This approach to ethics is known as the Divine Command theory. Human beings have been created as moral creatures in the likeness of God, and scripture provides practical guidance concerning moral living and decision-making. The Old Testament prophets particularly recognised that religion and morality go together and spoke out when Israel did not practise what it preached. True religion meant moral consistency.

Because we are seen as created in the image of God as moral beings, many have appealed to the conscience as a way God guides us in moral decision-making. Our conscience makes us feel guilt and remorse. However, human beings are morally flawed, as Paul says:

… for all have sinned and fall short of the glory of God.

(Romans 3: 23)

For some, the belief that we are morally flawed questions the role of our reasoning in moral decision-making. Others question the status of the role and authority of the scriptures as a source of moral guidance.

2 God as judge

a) God as law-giver

According to the Judaeo-Christian view, the original harmony between God and human beings has collapsed (Genesis 3), and there is a loss of immediate awareness of good and evil and of the ability to obey God's commands. The scriptures recount how God reveals his standards by means of laws. The best-known laws are the Ten Commandments (Exodus 20). These are seen as a summary of the standard to live by and are an expression of God's nature, will and character. The law is summed up as follows:

Hear O Israel: The Lord our God, the Lord is one. Love the Lord your God with all your heart and with all your soul and with all your strength.

(Deuteronomy 6: 4–5)

This is known as the *Shema*, which is the Hebrew word for hear – the first word of the verse. The whole verse is recited as the confession of the Jewish faith.

For Christians, the New Testament provides further guidance on right living.

" KEY QUOTES "

For God so loved the world that he gave his one and only Son, that whoever believes in him shall not perish but have eternal life.

(John 3: 16)

Good and upright is the Lord;
Therefore he instructs sinners in his ways.
He guides the humble in what is right
And teaches them his way.

(Psalm 25: 8–9)

TASK

What do you learn about God's goodness from each of these sources?
1 Kings 8: 56; Psalm 34: 8, 86: 5, 119: 68, 135: 3; 1 Timothy 4: 4; James 1: 17
Objective To develop and illustrate teaching on God's goodness

" KEY QUOTES "

Love your neighbour as yourself.
(Leviticus 19: 18)

The law will go out from me;
My justice will become a light to the nations.
(Isaiah 51: 4)

TASK

Find out about the importance of the Shema (Deuteronomy 6: 4–5) for a Jew.
What does this reveal about the nature of God?
Objective To understand the nature of God

66 █ KEY QUOTE █ 99

**But it is God who
judges;
He brings one down,
he exalts another.**

(Psalm 76: 7)

b) God as judge

God is righteous and so always acts in accordance with what is right. As we saw above, God himself is the final standard of what is right. His commands and judgements meet perfect standards of justice. As part of his sovereignty he judges; his apportioning of punishment is perfectly just. The Judaeo-Christian understanding is that God's judgements and punishments are designed to bring restoration, repentance and forgiveness. Many of the prophets in the Old Testament depict God's punishment as a sign of his love. For instance the prophet Micah says:

**Because I have sinned against him,
I will bear the Lord's wrath,
until he pleads my case
and establishes my right.**

(Micah 7: 9)

There is also the idea that God will act as judge on the last day.

The dead were judged according to what they had done as recorded in the books.

(Revelation 20: 12)

TASK

Read the following passages and find out why the people were being judged: Amos 2: 6–8; Micah 6: 10–11; Isaiah 1: 11–17, 5: 7, 23; Jeremiah 7: 9. What does this tell us about the character of God? Objective To understand the moral nature of God's judgement

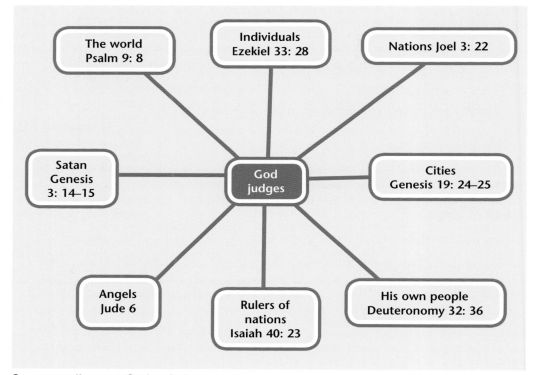

Summary diagram: God as judge

Reflection and assessment AO1

It is vital to bring together the information that has been covered so far and recognise how it can be transformed into effective examination-style revision and answers. The best way to do this is to ask the question: 'How am I going to be assessed on this information?'

Look back to page 7 in the Introduction to review the level descriptors for AO1. There is a description of the character and features for each level. The exam is marked with reference to descriptor levels.

The following key points, which are not in any particular order, are given in answer to the question:

Explain what the Bible teaches about the goodness of God.   (25 marks)

- God expects this goodness to be reflected in his creation, since we are made in his image.
- He can be relied upon.
- We are expected to show this goodness in our actions and will be punished by God if we do not.
- The Bible always shows God as good.
- God is good, not evil.
- To say that God is good is to say that which God approves is good.
- He is kind and compassionate.
- God is faithful and always does what is upright and just.
- He does what is worthy of approval and always acts in a way consistent with his character.
- Part of God's goodness is that he cannot ignore morally wrong acts. God is just and he must act consistently with his own character.
- The act of creation itself shows his goodness as he pronounces after each day 'it is good'.

Suggestion for further application of skills

Turn to the section on God as judge. Make a list of five key points to explain and summarise the ideas. With a partner, add further points to make your explanation more comprehensive; try to find and include relevant quotes from scholars, biblical texts or some further source of information to add at suitable places as examples to support and illustrate the points.

Now use this material to answer the question:

Explain what is meant by the concept of God as judge.   (25 marks)

TASK

Use these key points as a basis for a writing frame to answer the question:
Explain what is meant in the Bible by the 'goodness of God'.
          (25 marks)
Add two relevant quotes at suitable places.
Objective To practise the good 'selection and demonstration of clearly relevant knowledge' (AO1), aiming for an answer that is demonstrating 'understanding and engagement with the material' (level 5) through use of quotes or examples as evidence (AO1)

Part 3

A critical analysis of the issues

What are the issues that I am expected to consider and to analyse critically?

- A comparison between the Judaeo-Christian concept of God and that of Aristotle's Prime Mover
- Issues arising from the Judaeo-Christian concept of God, especially:
  - If God created the Universe, is he therefore responsible for everything that happens in it?
  - Does God command things because they are good or are things good because God commands them?

KEY QUESTIONS

- Is the ancient Greek idea about the Prime Mover similar to the Judaeo-Christian idea of God?
- Are there things God cannot do?

1 Comparison between the Judaeo-Christian God and the Prime Mover

The Judaeo-Christian understanding of God has been influenced by the ancient Greek traditions. However, the Greeks' approach was based more on philosophical arguments. The Judaeo-Christian approach was often more faith-based and included people's experiences of God.

One reason for such a difference in emphasis is that the Prime Mover is impersonal and disinterested in the affairs of human beings. Indeed, the Prime Mover is unaware of his creation and thinks only about himself. In contrast, the God of the Bible knows his creation intimately and is concerned about the actions of his creatures. God is active in the world, causing things to happen, whereas the Prime Mover attracts everything towards himself. This means that it is the object that is moving rather than the Prime Mover.

Though both are creators, the Prime Mover created from what was there. The Judaeo-Christian belief about creation is that God made it ex nihilo.

2 Concepts of the Judaeo-Christian God

a) Omnipotence

Most philosophers would say that there are things that even God cannot do. For instance, he cannot do what is impossible by definition, such as make circles square. Does this mean God is *not* omnipotent?

A few philosophers disagree. They say that God *can* do these things even though they are logically impossible. Most argue that the example given is not a limitation of God's power. Most linguistic philosophers would accept that circles are round by definition and to say they are square would be completely meaningless. To say that God can make a

TASK

Draw a diagram to highlight the similarities and differences between Aristotle's ideas about the Prime Mover and the Judaeo-Christian idea of God.

Objectives To clarify the two ideas and contrast and compare both ideas To help justify a point of view

square a circle is literally meaningless. Indeed, saying God is omnipotent is not the same thing as saying God can do anything. Once God has opted for a certain action then, by definition, other options are excluded and therefore impossible. For instance, by choosing to create the world, it becomes impossible to not create the world. Hence, being unable *not* to create the world, once it has been created, is not a lack of omnipotence.

b) Omniscience

There do seem to be some things that God cannot know. For instance, some say he cannot know his own decisions before he has made them.

Many argue that the solution to all instances of this type involve the problem of God and time. If God is timeless, he sees the past, present and future, all in the same moment. Others argue that such a relationship of God with time is nonsensical.

c) Omnipresence

God is often portrayed as a person. If this is correct then it would seem impossible that he could be everywhere. Aquinas attempted to resolve this problem by stating that God's presence everywhere meant there was unlimited scope for God's operative powers. In other words, God affects everything.

d) God's responsibility for everything that happens

It would seem that if God created the Universe and everything in it, then he must be responsible for not only the good things but also the evil things. The Genesis account of creation describes it as very good, yet it contains pain, disease and suffering. If God did make the Universe perfect at the start, then he has allowed it to go wrong and so is responsible.

The response to such a conclusion usually involves the problem of evil and the problem of free will. To examine the problem of evil, see Topic 4, parts 1 and 3, pages 91 and 109.

If God gives human beings free will, then we may choose to do evil and cause pain. It is true that God need not have given us free will, but some argue that it is better to have it than not to have it. Again, these issues are discussed more fully on pages 97 and 110.

e) The source of moral goodness

Plato wrote a dialogue called *Euthyphro*, in which Euthyphro takes his father to court, charging him with murder. His father failed in care and attention and allowed a worker to die. Socrates is at the court awaiting his own trial, so he engages him in dialogue about moral goodness. In the dialogue Socrates poses the question that has become known as the Euthyphro dilemma. Put in a Biblical context it can be expressed as:

Does God command things because they are good, or are things good because God commands them?

Put simply, does good exist independently, and separate from approval, or does good exist as a consequence of it being approved?

Either answer creates problems. If God commands things because they are good, then it implies there is a standard of goodness independent of God. In this case God is no longer the creator of everything. There is a standard of values outside of his control and creativity.

❝ KEY QUOTE ❞

To sin is to fall short of full activity. Therefore to be able to sin is to be able to fail in something ... It is because God is omnipotent that he cannot sin.

(Aquinas)

? KEY QUESTIONS

- Are there things God cannot know?
- Can God be everywhere at the same time?
- Is God responsible for all the evil that is in the world? If so, then how can he be described as good?
- Does God command things because they are good, or are things good because God commands them?

❝ KEY QUOTES ❞

is ... the pious or holy ... beloved by the gods because it is holy, or holy because it is beloved by the gods?
(Socrates speaking in Plato's *Euthyphro*)

Morality is not grounded ultimately in God's commands, but in his character, which then expresses itself in his commands.
(Scott Rae: *Moral Choices – An Introduction to Ethics*)

However, the alternative option is no less problematic. If whatever God thinks and does is simply by definition good, regardless of what it is, then does it make sense to praise God for his goodness?

Both views have supporters, Plato's idea of Forms would be consistent with the standard of goodness as independent of God, while accepting a relative view of morality would be consistent with the second view.

Others have proposed an alternative solution. They accept that there is an objective standard but the standard is not external to God, but internal. Morality is grounded in the character of God, who is perfectly good. His commands are rooted in his character. That is not the same thing as saying that God and Good are identical. God is not the very same thing as goodness. Goodness is an essential characteristic of God.

3 Possible conclusions

In assessing the Prime Mover and the concepts of the Judaeo-Christian God, it is important to reflect upon the arguments above and arrive at some appropriate conclusion. It may be that you accept none of those listed here, or just one of them, or you may have a different conclusion that is not listed. However, what is important is the way that you have arrived at your conclusion – the reasoning process.

From the above, here are some possible conclusions that you could draw.

a) The Prime Mover

1   The Prime Mover is totally different from the Judaeo-Christian God.

2   The Prime Mover is similar but not the same as the Judaeo-Christian God.

3   The Prime Mover is identical to the Judaeo-Christian God.

b) Concepts of the Judaeo-Christian God

1   The concepts are logically contradictory.

2   The concepts are problematic but can be resolved by narrowing the definitions.

3   The concepts are logical and consistent.

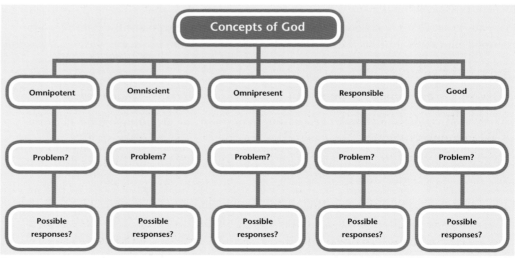

Summary diagram: Problems associated with the concept of God

EXAM TIP

Do not feel that you must reach a clear conclusion. Not being able to reach a clear conclusion is an acceptable answer. However, there has to be justification in your answer as to why no one particular conclusion could be fully supported.

This demonstrates critical evaluation by reasoned argument. (AO2)

TASK

Copy the diagram and fill in the last two rows of boxes.

Objective To consider some problems associated with the concept of God and to outline some appropriate responses in order to 'show understanding and critical analysis of different viewpoints' (level 5 descriptor AO2)

Reflection and assessment AO2

Earlier in this topic you considered the assessment objective AO1 focused on knowledge and understanding. The second way of being assessed is through assessment objective AO2. For this objective you need to be able to 'sustain a critical line of argument and justify a point of view'.

Look back to page 8 in the Introduction to review the level descriptors for AO2. There is a description of the character and features for each level. The exam is marked with reference to levels.

Look at the following sample answer – a response to the question:

Evaluate the claim that things are good because God commands them.   (10 marks)

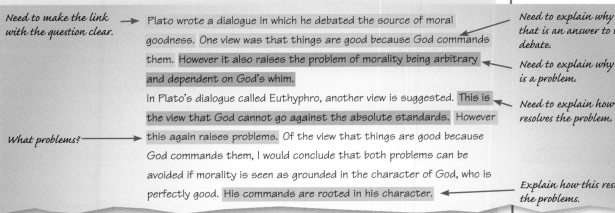

Need to make the link with the question clear. → Plato wrote a dialogue in which he debated the source of moral goodness. One view was that things are good because God commands them. However it also raises the problem of morality being arbitrary and dependent on God's whim.

In Plato's dialogue called Euthyphro, another view is suggested. This is the view that God cannot go against the absolute standards. However *What problems?* → this again raises problems. Of the view that things are good because God commands them, I would conclude that both problems can be avoided if morality is seen as grounded in the character of God, who is perfectly good. His commands are rooted in his character.

Need to explain why that is an answer to the debate.

Need to explain why this is a problem.

Need to explain how that resolves the problem.

Explain how this resolves the problems.

So what does it score?

In the exam the answer will be marked according to levels (see page 8 in the Introduction). Certainly there is some basic reasoning. The candidate clearly has an understanding of the main debate and is aware that each of the two classic horns of the dilemma has problems. However, the initial claim is not expanded. The problems posed are not explained, developed or responded to. There is a conclusion that does logically follow from what has been written, but it is not explained.

This would score a level 2 (an attempt to sustain an argument, views asserted but not successfully justified).

Suggestion for further application of skills

Consider the following question:

'The Prime Mover is identical to the Judaeo–Christian God.' Discuss   (10 marks)

Read the relevant pages again and list some key areas that would need to be discussed, indicating the possible conclusions. As a group, building upon the experience of the reflection and assessment task, see if you can create a plan for a higher-level answer. Individually, write this up under timed conditions and then compare answers with other members of the group.

Finally, compare the standard of your answer with that of the previous question. Are there any ways in which you can learn from one to develop the other further? Ask yourself which is the better answer and identify its good features.

> ### TASK
> **Using this answer and the comments, write a level 4 answer.**
> Objective To transform unsuccessful analysis and identify 'asserted views' that differentiate a level 2 response from higher levels

Part 1A

The ontological argument

What am I required to study?
- The ontological argument from Anselm and Descartes
- Challenges from Gaunilo and Kant

This means I am expected to know about:
- the two forms of Anselm's argument
- Anselm's understanding of God
- Gaunilo's analogy of the island
- Descartes' argument
- Descartes' understanding of existence as a perfection
- the challenge to the argument by Kant.

KEY WORDS

Ontology a branch of metaphysics dealing with the nature of being; the study of being, or what is
A posteriori from, or after, experience
A priori prior to, without reference to, experience

This section explores some of the main arguments for the existence of God. The **ontological** argument is usually presented as both a deductive and an *a priori* argument. It is expected that you will have an understanding of the difference between a deductive argument and an inductive argument, as well as the difference between an *a priori* argument and an *a posteriori* argument.

The forms of argument proposed by both Anselm and Descartes are required, as well as a particular challenge to each of them. Part 1B will assess the extent to which those challenges are successful.

It would be helpful to write your notes under the headings listed in 'This means I am expected to know about', as it is from these areas that the exam questions will be derived.

Remember that your studies will include elements of the *two* basic assessment objectives of:

- Knowledge and Understanding (AO1)
- Evaluation (AO2).

See pages 7–8 in the Introduction to remind yourself of these objectives.

The evaluation material is set out in Part 1B of this topic (page 50) and can be studied either alongside the AO1 material, as you work through this topic, or as a discrete topic.

1 Philosophical arguments

a) The form of the argument – deductive or inductive?

Consider the following.

- If Charles does his homework he will gain a grade A at AS religious studies.
- Charles does his homework.
- Therefore Charles gains a grade A at AS religious studies.

The form or structure of this argument is such that if both the first statement and the second statement (the **premises**) are true then it must follow that the final statement (the **conclusion**) must also be true. The conclusion is already contained in the premises. It is deduced from them. Hence the conclusion must follow. This form of argument is called a **deductive argument**.

However there is another form of argument.

- If Charles does his homework he will gain a grade A at AS religious studies.
- Charles gains a grade A at AS religious studies.
- Therefore Charles did his homework.

The form or structure of this argument is different. Even if the first statement and the second statement are both true, we cannot be certain about the conclusion. It is just possible that Charles cheated, or that the examiner marked the paper wrongly, or the wrong mark was put into the computer and sent out by the exam board. In fact, there could be a number of alternative explanations. If the premises are true then the conclusion does *not* have to follow from the premises, though it is consistent with them. In this case the conclusion is not deduced or subtracted from the premises, but is inducted or inferred. The conclusion does not necessarily follow.

This form of argument is called an **inductive argument**.

Hence a deductive argument with true premises offers certainty in proof, while an inductive argument with true premises offers only degrees of probability

b) The truth value of the premise – a priori or a posteriori?

Identifying the type of argument – deciding if it is deductive or inductive – does not, in itself, prove whether the conclusion is true or false. We must also decide whether the individual premises are true or false. Types of argument merely tell you about the logical connection between the premises and the conclusion. How then do we decide about the truth value of the premises?

Consider the following premise.

- Charles gains a grade A at AS religious studies.

How do I go about finding out if that is true? I would have to go and check in some way – maybe by looking at a list of published results or asking to see the certificate that the exam board gave Charles. I cannot assume that Charles has a grade A at AS religious studies. I would need to make some kind of investigation. I could only conclude the **truth value** in the light of some experience, for example, seeing the certificate. If this is the case then the premise is said to be *a posteriori* (after experience).

Some premises may be such that their truth value can be decided without reference to experience.

Consider the following premise.

- The circle is square.

I do not need to investigate the truth of whether a circle is square. I know that the premise is false. By definition, a circle is round, not square. Premises such as these are called *a priori*, meaning that their truth value can be determined without reference to any experience or any investigation.

KEY WORDS

Premise a statement that forms part of an argument from which a conclusion is drawn
Conclusion a statement that purports to be drawn from a set of premises
Deduction a process of reasoning by which the conclusion is shown to follow necessarily from the premises
Induction a process of reasoning that draws a general conclusion from specific instances

TASK

Make up two deductive arguments and two inductive arguments. Think about how you would decide whether they were true.
Objective To check understanding of the difference between the two types of argument

KEY WORDS

Truth value whether a statement is actually true or false

c) The nature of concepts – analytic or synthetic?

This is a distinction that Kant introduced and is relevant to his challenge to the ontological argument.

Consider the following premise.

- All bachelors are unmarried.

This premise does not contain any new information about bachelors – it merely clarifies the term or concept of bachelors. The concept of bachelor already contains the property of marital state. Such premises are called **analytic**.

Now consider this premise.

- All bachelors are married.

This is also an analytic statement since the concept of marital state is contained within the concept of bachelor. The truth value – in this case it is false – does not affect whether or not it is analytic. In the same way, the premise used earlier about the circle being round is also analytic, since the concept of roundness is contained in the property of circle.

Consider the following premise.

- Peter is a bachelor.

This premise contains new information about the concept of Peter. He has a particular marital state (single). There is nothing in the concept of a particular person that tells you their marital state. People can be either married or single.

Premises that add new information to the concept are called **synthetic**.

d) Philosophical arguments and the arguments for the existence of God

Three of the classic arguments for the existence of God attempt to demonstrate the existence of God from some observation or experience of the Universe.

- The **cosmological argument** infers God from the existence of the world or from phenomena within it, such as causality.
- The **teleological argument** infers a designer from the occurrence of order and regularity in the world.
- The **moral argument** infers God as the explanation for moral consciousness or the guarantor for the highest good.

Because these all involve claims about the world that can be investigated empirically, by the senses, or be verified by experience, they are *a posteriori* arguments. Thus they contain premises that are based on experience, such as order in the world or moral consciousness.

In contrast the ontological argument (which we shall be studying in the next section) is *a priori*. Such premises are prior to any experience of the world, and are not verified by experience.

Traditionally, the arguments for the existence of God have all been regarded as deductive and flawed. However, in more recent years the *a posteriori* arguments have been presented as inductive and are assessed in terms of persuasiveness. Swinburne, in particular, has taken this approach in his book, *The Existence of God*. The cumulative approach in considering all the arguments together as persuasive of God's existence is another trend of the last century.

KEY WORDS

Analytic statements statements of which the truth value is determined by the definition of their concepts

Synthetic statements statements of which the truth value cannot be determined by the definition of their concepts

KEY IDEA

Deductive arguments offer proof while inductive arguments only offer probabilities.

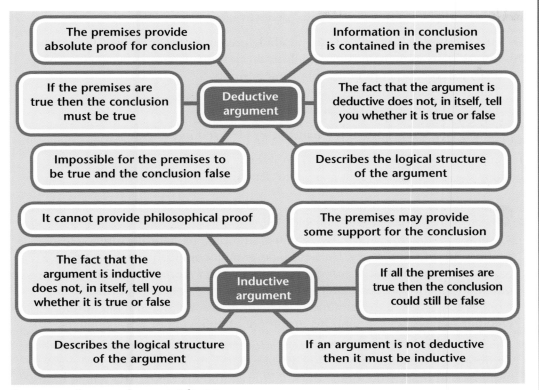

Summary diagram: Argument forms

TASK

Use the terms *a priori*, *a posteriori*, *analytic* and *synthetic* to identify the following statements.
- Worthing is in West Sussex.
- 2 + 3 = 5
- Every event has a cause.
- I have two hands.

Objective To check understanding of key terms

2 Arguments for the existence of God

Arguments to prove God's existence have rested on two main approaches. The first starts from our experience of the world, and draws inferences from such observations. The cosmological and teleological arguments are examples that use this approach. The second approach examines the very concept of God. This is the approach of the ontological argument, the first of the arguments on which we are going to focus.

3 Anselm's ontological argument

a) Historical background

Ontological literally means concerned with being. The ontological argument differs from all other proofs. It is deductive rather than inductive in form. Its premises are *a priori* – its truth value is judged without reference to experience or investigation. The argument does not appeal to some feature of the Universe but rather focuses on the concept of God.

b) Anselm's ontological argument

i) The first form

Anselm began by defining God as 'a being than which nothing greater can be conceived'. If this being is the greatest, then it must be more than merely something existing in people's thoughts. It is possible to think of something greater than a mere idea. If God is the greatest, then he must really exist separately from people's imaginations. He must exist actually, in reality. In summary, the concept of God must include actual existence.

 KEY IDEA

The ontological argument is based on the concept of God, not on inferences from observations.

❝ KEY QUOTE ❞

God is a being than which nothing greater can be conceived.

(Anselm)

KEY IDEA

Existence adds to greatness.

 KEY QUOTE 99

I believe in order to understand.

(Anselm)

 KEY WORDS

Necessary being a being that, if it exists, cannot *not* exist, whose non-existence would be a self-contradiction (This is its sense in the ontological argument. It can also be used in the causal sense, of a being who is required as an explanation.) **Contingent** that which need not be, that which could have been different; something that has dependency

---

EXAM TIP

Where appropriate, express a philosophical argument in argument form with premises and conclusion. This demonstrates understanding through the use of correct language and terminology. (AO1)

EXAM TIP

Remember that Anselm's argument has two parts to it. Make clear how the two parts differ. This demonstrates clear relevant knowledge and understanding. (AO1)

The ideas may be expressed as a formal deductive argument.

- God is the greatest possible being (nothing greater can be conceived).
- If God exists in the mind alone (only as an idea) then a greater being could be imagined to exist, both in the mind and in reality.
- This being would then be greater than God.
- Thus God cannot exist only as an idea in the mind.

Therefore, God exists both in the mind, as an idea, and in reality.

In summary, it is self-contradictory to be able to conceive of something than which nothing greater can be thought and yet to deny that this exists in reality.

> **KEY PROFILE: ANSELM (1033–1109)**
>
> Anselm was Italian by birth. A Benedictine monk, he later became Archbishop of Canterbury. He wrote many philosophical and theological works. The ontological argument appears in *The Proslogion*. Near the beginning is the famous statement that sums up Anselm's approach: 'I believe in order to understand.' However, there is much debate about whether Anselm was aiming his argument at believers or non-believers.
>
> Anselm recounts how he came to the argument. He prayed for a single, short argument by which to prove almost everything about God. 'Suddenly one night during matins the grace of God illuminated his heart. The whole matter became clear to his mind, and a great joy and exultation filled his inmost being'. What he had received was the 'ontological proof'.

ii) The second form

Anselm developed his argument to seek to demonstrate that it was impossible to conceive of God as not existing. Put another way, Anselm argued that God has necessary existence. He also believed that God is not limited by time.

The argument is that this state of necessary existence is greater than a being who comes and goes out of existence. Given that God is the greatest conceivable being, he must therefore have necessary existence. The deductive argument is as follows.

- God is the greatest possible being so nothing greater can be conceived.
- It is greater to be a **necessary being** (cannot *not* be) than a **contingent** being (can cease to exist).
- If God exists only as a contingent being, so can therefore be imagined not to exist, then a greater being could be imagined that cannot be conceived *not* to exist.
- This being would then be greater than God.
- God is therefore a necessary being.

Therefore, God must exist in reality.

In summary, God must be a necessary being, meaning that he cannot *not* exist. It would be a logical contradiction to claim that God does not exist if he has necessary existence.

4 Anselm's understanding of God

Anselm defines God as the greatest possible being, and then concludes that God must exist. God must have necessary existence rather than contingent existence.

The ontological argument, therefore, claims to reveal the logic that the concept of God includes the concept of existence. God must have existence. This is necessary existence. Necessary statements claim that those things must be the way they are. They could not be otherwise. If God has necessary existence, then he *cannot* not be.

In contrast to this is the idea of contingency. If something is contingent then it need not be. An example of a contingent truth is: 'Gordon Brown is Prime Minister of the United Kingdom in the year 2008.' It is true but there is nothing necessary about the state of affairs it describes. Had Tony Blair not resigned it would be he and not Gordon Brown who were Prime Minister.

5 Descartes' ontological argument

In *Meditation 5*, Descartes argued that there were some qualities that an object necessarily had, otherwise it would not be that object. He considered a triangle that must have three angles adding up to 180 degrees. Equally, the notion of a hill or slope demands the idea of a valley. In the same way, existence cannot be separated from the concept of God.

This can be set out as a formal deductive argument.

- God, a supremely perfect being, has all perfections.
- Existence is a perfection.

Therefore God, a supremely perfect being, must exist.

In summary, existence is a perfection and, as God is defined as having all perfections, God must have existence. Descartes thought that theorems could be proved about triangles, whether or not there were any triangular things in the world. Similarly, theorems could be stated about God, whether or not there was a God. The theorem that God is a supremely perfect being, however, leads to the conclusion that God must actually exist.

KEY PROFILE: DESCARTES (1596–1650)

Descartes is regarded as the founder of modern philosophy. He wrote *Meditations* and in it proposed his philosophical arguments for a unified and certain body of human knowledge. He broke free from the dogmas of Aristotle and supported instead the new age of science. Descartes favoured independent enquiry from first principles and asserted only that which could be known to be certain. Key to his argument was the ontological argument to prove the existence of God, since if there were a God it would guarantee that we would not be deceived.

6 Descartes' understanding of existence as a perfection

Like Aristotle, Descartes considered the nature of God – God's essence. But discussing the nature of something seems to assume that the thing exists and therefore

KEY IDEA

The concept of God cannot be separated from the concept of existence.

KEY QUOTE

God is a supremely perfect being.

(Descartes)

EXAM TIP

Marks are awarded for the understanding of arguments, not for irrelevant biographical details. This demonstrates relevant selection and clear understanding through the use of evidence. (AO1)

45

KEY QUESTION

What is the difference between Anselm's form of the ontological argument and Descartes' ontological argument?

" KEY QUOTE "

The fool says in his heart there is no God.

(Anselm)

KEY PERSON

Gaunilo was an eleventh-century Benedictine monk who challenged Anselm's ontological argument by his counter-example of the greatest conceivable lost island.

KEY IDEA

If ontological argument is valid, then it would mean that if you conceive of the greatest of anything, then it must exist.

begs the question about its existence. However, Descartes avoided this criticism because he distinguished between a thing's essence and its existence. According to medieval philosophy, it was possible to determine what something was, its essence, independently of knowing whether it existed. Descartes defined God as a supremely perfect entity with such properties as being all-powerful, all-knowing. All of these perfect properties would be meaningless without the existence. Thus for Descartes, when we think about the essence of God, existence is inseparable. If God is perfect then it means he lacks nothing. Therefore he cannot lack existence. In this sense, God has necessary existence.

Anselm refers to God as 'a being than which no greater can be conceived'. He then focuses on the difference between existing in the mind and existing in reality. If God did not exist, then a being greater than God would be possible. This line of argument does not depend on any theory of absolute objective greatness.

In contrast, Descartes refers to God as 'having all perfections' and focuses on the fact that when we consider the idea of God it forces us to conclude that he exists. This approach contains the idea of absolute objective perfection.

7 Gaunilo's challenge

a) 'On behalf of the fool'

Anselm begins his argument by defining what he means by God. He argues that in denying God even fools have a concept of what they are denying. By fool Anselm meant atheist. The reasons for this connection of words are stated here.

1 Psalm 14: 1 says the fool says there is no God.

2 When the fool thinks clearly about the idea of God he will realise that God must exist!

Anselm's ontological argument did not go unchallenged. **Gaunilo**, a contemporary of Anselm and a fellow Benedictine monk, wrote a response entitled *On Behalf of the Fool*.

b) The analogy of the island

Firstly, Gaunilo challenged Anselm on the grounds that it was not possible to conceive of God. In other words, the argument could not even begin since human beings are unable to conceive of God.

His more famous objection was an attempt to reduce the argument to absurdity. He attempted to use the same logical framework as Anselm. He substituted the words 'the greatest conceivable lost island' for 'the greatest conceivable being'. By the same argument, Gaunilo claimed that such a lost island must exist. In other words, he challenged the argument by saying that if you conceive of the greatest of anything then it seems that it must exist, on the grounds that it is greater to exist in reality than in the mind only. Gaunilo concluded:

> ... I know not which I ought to regard as the greater fool: myself, supposing that I should allow this proof; or him, if he should suppose that he had established with any certainty the existence of this island.

Perhaps underpinning Gaunilo's objection was the rejection of the idea that somehow you could define something into existence. There seems to be some sleight of hand involved in moving from a definition to a real existence.

Many argue that filling out a concept and showing that there really is something to which the concept refers are two quite different processes and that the first does *not* lead to the second. Remember that the ontological argument alleges that we cannot explain the concept of God properly without coming to the conclusion that God exists.

8 Kant's challenge

a) Real predicates

To understand **Immanuel Kant's** challenges to the ontological argument it is necessary to understand what he meant by **real predicates**. A sentence consists of a subject and a predicate. Consider the sentence: 'Alison has a daughter called Elizabeth.' Then 'Alison' is the subject and 'has a daughter called Elizabeth' is the predicate. A real predicate enlarges or expands or adds to our concept of the subject. The fact that Alison has a daughter called Elizabeth adds to the concept of Alison. Hence it is a real predicate.

b) Existence is not a real predicate

Kant made the point that existence is not a real predicate. It does not tell us what an object is like – it does not enlarge, expand or add to our concept of the subject. This argument is often expressed as: 'Existence is not a great-making quality.' Kant argued that to say a concept existed was merely to state that it had actuality. It adds nothing to the concept. Since the real contains no more than the merely possible, a concept is not made greater by asserting that it corresponds to a reality.

We do not add anything to the concept when we declare that it *is*. Otherwise it would not be exactly the same thing that exists. It would be something more than we had thought of in the original concept. We could not say that the exact object of my imagination really exists.

Many think that to say that something exists defines it as having the property of a number. Effectively, this denies the number zero. **Bertrand Russell** made a similar point. He used the example: 'Cows exist but unicorns do not exist.' He said that he was not talking about cows, saying that they have the attribute of existence, or that unicorns lack this attribute. Rather, he was talking of the concepts of a cow and a unicorn and saying that one of them is actually there and one of them is not.

Gottlob Frege argued in a similar way, saying that in the sentence: 'God exists,' the subject is really 'the concept of God', and the predicate is 'applies to something'. When expressed in this way, it becomes clear why existing is not a property.

c) Analytic existential statements can be denied without contradiction

An **analytic existential proposition** is an analytic statement about existence. The ontological argument claims that 'God exists' is:

1   analytic – the concept of God necessarily contains the concept of existence, so the predicate is already contained in the subject

2   existential – the proposition is about existence, God's existence.

Given that necessary existence is part of the concept of God, it appears a logical contradiction to say: 'God does not exist.' It is the same thing as saying: 'An existing God does not exist.' Such a statement is nonsense. It seems that to deny an analytic existential statement is nonsense since it leads to a logical contradiction.

KEY PERSON

Immanuel Kant (1724–1804) was a German philosopher who removed the last traces of the medieval world view from modern philosophy.

KEY WORDS

Real predicate something that adds to our concept of the subject

Analytic existential propositions propositions that are about existence and are analytic, having the property that no new information is added

KEY PERSON

Bertrand Russell (1872–1970) was a British philosopher who argued that everyday grammar can confuse us into thinking that a certain entity exists; for example, referring to the present King of France can mislead people into thinking that there is an existing King of France.

KEY PERSON

Gottlob Frege (1848–1925) was a German logician, mathematician and philosopher.

❝ KEY QUOTE ❞

We cannot define something into existence – even if it has all the perfections we can imagine.

(Hume)

 KEY IDEAS

Existence is not a great-making quality.

❝ KEY QUOTE ❞

A hundred real thalers do not contain the least coin more than a hundred possible thalers.

(Kant)

NB A thaler was an old German silver coin.

Kant proposed that no such contradiction arose if you rejected both subject and predicate: 'For nothing is left that you can contradict.' He explained that: 'It would be self-contradictory to posit a triangle and yet reject its three angles, but there is no contradiction in rejecting the triangle together with its three angles.'

Thus, there is no contradiction in claiming that there is not a being who, in reality, has the property of necessary existence. Definitions only tell us what God would be like *if* he existed. It cannot establish whether he does in fact exist. One can move from a concept of imagination to a concept of reality but not from a concept of reality to one of imagination. To express it another way, if God exists he will have necessary existence, but it is not a contradiction to say that such a concept does not have an actuality.

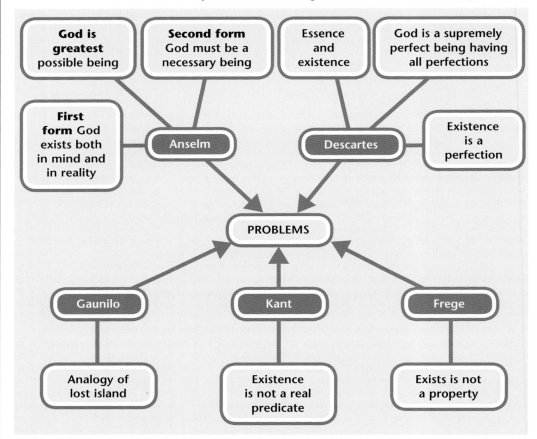

Summary diagram: Ontological arguments

Reflection and assessment AO1

It is vital to bring together the information that has been covered so far and recognise how it can be transformed into effective examination-style revision and answers. The best way to do this is to ask the question: 'How am I going to be assessed on this information?'

Look back to page 7 in the Introduction to review the level descriptors for AO1. There is a description of the character and features for each level. The exam is marked with reference to levels.

Look at the following sample answer – a response to the question:

Explain Descartes' ontological argument. (25 marks)

Material about Descartes needs to relate to the focus of the question. Biographical detail about philosophers is usually irrelevant and wastes time. For every minute spent on writing an irrelevancy, there is a minute lost of writing something relevant.

The illustration needs explaining and linking back to Descartes' ontological argument.

This is evaluative and the question only asked for the outline of the argument (AO1/ AO2). For this question, no marks would be awarded for any critical evaluation.

Descartes lived in 17th century in France and was famous for his phrase 'I think therefore I am'. He argued for God's existence using an argument that resembled that by Anselm. God was the greatest conceivable thing. Existence was part of perfection, so God being perfect must exist. He likened this argument to a triangle and three angles. The argument is deductive and is therefore proof that God exists. Kant criticised it on the grounds that existence is not a real predicate.

The wrong definition. Students often get confused between the arguments of Anselm and Descartes. Check on pages 45–6 for the differences between them. The correct definition needs explaining.

The argument needs setting out as a formal argument with premise and conclusion. It also needs to be explained.

It is only proof if it is a sound and valid argument. The type of argument does not demonstrate its truth value.

In the light of these comments, now write a level 4 answer.

Suggestion for further application of skills

Look at an essay that you have recently completed.

1   Underline in green what could have been omitted or is repeated.
2   Underline in blue any evaluation words.
3   Underline in red key phrases.
4   Identify strengths and weaknesses.
5   Identify how the essay could be improved.

Part 1B
A critical analysis of the issues

What are the issues that I am expected to consider and to analyse critically?

- The strengths of the ontological argument
- The weaknesses of the ontological argument

1 Strengths of the ontological argument

a) It holds out the hope of a proof

The ontological argument is a deductive argument. If **valid**, it will be proof for both believer and non-believer. It is not a question of weighing up the probabilities. Remind yourself about deductive arguments by looking back at page 41.

b) It provides the same starting point for everyone

It has an entry point for everyone, both believer and non-believer. Even the atheist who denies that there is such a being as God must have an understanding of the concept of God, to be able to reject belief in God.

c) It fits in with the cosmological argument

There is a Universe but it did not have to exist. Thus it displays the characteristic of contingency. It need not have been, but it is. Therefore, we seek an explanation for why it is, since it did not have to be! This demand for an explanation is the heart of the cosmological argument, see page 56.

Whatever provides the ultimate explanation, or the first cause, must be non-contingent or necessary. That is the attraction of the ontological argument. It argues for a necessary being that requires no more explanation, It is a classic 'the buck stops here' argument.

This fits in with the cosmological argument, which sought an ultimate explanation, one that did not require a further explanation. The ontological argument provides that source – a necessary being.

d) It is an intriguing argument that continues to be debated

There are numerous modern forms of the argument. Probably the most popular involves **possible worlds**. The idea of possible worlds focuses on the modality: the necessity, impossibility or possibility of statements. This approach is known as the **modal** form. To test for logical impossibility we need to think of a possible world in which the statement is true. If we can, then the statement is not logically impossible. For example, consider the statement: 'Peter Cole became Prime Minister of the United Kingdom in 2004.' This is not logically impossible since we can imagine a possible world where this happened. It just never happened in this world. So although the statement is not true, neither is it a logical impossibility.

? KEY QUESTIONS

- How successful is the ontological argument?
- Does the ontological argument prove the existence of God?

KEY WORDS

Valid a logically correct argument
Possible world anything that can be conceived of, or is logically consistent
Modal relating to the form of a thing, for example, necessary, possible

Now consider the statement: 'Colin and Simon are taller than each other at the same time.' There is no possible world where we could imagine this could be true. Hence this statement is a logical impossibility.

In a similar way we can talk about logical necessity. For a statement to be logically necessary, it would have to be true in all possible worlds.

A modern version of the ontological argument uses this approach.

- There is a possible world, in which there exists a being with maximal greatness, existing in every possible world, and excellence, having such properties as omniscience and omnipotence.
- Therefore, in any possible world this being has maximal excellence.
- Our world is a possible world since our world exists.

Therefore, in our world there is this being.

e) The challenges by Gaunilo fail

In reply to Gaunilo, Anselm pointed out that God was of a different order of being to everything else. There are two types of existence: existence that can fail to be called the contingent existence, and existence that cannot fail to be, the necessary existence.

God cannot come and go out of existence. God has necessary existence (cannot *not* be) unlike everything else, because everything else is contingent.

Because God is a totally different being in terms of his existence, the ontological argument works only for God. Everything else is contingent or *not* necessary.

Criticism about the definition of God also fails. Most agree that the definition that Anselm used is not nonsense. It does convey meaning. Whatever one believes about God, it seems reasonable to say that nothing can be thought to be greater than God.

Gaunilo's example of the 'greatest conceivable lost island' has been branded as incoherent. Firstly, because it is purely a matter of individual taste as to which properties make an island the greatest conceivable, for instance, what would the climate be? Secondly, these great-making properties have no intrinsic maximum. For instance, how many palm trees would the island have to have in order to qualify as the greatest conceivable island?

Gaunilo also failed to account for the nature of God's being. He equated it with the island, which is a thing. However, God is not a thing, like an island. God's being is in a very different category.

f) The challenges by Kant fail

The claim that existence is not a real predicate, as it adds nothing to the concept, has been challenged. Stephen Davis notes that:

Of the real hundred thalers, my concept of them includes the property of having-purchasing-power-in-the-real-world. My concept of a hundred thalers does not have that property.

In essence, then, the concept I have of the hundred thalers, that exist only in my mind, does not have the property of enabling me to purchase anything in the real world. In contrast, the concept of the real hundred thalers has the property of enabling purchases

---

EXAM TIP

By presenting the argument in logical form, it becomes easier to challenge.

- Are the premises true?
- Even if the premises are true, does the conclusion necessarily follow?

This demonstrates the use of correct language and terminology, and critical evaluation by reasoned argument. (AO1, AO2)

KEY QUESTIONS

- **Is the definition of God coherent?**
- **Who is the fool, Anselm or Gaunilo?**

in the real world. So Stephen Davis is arguing that existence does add a great-making quality. In the case of the real thalers, it permits purchases of real items in the real world.

Indeed, Kant himself seems to contradict himself. He claims that it is not possible to reach a conclusion about existence by merely examining the concept. If Kant is correct, then it is necessary to investigate the world empirically to find out about existence. It means that existence is not contained in the concept and so shows that existence must add something to the concept. Hence it is a real predicate.

Supporters of the ontological argument have argued that it *is* possible to have analytic existential propositions. They cite such examples as: 'A number greater than a million exists,' and 'Science-fiction characters do not exist,' as analytic existential propositions.

TASK

Doctor Who is more powerful and knowledgeable in the fictional world of *Dr Who* than Peter Cole is in this world. So is Dr Who greater than Peter Cole, even though Peter Cole exists and Dr Who doesn't? Discuss.

Objective To experience the complexities of the ontological argument

How real is Doctor Who?

2 Weaknesses of the ontological argument

a) Its starting point is flawed

Anselm's description of God as a being of whom 'nothing greater can be conceived' is rejected by many as incoherent.

The possible incoherency arises in a number of areas.

- How can God be omniscient? Can he know my future choices? Can God set himself a problem that he cannot solve?
- If God is timeless, does that mean he is outside of time? If so, then how can he act in time?

- If God is all-powerful, then can he do anything? If so, can he do what is wrong? Can he build a stone that he cannot lift?
- If God never changes, can he change his mind?
- No being could be both omniscient and omnipotent since an omnipotent being could make a creature who had a secret unknown to anyone but itself, while an omniscient being must know every secret.

Perhaps a stronger criticism concerns the idea of the greatest or most perfect being. Do we really have a concept of this? Does the property of most loving have a maximum? Is there an intrinsic maximum for loving?

b) The existence of God eliminates the need for faith

If God is proved then there is no room for faith. Indeed, many claim that a religious belief cannot be subjected to proof. If God requires us to have faith then, they would claim, there cannot be a conclusive proof for God's existence.

c) God is not an external being

Others would argue that God is not an additional being but rather a word used to describe a sense of ultimate meaning to life. God is not an object, not a thing. God represents what is most important to us.

3 Possible conclusions

When assessing the ontological argument, it is important to reflect upon the arguments previously discussed and arrive at some appropriate conclusion. It may be that you accept none of these listed here, or just one of them, or you may have a different conclusion that is not listed. However, what is important is the way that you have arrived at your conclusion – the reasoning process.

From the preceding discussions, here are some possible conclusions you could draw.

1 The ontological argument is successful and proves the existence of God. There are various arguments that are described as ontological. It could be one particular form of the argument that is regarded as successful or it could be the general approach shared by them all.

2 The ontological argument fails to prove the existence of God. This could refer to one particular form of the argument. The fact that one argument fails does not prove that all forms of the ontological argument fail.

3 The ontological argument does not prove that God exists. However, it is persuasive, especially when considered alongside the cosmological argument – or other arguments for the existence of God. It forms part of the cumulative case for the existence of God.

4 The success or failure of the ontological argument is still being debated. The argument remains a live issue in philosophical circles and no agreed conclusion has yet been reached.

5 The whole concept of trying to demonstrate that God exists is nonsensical. It is to misunderstand the meaning of the word God. God is not an object or a thing. It is a word used to encapsulate that which is most important to us.

? KEY QUESTIONS

- **Does proof remove the need for faith?**
- **Is God an objective reality or just a word we use to describe our ideals and goals?**
- **Does the ontological argument prove anything?**

66 KEY QUOTE 99

The idea of a personal God is an anthropological concept which I am unable to take seriously.

(Einstein)

EXAM TIP

Make sure that you explain how your criticism weakens the argument. Avoid just stating a criticism and leaving it to the examiner to work out why it is valid. This demonstrates justifying a point of view. (AO2)

Reflection and assessment AO2

Earlier in this topic we considered the assessment objective AO1 focused on knowledge and understanding. The second way of being assessed is through assessment objective AO2. For this objective we need to be able to 'sustain a critical line of argument and justify a point of view'.

Use the writing frame provided to help you answer the question below.

As you progress through the book, the amount of support in these sections will be gradually reduced in order to encourage the development of your independence and the honing of your AO2 skills.

Critically assess Gaunilo's challenge to Anselm's ontological argument. (10 marks)

Key points

- Always point out the *case in support* of the argument and the *case against* the argument.
- Always *respond to* and *assess* each point as you proceed through the answer so you show *critical analysis*.
- *Avoid* just listing points.
- *Always use juxtaposition* and *integrate* the views so you show *engagement*.
- Keep relating the material back to the *focus* of the discussion.
- Always give a clear weighing up, leading to an *appropriate conclusion* even if the conclusion is that both sides are equal.
- Remember that the case against can include better *alternatives* as well as *weaknesses* of the case in support.

Writing frame

Anselm defined God as ...

The thrust of Anselm's ontological argument is ...

Anselm made reference to the 'fool'. By this he meant ...

Gaunilo challenged Anselm's definition of God by saying that ...

A reply to this criticism of the definition is ...

More recent criticism of Anselm's definition has centred around the problem of ...

Gaunilo's analogy of the lost island challenged Anselm's argument because ...

Anselm replied that God was a different order of being. This was a reply to Gaunilo's criticism because ...

The charge of incoherency has been levelled against Gaunilo's analogy of the lost island. It is incoherent because ...

Overall, it seems that ...

Although quite basic, this writing frame does focus on critical analysis. It is better to deal with three or four criticisms in some detail, than to compile a longer list with very brief comment. It is also important to make clear in what way your criticism challenges the argument or view.

Suggestion for further application of skills

Construct your own writing frame for the question:

Critically assess Kant's challenge to the ontological argument.　　　(10 marks)

Part 2A

The cosmological argument

What am I required to study?

■ The cosmological argument from Aquinas and Copleston

■ Challenges from Hume and Russell

This means I am expected to know about:

■ Aquinas' argument of the unmoved mover

■ Aquinas' argument of the uncaused causer

■ Aquinas' argument from possibility and necessity

■ Copleston's cosmological argument

■ the challenges to the argument by Hume

■ the challenges to the argument by Russell.

This section continues to explore some of the main arguments for the existence of God. The cosmological argument has many different forms but the exam requires a study of only two – those of Aquinas and Copleston. Particular challenges to these arguments will also be examined. Part 2B will assess the extent to which those challenges are successful. It would be helpful to write your notes under the headings listed in 'This means I am expected to know about', as it is from these areas that the exam questions will be derived.

Remember that your studies will include elements of the *two* basic assessment objectives of:

■ Knowledge and Understanding (AO1)
■ Evaluation (AO2).

See pages 7–8 in the Introduction to remind yourself of these objectives.

The evaluation material is set out in Part 2B of this topic (page 63) and can be studied either alongside the AO1 material, as you work through this topic, or as a discrete topic.

1 Introduction

The cosmological argument attempts to infer the existence of God from the existence of the cosmos or from phenomena within it. The claim is that the Universe cannot account for its own existence and so the argument seeks causes that have their solution in the existence of God. The arguments are *a posteriori* (see pages 40–2) and so, at best, lead to probabilities rather than proofs.

2 Aquinas' cosmological argument

a) The First Way – the unmoved mover

Thomas Aquinas wrote a compact form of the arguments for God and these have become known as the *Five Ways*. The first three ways are varying forms of the cosmological argument.

 KEY PROFILE: THOMAS AQUINAS (1225–1274)

A Dominican friar and prolific writer, Aquinas argued that all human understanding was ultimately based on what had been revealed by God. However, it was necessary for humans to have rational thought in order to understand God's revelations. Aquinas thus combined faith and reason. His arguments for Christianity used **Aristotelian** philosophy.

His famous *Five Ways* summarised five arguments for the existence of God. Each of his 'proofs' assumes the existence of a God who is uncreated and independent of the Universe. This means that though God is not reliant on the Universe for his existence, the Universe is reliant on God for its existence.

KEY WORD

Aristotelian of, or relating to, Aristotle

KEY IDEA

Aquinas' argument is about dependency and sustaining, rather than on beginnings.

EXAM TIP

Remember that the exam is testing your understanding of philosophy, rather than the life and times of Aquinas, so avoid including irrelevant biographical details in your answer. This demonstrates selection of clearly relevant knowledge. (AO1)

The First Way is also called the unmoved mover, the unchanged changer or the prime mover. It focuses on the idea of change or motion, by which Aquinas means the process by which an object acquires a new form. An object has the potentiality to become something different, so movement or change is the actualisation of that potential. For instance, wood is potentially hot, and for a piece of wood to become hot it has to be changed by fire. Clearly, nothing can be both potential and actual at the same time. There is a transition from one state to the other. Some change or movement takes place. What is potentially *x* is not actually *x*, yet the actually *x* can only be produced by something that is potentially *x*. Whatever is moved or changed must be moved or changed by another, which itself was moved or changed. If we trace back far enough we must arrive at a first mover, moved by no other. This first mover must also contain all actuality and no potentiality. According to Aquinas, this is what we understand to be God. This can be expressed in argument form.

- Nothing can move or change itself.
- Everything that is in motion or change is moved or changed by something else.
- Infinite regress of movers or changers is impossible.

Therefore, there must be a first mover or changer – God.

Aquinas was not arguing that the Universe necessarily had a beginning. He thought it did, but said that you could not reason that out as it was revealed doctrine. Rather, his emphasis was on dependency. Christian theology has always taught that God sustains the Universe. In other words, if God ceased to exist then the Universe would also cease. There must be an initiator of the change whose continued existence is depended upon. An analogy of this type of causal relationship is of a performance that depends on the continued existence of actors. Such a causal relationship is known as hierarchical.

KEY IDEAS

Difference between the First Way and the Second Way
- In the First Way, the mover (changer) produces the various stages through which changeable things pass, and produces another state of something.
- In the Second Way, the causer produces the existence of the thing.

KEY WORD

Contingent being a being that either in fact exists, but might not have, or that does not in fact exist, but might have.

b) The Second Way – the uncaused causer

The Second Way focuses on cause and existence. It has a structured argument, similar to the First Way. Neither argument is original to Aquinas, in that they are both adapted from Aristotle. The argument states that nothing could be the cause of itself. The reason is that it would already have had to exist in order to bring itself into existence. This would be impossible. Therefore, if we trace back far enough, there must be a first cause, caused by no other. According to Aquinas, this is what we understand to be God. Again, this can be expressed in argument form.

- Nothing can be the cause of itself.
- Infinite regress of causes is impossible.

Therefore there must be a first cause – God.

Again, Aquinas was arguing for a hierarchical chain of causes rather than a linear chain.

c) The Third Way – possibility and necessity

For Aquinas, anything that had a property was referred to as a *being*. The world consists of contingent items, that is, beings that have a possibility of ceasing to exist. In a finite period of time a possibility need not be realised. However, in an infinite amount of time all possibilities occur. This means there will have been a time when all **contingent beings** will have ceased to exist. But if at one time there had been nothing, then there would still not be anything now, for things cannot come into existence by themselves. However, there are contingent beings existing now, so there must be something non-contingent or necessary. This necessary being sustains the existence of contingent beings. According to Aquinas, this necessary being is what we understand to be God. This can be expressed in argument form.

- Some contingent beings exist.
- If any contingent beings exist, then a necessary being must exist.

Therefore, a necessary being exists, namely God.

This argument contains the idea that if something is possible, then that possibility must be realized, given infinite time.

KEY IDEA

The principle of sufficient reason: There is a complete explanation for everything.

KEY IDEA

The difference between factually necessary and logically necessary
The First Cause sees God as a factual necessity, as the causal explanation to the Universe. This means that God is seen as a being who is not dependent on any other for his existence. He is a contingent being that is causeless, and it would not be a logical contradiction if such a being did not actually exist.
In contrast, the ontological argument sees God as a logical necessity, whose non-existence would be a logical contradiction.

3 Copleston's cosmological argument

a) The radio debate

In 1948, a radio debate was broadcast in which **Frederick Copleston** and Bertrand Russell (1872–1970) discussed the cosmological argument. Copleston was a Jesuit priest and professor at Heythrop College and strongly supported the argument, while Russell, a British philosopher, opposed it. The form of the cosmological argument that Copleston defended was one based on contingency and the principle of sufficient reason. It was an argument that, in basic form, was originally presented by Leibniz (1646–1716). Key to Copleston's argument was the appeal for explanation.

 KEY PROFILE: FREDERICK COPLESTON (1907–94)

Copleston was a Jesuit priest and writer of philosophy. He was also well known for his several radio debates on philosophy. In particular, he debated with the philosophers Bertrand Russell and A.J. Ayer, both of whom were non-believers.

One of his great contributions is his nine-volume *History of Philosophy* (1946–75).

b) Copleston's argument

The key steps in his argument are summarised here.

- There are at least some beings in the world that do not contain in themselves the reason for their existence.
- The totality of the world comprises such objects. There is no world distinct from these objects.
- The explanation for the world must therefore be found externally to it.
- The reason must ultimately be an existent being that contains within itself the reason for its own existence.

That reason is that it cannot *not* exist. It is a necessary being – God.

So, only God, a necessary being, can be the complete explanation for the existence of the Universe that contains contingent items. It is the explanation that requires no further explanation.

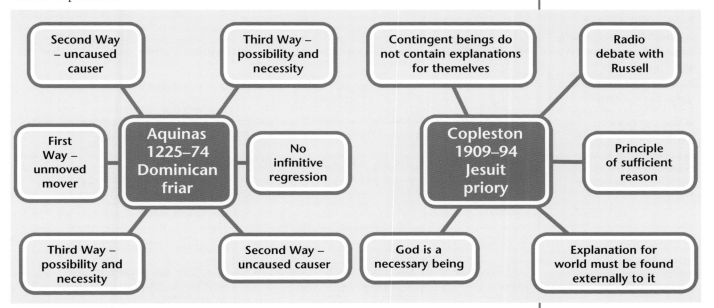

Summary diagram: Aquinas and Copleston

KEY WORD

Empiricist a person who takes the view that the dominant foundation of knowledge is experience

66 KEY QUOTE 99

Every man who exists has a mother ... therefore the human race must have a mother, but obviously the human race hasn't a mother – that's a different logical sphere.

(Russell)

TASK

In the radio debate, Russell supports his view that not everything has a cause, by appealing to science. How might science support this view? How might science support the opposite view, namely that everything does have a cause?

Objectives To engage in the debate about causes

To appreciate how science can be used both for and against the view

4 Challenges to the cosmological argument

a) Hume's challenges

i) Rejection of the idea that we cannot know anything about cause

David Hume was an **empiricist**. He viewed experience as the foundation of knowledge and so, when he came to consider causation, he claimed that we could not experience the actual cause. Human beings, in their imagination, make the connection between cause and effect. Two events follow, one from the other, and our minds, through habit, make a connection between them. This is what Hume understood by cause.

This demand, that experience is required for knowledge, led Hume to question other aspects of the argument. He argued that, because we do not have any direct experience of the creation of universes, we are unable to make conclusions about the creation of this Universe.

If we use the cosmological argument we have gone beyond our experiences, which Hume would not allow. We began with familiar concepts of the Universe that come from our regular experiences, and concluded with concepts far beyond human experience – a necessary being.

> **KEY PROFILE: DAVID HUME (1711–76)**
>
> A Scottish empiricist philosopher, Hume became interested in philosophy as a young student at Edinburgh University. In his own lifetime, he was better known for his volume on the *History of England*. His contribution to philosophy was not recognised until after his death.
>
> Hume was very sceptical about what we could actually know and was an agnostic about the existence of God. His lack of a clear belief in God seemingly barred him from becoming professor at either Edinburgh or Glasgow University.

ii) Rejection of the idea of moving from individual causes to a cause for the totality

Hume rejected the argument that we could make the move from saying that every event in the Universe has a cause, to the claim that the Universe has a cause. One cannot move from individual causes to the claim that the totality has a cause. In fact, Hume argued that when the parts are explained the whole is explained.

iii) Rejection of the idea of a beginning to the Universe

Hume questioned whether the Universe had a beginning. He suggested that perhaps it has always existed. In such a case it would be meaningless to ask about a cause. Modern cosmology does allow for an infinite past history of the Universe, since it is consistent with current scientific understanding to have an infinite series of expanding and contracting Universes. This is known as the Oscillating Universe Theory.

iv) Rejection of the idea of the Christian God as the necessary being

Hume saw no reason to conclude that, even if the Universe did have a cause, that cause must be the Christian God. The cosmological argument tells us nothing about the attributes of the necessary being. Hume suggested that it could be argued that the cause of the Universe is a committee of gods.

b) Russell's challenges

i) Rejection of the principle of sufficient reason

Bertrand Russell questioned the claim that there was a reason for everything. In particular, he challenged the view that the Universe required an explanation. Indeed, he went even further and argued that any talk of the cause of the Universe as a whole was meaningless. He argued that: '… the Universe is just there, and that's all.' In other words, there was no explanation. It is just a brute fact.

ii) Rejection of the idea of moving from individual causes to a cause for the totality

Like Hume, Russell rejected the argument that made the move from saying that every event in the Universe has a cause to the claim that the Universe has a cause. One cannot move from individual causes to the claim that the totality has a cause. He used an illustration to demonstrate his argument.

> **To say that every person who exists has a mother does not then imply that the human race must have a mother.**

Technically, this error of logic is a **fallacy**, known as the fallacy of composition. The error is to conclude, mistakenly, that since the parts have a certain property, the whole likewise has that property.

KEY PROFILE: BERTRAND RUSSELL (1872–1970)

A British philosopher, logician and mathematician, Russell is regarded as one of the founders of analytic philosophy. In 1950 he won the Nobel Prize for Literature. He was well known for his anti-war and anti-nuclear protests and remained active in public life until his death at the age of 97.

iii) Rejection of the notion of a necessary being

Russell claimed that the word necessary could not meaningfully be applied to things, only to analytic propositions (see page 42). He therefore rejected the notion of necessary being, and the idea that existence is a real predicate (see the discussion on this on page 47).

Reflection and assessment AO1

It is vital to bring together the information that has been covered so far and recognise how it can be transformed into effective examination-style revision and answers. The best way to do this is to ask the question: 'How am I going to be assessed on this information?'

Look back to page 7 in the Introduction to review the level descriptors for AO1. There is a description of the character and features for each level. The exam is marked with reference to levels.

KEY QUOTES

… the Universe is just there, and that's all.

(Russell)

If one refuses to even sit down at the chessboard and make a move, one cannot, of course, be checkmated.

(Copleston to Russell)

KEY WORD

Fallacy unsound reasoning

TASK

Use these key points as a basis for a writing frame to answer the question:
Explain Russell's criticisms of the cosmological argument.
(25 marks)

Add one other argument by Russell. Where necessary, expand your answer so you explain rather than just make statements.

Objective To develop an awareness of what will constitute a very good answer (levels 4–5) by gradually building up a response

Look at the key points, below, in answer to the question:

Explain Russell's criticisms of the cosmological argument. (25 marks)

You will need to refer to these points, which are not presented in any particular order, to complete the task.

- Every event has a cause.
- The cosmological argument commits the fallacy of composition.
- Russell criticised the cosmological argument in a radio debate with Copleston.
- Only God, a necessary being, can be the complete explanation for the existence of the Universe that contains contingent items.
- To say that every person who exists has a mother does not then imply that the human race must have a mother.
- One cannot move from individual causes to the claim that the totality has a cause. He used an illustration to demonstrate his argument.
- The argument that Russell was attacking was one based on the principle of sufficient reason.
- Russell claimed that the word necessary could not meaningfully be applied to things, only to analytic propositions.

Unit 1
Topic 3
The philosophy of religion
Traditional arguments for the existence of God

Part 2B
A critical analysis of the issues

What are the issues that I am expected to consider and to analyse critically?

- The strengths of the cosmological argument
- The weaknesses of the cosmological argument

1 Strengths of the cosmological argument

a) It gives an explanation

We seek an explanation for everything else, so why not for the Universe? Indeed, science works on the basis that everything has an explanation. That is what scientific enquiry assumes is the case. It brings into sharp contrast the two ways of looking at the Universe. Either it is inexplicable or it is intelligible. If there is an explanation, it is possible that it could be contained in God.

b) It fits in with the ontological argument

The ontological argument explored the idea of a necessary being. The cosmological argument leads to the idea of a necessary being. Although the cosmological argument, by itself, does not lead to a fully defined God in the Christian sense, it can be seen as an important element of a cumulative argument. When all the arguments for the existence of God are taken together, they all point to the same conclusion – God. Taken together they fill out the attributes of the necessary being.

c) Science supports the view that the Universe had a beginning

Modern cosmology suggests that the **Big Bang** implies a finite past history of the Universe. Support for such a theory includes the evidence that the Universe is expanding, which suggests that it had a starting point.

d) Philosophy supports the view that the Universe had a beginning

If the Universe had no beginning, then an infinite number of past moments of the Universe's history have elapsed, and they are being added to as time goes on. But it is impossible to add to an infinite number of things. For instance, if we have an infinite number of dogs, we cannot add to that number of dogs by introducing another dog. Likewise, if an infinite number of past moments of the Universe have elapsed, then neither can be increased. Yet the Universe continues to exist. Moments continue to be added. This implies that the Universe had a beginning. Furthermore, if the Universe had no beginning, then an infinity of years will have passed, which is impossible.

> ## KEY QUOTE
> An expanding Universe does not preclude a creator, but it does place limits on when he might have carried out his job!
>
> (Stephen Hawking)

> ## KEY QUESTIONS
> - Does everything have an explanation?
> - Is the necessary being God?
> - Is God the same God as the Christian God?
> - Did the Universe have a beginning or has it always existed?

> ## KEY WORD
> **Big-Bang theory** the theory of an expanding Universe that began as an infinitely dense and hot medium at some finite time in the past; the initial instant is called the Big Bang

KEY QUESTION

Is a Universe with no beginning, possible?

TASK

'God is part of the Universe.'
List some points that support this view and list some points that oppose such a view.
Objective To understand the issues involved in studying God's relationship to the Universe

e) The challenges by Hume fail

Hume's view concerning causes has come under criticism. He claimed that our minds make the connection of cause when one event constantly follows another. However, even when one event follows another, we distinguish between the ideas of both cause and coincidence. This suggests they are different things. Night and day are two events that constantly follow one another but we would not claim that one causes the other. Sometimes two events are regarded as causally related yet do not always follow one after the other. For instance, we reason that staring at a computer screen sometimes causes headaches.

Hume argued that perhaps the Universe never had a beginning. For criticism of this see the previous sections, c) and d) above.

f) The challenges by Russell fail

For discussion about Russell's rejection of the notion of a necessary being, see the section on the ontological argument, page 40.

2 Further weaknesses of the cosmological argument

a) Aquinas' arguments rely on ancient ideas

Aquinas' arguments rest on assumptions that are no longer widely held. Much was based on Plato and Aristotle, many of whose ideas and theories have long since been rejected as being pre-scientific.

b) A contradiction

If it is claimed that everything requires a cause, then how can God be seen as an exception – an uncaused causer? If God can be an exception, then why are there not other exceptions?

In reply, it is argued that Aquinas did not see God as just another thing, like everything else in the Universe. God is of a totally different order and not subject to the same conditions as the Universe.

c) The problem of infinity

Many argue that to treat infinity as though it were a number is to misunderstand the word. Infinity is a concept. Hence it is meaningless to speak of 'adding more moments of time'.

d) More than one cause

Why cannot the different forms of the *Three Ways* each lead to a different kind of God? Why must the regress lead to just one first cause? Independent happenings might lead back to causes that are independent of each other. Therefore, there could be many causes. Even if the first cause were God, he could have ceased to exist later. After all, a mother causes a child but then dies.

e) The Universe is not contingent

The Universe is matter and energy, and is eternal. Particular objects come and go out of existence, but the matter of which they are composed is forever and exists necessarily. It could not have failed to exist. There is no reason – it is just brute fact. Thus, the great ultimates of the Universe are about matter, not about a metaphysical being called God.

KEY QUESTION

If everything has a cause, what caused God?

f) God is not an external being

Others would argue that God is not an additional being but rather a word used to describe a sense of ultimate meaning to life. God is not an object, not a thing. God represents what is most important to us.

3 Possible conclusions

When assessing the cosmological argument, it is important to reflect upon the arguments previously discussed and arrive at some appropriate conclusion. It may be that you accept none of these listed here, or just one of them, or you may have a different conclusion that is not listed. However, what is important is the way that you have arrived at your conclusion – the reasoning process.

From the preceding discussions, here are some possible conclusions you could draw.

1 The cosmological argument is successful and proves the existence of God. There are various arguments described as cosmological. It could be one particular form of the argument that is regarded as successful or it could be the general approach shared by all the arguments.

2 The cosmological argument does not prove that God exists. However, it is persuasive, especially when considered alongside the other arguments for the existence of God. It forms part of the cumulative case for the existence of God.

3 The cosmological argument fails to prove the existence of God. This could refer to one particular form of the argument. The fact that one argument fails does not prove that all forms of the cosmological argument fail. (Although other forms of the argument are not required to be studied in detail, it would be useful to be aware that other formulations exist, for example, Kalam, see below.)

4 The Universe is a brute fact. No explanation is required.

5 The success or failure of the cosmological argument is still being debated. The argument remains a live issue in philosophical circles and no agreed conclusion has yet been reached.

6 The whole concept of trying to demonstrate that God exists is nonsensical. It is to misunderstand the meaning of the word God. God is not an object or a thing. It is a word used to convey that which is most important to us.

KEY IDEA

The Kalam argument
This form of the cosmological argument is Islamic in origin, dating back to about ce850, and was devised by a group that belonged to the Islamic Kalam tradition of philosophy. However, the argument has had a revival in the late twentieth century, mainly through the writings of William Craig.

The argument claims that everything that begins to exist has a cause for its existence and, since it began to exist, the Universe has a cause of its existence. Behind the entire Universe there exists a cause that brought it into being. This cause is God.

TASK

What is meant by 'the Universe'?
Is it possible to envisage the total absence of matter and space?
Give reasons.
Did the Universe have to exist or could there have been nothing at all?
Objective To develop deeper understanding of the complexities of the cosmological argument

KEY IDEAS

Swinburne distinguishes between scientific explanations (such as laws of nature) and personal explanations. Personal explanations are about intentions and address the question; 'Why …?', whereas scientific explanations do not involve intentions but address the question: 'What …?'.
The **Kalam** argument claims that transcending the entire Universe there exists a cause that brought the Universe into being. This cause is God.

Reflection and assessment AO2

Look back to page 8 in the Introduction to review the level descriptors for AO2. There is a description of the character and features for each level. The exam is marked with reference to levels.

Look at the following sample answer – a response to the question:

To what extent was Hume successful in challenging the cosmological argument?
(10 marks)

The cosmological argument by Aquinas consists of the first three Ways of his Five Ways. Aquinas lived in Italy and was a prolific writer. His dates are 1225 to 1274. He attempted to apply the philosophy of Aristotle to Christianity. His First Way involved the unmoved mover. The Second Way involved the uncaused causer and the Third Way centred on the need for a necessary being to sustain the existence of contingent beings.

Hume saw that at the heart of the arguments was the idea of cause. Hume was an empiricist and so rejected the whole idea of cause. Indeed he claimed it was impossible to conclude anything about the creation of the Universe since we have no experience of such an event.

He also claimed that the argument was flawed because of the fallacy of composition.

However his own arguments have been challenged, particularly about causation. Hume clearly was not successful since the cosmological argument continues to be argued and believed. There are other arguments that weaken the case for the cosmological but these were not made by Hume eg. the Universe is not contingent.

This is not relevant. Need to focus on the question slant.

Need to draw out the underlying thrust and basis of the argument.

It is good that the candidate did not write out in full the argument but highlighted the main thrust.

Need to explain his view about cause and how this then relates to a challenge to the cosmological. It should not be the task of the examiner to work it out.

Again it needs unpackaging so it is clear how this challenges the argument.

A good example of a 'hit and run' answer. No explanation is given and no link made to the argument.

There are other arguments by Hume that have not been discussed.

Requires brief explanation why this is an argument against the cosmological.

Need to explain how causation was challenged and whether that challenge was successful.

Not in itself evidence Hume was unsuccessful. Perhaps other forms of argument used now; for example, Kalam.

So what does it score?

In the exam the answer will be marked according to levels (see page 8 in the Introduction). Certainly there is some basic reasoning. The candidate clearly has an understanding of the main cosmological arguments by Aquinas but needed to have identified the heart of the first two ways. It is important to do this so that the force of Hume's arguments can be clearly seen. There is some awareness of

Hume's attack but anyone not having studied this area would not have been much wiser after reading this answer. It is important to explain how the argument is challenged and not to leave it to the examiner/reader to work it out. Phrases such as 'fallacy of composition' need to be explained and related back to the argument to draw out why that is a challenge. There is a conclusion that does logically follow from what has been written, but it is not developed.

This would score a higher level 2 (an attempt to sustain an argument, views asserted but not successfully justified).

Suggestion for further application of skills

Look at an essay that you have recently completed.

1 Underline in green what could have been omitted or is repeated.
2 Underline in blue any evaluation words.
3 Underline in red key phrases.
4 Identify strengths and weaknesses.
5 Identify how the essay could be improved.

TASK

Using this answer and the comments, write a level 4 answer.

Objective To develop an awareness of what will constitute a very good answer by gradually building up a response that 'uses a range of evidence to sustain an argument' (level 5 descriptor)

Part 3A

The teleological argument

What am I required to study?

- Teleological arguments from Aquinas and Paley
- Challenges from Hume, Mill and Darwin

This means I am expected to know about:

- Aquinas' argument 'from the governance of things'
- Paley's argument by analogy (*qua* purpose)
- Paley's argument by evidence (*qua* regularity)
- the challenges to the argument by Hume
- the challenges to the argument by Mill
- the challenges to the argument by Darwin.

KEY WORD

Qua **A Latin word meaning 'as relating to'**

This section continues to explore some of the main arguments for the existence of God. The teleological argument has many different forms but the exam requires a study of only two – those of Aquinas and Paley. Particular challenges to these arguments will also be examined. Part 3B will assess the extent to which those challenges are successful.

It would be helpful to write your notes under the headings listed in 'This means I am expected to know about', as it is from these areas that the exam questions will be derived.

Remember that your studies will include elements of the *two* basic assessment objectives of:

- Knowledge and Understanding (AO1)
- Evaluation (AO2).

See pages 7–8 in the Introduction to remind yourself of these objectives.

The evaluation material is set out in Part 3B of this topic (page 77) and can be studied either alongside the AO1 material, as you work through this topic, or as a discrete topic.

1 Introduction

KEY WORD

Teleological explanation by reference to end, goal or purpose

In the last section, the cosmological argument attempted to infer the existence of God from the existence of the cosmos. It centred on the claim that the Universe cannot account for its own existence. The **teleological** argument is similar in approach. The argument is popular and much used. It infers the existence of God from a particular character of the world, namely the presence of order, regularity and purpose. Such features are seen as marks of design and so the argument concludes that God must be the source of that design. The kind of example that is often cited as evidence for design is the human eye, and also the solar system with the planets revolving in their predictable orbits.

Teleological is derived from the Greek words *telos*, meaning end, purpose or goal, and *logos*, meaning reason. Thus it is an explanation by reference to some purpose or end. Nature is viewed as directed in order that something beneficial may result.

2 Aquinas' teleological argument

Aquinas wrote his *Five Ways*, of which the teleological argument was the Fifth Way.

> **The Fifth Way is taken from the governance of the world. We see that things that lack knowledge, such as natural bodies, act for an end, and this is evident from their acting always, or nearly always, in the same way, so as to obtain the best result. Hence it is plain that they achieve their end, not fortuitously, but designedly. Now whatever lacks knowledge cannot move towards an end, unless it be directed by some being endowed with knowledge and intelligence; as the arrow is directed by the archer. Therefore some intelligent being exists by whom all natural things are directed to their end; and this being we call God.**

The heart of this argument is that non-intelligent material things produce beneficial order, and therefore require an intelligent being to bring this about – God. It follows Aristotelian thinking about final cause – the purpose for which the thing exists or was produced (see pages 17–18). Aquinas' views about nature included thinking that things develop toward the realisation of ends that are internal to their own natures. An archer must direct an arrow. In the same way, God must direct nature. Aristotle's God did not appoint the ends. They just were there. Aquinas argued that there cannot be purposefulness without a guiding intelligence. This can be expressed in argument form as below.

- There are beings without knowledge that act for ends.
- If a being without knowledge acts for an end, then it must be because it is directed by a being with knowledge and intelligence.

Therefore, there must be a being with knowledge and intelligence – God.

3 Paley's teleological argument

William Paley presented a different approach to teleology. His influential book, *Natural Theology: or Evidences of the Existence and Attributes of the Deity, Collected from the Appearances of Nature*, first published in 1802, expounded the belief that the nature of God could be understood by reference to the natural world, which was God's creation. He likened the workings of biological organisms to machines made by an intelligent being. It reflected the contemporary thinking about a mechanistic Universe. His teleological argument comprises two parts.

a) Design qua purpose

At the time of Paley the pocket watch had just been invented and was an object that impressed people. Paley used the **analogy** of the watch to illustrate his argument. It was by no means original, although through Paley it became well known.

EXAM TIP

Where appropriate, express a philosophical argument in argument form with premises and conclusion. This demonstrates understanding through the use of correct language and terminology. (AO1)

KEY WORD

Analogy a comparison of two or more things to show how they are similar

EXAM TIP

If you are asked about Paley's argument, do not just narrate the story of the watch found on the heath. You need to draw out from the account what the actual argument is – explain the analogy and what it is implying. This demonstrates relevant knowledge and understanding through the use of evidence and examples. (AO1)

 KEY PROFILE: WILLIAM PALEY (1743–1805)

Paley was a clergyman who, in 1782, was appointed Archdeacon of Carlisle. He became well known for his writings on philosophy and Christian apologetics. His 1794 book, *A View of the Evidence of Christianity*, was required reading at Cambridge University until the 20th century. Charles Darwin, in his autobiography wrote:

> **... In order to pass the BA examination, it was, also, necessary to get up Paley's** *Evidences of Christianity*, **and his** *Moral Philosophy* **... The logic of this book and, as I may add, of his** *Natural Theology* **gave me as much delight as did Euclid.'**

Though Paley's material was not particularly original, his clear style made it popular and widely read. Some years earlier, David Hume had criticised forms of the teleological argument such as Paley's. However, Hume's writings sold little and so were not well known. It was not until much later that Hume's philosophical writings became popular.

Suppose you were crossing a heath and came across a watch. Paley argued that even if you had never seen a watch before, you would know that this instrument did not happen by chance, but must be the result of the work of an intelligent mind. All the parts fit together and achieve the purpose of telling time. The watch must have had an intelligent and skilled maker who designed it to do what it does. The watch demands a watchmaker, and no entirely naturalistic explanation would be acceptable. Likewise, the way the Universe fits together for a purpose, demands an intelligent designer. The designer would have to be God.

Paley also supported his argument by giving further examples of complex purposeful design found in nature. For instance, he referred to the eye as being designed for the particular purpose of seeing. Paley regarded both the watch and the Universe as teleological systems that required an intelligent mind to bring them into being.

This argument can be expressed as below.

- There exist in nature many examples of **beneficial order**.
- Beneficial order is best explained as the result of an intelligent designer.

Therefore, nature is probably the result of an intelligent designer – God.

Alternatively, an argument could focus on the analogy aspect.

- Objects in nature are analogous to manufactured machines.
- Manufactured machines are the result of intelligent design.
- Analogous effects will have analogous causes.

Therefore, objects in nature are the result of something analogous to intelligent design – God.

 KEY WORD

Beneficial order a regular arrangement that produces an advantage or assistance

❝ KEY QUOTE ❞

Were there no examples in the world of contrivance except the eye, it alone would be sufficient to support the conclusion ... of an intelligent creator.

(Paley)

The analogous argument rests on the idea that similar effects imply similar causes.

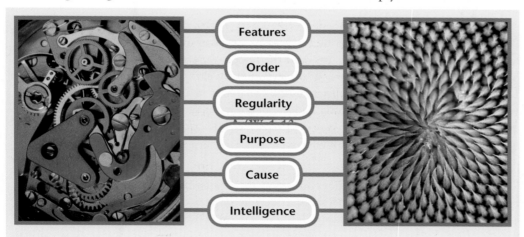

Features

Order

Regularity

Purpose

Cause

Intelligence

Like effects imply like causes

EXAM TIP

Remember that the exam is testing your understanding of philosophy rather than the life and times of Paley, so avoid including irrelevant biographical details in your answer.
This demonstrates selection of clearly relevant knowledge. (AO1)

Paley was aware of criticisms made against this approach (possibly those made by David Hume) and so, to offset them, he claimed that the argument was not weakened if:

■ we had never seen a watch before
■ we found that the mechanism did not always work perfectly
■ there were parts of the machine the function of which we did not understand.

b) *Design* qua *regularity*

Besides purpose, Paley also argued that the regularity observed in the Universe required the idea of an intelligent mind as explanation. He used as evidence scientific findings from his own time, from astronomy and from Newton's laws. An instance of this was the way in which the planets obeyed laws in their movements. The whole Universe, and all its parts, seemed ordered and acted in a regular and predictable way according to fundamental laws. The agent responsible for such order must be God.

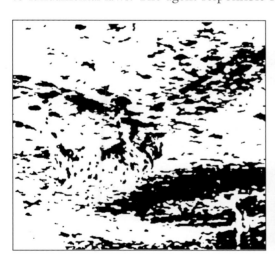 

Designed or not?

TASK

Which of the pictures, if either, is designed? How did you decide?
Objectives To appreciate the problem of recognising design
To consider what an undesigned Universe would look like
(To find out which, if either, is designed, turn to page 76.)

4 Challenges to the teleological argument

a) Hume

Paley's argument was published in 1802, some 26 years after the death of Hume. In his lifetime Hume had strongly attacked the teleological argument and many felt that his criticisms against Paley's form of the argument were valid. His criticism appeared in *Dialogues Concerning Natural Religion*, a book that was not published until 1779, three years after Hume had died. Hume had deliberately delayed publication until after his death because he felt the book was controversial. His criticisms of the argument cover several points, as discussed below.

i) An unsound analogy

The strength of the argument depends upon the similarity between the things held to be analogous – the machine and the world. The greater the similarity, the stronger is the argument; the weaker the similarity, the weaker is the argument. But, said Hume, the two analogies are far apart. Our world is *not* like a machine at all since it is composed of vegetables and animals. It is more organic than it is mechanical.

Neither is it philosophically sound to argue that intelligence is the necessary governing principle behind the world. Hume pointed out that there were lots of alternative governing principles, such as generation, vegetation and gravity. Why should one of these not be the dominant principle? Indeed, why should different principles not rule over their own natural domains: vegetation in plants, generation in animals, gravity in movements of planets? We cannot project from one limited area to another part or to the whole of nature.

Hume re-emphasised the point that the world did *not* closely resemble something man-made. If we see a house we conclude with certainty that it had an architect or builder. This is because we have seen it being built. We cannot infer from this that the Universe bears a similar cause (intelligence), because it does not bear close resemblance to a house. Hume pointed out that a number of people are involved in designing a house so perhaps, by analogy, there could be a team of gods who designed the world.

ii) Similar effects do not necessarily imply similar causes

Hume goes further by questioning whether it is a sound notion that similar effects result necessarily from similar causes. To know that an orderly Universe must arise from intelligence and thought, we would have to have experienced the origin of the world. Why should similar effects not be the result of different causes?

iii) Other possible analogies

This has already been hinted at in i) above. Hume argued that: 'the world plainly resembles more an animal or a vegetable than it does a watch or a knitting loom'. In particular, he argued that the world could be compared to a carrot. The relevance of this is that if the analogy is made with the carrot then the mark of design in the world could be caused by something similar to generation or vegetation. The natural world may possess some inner self-regulation and growth. Had Hume lived long enough he may well have joined forces with Darwin. **Darwinism** sees beneficial adaptations explained in non-personal terms by means of natural selection.

Indeed, Hume argued that, at its base, intelligence is itself caused by the process of generation. Surely the process of causes continues, since intelligence requires a cause. Hence you end up with an infinite regression of causes.

? KEY QUESTIONS

- **Was Hume an atheist?**
- **Is intelligence the only cause of order and regularity?**
- **Is the world more organic than mechanical?**
- **Do similar effects necessarily imply similar causes?**
- **Does intelligence require a cause?**

TASK

Think of examples in which things that have similar effects do not have the same cause.

KEY WORD

Darwinism the theory of natural selection to account for changes in nature

iv) Analogy makes God more human than divine

The more you press the analogy of the manufactured machine, such as a watch, with the Universe, the more human you have to make God (similar effects imply similar causes). Consider these arguments.

- We cannot ascribe infinity to God because, as the cause ought only to be proportional to the effect, the effect is not infinite.
- Likewise perfection cannot be ascribed to God. It is impossible for us to tell whether this system contains any great faults. Even if the system were perfect, it is not certain whether all the excellences can be ascribed to the workmen. For instance, many worlds might have been botched and bungled before this system was made.

Hume drove his point home by suggesting the following.

This world is very faulty and imperfect, and was only the first rude essay of some infant deity who afterwards abandoned it, ashamed of his lame performance; it is the work only of some inferior deity and is the object of derision to his superiors; it is the production of old age in some superannuated deity, and ever since his death has run on from the first impulse and active force which he gave it …

v) Analogy leads to a non-moral God

Hume listed some unpleasant features of nature, for example, earthquakes, war and disease, and questioned how the planning and design could be that of a just and good God. Workmen have to be judged in proportion to the quality of the work produced. Equally, Hume argued that you cannot attribute to the cause anything more than is sufficient to produce the effect. He claimed that a more plausible hypothesis was that of a God who had no moral character. Alternatively, there could be two forces, one good and one evil.

vi) Other explanations for apparent order

Hume suggested that we cannot be sure that the so-called organised Universe is not the result of some blind, cosmic accident. Indeed, any Universe is bound to have the appearance of design. There could be no Universe at all if the parts of it were not mutually adapted to some degree.

b) Mill

In *Nature and Religion* (1874), **John Stuart Mill** focused on a criticism that Hume had identified earlier. This was the occurrence of disorder in the Universe. In particular, Mill argued that in nature various atrocities occur that go unpunished. He concluded from this that such things could not result from an intelligent designer who had the attributes of the Christian God. Mill saw natural evil as evidence against God as designer. The work of nature that is destructive and random shows that we do not live in a benevolent world designed by a moral God. He draws the parallel with our reaction to human beings who acted in a similar way to nature. We would demand justice. For further information, read the section on the problem of evil, on page 91.

TASK

Think of some examples of analogies where the effects are the same but the cause is different.

Objective To understand the weakness of argument by analogy

---

66 **KEY QUOTES** **99**

Nearly all the
things which men
are hanged or
imprisoned for doing
to one another are
nature's everyday
performances.

(Mill)

Nature red in tooth
and claw.

(Mill)

All which people
are accustomed
to deprecate as
'disorder' and its
consequences,
is precisely a
counterpart of
nature's ways.
Anarchy and the
reign of terror are
overmatched in
injustice, ruin, and
death by a hurricane
and a pestilence.

(Mill)

… Darwin made it
possible to be an
intellectually fulfilled
atheist.

(Dawkins)

 KEY PROFILE: JOHN STUART MILL (1806–73)

Mill is probably best known for his writings on *Utilitarianism*, which held that one must always act so as to produce the greatest happiness for the greatest number of people, and for his defence of free speech and liberty in his book, *On Liberty*. However, he also wrote an influential book in which he argued that evil counted against belief in a designer God. Indeed, the amount of goodness in nature is far outweighed by the amount of suffering.

During his life he served as a member of Parliament and was godfather to Bertrand Russell.

c) Darwin

With the publication of Darwin's *Origin of Species* (1859), many regarded the teleological argument as no longer convincing. Darwin's theory described a way of understanding the natural world whereby its complex biological functions no longer required an intelligent designer to account for apparent order.

Firstly, Darwin identified that variations occur in offspring within a species. These are accidental. Secondly, he argued for natural selection, which involved the theory of the survival of the fittest. This is the theory that the organisms that are best able to survive, for example, find food, avoid predators, pass on their genetic traits. The combining of variation and survival leads eventually to the emergence of organisms that are suited to their environment. They will have the appearance of design but will be the result of evolving by variation and survival. God becomes an unnecessary hypothesis.

Darwin demonstrated that order was not necessarily evidence of purpose and design. Order could result from blind chance.

This challenge, which offers a naturalistic explanation for the features of the Universe without recourse to the supernatural, has continued to be voiced. Among the most well known and most vocal is Richard Dawkins.

A true watchmaker has foresight; he designs his cogs and springs, and plans their interconnections, with a future purpose in his mind's eye. Natural selection, the blind, unconscious, automatic process which Darwin discovered, and which we now know is the explanation for the existence and apparently purposeful form of all life, has no purpose in mind. It has no mind and no mind's eye. It does not plan for the future. It has no vision, no foresight, no sight at all. If it can be said to play the role of the watchmaker in nature, it is the *blind* watchmaker.

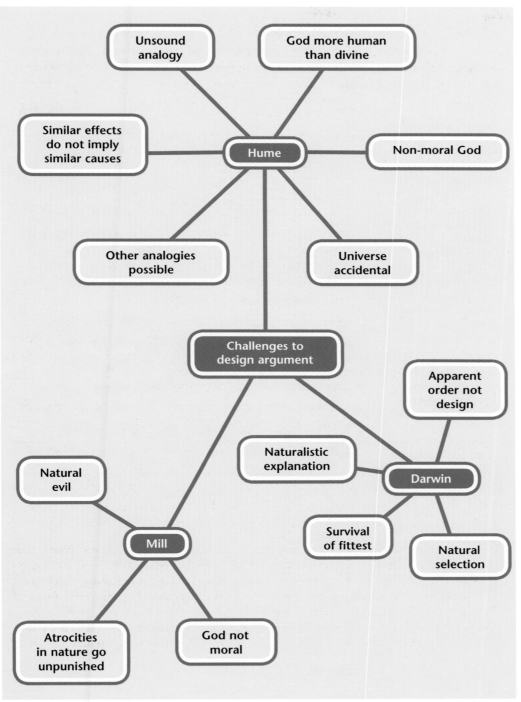

Summary diagram: Challenges to the design argument

Reflection and assessment AO2

It is vital to bring together the information that has been covered so far and recognise how it can be transformed into effective examination-style revision and answers. The best way to do this is to ask the question: 'How am I going to be assessed on this information?'

Read the following question and the answer that follows. Then complete the task that is in the margin.

Outline Paley's teleological argument. (25 marks)

Strength: Technical terminology and awareness that there are two aspects to Paley's argument, the other being focused on regularity.

Strength: The analogy is expressed in a concise way. It has not been embellished.

Development: This is not explained. Need to make clear that purposeful machines require a maker.

Development: Perhaps need to make clear why God.

Paley was an 18th-century Anglican clergyman. Paley agreed with the design argument. He argued design qua purpose using an analogy. In the watch analogy, Paley comes across it on a heath amongst the grass. He says, 'If you saw a stone and wondered how it came to exist, you could happily say that it was through chance factors like wind and rain. You would not come to the same conclusion about a watch. When you come to inspect the watch, we perceive that its several parts are framed and put together for a purpose. From this therefore, Paley believes that the watch must have a designer.

As a result of the watch having a designer, Paley believes that the Universe must have a designer. For Paley, the designer is God. Much like the watch, the Universe is so well put together and appears to have purpose, that there must be a designer behind it. Paley uses the watch analogy, to show that everything in the Universe has been designed and therefore has a designer.

Paley believes that you may not know the purpose of something but you know it has a purpose and therefore a designer. As part of his design qua regularity, Paley shows the orderliness of the orbiting planets and laws of nature to prove that there must be a designer. The designer is an external force and for Paley the explanation is God.

TASK

Look at the sample answer. In groups, analyse the answer by writing down the word or phrase from the essay in one column and the appropriate comment in the other column. Some comments have already been marked.

Objectives Critical analysis of an essay and awareness of different level demands Peer assessment

Answer to task on page 71: The first picture is designed. If you turn it upside down you will see a picture of a Dalmatian dog.

Suggestion for further application of skills

As a group, rewrite the answer so that it can score level 5 (check the level descriptors again on page 8 in the introduction).

Part 3
A critical analysis of the issues

What are the issues I am expected to answer and to analyse critically?

■ The strengths of the teleological argument

■ The weaknesses of the teleological argument

1 Strengths of the teleological argument

a) It gives an explanation

We seek an explanation of everything else, so why not of the Universe? The teleological argument answers the question: 'Why is the Universe the way it is?' Science works on the basis that everything has an explanation. That is what scientific enquiry assumes is the case. This brings into sharp contrast the two ways of looking at the Universe – either it is accidental or it is deliberate and purposeful.

b) It fits in with the other arguments for God's existence

Although the teleological argument, by itself, does not lead to a fully defined God of the Christian understanding, it can be seen as an important part of a cumulative argument. When all the arguments for the existence of God are considered, they point to the same conclusion – God. Taken together they fill out the attributes of the necessary being.

c) Recent scientific findings support it

Recent science has shown how finely balanced the Universe is. For instance, it has identified what are called cosmological constants. These are things such as the gravitational constant, the speed of light, the basic properties of elementary particles and the Planck constant. All these constants could have been different and are in most cases causally unrelated to each other, but each must fall within a very narrow range, if life is to be possible. If any had changed a small amount then life as we understand it would not have emerged. This strongly supports the view that the Universe is not an accident but has a design.

d) The challenges by Hume fail

i) An unsound analogy
There appears to be purpose in nature, and the watch displays purpose, so supporters of the argument would claim it was a sound analogy. Purpose shouts for an explanation.

Even if compared to a vegetable, which Hume suggests, it could be argued that the vegetable shows features of design, so who or what designed the vegetable?

? KEY QUESTIONS
- Does everything have an explanation?
- Do all the arguments lead to the *same* God?
- Is God the same God as the Christian God?
- Could the cosmological constants have been different?
- Does the claim to uniqueness mean that we are unable to investigate it?

❝ KEY QUOTE ❞
As we look out into the Universe and identify the many accidents of physics and astronomy that have worked together to our benefit, it almost seems as if this same Universe must in some sense have known that we were coming.

(Dyson)

TASK

Use the analogy of a work of art and the Universe to express the design argument.
List its strengths and weaknesses as an argument.
Outcome To help understand analogous arguments and how they function

KEY QUESTION

Is God the God of Christianity?

TASK

In groups, discuss whether the watch analogy refers to the parts of the Universe or the whole Universe. What problems does each raise about 'purpose'?
Outcome To understand Paley's analogy and its problems

KEY IDEA

Ockham's razor is the philosophical principle that states that entities should not be multiplied beyond necessity. The name derives from the idea of 'shaving off' those entities that are not needed. This principle is also extended to recommend, where there are multiple theories, selecting the simplest theory – the one that introduces fewest assumptions and fewest entities.

It seems unreasonable of Hume to say that no questions can be asked about the origin of things that are unique. Scientists try to account for things that are unique and the Universe shares many characteristics with its parts.

ii) Similar effects do not necessarily imply similar causes

The obvious cause of beneficial order and purpose and regularity is intelligence. There would have to be good reasons why this should not be the case and why an alternative should be considered.

iii) Other possible analogies

Supporters of Paley have, in fact, offered other analogies. For example, instead of a machine they propose a work of art. This would allow the idea of beauty also to be a common feature. We evaluate works of art in a different way from how we evaluate mechanical efficiency. Beauty is not just about efficiency. This analogy has the added attraction of embracing such a wasteful process as evolution.

iv) Analogy makes God more human than divine

It could be argued that making God more human is actually contrary to the analogical argument. It is a non-explanation, proposing a material God as an explanation for the material order in the Universe, since the material God already possesses this order.

Given that the argument is analogical, it does not demand a direct relationship between human designers and God.

Finally, the claim that the analogy leads us to suppose a whole community of gods can be challenged, on the basis of **Ockham's razor**. This principle of reasoning assumes that entities are not to be multiplied beyond necessity.

v) Analogy leads to a non-moral God

The teleological argument is part of a cumulative argument and does not claim to demonstrate all the attributes of God in each part of the argument. Supporters would point challengers in the direction of the moral argument for the existence of God (see page 82). See also the section on the problem of evil, on page 91.

vi) Other explanations for apparent order

Swinburne has challenged the argument of those who maintain that, unless the Universe was an orderly place, people would not be around to comment on its existence and there is nothing in the fact that people find order. What else could they find?

Swinburne deals with this position by pointing out that the existence of an observer has no bearing on the probability of the occurrence of the events being observed. If a series of highly improbable events gives rise to an observer who can note this improbability, they are nonetheless improbable. He uses an illustration to make clear his point.

Suppose that a madman kidnaps a victim and shuts him in a room with a card-shuffling machine. The machine shuffles ten decks of cards simultaneously and then draws a card from each deck and exhibits the ten cards simultaneously. The kidnapper tells the victim that he will shortly set the machine to work and it will exhibit its first draw, but that unless the draw consists of an ace of hearts from each deck, the machine will simultaneously set off an explosion which will kill the victim, in consequence of which he will not see which cards the machine drew. The machine is then set to work, and to the amazement and relief of the victim the machine exhibits an ace of hearts drawn from each deck. The victim thinks that this extraordinary fact needs an explanation in regard to the machine having been rigged in some way. But the kidnapper, who now reappears, casts doubt on this suggestion. 'It is hardly surprising,' he says, 'that the machine draws only aces of hearts. You could not possibly see anything else. For you would not be here to see anything at all, if any other cards had been drawn.'

But of course the victim is right and the kidnapper is wrong. There is indeed something extraordinary in ten aces of hearts being drawn and it clearly needs an explanation. The fact that this peculiar order is a necessary condition of the draw being perceived at all makes what is perceived no less extraordinary and in need of explanation. The teleologist's starting point is not that we perceive order rather than disorder, but that order rather than disorder is there. Maybe only if order is there can we know what is there, but that makes what is there no less extraordinary and in need of explanation.

e) The challenges by Mill fail

Many challenge Mill's claim, which seems to equate nature's crimes with humanity's crimes. The difference is one of intention. Nature does not act with intention in the way that human beings do. This seems like a flaw in Mill's argument.

His understanding of disorder has also been questioned. Disorder can be subjective. Even if there were disorder (evil), it may be part of God's greater plan. See also the section on the problem of evil, on page 91.

f) The challenges by Darwin fail

Without doubt, the theory of natural selection has been regarded as a major challenge to the teleological argument. However, various responses have been made in reply.

- Evolution is only a theory and not proven. The theory is seen as wrong.
- There is a jump from moving from a description of how natural selection operates upon existence, to the assumption that natural selection also provides the explanation for that existence. As Tennant said: 'The survival of the fittest presupposes the arrival of the fit.'
- There can be no origin of species without a mechanism that is itself teleological. This system needs an explanation. Natural selection cannot give it. The explanation is God. God is the designer of the process of natural selection.
- New versions of the teleological argument are now popular. They focus on things such as the fine tuning of the Universe, or irreducible complexities. (See the section about intelligent design, pages 105–6.)

Swinburne accepted that the arguments used by Paley about the complex structure of plants and animals, to which he refers as spatial order, were not convincing since Darwinism could account for these features. Instead, Swinburne focused on temporal order, by which he meant the laws of nature throughout the Universe. The Universe is orderly, yet it could have been chaotic.

Nature seems to conform to a formula. If there is an explanation to account for this, then it cannot be a scientific one because we explain the operation of scientific laws in terms of more general scientific laws. The best explanation and the simplest is a personal explanation rather than scientific laws – God.

KEY PERSON

William of Ockham (1288–1349) was a Franciscan monk who studied philosophy and theology and to whom the principle known as 'Ockham's razor' is attributed.

66 **KEY QUOTE** 99

The teleologist's starting point is not that we perceive order rather than disorder, but that order rather than disorder is there.

(Swinburne)

KEY QUESTIONS

- Does the Universe have to be ordered?
- Can evil exist if there is a God?
- Did God design the evolutionary process?
- Are there such things as irreducible complexities?

66 **KEY QUOTE** 99

So either the orderliness of nature is where all explanation stops, or we must postulate an agent of great power and knowledge … the simplest such agent is … God.

(Swinburne)

79

66 ■ KEY QUOTE ■ 99

... far from being
the 'terminus'
of the quest for
intelligibility and
explanation in the
Universe, God is the
terminal illness of
reason.

(Atkins)

 KEY QUESTION

Would any world,
whatever its form,
have the appearance
of being designed?

2 Weaknesses of the teleological argument

a) Not a proof

The teleological arguments tend to be expressed as inductive arguments and so are about probabilities rather than deductive proof.

b) An undesigned Universe

Linguistic philosophy has focused on the issue of whether statements are meaningful. One claim is that a meaningful statement is one where we know what would disprove it. Hence, until we can say what the world would have to be like, not to be designed, we cannot conclude that the world is designed.

c) God is not an external being

Others would argue that God is not an additional being but rather a word used to describe a sense of ultimate meaning to life. God is not an object, not a thing. God represents what is most important to us.

3 Possible conclusions

When assessing the teleological argument as evidence for God's existence, it is important to reflect upon the arguments previously discussed and arrive at some appropriate conclusion. It may be that you accept none of these listed here, or just one of them, or you may have a different conclusion that is not listed. However, what is important is the way that you have arrived at your conclusion – the reasoning process. From the preceding discussions, here are some possible conclusions you could draw.

1   The teleological argument is successful and proves the existence of God. There are various arguments that are described as teleological. It could be one particular form of the argument that is regarded as successful or it could be the general approach shared by them all.
2   The teleological argument does not prove that God exists. However, it is persuasive, especially when considered alongside the other arguments for the existence of God. It forms part of the cumulative case for the existence of God.
3   The teleological argument fails to prove the existence of God. This could refer to one particular form of the argument. The fact that one argument fails does not prove that all forms of the teleological argument fail.
4   The Universe is inexplicable. It has no explanation and it does not need one. It just is.
5   The success or failure of the teleological argument is still being debated. The argument remains a live issue in philosophical circles and no agreed conclusion has yet been reached.
6   The whole idea of trying to demonstrate that God exists is nonsensical. It is to misunderstand the meaning of the word God. God is not an object or a thing. It is a word used to encapsulate that which is most important to us.

Reflection and assessment AO2

Look back to page 8 in the Introduction to review the level descriptors for AO2. There is a description of the character and features for each level. The exam is marked with reference to levels.

Look at the following sample basic answer – a response to the question:

'Darwinism, rather than God, is a better explanation of purpose in the world.' Discuss. (10 marks)

A *basic* answer might deal with the question by:

- stating how Darwinism explains apparent order and purpose in the world
- giving some basic explanation why, therefore, God is redundant as an explanation
- drawing a simple conclusion that the claim is true.

Suggestion for further application of skills

Now use what you have done to create the ideal plan for the question:

'That God created the world is the simplest and best explanation for the universe.' Discuss. (10 marks)

Now try answering this question under timed conditions and use the ideal plan to do some peer assessment. Mark each other's work, identifying strengths and areas for development.

TASK

Look at the basic answer opposite. Try to work out how a developed answer would deal with the question, by adding two or three more bullet points.
Now develop this answer to indicate how a higher-level answer would deal with the question, by adding further bullet points. Remember to keep the bullet points focused on the question. For the higher level, the evaluation should show a range of evidence to sustain an argument and show understanding of critical analysis of different viewpoints, for a well-constructed and organised answer.
Objective To develop awareness, by gradually building up a response, of what constitutes a higher-level answer using a range of evidence to sustain an argument (AO2 level 5)

Part 4A

The moral argument

What am I required to study?

- The moral argument from Kant
- Psychological challenges from Freud

This means I am expected to know about:

- Kant's form of the moral argument
- Kant's concept of the *summum bonum*
- Kant's inferences about innate moral awareness
- Freud's challenges to the moral argument
- Freud's view that moral awareness comes from sources other than God.

This section continues to explore some of the main arguments for the existence of God. The moral argument has many different forms but the exam requires a study of only one – that of Kant. Freud's challenge to this argument will also be examined. The debate about the source of moral awareness is a central issue. Part 4B will assess the extent to which Freud's challenge is successful.

It would be helpful to write your notes under the headings listed in 'This means I am expected to know about', as it is from these areas that the exam questions will be derived.

Remember that your studies will include elements of the *two* basic assessment objectives of:

- Knowledge and Understanding (AO1)
- Evaluation (AO2).

See pages 7–8 in the Introduction to remind yourself of these objectives.

The evaluation material is set out in Part 4B of this topic (page 88) and can be studied either alongside the AO1 material, as you work through this topic, or as a discrete topic.

1 Introduction

a) Kant's approach

Having examined the traditional arguments for God, Kant found them flawed, though the teleological probably impressed him most. For him, the route to God was more likely to be through our own experience and human reason. He argued that the mind determines the way in which we experience things, rather than external things in themselves. All we know comes from sense experiences organised by our minds. We cannot know things in themselves, but only things as we perceive them to be.

❝ KEY QUOTE ❞

Two things fill the mind with ever new and increasing admiration and awe ... the starry heavens above me and the moral law within me ...

(Kant)

Kant held that the categories by which we understand the world, such as space, time, and causality were *not* derived from experience. Rather, the mind imposes categories on all its experiences.

Empirical evidence about the world is unreliable and can never lead to certainty. The starting point needs to be from within our own experience; for Kant that is the experience of moral choice. He thought that from the experience of moral choice it was possible to reason that there was a God. One of the implications of the experience of moral choice, through pure reasoning, was the conclusion that God must exist.

 KEY PROFILE: IMMANUEL KANT (1724–1804)

One of the main focuses of Kant's philosophy concerned the question of what we can know. His great contribution was to argue that the mind plays an active role in structuring reality.

In his discussions about morality, Kant saw that it was the motivation rather than the outcome that determined whether the act should be judged moral. The reason for this was that intentions could be controlled whilst outcomes could not.

For Kant, the belief in God was a practical necessity. The idea of God could not be separated from the relation of happiness with morality. It was this connection that made the moral world intelligible.

b) Some key terms

To understand Kant's moral argument it is necessary to understand the terms in which he expresses it, as they underpin his thinking and reasoning.

- **Practical reason** – the human ability to decide through reflection on an appropriate course of action. It develops and guides the good will rather than trying to achieve happiness.
- **Autonomy of the will** – the ability of the will to choose maxims for itself independently of any desires that originate from our own nature.
- **The good will** – a will that is intrinsically good, with motives that are always right. It acts from duty rather than just conforming to duty.
- **Freedom** – the ability to be able to follow our own rational principles instead of our desires. This means that we can act on categorical imperatives.
- *Summum bonum* – the highest good. It is an end in itself and at the same time contains all other goods. The essence of it is virtue but it is not complete until it includes happiness.
- **Categorical imperative** – a principle for testing whether something is right or wrong. It is a demand to act in a certain way for its own sake, rather than for some other purpose, for example, 'Act only on that **maxim** which you can at the same time will to be a universal law.'

Being **moral** is a case of following the categorical imperative. A genuinely moral action is one that is done according to a maxim that we can will to be universal law. Thus an immoral action is one of which the underlying maxim cannot be intelligibly willed to be universal law, for example, lying to suit my own ends would not be wise for a universal law.

 KEY WORDS

Categorical imperative an unconditional moral law that applies to all rational beings and is independent of any personal motive or desire (For Kant, *the* categorical imperative was the principle that one should act on a maxim only if one can will that it becomes a universal law.)

Summum bonum the ultimate end or goal to which human beings ought to aspire; comprises both virtue and happiness

Maxim a general rule or principle governing the action of a rational person

Moral relating to human behaviour and what ought and ought not to be done

TASK

Find out what other categorical imperatives Kant stated.

Do you think they are workable as a universal law? Give reasons for your view.

Objective To develop understanding of the concept of categorical imperatives

EXAM TIP

Kant's moral argument includes lots of technical words. You will be expected to use them in your answers where appropriate. Make sure you use them accurately and explain them.
This demonstrates use of correct language and terminology. (AO1)

? KEY QUESTION

Are we under an obligation to achieve goodness?

This is the test for good and bad actions. Reason, not feeling, is the guide and good acts are obligatory because they are rational.

c) Kant's argument

The argument for God can be presented using the following steps.

- Our moral experience shows that we are under an obligation to achieve goodness or virtue – not merely an average level of morality but the highest standard possible. We recognise an obligation to achieve what is best – real virtue.
- Beyond this, we recognise also that true virtue should be rewarded by happiness. It would not be a rationally satisfying state of affairs if happiness came to the unvirtuous or unhappiness to the virtuous. If people were virtuous but were also in pain and misery, their virtue would still be valuable but, nevertheless, the total situation would not be the best possible.
- The desired state of affairs in which humankind is both virtuous and happy is called by Kant the *summum bonum* or highest good. This we recognise to be what ought to happen.
- Now, in Kant's famous argument, ought implies can – an obligation to achieve something implies the possibility that the goal can be achieved, otherwise there can be no obligation. It has to be possible, therefore, for the *summum bonum* to be achieved.
- However, while humans can achieve virtue, it is clearly outside their power to ensure that virtue is rewarded or coincides with happiness.
- Thus it necessitates the existence of God as the one who has the power to bring virtue and happiness into harmony. Such rewarding with happiness clearly does not take place before death. So Kant argued that there must be survival after death.

Note that Kant was not arguing that morality did not exist if God's existence is denied. For Kant, the fact that it is a duty or obligation is sufficient reason to do it. However, he thought that God was demanded, if the goal of morality was to be realised.

For further discussion on this topic, see Unit 2, *Ethics*, page 159.

EXAM TIP

The exam requires *only* Kant's form of the argument. Do not attribute more popular forms of the argument to Kant.
This demonstrates selection and relevant knowledge skills. (AO1)

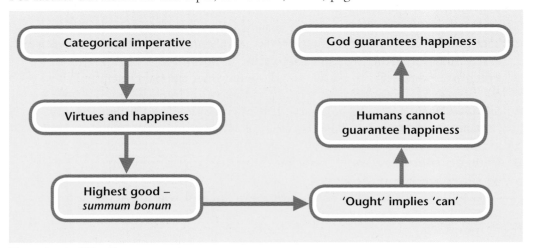

Flow chart of Kant's argument

2 Possible weaknesses with the argument

a) Ought implies can

Kant argued that ought implies can. If he meant that it was logically possible to bring about the *summum bonum*, then all he was saying was that it was not a logical contradiction. But just because it is not a logical contradiction does not therefore mean that it actually happens. If he meant that it actually happens, we can ask the questions: 'Why must it? How can anyone know?' In effect, we question his assumption.

b) Why God?

Why make the assumption that only God can bring about the highest good? 'Why not a pantheon of angels?' suggests Brian Davies.

c) Why happiness?

Why make the assumption that virtue must be rewarded with happiness?

d) Other explanations

Sense of duty can be explained by other means, for example, *socialisation*.

3 Freud's challenge to the moral argument

As already noted, the moral argument is weakened if another explanation can be given for our moral awareness and sense of duty. One person who gave a naturalistic explanation of moral awareness was **Sigmund Freud**. According to him, socialisation, not reason, formed the basis of our sense of morality.

> ### KEY PROFILE: SIGMUND FREUD (1856–1939)
>
> Sigmund Freud was born in Moravia, in what is now the Czech Republic. He spent most of his life in Vienna but, in 1937, being Jewish, he was forced to flee to London from the invading Nazis. In Vienna he worked as a doctor, specialising in neurological disorders. Freud realised that symptoms that did not have an organic or bodily basis nevertheless were as real as though they had. So began his search for treatment in which he developed his psychoanalytical method. The goal of the therapy was to bring to consciousness repressed thoughts and feelings. He regarded dreams as a way into the unconscious. He dismissed the idea that God was the source of moral awareness.

a) Freud's structure of the mind

Freud saw personality as having three aspects that work together to produce all our complex behaviours:

- **Id –** the primitive mind, which contains all the basic needs and feelings. It functions in the irrational and emotional part of the mind. It is also the unconscious self. This reflects the child's 'I want'.
- **Ego –** this develops out of a growing awareness that you can't always get what

? KEY QUESTIONS

- **Does ought imply can?**
- **Is God the only thing that can bring about the highest good?**
- **Why assume virtue must be rewarded with happiness?**

❝ KEY QUOTE ❞

I found in myself a constant love for my mother, and jealousy of my father. I now consider this to be a universal event in childhood.

(Freud)

TASK

Find out how Oedipus came to murder his father and marry his mother.

How does this story relate to Freud's psychoanalytical method?

Objective To help understanding of the Oedipus complex

 KEY PERSON

Sophocles was born around 497BCE, and was a Greek tragedian. His most famous work is the *Oedipus Cycle*, which consists of three plays, one of which is *Oedipus Rex*.

you want. It functions with the rational part of the mind and controls the id. This reflects adulthood.

■ **Superego** – the last part of the mind to develop and seen as the moral part of the mind. It is the unconscious mind and itself consists of two parts:
   – the ego-ideal, which praises good actions
   – the conscience, which makes you feel guilty for bad actions.

The ego-ideal is what the child's parents or society approve of or value; it provides rules for good behaviour. In contrast, the conscience provides rules about what constitutes bad behaviour. These rules evolve from a child's perception of the extent to which parents and society show disapproval or lack of value of certain behaviour. Freud understood psychological conflicts as conflicts between the id and the superego, in which the ego was trying to negotiate between them.

b) Source of moral awareness

Freud's analysis of the mind provides him with his explanation of moral awareness. There is no sense of duty or good will, as with Kant, but rather the conscious mind of the ego battling between the subconscious primitive desires of the id and the demands of society and parents of the superego. When conflict arises we internalise it and speak of conscience.

Kant thought in terms of absolutes and *summum bonum*. Freud thought in terms of relative and unnecessary guilt. Indeed, Freud argued that our moral awareness cannot be from God since we all have different opinions about ethical issues.

c) The Oedipus complex

Central to Freud's understanding of the structure of the mind and of conscience is the Oedipus complex. He sought to show that this pattern of development of the mind reflected the stages of progression into adult sexual maturity. He named his theory the Oedipus complex, after the famous Greek tragedy *Oedipus Rex* by **Sophocles**. In the story, Oedipus unwittingly murdered his father and married his mother. Freud saw in this story a parallel with the developing ego. He believed the Oedipus story was popular and remains popular because it bears witness to the universal experience of this Oedipal complex.

Freud argued that, at the Oedipal stage, usually from three to five years old, the child experiences an erotic attachment to one parent and hostility toward the other parent. The resolution of the jealousies and angers towards both parents forms the nucleus of the superego, the conscience. Freud linked this phase and the repression of desire with the origin of guilt. He argued that most mental disorders find their roots in events at this stage of development. So the origin of conscience, values and guilt go back to experiences in childhood and particularly in the progression into adult sexual maturity.

Reflection and assessment

It is now time to channel the information you have considered in a more focused way. In order to do this, once again you need to ask yourself the question: 'How am I going to be assessed on my use of this information?'

In the examination you will be assessed by levels of response (see pages 7–8). Below is an examination-style question about the moral argument. Beneath it are three sets of bullet points under the headings 'basic', 'developed' and 'higher'. A basic answer relates to levels 1 and 2. The developed answer can score level 3 or possibly the lower requirements for level 4. The higher level scores from level 4 up to the maximum.

Read the following question and complete the task. To do the task you will need to look back at the level descriptors given in the Introduction (pages 7–8).

Explain Kant's moral argument. (25 marks)

Basic	Developed	Higher
• Feeling of duty or obligation • Highest good • God is needed for ultimate happiness	• True virtue is rewarded by happiness by God (*summum bonum*) • Ought implies can • Reward comes in another realm, after death	• Clarification that moral argument urges action to aim for the highest possible standards • Discussion of the link between happiness and virtue and the reasoning behind this • Some discussion of the precise meaning of obligation – the ability to exercise the obligation • An understanding of the idea that it is beyond human control to bring about the balance between happiness and virtue

Suggestion for further application of skills

Using the question and notes above, create a plan and then write up your answer under timed conditions. After grading it would be beneficial to photocopy the best answers (one for each essay) and, as a group, consider what makes them good. Use this time of reflection to revisit your own work and improve it through redrafting it.

TASK

From what you have so far learned about levels of response, create a list of points for a developed-level answer (level 3). Improve this further for a higher-level answer. You can then create writing frames and fully drafted answers for the whole question.
Outcomes Gradually to build up and improve on an answer
To develop appreciation of the difference between a level 3 answer and a level 4–5 answer

TASK

Consider the following question:
Explain the challenges made to the moral argument. (25 marks)
Study the example of what could be given for 'basic', 'developed' and 'higher' for the question about the moral argument, opposite. Add to this list as a group. Now, in small groups, work out what could be included for 'basic', 'developed' and 'higher' for the question about the challenges made to the moral argument. You could swap ideas between groups, to finalise your notes, or each group could take the 'basic', 'developed' and 'higher' sections in turn and discuss your notes.
Objective To develop an awareness of what will constitute a very good answer (levels 4–5) by gradually building up a response

Part 4B

A critical analysis of the issues

What are the issues that I am expected to consider and to analyse critically?

- The strengths of the moral argument
- The weaknesses of the moral argument

? KEY QUESTIONS

- Do we have an innate sense of right and wrong?
- Are we obliged to act in a certain way?
- Can there be morality without a God?

TASK

Do you agree with John Hick's argument about the implications for morality if there is no God?

Can you think of a reply to his argument?

Objectives To develop the skill of responding to arguments
To develop the skill of challenging views

1 Strengths of the moral argument

a) Our experience

The moral argument makes sense of our own experience of right and wrong. Generally, we all seem to have an innate moral sense. Although we may disagree over details, there are fundamental moral principles that we all share.

b) Obligation

Most people feel there are certain obligations about how they should behave. Obligation, obedience and guilt are only meaningful if there is a person to whom responsibility is due.

To deny that God exists is to deny the source of authority for good moral behaviour and to deny the ultimate sanction against evil behaviour. Therefore, there would be no reason to behave in a good way; there would be no reason not to act according to our own whims. John Hick points out that on humanist presuppositions, it would be inconsistent to praise self-sacrifice for the sake of the human community since: '... it is unreasonable for anything to be of more value to a man than his own existence' (*Arguments for the Existence of God*, 1970). In other words, it becomes very difficult to justify ultimate self-sacrifice if God does not exist.

c) The challenge of Freud fails

- The view that our conscience is in some way an independent witness to our behaviour has been challenged. Freud seems to depict conscience as some kind of internal judge.
- Conscience is not something that suddenly comes into existence in humans at five or six years old. Moral awareness is a gradual and continuing process.
- Freud's theory involving id, ego and superego seems unnecessarily complex. There are much simpler explanations.
- There is no scientific evidence to support Freud's theories about the mind and brain. His theories were based on limited observations from primarily upper-class Austrian women living in a strict era of the 1900s.
- Atheism is also open to psychological explanation.

d) Part of the cumulative argument

Taken with other arguments for the existence of God, the moral argument highlights an attribute of God, a moral being. Often appeal is made to the Ockham's razor approach, which claims that unnecessary entities should be erased. The solutions to all the questions raised by the theistic arguments, such as cause, order, regularity and morality, is the one entity, called God. This is regarded as a simpler solution, since it only requires the single entity – God – for a solution to *all* the arguments. Various analogies have been used to illustrate this approach. For instance, if you have a leaky bucket (inductive argument for God's existence) and insert other leaky buckets inside (more arguments for God's existence), then the leaks are sealed – the arguments gain strength.

2 Further weaknesses of the moral argument

a) Other explanations for moral awareness

Objectively binding moral laws can have other sources than God. For instance:

- **Cultural relativism** – every society approves and disapproves of particular actions and teaches its young to think of such actions as right or wrong. Which acts are designated right or wrong differs from one culture to another. Thus morality is a product of human culture. The reason we feel guilt comes from socialisation, for example, values taught to us when we were children.
- **Emotivism** – when people state that an act is wrong they are not stating a fact, but merely giving voice to their own emotion or attitude about the act.
- **Evolution** – human beings who have the notion to be kind, helpful, etc. are more likely to survive in the process of natural selection. This characteristic has been genetically transmitted.

Even if the moral law requires a source of authority and sanction, this does not mean that there *is* a source or sanction. What I require to be the case hardly brings the case into reality.

b) The cumulative approach is flawed

It is debatable as to whether the introduction of the entity we call God is really a simpler answer, given the complexities of the concept of God. Also $0 + 0 = 0$ (A failed argument added to another failed argument results in both failing.)

c) God is not an external being

Others would argue that God is not an additional being but rather a word used to describe a sense of ultimate meaning to life. God is not an object, nor a thing. God represents what is most important to us.

3 Possible conclusions

When assessing the moral argument as evidence for God's existence, it is important to reflect upon the arguments previously discussed and arrive at some appropriate conclusion. It may be that you accept none of these listed here, or just one of them, or you may have a different conclusion that is not listed. However, what is important is the way that you have arrived at your conclusion – the reasoning process.

From the preceding discussions, here are some possible conclusions you could draw.

? KEY QUESTIONS

- **What is a conscience?**
- **Is God a simple solution?**
- **Is the cumulative argument persuasive?**
- **Can objectively binding moral laws have other explanations other than God?**
- **Is God a simpler explanation?**

KEY IDEA

The principle of Ockham's razor states that the explanation of any phenomenon should make as few assumptions as possible, eliminating those that make no difference in the observable predictions of the explanatory hypothesis or theory.

EXAM TIP

Make sure that you explain how your criticism weakens the argument. Avoid just stating a criticism and leaving it to the examiner to work out why it is. This demonstrates justifying a point of view. (AO2)

KEY QUOTE

If the only way open to us for the knowledge of God were solely that of the reason, the human race would remain in the blackest shadows of ignorance.

(Aquinas)

1 The moral argument is successful and proves the existence of God.

2 The moral argument does not prove that God exists. However, it is persuasive, especially when considered alongside the other arguments for the existence of God. It forms part of the cumulative case for the existence of God.

3 The moral argument fails to prove the existence of God. This could refer to Kant's form of the argument. However, there are other forms, for example, obedience and guilt are only seen to be meaningful if there is a person to whom responsibility is due. The fact that one argument fails does not prove that all forms of the moral argument fail.

4 Morality can be accounted for in purely naturalistic terms.

5 The success or failure of the moral argument is still being debated. The argument remains a live issue in philosophical circles and no agreed conclusion has yet been reached.

6 The whole concept of trying to demonstrate that God exists is nonsensical. It is to misunderstand the meaning of the word God. God is not an object or a thing. It is a word used to encapsulate that which is most important to us.

Reflection and assessment AO2

It is vital to bring together the information that has been covered so far and recognise how it can be transformed into effective examination-style revision and answers. The best way to do this is to ask the question: 'How am I going to be assessed on this information?'

Look back to page 8 to review the levels of response descriptors for AO2. There is a description of the character and features for each level. The exam is marked by reference to levels.

Look at the key points, listed here, in answer to the question:

'Moral awareness demands the existence of a God.' Discuss.   (10 marks)

You will need to refer to these points, which are not presented in any particular order, to complete the task.

- *Summum bonum* is virtue plus happiness.
- Happiness requires God to guarantee it.
- Ought implies can.
- Only the existence of God can account for moral awareness.
- Freud saw upbringing as the source of behaviour development.
- There is no innate sense of right and wrong.
- Freud's understanding of conscience is flawed.

Suggestion for further application of skills

Read again the discussion about possible conclusions, above. In groups, design a flow chart that clearly provides the evidence for each conclusion, drawing upon the key issues covered in this section.

TASK

Use the key points, opposite, as a basis for a writing frame to answer the question opposite.

The list is deliberately basic. At this stage you should be able to identify the fact that it contains the general issues but does not have the detail of development, which you will need to add. Remember to add relevant quotes and questions at suitable places. The final product should show evidence of a sustained argument and critical analysis of more than one point of view.

Objective To encourage the development of an answer that shows understanding and critical analysis of different viewpoints (level 5 descriptor)

Part 1

The problem of evil

What am I required to study?

- The problem of evil

This means I am expected to know about:

- the nature of the problem of evil
- natural and moral evil
- the classic theodicies' response to:
  - God's responsibility for the existence of evil in the world
  - the origins of evil
  - the role of human free will
- criticisms of each theodicy.

The problem of evil is a vast topic and there have been many attempts at resolving it. This section concentrates on explaining what the problem is and focuses on three particular aspects of the problem addressed by two classic theodicies: those of Augustine and Irenaeus.

It would be helpful to write your notes under the headings listed in 'This means I am expected to know about', as it is from these areas that the exam questions will be derived.

Remember that your studies will include elements of the *two* basic assessment objectives of:

- Knowledge and Understanding (AO1)
- Evaluation (AO2).

See pages 7–8 in the Introduction to remind yourself of these objectives.

The evaluation material is set out in Part 3 of this topic (page 109) and can be studied either alongside the AO1 material, as you work through this topic, or as a discrete topic.

1 The nature of the problem of evil

a) The logical problem

In his *Confessions*, Augustine (CE354–430) expressed the classic dilemma of the problem of evil as: 'Either God cannot abolish evil, or he will not; if he cannot then he is not all-powerful; if he will not then he is not all-good.'

If one accepts that God is both all-powerful and good, then the assumption is that a good God would eliminate evil as far as he is able. Given that he is all-powerful, he should therefore eliminate it all. However, evil exists. Clearly, God has the means (power) and the motivation (love, goodness) to eliminate evil. So why doesn't he?

> 66 **KEY QUOTE** 99
>
> **Either God cannot abolish evil, or he will not; if he cannot then he is not all-powerful; if he will not then he is not all-good.**
>
> **(Augustine)**

EXAM TIP

It is not sufficient just to say that God is all-powerful and all-loving, therefore the existence of evil causes a problem. You need to spell out why those attributes of God – power and love – are seen as inconsistent with the existence of evil.

This demonstrates relevant understanding through use of evidence and examples. (AO1)

KEY WORDS

Argument a set of statements such that one of them (the conclusion) is supported or implied by the others (the premises)

Classical theism the belief in a personal deity, creator of everything that exists and who is distinct from that creation

Theodicy a justification of the righteousness of God, given the existence of evil

EXAM TIP

In an essay you need to illustrate these categories of moral and natural evil, explaining why they are described as evil.

This demonstrates relevant understanding through use of examples. (AO1)

When put in its simplest form, this **argument** it is seen as essentially a logical problem, expressed by means of three premises and a conclusion.

God is all powerful,
God is all good,
God opposes evil.
Therefore evil does not exist in the world.

A theist would agree with the premises, yet few would agree with the conclusion. They would admit that evil exists. There is therefore a contradiction and the logical reasoning suggests that one of the premises is wrong. However, that would deny **classical theism**, which argues that God is all-good and all-powerful.

Remember these arguments.

- God's omnipotence includes God's omniscience: for a God who can do anything, but does not always know what is the best way of doing it, might be said to be less than all-powerful.
- God cannot do the logically impossible, for example, make square circles. Neither can he do what is inconsistent with his nature. (Some of these points are debatable.)
- The premise that God is all-good implies that he opposes evil and will wish to remove it.
- The problem is really only a problem for the believer in God, since if there is no God there is no problem.

b) Moral and natural evil

The illustration of evil is an important aspect of exploring the problem since different types of evil raise different philosophical issues. It is usual to divide evil into:

- moral – in which responsible actions cause suffering or harm, for example, murder, stealing, lying
- natural – in which events cause suffering but over which human beings have little or no control, for example, earthquakes and diseases. At various times certain events have been used as classic illustrations of natural evil. At one stage it was the Lisbon earthquake of 1755, but in the present day it is the 2008 Chinese earthquake, the 2004 Asian tsunami, AIDS or cancer.

The problem of suffering has a slightly different emphasis. It focuses on the experience of evil. It raises different questions because of the experience. It deals with the problem on a more personal level – how the individual responds to suffering. The questions that are raised here are more of the form: 'Why me? Why now? Why this particular form? Why this intensity? Why this length of time?' They are questions that struggle to find purpose and explanation in what is being experienced.

Quite clearly, the rather academic and cold discussion about the philosophical problems of evil are often inappropriate for someone battling with their own personal pain and grief.

In Western philosophy there have been two main **theodicies**, those of Irenaeus (CE130–202) and Augustine (CE354–430).

The Asian tsunami of December 2004

TASK

The photo shows part of the Asian tsumani of December 2004. Explain why such an event is an example of natural evil.

List the similarities *and* the differences between natural and moral evil.

Objective To understand the perceived differences between natural and moral evil

Some make further groupings such as physical, which refers to pain itself and mental anguish, and metaphysical, which refers to imperfection and contingency as a feature of the cosmos.

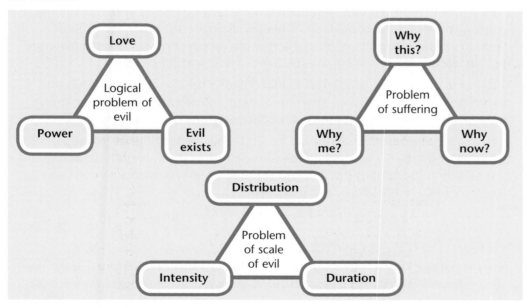

Summary diagram: The problem of evil

❝ KEY QUOTE ❞

Nearly all the things which men are hanged or imprisoned for doing to one another, are Nature's everyday performances.

(J.S. Mill)

66 ■ **KEY QUOTE** ■ **99**

And God said: 'Let us make man in our image, after our likeness.'

(Genesis 1: 26 RSV)

KEY PERSON

John Hick (1922–) is an English theologian and philosopher who has been influential in popularising a soul-making theodicy. He has also argued for religious pluralism. Hick has developed the Irenaeus theodicy in his book, *Evil and the God of Love*.

2 The classical theodicies

a) *Irenaeus' theodicy (soul-making)*

In the writings of Irenaeus there appears the idea that human beings were not created perfect but are developing towards perfection. Irenaeus made a distinction between the image and the likeness of God (Genesis 1: 26). Adam had the form of God but not the content of God. Adam and Eve were expelled from the Garden of Eden because they were immature and needed to develop; they were to grow into the likeness (content) of God. They were the raw material for a further stage of God's creative work.

The fall of humanity is seen as an inevitable part of growing up and maturing. This process takes place as free persons make decisions about their lives and the world in which God has placed them, so the emphasis in this theodicy is soul-making.

Irenaeus himself never developed a full theodicy as such, but his approach represents that put forward in recent times by **John Hick**. Hick sees the first phase of God – making humankind in his image – as the culmination of the evolutionary process, whereby a creature has been evolved who has the possibility of existing in conscious fellowship with God. The second phase involves making moral, responsible choices in concrete situations. It is a necessary pilgrimage within the life of each individual.

An essential part of this theodicy is that this process is worthwhile because of the eventual outcome. Hick argued that, if the process is not completed in this life, then there is another life in another realm to which we go, until the process is complete. Thus, all will eventually succeed.

 KEY PROFILE: IRENAEUS BISHOP OF LYON (CE 130–202)

Irenaeus is thought to have been a Greek from Smyrna (what is now the region of Izmir in Turkey). He was raised in a Christian family and became the second Bishop of Lyon. Almost all of his writings were directed against Gnosticism, which he considered a heresy. Gnosticism preached a hidden wisdom or knowledge that was only given to a select group. This knowledge was necessary for salvation or escape from this world.

One of his most influential arguments concerns the conception of human beings as created imperfect. This theory later influenced eastern theology and was used by John Hick for his modern soul-making theodicy.

Irenaeus is referred to as an Early Church Father. This is the term used of the early and influential theologians and writers in the Christian Church, particularly those of the first five centuries of Christian history. It does not generally include the New Testament authors.

b) *Augustine's theodicy (soul-deciding)*

Augustine did not have a fully worked-out theodicy as such. He approached the issue of the problem of evil from a variety of angles and these general ideas have been the basis of a number of Augustinian-type theodicies, which reflect the traditional Christian approach.

His main themes are summarised here.

- Creation is good.
- Humans beings were created perfect.
- Human beings have free will.
- Human beings used their free will to turn away from God (The Fall).
- God makes possible repentance and salvation.

The emphasis is on soul-deciding: those who do not turn back to God are condemned to hell.

This approach to the problem of evil is identified as a soul-deciding theodicy, since our response to evil and God's rescue plan of salvation – belief in Jesus and his death for us – determines what happens to us when we die.

 KEY PROFILE: AUGUSTINE (CE354–430)

Augustine was Bishop of Hippo and is regarded as the first major Christian philosopher. He was distinctive in that he thought through philosophical issues in the light of his faith and his understanding of the Bible. His various approaches on the issue of the problem of evil can be found mainly in *The City of God* and in his autobiography, *The Confessions*.

3 How the theodicies address issues

a) The origins of evil

The actual origin of evil is part of the problem of evil. If God created or caused all things then clearly he is the originator of evil. The fact that God is all-powerful and so all-knowing also raises problems about our free will and hence our responsibility for doing evil.

In both the Irenaeus and the Augustine theodicies, the origin of evil is traced back to the Fall, described in Genesis 3. However, for Irenaeus it is seen as a necessary part of the growing and maturing process.

In contrast, Augustine sees it as a falling from perfection that can only be reversed by accepting God's rescue plan of salvation through Jesus.

As God is the author of everything in the created Universe, it follows that evil is not a substance, otherwise it would mean that God created it, which Augustine rejects. Thus, for Augustine, evil is a privation, or the absence or lack of something that ought to be there. It is the malfunctioning of something that in itself is good; for instance, sickness is a real physical lack of good health. Evil cannot exist in its own right. Evil happens when something renounces its proper role in the divine scheme and ceases to be what it is meant to be. Hence, moral evil is the privation of right order in the human will.

Our rebellion against God has affected all of creation and distorted it, so that our environment is not as God intended it (Romans 8: 22). In addition, Augustine saw natural evil caused by fallen angels who, by their free decisions, wreak havoc.

EXAM TIP

Remember that most questions will not require a full account of the theodicy. Select those aspects of the theodicy that are relevant to the particular focus of the question. This demonstrates selection skills. (AO1)

" KEY QUOTES "

You are free to eat from any tree in the garden; but you must not eat from the tree of the knowledge of good and evil, for when you eat of it you will surely die.

(Genesis 2: 16–17)

We know that the whole of creation has been groaning as in the pains of childbirth right up to the present time.

(Romans 8: 22)

The Lamb, William Blake

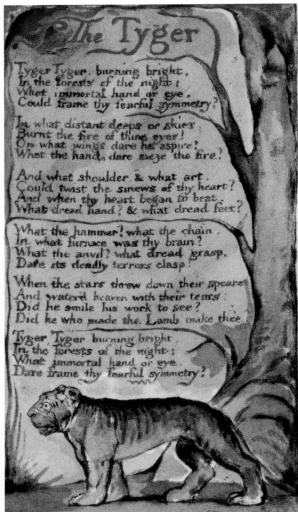

The Tyger, William Blake

b) God's responsibility for the existence of evil

For Irenaeus, the existence of evil is positive and God is responsible for it. The justification is that evil leads to a greater good. It is the means by which human beings progress and mature. It is through suffering that character and virtues are often developed. Some moral goods, such as courage, compassion and forgiveness, are responses to evils and hence could not exist without them. Sometimes this is referred to as a second-order good. The moral goods are those that result from alleviating, resisting and overcoming evil and involve intelligent and informed responses to evils. This could be seen as a necessary part of the soul-making process. Hick comments that the value of this world is:

> **… to be judged, not primarily by the quantity of pleasure and pain occurring in it at any particular moment, but by its fitness for its primary purpose, the purpose of soul-making.**

(*Evil and the God of Love*)

TASK

Read William Blake's poems, *The Lamb* and *The Tyger*.

What do you think these poems say about the problem of evil?

Objective To appreciate some of the problems that evil poses in relation to God's existence

In contrast, the Augustine theodicy sees evil as something negative and an unwelcome intruder. Evil spoils the perfect world that God created. The death of Jesus is seen as the ultimate solution to evil. In some way, through that event, evil is overcome. The Bible claims that linking your life with God starts putting evil in reverse, so that in heaven pain and suffering will be totally absent.

c) The role of free will

In the Irenaean theodicy, the existence of evil gives people freedom to come to God. God deliberately creates a world in which it is not immediately and overwhelmingly evident that there is a God. This is called an **epistemic distance**. The world is ambiguous and it could be reasoned that there is no God, equally as strongly as that there is a God. Human goodness that has come about through the making of free and responsible moral choices, in situations of difficulty and temptation, is more valuable than goodness that has been created ready-made.

Equally, if humans had been created in the direct presence of God they could have no genuine freedom. Hence the need for the epistemic distance that evil provides. It is best that free beings freely choose to love God.

For Augustine, free will plays a vital role in understanding the existence of evil in the world. It is deemed better to have free will than not to have free will. Indeed, moral beings require free will if the word 'moral' is to have any meaning. However, with that freedom comes the capability of actualising evil. It is free will, wrongly enacted, that spoils God's perfect creation. God foresaw humankind's fall 'from the foundation of the world' and planned their redemption through Christ.

4 Criticisms of the theodicies

a) Irenaeus' theodicy (soul-making)

1 If the end result is guaranteed by God, what is the point of the pilgrimage? Indeed, if there is universal salvation then do we have free will to refuse to mature?

2 Does the end justify the means? The suffering experienced, for example, at Auschwitz, cannot justify the ultimate joy. Undoubtedly, in the Holocaust, people were ruined and destroyed more than made or perfected. It is hard to see how this fits God's design and human progress.

3 Could not the greater goods be gained without such evil or suffering?

4 As a Christian theodicy, it seems to make the **atonement** superfluous and unnecessary.

5 Several criticisms involve suggestions of better ways to achieve this process. For example, why did the natural environment have to be created through a long, slow, pain-filled evolutionary process? Why could an omnipotent God not do it in 'the twinkling of an eye'? Equally, if we go on to another life to reach maturity, then why did God not simply make our earthly spans much longer, so that we could reach the Celestial City on Earth, or at least get closer? Indeed, is there any evidence for other lives?

KEY WORDS

Epistemic distance God is hidden and so this allows human beings to choose freely

Atonement the reconciliation of human beings with God through the sacrificial death of Christ

TASK

Read the various criticisms of the theodicies and try to think of some replies to answer those criticisms.

Objective To develop evaluative skills by responding to the criticisms

EXAM TIP

It is important not to mix up the two theodicies. Although they have some similarities, remember that the Augustinian is *from* perfection whereas the Irenaean is *to* perfection.

b) Augustine's theodicy (soul-deciding)

1 Modern science rejects the idea of humanity's fall from perfection. Rather, it suggests an evolutionary development. A literal approach seems to contradict modern science.

2 If humans are finitely perfect then, even though they are free to do so, they need not sin. If they do then they were not flawless to start with, so God must share the responsibility of their fall. Note that Augustine argues that some angels were predestined to fall. If this view is not accepted then how did angels fall, given that they were perfect? Surely in a perfect world they would have no reason to sin?

3 It is hard to clear God from responsibility for evil since he chose to create a being whom he foresaw would do evil.

4 The existence of hell is not consistent with an all-loving God. The idea of hell seems contrary to a loving and good God.

5 Augustine's view of evil as a privation is challenged. It is not sufficient to say that it is a lack or absence. Many would argue that it is a real entity.

6 If everything depends on God for its existence, then God must be causally involved in free human actions. Do we have free will?

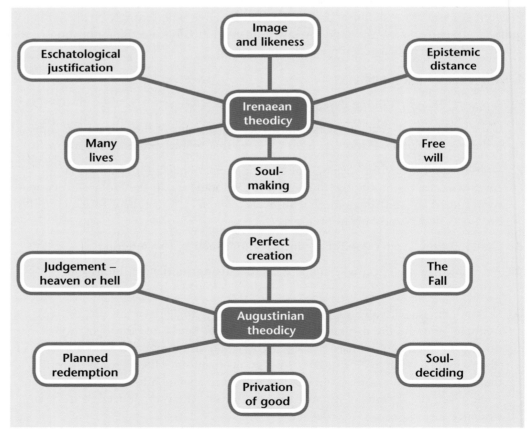

Summary diagram: The theodicies

Reflection and assessment AO1

It is vital to bring together the information that has been covered so far and recognise how it can be transformed into effective examination-style revision and answers. The best way to do this is to ask the question: 'How am I going to be assessed on this information?'

Look back to page 7 in the Introduction to review the level descriptors for AO1.

Look at the following sample basic answer, which is a response to the question:

Explain what is meant by the problem of evil.   (25 marks)

The *basic* answer would deal with the question in the following way:

- State the basic problem that a good and powerful God should stop evil. Yet evil exists.
- Give some basic indication of evil in terms of natural/moral evil.

Now indicate how a *developed* answer would deal with the question by adding two or three more bullet points.

Now go on to develop this answer to indicate how a *higher* answer (level 4–5) would deal with the question by adding further bullet points. Don't forget to keep the bullet points focused on the question.

Suggestion for further application of skills

Create a plan for the question:

Explain how Augustine's theodicy accounts for natural evil.   (25 marks)

Then write up your answer under timed conditions. Working in a group, compare your answers. Photocopy the best answers and, still as a group, consider what makes them good.

Use this time of reflection to revisit your own work and improve it by redrafting it.

Part 2
Origin of the Universe

What am I required to study?

- Religion and science

This means I am expected to know about:

- scientific and philosophical views on the creation of the Universe; particularly the debate between Creationism and the Big-Bang theory
- Darwinism and various developments of evolutionary theory
- Intelligent design and Irreducible complexity
- religious responses to challenges posed by scientific views.

This is a religious studies exam rather than a science exam. It is important that you have a good understanding of the possible conflicting ideas of science and religion. It is helpful to understand the philosophical conflicts that may occur and to appreciate why such conflicts exist. Some of the material we use will link up with earlier sections on this topic, for example, the cosmological and teleological arguments for the existence of God, whilst other material will have a link with the topic of God as Creator.

It would be helpful to write your notes under the headings listed in 'This means I am expected to know about', as it is from these areas that the exam questions will be derived.

Remember that your studies will include elements of the *two* basic assessment objectives of:

- Knowledge and Understanding (AO1)
- Evaluation (AO2).

See pages 7–8 in the Introduction to remind yourself of these objectives.

The evaluation material is set out in Part 3 of this topic (page 109) and can be studied either alongside the AO1 material, as you work through this topic, or as a discrete topic.

1 Scientific and philosophical views on the origin of the Universe

a) Introduction

Many scientists believe in a creator and just as many do not. Similarly, religious people hold many different views on the origin of the Universe. It is therefore difficult to be precise about what science or religion says about the origins of the Universe.

Cosmology is the scientific study of the origin and nature of the Universe. The Universe, which is more than just our Solar System: it includes every physical thing that exists. Theories about the origins of the Universe could raise questions about the meaning and value of human life; therefore, religious belief and scientific study may overlap.

KEY WORD

Cosmology the scientific study of the origin and nature of the Universe

b) The Big-Bang theory

i) The theory

There are really only two options to choose from when considering the origin of the Universe. Either it has always existed, or it began at a particular moment in the past. The idea that the Universe has always existed is not now a widely held view. The evidence points more to the Universe having a beginning. The current popular scientific theory about how the Universe began is called the Big-Bang theory.

Some 13.7 billion years ago there was an event that we call the Big Bang. The Universe came into existence after the explosion of an infinitely small and infinitely dense ball of energy, called a space–time singularity. This should not be thought of as a fireball somewhere in space. It did not appear in space: rather, space began inside the singularity. Before this, nothing existed, not space, time, matter, energy – nothing. What existed prior to the Big Bang is unknown. Mathematical models have attempted to describe physical processes associated with the Big Bang to within 10^{-43} seconds of its start. At that stage, infinite density is almost reached and known laws of physics cease to function.

After the initial appearance of the singularity, it inflated – this was the Big Bang. It expanded and started to cool. After some 300 000 years, the fundamental forces of physics (gravity, electromagnetism, nuclear) began to emerge. From sub-atomic particles, hydrogen and helium were formed. As the cooling continued, galaxies and stars were formed, followed by planets and the earliest life-forms.

ii) The evidence

- Galaxies appear to be moving away from us at speeds proportional to their distance. This is Hubble's Law, named after **Edwin Hubble** who discovered this phenomenon in 1929. He noticed that galactic light is slightly distorted in colour – a phenomenon known as red-shift. This suggests rapid recession, with every galaxy moving away from every other one. This is consistent with the idea of an expanding Universe.

- The idea of an expanding Universe is consistent with Albert Einstein's theories about gravity. He argued that gravity stretches or distorts space and time. The galaxies are not moving about through space. Rather, intergalactic space is being inflated. A helpful analogy is a balloon. The Big Bang is not like a balloon popping and releasing its contents, but more like a balloon being blown up and so continually growing.

- Steven Hawking, George Ellis and Roger Penrose investigated the application of Einstein's theory of relativity to notions of time and space. They concluded that time and space had a finite beginning that corresponded to the beginning of matter and energy.

- The Big-Bang theory suggests that the Universe was initially extremely hot. If that was so, we should be able to find some remnant of this heat. In 1965, Arno Penzias and Robert Wilson discovered cosmic microwave background radiation, which they thought was this remnant.

- The Big-Bang theory implies that heavy elements would have formed later than lighter elements such as hydrogen and helium. The occurrence of hydrogen and helium in the Universe supports this expectation.

KEY PERSON

Edwin Hubble (1889–1953) demonstrated the existence of other galaxies besides the Milky Way and, through investigating distances, pushed the frontiers of the Universe to hundreds of millions of light years; he also found observational proof that the Universe was expanding (the redshift).

TASK

Find out what happens to time clocks when you move in space. How does this support the Big-Bang theory?
Outcome To improve understanding of the Big-Bang theory

■ The Universe is becoming more and more disordered as time passes. This is consistent with the second law of thermodynamics and so suggests that the Universe did not always exist. It had a beginning.

The original theory was suggested by George Gamow, Ralph Alpher and Robert Herman in 1948. The term Big Bang was coined by Fred Hoyle in a radio interview in 1950.

TASK

The photo is of the CERN accelerator complex. Find out what the initials CERN stand for and what work is done at the complex. What connection has this with the Big-Bang theory?

Outcome To understand the Big-Bang theory

The CERN accelerator complex

c) Creationism

Creationism, as it is normally understood, is a belief that the Universe and life were created by God over a very short period of time. The view is anti–evolutionary because it suggests a sudden and complete process rather than one that stretches for countless millions of years. It is often associated with a very literal interpretation of religious texts, such as the creation account in Genesis.

d) The Genesis account

The main source for the Christian view of creation of the Universe (and life) is the early chapters of Genesis. It depicts God as creating the Universe (and life) in eight divine acts over a period of six days.

TASK

Read Genesis 1: 1 to 2: 3 and make a list of the things created on each day.
Now read Genesis 2: 4–23. Can you see any problems arising from comparing the two accounts?
Can you suggest any solutions to those problems?

Outcome To develop understanding of the problems of interpreting religious texts

■ Let there be light … (Genesis 1: 3)
■ Let there be an expanse between the waters ... (Genesis 1: 6)
■ Let the waters under the sky be gathered together ... (Genesis 1: 9)
■ Let the land produce vegetation ... (Genesis 1: 11)
■ Let there be lights in the expanse of the sky ... (Genesis 1: 14)
■ Let the waters teem with living creatures, and let birds fly ... (Genesis 1: 20)
■ Let the land produce living creatures ... (Genesis 1: 24)
■ Let us make man in our image ... (Genesis 1: 26)

It is important to note that a substantial majority of those who would call themselves Christians do not take a strictly literal view of the Genesis account of creation and would accept some kind of evolutionary process (see section 2 below).

To remind yourself about what this account teaches concerning God as Creator and what it reveals about God's nature, look back at Topic 2, Part 1, on page 27.

e) Areas of possible conflict between the Big-Bang account of creation and a literal interpretation of the Genesis account

i) Significance of Earth

The Genesis account has Earth as the focus of the account. In contrast, the Big-Bang theory of an expanding Universe places less emphasis on the importance of Earth.

ii) Independence from God

Even if God was responsible for the Big Bang, it could be argued that the Universe has been shown to be mechanistic and runs along lines of perpetual motion, so is independent of God. The religious view is more that God is sustainer and maintains the workings of the Universe.

iii) Difference in order

The order in the Genesis account does not follow the order of that of the Big-Bang theory. For instance, in the Genesis account, Earth predates the Sun and stars by three days.

iv) Difference in purpose

The Big Bang might or might not have been caused by a deity and, therefore, might or might not have had a purpose to it. The Genesis account assumes a deliberate intentioned creation, which God deemed very good. The world was made for a purpose.

2 Attempts at reconciling different approaches

Biblical literalists believe that the seven days in the Genesis account correspond exactly to 24-hour days of history during which God created the world. This results in understanding the creation not in terms of billions of years but rather thousands. Such a view is often referred to as Young Earth creationism. Some supporters of this view argue that, by working back through the Biblical genealogies, the actual date of creation can be established. The classic dating was calculated by Bishop James Ussher as the nightfall preceding 23 October 4004BCE.

Clearly, if a Young Earth view is taken, then it is difficult to see how the scientific account and the religious account can be reconciled. However, various other understandings and interpretations have been given to the Genesis account that make possible some reconciliation between the scientific and religious approaches. Many believe in God as the Creator without taking a strictly literal view of the whole of Genesis 1–3. Some of the various theories of such people are described here, although this list is not exhaustive.

a) Progressive creationism (Day–Age theory)

This response holds that each day of creation week represents a long age (millions or even billions of years) in which God acted upon creation. They see no reason to interpret the days in a literal sense, since God's time is not the same as our time.

b) Gap theory

Many argue that a gap should be inserted between Genesis 1: 1 and Genisis 1: 2. This then accommodates geological time.

c) Framework interpretation

This response sees Genesis 1 as written to provide a theology of creation opposing myths from pagans. It is not to be taken as a scientifically or historically accurate record. This is often expressed as: 'Science answers the *how* question, while religion answers the *why* question.'

❝ KEY QUOTES ❞

So long as the Universe had a beginning, we could suppose it had a creator.
(Stephen Hawking)

The intention of the Holy Ghost is to teach us how one goes to heaven, not how heaven goes.
(Galileo)

[1]In the beginning God created the heavens and the Earth. [2]The Earth was without form and void, and darkness was upon the face of the deep; and the Spirit of God was moving over the face of the waters. [3]And God said, 'Let there be light' and there was light.
(Genesis 1: 1–3)

103

d) God as source of the Big Bang

The Big-Bang theory is seen as consistent with the claim that there is a God. The theory says that the Universe had a beginning, and that both time and space came from nothing. This is seen as a parallel to the beginning of Genesis. God is seen as the explanation of the Big Bang. Indeed, in 1951 Pope Pius XII declared approval for the Big-Bang theory, based on this understanding.

3 Scientific and philosophical views on the origins of life

a) The theory of evolution

Darwin's theory provided a way of understanding the natural world, in which its complex biological functions no longer required an intelligent designer to account for apparent order.

Firstly, Darwin identified that variations occur in offspring within a species. These are accidental. Secondly, he argued for natural selection, which included the theory of the survival of the fittest. This proposes that organisms that are best able to survive – for example, finding food, avoiding predators – pass on their genetic traits. The combination of variation and survival leads eventually to the emergence of organisms that are better suited to their environment. Over time, beneficial mutations accumulate and the result is an entirely different organism. This may have the appearance of design, but is the result of organisms evolving by variation and survival. God becomes an unnecessary hypothesis.

Darwin demonstrated that order was not necessarily evidence of purpose and design. Order could result from blind chance.

b) The Genesis account

This describes each species as being complete and created separately, rather than progressing and developing into different species. (For details of the order see section 2, above.) The literal interpretation of Genesis is associated with creationist theories and is particularly supported by those who take the text of scriptures as literal.

In particular, human beings are seen as being made in the image of God with the faculty of having a relationship with God. This marks out human beings as different from the rest of creation.

> **KEY QUOTE**
>
> **After Darwin we are bound in the end to be committed to a non-dualistic view of both the human being and the world.**
>
> (Don Cupitt)

> **KEY QUESTION**
>
> **Does Darwinism have a religious basis, since it claims that there is no purpose or intelligence behind the Universe?**

> **TASK**
>
> The picture is *The Creation of Adam* by Michelangelo, which forms one of the panels of the ceiling of the Sistine Chapel. Research the painting on the internet to find out how the figures have been interpreted and what the artist might be saying about this creation story.
>
> Outcome To understand interpretations of the Genesis account

The Creation of Adam, Michelangelo

4 Attempts at reconciling different approaches

a) Progressive creationism (Day–Age theory)

As already discussed, this belief holds that each day of creation week represents a long age (millions or even billions of years) in which God acted upon creation. There is no reason to interpret the days in a literal sense since God's time is not same as our time. Holders of this view would accept much of what would be called micro-evolution, adaptation within a species and even some larger changes. But macro-evolutionary changes such as a bird evolving from a fish are not seen as a viable process. In particular, human beings are special creations and are not evolved from another species.

b) Theistic evolution

This takes the Genesis account as religious and theological rather than historical and scientific. Evolution is seen as the mechanism God used to bring about life and human beings. This therefore retains the theistic belief that the world is ultimately the result of divine creation. Some theistic evolutionists prefer to call it Evolutionary Creation. It emphasises their belief in a creator whilst still accepting evolution.

In 1996, Pope John Paul II made a statement about evolution. He seemingly accepted the idea although he did not identify the actual mechanism. The Pope stated that humankind was created in the image and likeness of God, and so he reinforced the Catholic teaching of earlier popes, such as Pius XII, that God infuses souls into human beings, regardless of what process he might have used to create our physical bodies. Science, the Pope insisted, can never identify for us 'the moment of the transition into the spiritual'. He argued that such a matter was for religion, not science.

More recently, in July 2007, Pope Benedict XVI said that the theory of evolution has strong scientific proof, but the theory does not answer the question: 'From where does everything come?'

c) Intelligent design

i) What is Intelligent design (ID)?
This view argues that an intelligence is necessary to explain the complex, information-rich structures of biology and that this intelligence is empirically detectable. It is an elaboration of Paley's 'eye' example (see page 70).

ii) What is the evidence for ID?
There are three main thrusts.

Irreducible complexities
This means that all the parts of a system must be in place at once for the system to work. The different parts could not have arisen separately, or at different times, by a process of gradual change such as evolution. It is claimed that many examples of biochemical systems reflect irreducible complexity. The originator of this approach is Michael Behe.

Specified complexities
This argues that design is implied any time that two criteria, namely complexity and specification, are satisfied. Behe argued that we should infer ID when we see what he calls specified complexity. By this, he means that we detect ID in events that are highly improbable (thus complex) and that also correspond to some independently

❝ KEY QUOTES ❞

If it can be demonstrated that any complex organ existed, which could not possibly have been formed by numerous, successive, slight modifications, my theory would absolutely break down.

(Darwin)

Thus while I argue for design, the question of the identity of the designer is left open.

(Michael Behe)

given pattern (thus specified). Some structures can be explained in terms of natural laws that do not necessarily point to design. For instance, we cannot conclude that, on the basis of scientific evidence, natural selection was designed. It may have been, but it is not necessarily so. However, ID claims that other structures show obvious design. These are the structures that have the characteristic of irreducible complexities and that perform a specified task.

An illustration that might help to explain this idea involves placing seaweed on a sandy beach, to make it appear that the seaweed has been thrown up by the tide. If you had seen me place the seaweed on the beach you would have known it was not there by chance. But you cannot deduce this by just seeing the seaweed lying on the beach. The fact it had been placed there is not obvious. However, if you laid out the seaweed to spell out 'Welcome to Worthing', such an arrangement would point to design. The claim is that specified complexities are of this second type of arrangement.

Evidence not theory

Supporters of ID claim that the debate is about evidence. Are there any examples of irreducible complex systems? It is claimed that, as a scientific theory, ID is a more adequate scientific explanation of the biological evidence than the theory of evolution. ID is not creationism. It does not say anything about the nature of the source of design, though it could be seen as pointing towards theism.

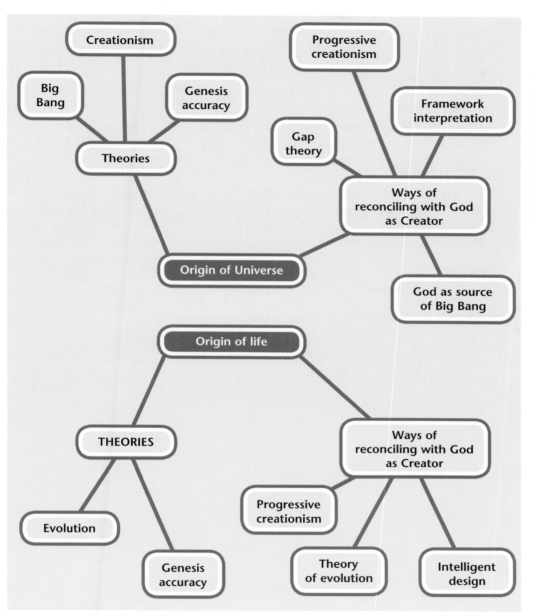

Summary diagram: Science

Reflection and assessment AO1

It is now time to channel the information you have considered in a more focused way. In order to do this, once again you need to ask yourself the question: 'How am I going to be assessed on my use of this information?'

Read the following question and complete the task. To do the task you will need to look back at the level descriptors given on page 7 in the Introduction.

Explain the ways in which the scientific account of the origin of the Universe differs from that given in Genesis. (25 marks)

Use what you have so far learned about levels of response, writing frames, mark schemes and essay plans, to do this task.

1 Split into small groups.
2 Within the group, use lists bullet points to create a five-level response in answer to the question:
   Explain the ways in which the scientific account of the origin of the universe differs from that given in Genesis.   (25 marks)
3 Then each person in the group should take one set of bullet points and use it to write up a paragraph.
4 Put the paragraphs together as an answer and swap with another group.
5 After the receiving group has commented on the work it is returned to the original group.
6 Review the comments and use them to improve the answer.

Objective Collaborative learning and peer assessment for examination focus on AO1

Suggestion for further application of skills

In your revision sessions, use this approach as a basis for re-visiting the other topics. This does not only apply to specific focus on questions but is also a way to create some quality summaries that demonstrate the skills relevant to AO1.

Part 3
A critical analysis of the issues

What are the issues that I am expected to consider and to analyse critically?

- A comparison between the two theodicies
- The strengths of each of the two theodicies
- The weaknesses of each of the two theodicies
- The strengths of the challenge by science to religious ideas about the origin of the Universe and life
- The weaknesses of the challenge by science to the religious ideas about the origin of the Universe and life

1 The two theodicies compared

a) Similarities

- Both are seen as Christian approaches.
- Both are based on the Genesis story.
- Both see moral evil as the fault of human beings.
- Both justify God.

b) Differences

Augustinian	Irenaean
Soul-deciding	Soul-making
Looks to past for explaining origin of evil	Looks to future (heaven) for the justifying of evil
The Fall is central	The Fall is not central – the key is the two-stage image and likeness
Natural evil is consequence of moral evil	Natural evil is deliberate from God as part of epistemic distance and soul-making environment
There is a hell	There is no hell
Not all go to heaven	All reach heaven eventually
One life and then death	Many lives
The Universe is not how God intended it	The Universe is how God intended it
The death of Jesus is central to salvation	The death of Jesus is not significant

2 Strengths and weaknesses of Augustinian theodicy

a) Strengths

The Augustian theodicy is attractive to those who accept authority of Scripture, as the Genesis account is central to Augustine's argument.

EXAM TIP

Make sure that you explain how your criticism weakens the argument. Avoid just stating a criticism and leaving it to the examiner to work out why it is.
Equally, if it has a strength then explain what makes it a strength.
This demonstrates justifying a point of view. (AO2)

KEY QUESTIONS

- **In what ways are the two theodicies similar?**
- **In what ways are the two theodicies different?**
- **How is natural evil explained?**
- **What is the significance of Jesus in each of the theodicies?**
- **Can there be morality without freedom?**

KEY WORD

Counter-argument an argument that sets out to refute another argument

The view that evil is not a substance, and therefore not created by God, seems to free God from responsibility for evil.

Augustine seems to account successfully for the occurrence of natural evil.

Part of its strength is that some criticisms against it fail (see page 98 for criticisms).

- The question of why God did not create free beings who could not sin can be answered in this way. It is logically impossible for God to create another being who, by necessity, freely performs only actions that are good. For God to cause such creatures only to do right and never wrong would be a contradiction of the idea of their free choice. They would simply not be free beings. Others have argued along different lines, pointing out that, even if it is logically possible, not everything logically possible is actually achievable. Love cannot be programmed. The fact that heaven is pictured as comprising people who never sin suggests that perhaps God could have created such beings on Earth. However, people will be in heaven by their own choice having chosen to forgo the opportunity to sin.

- Many see love as the key to answering the criticism that God should not have created beings whom he knew would commit evil. God wishes to enter into loving relations with his creatures, but genuine love is an expression of the free commitment of both parties. Love between God and his creatures is therefore possible only if the creatures are free to reject his love as well as respond to it. Without freedom, we could not share in God's goodness as we could not freely love him. Nevertheless, the creation of free creatures involved the risk that persons would misuse their freedom and reject the good, and this is what happened. God could have chosen to make a world without free creatures in it, but the creatures would be robots, and therefore it would be a non-moral world. It may be physically better but it cannot be regarded as morally better, since it is non-moral.

b) Weaknesses

The centrality of Genesis 1–3 to the theodicy weakens the argument, as the literal interpretation of Genesis seems contrary to modern thinking about origins. Another criticism has come from D.Z. Philips. He focuses on the fact that this theodicy demands that God allows certain evils to take place for the sake of a future good. This implies that God has planned the evil. Philips concludes that God's 'evil nature is revealed'.

Many of the criticisms listed on page 98 may not seem to have satisfactory **counter-arguments**.

3 Strengths and weaknesses of Irenaean theodicy

a) Strengths

Irenaean theodicy seems consistent with modern thinking about the origins of life.

The focus on seeing Earth as a suitable environment for making free choices seems to remove blame from God for creating evil. A paradise environment would have led to a non-moral world. No second-order goods could have been developed (see page 96).

All evil is justified since all ultimately achieve the goal of heaven.

Part of its strength is that some criticisms against it fail (see page 97 for criticisms). For instance, the criticism that, as a Christian theodicy, it seems to make the atonement superfluous and unnecessary, can be answered by the argument that Jesus is an example of a human being who has the content of God. Perhaps a more Christian approach would be to see the theodicy more in terms of faith-making than soul-making.

b) Weaknesses

Many voice unease about what appears to be a lack of fairness in the workings of the theodicy. For instance, is it just that all achieve the goal of heaven? It makes God the author of evil and suffering, and this suffering often seems disproportionate and unfair.

In addition, many commentators would argue that several of the criticisms listed on page 97 do not seem to have satisfactory counter-arguments.

4 Possible conclusions about the problem of evil

When assessing the problems of evil, it is important to reflect upon the arguments previously discussed and arrive at some appropriate conclusion. It may be that you accept none of these listed here, or just one of them, or you may have a different conclusion that is not listed. However, what is important is the way that you have arrived at your conclusion – the reasoning process.

From the preceding discussions, here are some possible conclusions you could draw.

1   There are no adequate solutions to the problem of evil.
2   There is a solution to the problem of evil, but it points to a God who is either not all-powerful or not all-loving.
3   The Augustinian theodicy is an adequate answer to the problem of evil.
4   The Irenaean theodicy is an adequate answer to the problem of evil.
5   There are other theodicies, such as the Process theodicy, that offer a more satisfactory solution to the problem of evil.

5 Possible conclusions about scientific and philosophical views on the origin of the Universe

When assessing the scientific and philosophical views of the origin of the Universe, it is important to reflect upon the arguments previously discussed and arrive at some appropriate conclusion. It may be that you accept none of these listed here, or just one of them, or you may have a different conclusion that is not listed. However, what is important is the way that you have arrived at your conclusion – the reasoning process.

From the preceding discussions, here are some possible conclusions you could draw.

1   It is not possible to know the cause of the beginning of the Universe as the event is beyond empirical investigation.
2   It is possible to know the cause of the beginning of the Universe by producing a theory that is consistent with the evidence.
3   The beginning of the Universe has a naturalistic explanation.
4   The beginning of the Universe has a supernatural explanation based on God.
5   Religious texts interpreted literally are the source for finding out about the beginning of the Universe.
6   The Big-Bang theory and belief in God are contradictory.
7   The Big-Bang theory is consistent with a belief in God and a figurative interpretation of religious texts.

? KEY QUESTIONS

- Is all evil justified?
- Did the death of Jesus achieve anything? Or did he die needlessly?

EXAM TIP

Do not just give a list of criticisms like some shopping list. It is far better to discuss and develop three or four criticisms, explaining and responding to them, than to give a list of seven or eight.

This demonstrates a process of reasoning and a sustained argument. (AO2)

6 Possible conclusions about scientific and philosophical views on the origin of life

When assessing the scientific and philosophical views on the origin of life, it is important to reflect upon the arguments previously discussed and arrive at some appropriate conclusion. It may be that you accept none of these listed here, or just one of them, or you may have a different conclusion that is not listed. However, what is important is the way that you have arrived at your conclusion – the reasoning process.

From the preceding discussions, here are some possible conclusions you could draw.

1   It is not possible to know how the beginning of life came about.
2   The beginning of life has a naturalistic explanation.
3   The beginning of life is explained by evolutionary theory and is not consistent with a belief in God.
4   The beginning of life is explained by evolutionary theory and is consistent with a belief in God and a figurative interpretation of religious texts.
5   The beginning of life is explained by the theory of Intelligent design.
6   The beginning of life is explained by a literal interpretation of religious texts, for example, Genesis 1–3.

Reflection and assessment AO2

It is now time to channel the information you have considered in a more focused way. In order to do this, once again you need to ask yourself the question: 'How am I going to be assessed on my use of this information?'

Look back to page 8 to review the levels of response descriptors for AO2. There is a description of the character and features for each level. The exam is marked by reference to levels.

Look at the key points, below, in answer to the question:

'The Augustinian theodicy fails to explain the problem of evil.' Discuss.

(10 marks)

You will need to refer to these points, which are not presented in any particular order, to complete the task.

- God foresaw the Fall.
- Evil is a privation.
- Not all are saved, so God is not all-loving.
- God is omnipotent, all good and opposes evil. Therefore evil does not exist in the world.
- Augustinian theodicy is soul-deciding.
- Why not make us flawless and perfect, so we would not fall?

Suggestion for further application of skills

You will now be focusing on revision skills and, more importantly, past questions. Now you have developed your skills in essay preparation to this stage, return to other topics of critical analysis (AO2 sections) and consider some of the key questions. Aim to build up some responses based around these key questions.

TASK

Use the key points opposite as a basis for a writing frame to answer the question. The list is deliberately basic. At this stage you should be able to recognise that it contains the general issues but does not have the detail for development. You will need to add this. Remember to add relevant quotes and questions at suitable places. The final product should show evidence of a sustained argument and critical analysis of more than one point of view.

Objective To build together an argument that uses a 'range of evidence to sustain an argument' (AO2 level 5)

Part 1

The language of ethical theories

What am I required to study?

■ The concepts of absolute and relative morality

■ The concepts of deontological and teleological

This means I am expected to know about:

■ what it means to call an ethical theory absolute and objective

■ what it means to call an ethical theory relative and subjective

■ the meaning of the terms deontological and teleological.

In this introductory topic we start by exploring some key terms in the study of ethical theories. In Part 2 we shall assess the strengths and weaknesses of such approaches. In later topics we consider specific ethical theories in detail and their application to the issues of abortion, euthanasia, genetic engineering, and war and peace. It would be helpful to write your notes under the headings listed in 'This means I am expected to know about', as it is from these areas that the exam questions will be derived.

Remember that your studies will include elements of the *two* basic assessment objectives of:

■ Knowledge and Understanding (AO1)

■ Evaluation (AO2).

See pages 7–8 in the Introduction to remind yourself of these objectives.

The evaluation material is set out in Part 2 of this topic (page 117) and can be studied either alongside the AO1 material, as you work through this topic, or as a discrete topic.

1 What is an ethical theory?

a) Ethics versus morals

In current usage there is a tendency to treat the two terms ethics and morals as interchangeable. However, their origins each indicate a different focus. The study of **ethics** examines the guiding principles that direct an action. It is a theory or system of moral values. Ethics not only directs a person how to act if they wish to be morally good, but also sets before that person the obligation of doing good rather than evil.

In contrast, **morality** is the application of these guiding principles, leading to appropriate conduct in particular situations such as war or genetic engineering. In this way, ethics can be seen as the philosophical treatment of morality.

KEY QUESTION

Is there a difference in meaning between 'ethics' and 'morals'?

KEY WORDS

Ethics a theory or system of moral values **Morality** the application of an ethical theory to produce appropriate conduct; conformity to moral principles

b) Right versus wrong

Suppose a terrorist bursts into a house and threatens to shoot the son if his father does not give vital information to the terrorist that will lead to the death of the leader of the country. What should the father do? If he refuses, then his son will be shot and he himself may also be killed. Yet, if he gives the information, it is almost certain that the leader of the country – a leader who has achieved great things for the country – will die. His death could result in the outbreak of civil war.

What are the guiding principles that will help the man decide what action to take? How were the guiding principles derived?

This framework of guiding principles is called an ethical theory. Acting consistently within this framework is acting morally. Sometimes we may choose to act contrary to our framework and so be said to be acting immorally. Disagreements about what is a moral action and what is not show that different people have different sets of guiding principles. Hence, one action may be seen as moral, often referred to as **right**, while others may judge the same action as immoral, or **wrong**.

In ethics, right and wrong generally have stronger meanings than just error or misjudgement. There is often an implied 'going against character' or failing to be the sort of person you should be. There is a standard of which you have fallen short. There is an indication that you have done something that you are obliged *not* to do.

2 Grouping ethical theories

Philosophers have identified common links between the various ethical theories and have categorised them into groups.

a) Absolutist versus relativist

Absolutists believe that there exists a standard of right and wrong that is fully and totally binding on all human beings. Those who are religious may feel that this absolute standard proceeds from the mind and will of a supreme being. Those who are not religious may believe that the standard simply exists.

Relativists believe that there is no absolute right or wrong. They do not see morality as imposing a binding obligation on human beings to behave in a particular way. They see morality as the response of human communities to issues of how to behave in relation to each other. There are no absolute rules, but there are norms of behaviour that promote goodwill and happiness or some other desirable objective.

A relativist can say that she finds a certain course of action unjust or morally wrong, but it is difficult for her to conclude that someone else should feel that this action was wrong. To the absolutist, a wrong course of action is something that they are under a binding and absolute obligation *not* to do.

Whereas the absolutist would have to say: 'This is wrong for me and for you and for everyone,' the relativist could say: 'This is wrong for me but may be right for you,' which is something the absolutist could never say.

There is some ambiguity in the terms absolutist and relativist in that they are not always mutually exclusive but can overlap; for example, relativist systems may have an absolutist element. Hence, moral relativists might agree on very basic human values, such as respect for property, even though they may interpret this very differently.

? KEY QUESTION

How do we decide our guiding principles?

TASK

Identify some of the possible guiding principles that people may use.

What do these imply about the sort of character they aim to be?

Objective To identify the link between ethics and the views of ideal human character

---

 KEY WORDS

Right (in Ethics) doing what is morally acceptable

Wrong (in Ethics) failing to do what you should do

Absolutist an ethical system involving rules that are to be followed by all people at all times, in all circumstances

Relativist an ethical system that has no fixed rules but each action depends on the situation

b) Subjective versus objective

In ethics, a theory is described as **subjective** if its truth is dependent on the person's view. This is very different from saying that an ethical theory is relativist, since this describes the range of the truth and does not hold true in all situations.

A theory is described as **objective** if its truth is independent of a person's view. Again, this is very different from saying that an ethical theory is absolutist, since this describes the range of the truth and it holds true in all situations.

It seems natural to link subjective with relativist, since both terms imply freedom of choice of the individual: nothing is fixed and immovable. However, there is also a sense in which subjective can be linked to absolutist. For example, you might conclude that no ethical theory can be absolutist since our values stem from our own feelings and choices. However, you may also think that some of those feelings and choices are universal to human beings, and so apply to everyone. This implies that it is not a contradiction to have an ethical theory that is subjectively grounded but holds to absolute values.

c) Deontological versus teleological

The dilemma of the father facing the terrorist (page 114) raised questions about the consequences of various actions that could be taken. Indeed, it is often the case that thinking about the consequences of a particular action persuades us whether or not to take that action. Such an approach, that focuses on the consequences, is called a **teleological ethical theory**. Teleological comes from the Greek, meaning end or purpose. In such theories, the rightness or wrongness of an action is identified by the consequences it produces. If the theory held that the action that best resulted in 'the good of the majority' was the criterion for judging right action, then the right action would be the one that resulted in the most good for the majority. It is the result, not the act itself, that decides the right action to take. This approach is also called **consequentialism**, since it claims that the value of the consequences of our actions is decisive for their moral status as right or wrong.

Deontological comes from the Greek, meaning obligation or duty. In such theories there is a relationship between duty and the morality of human actions. Therefore, **deontological ethical theories** are concerned with the acts themselves, irrespective of the consequences of those acts. For instance, a deontologist might argue that murder was wrong whatever the situation or consequence, and therefore euthanasia was morally wrong. It is not such things as feelings of happiness, or good for the greatest number, that decide a right action, but rather that certain acts are *intrinsically* right or wrong. These wrong acts go against our duty or obligation.

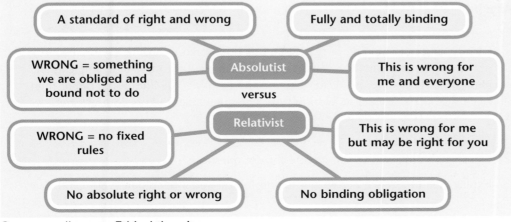

Summary diagram: Ethical theories

KEY WORDS

Subjective having its source within the mind; a particular point of view, dependent on the subject
Objective external to the mind, real or true regardless of subject and their point of view
Teleological ethics any ethical system that is concerned with consequences of actions
Consequentialism another name for teleological ethics
Deontological focusing on the rightness or wrongness of actions themselves, rather than the rightness or wrongness of the consequences
Deontological ethics any ethical system that is concerned with the act itself rather than the consequences of the act

? KEY QUESTIONS

- Can an ethical theory be absolutist *and* subjective?
- Can an ethical theory be relativist *and* objective?
- What is the difference between deontological and teleological ethics?

Reflection and assessment AO1

It is vital to bring together the information you have covered so far and recognise how it can be transformed into effective examination-style revision and answers. The best way to do this is to ask the question: 'How am I going to be assessed on my use of this information?'

The first way is through assessment objective 1 (AO1). For this objective you need to be able to 'select and clearly demonstrate the relevant knowledge and understanding through the use of evidence, examples and correct language and terminology'.

Use the writing frame provided below to answer this question:

Explain the difference between absolutist and relativist ethics.   (25 marks)

In later units of the book, the amount of support in these sections will be gradually reduced in order to encourage the development of your independence and the honing of your AO1 skills.

Key points

- Use the correct *technical language* to refer to ethical theories.
- Always give an *example* of the term.
- Relate the example to the meaning so that it shows *understanding* of the meaning.

Writing frame

An absolutist believes ...

An example of an absolutist ethical system is ...

This is described as an absolutist ethical system because ...

A relativist believes ...

An example of a relativist ethical system is ...

This is described as a relativist ethical system because ...

One difference between the absolutist and relativist approach to ethics is ...

Another difference is ...

Whereas the absolutist would have to say: 'This is wrong for me and for you and for everyone,' the relativist could say: '...'

Clearly, an understanding of the two terms is required to enable any discussion of the differences. The best way to explain each term is to use an example as an illustration. However, be aware that you must explain the illustration rather then leave it to the examiner to work it out. The differences then become clearer.

Suggestion for further application of skills

Construct your own writing frame for the question:

Explain the difference between a deontological and a teleological ethical theory.
                (25 marks)

Part 2

A critical analysis of the issues

What are the issues that I am expected to consider and to analyse critically?

■ The strengths and weaknesses of an ethical system that is absolute and objective

■ The strengths and weaknesses of an ethical system that is relative and subjective

1 Strengths of an ethical system that is absolute and objective

a) It recognises universal laws

There seems to be common recognition that certain acts are morally wrong. This is reflected in such institutions as the International Court of Justice at The Hague and the *United Nations Declaration of Human Rights*.

b) Judgement is possible

Given that rules are fixed, it is possible to judge people by this common standard of acceptable action.

c) It provides justification for acting

Morality seems to demand some sort of obligation. If there is a fixed moral code then there is an obligation to act in that way.

d) It gives clear guidelines

The rules are fixed and clear to apply.

2 Weaknesses of an ethical system that is absolute and objective

a) What is the source of the absolutes?

One answer could be 'God'. However, there are those who do not accept this answer. It is difficult to see what they can refer to as a source of absolute moral authority.

b) Is there conflict between absolutes?

Relativists might argue that it is sometimes difficult to avoid a clash between two values that are held by others to be absolutes. For example, was the attempted assassination of Hitler morally justifiable? To assassinate him would be murder but to allow him to continue would be to allow evil to continue.

c) It ignores circumstances

The application of absolutist morality seems rather cold and ignores a person's circumstances. Surely all situations are different and need to be viewed from other people's positions?

? KEY QUESTIONS

● Are there fixed moral laws?
● Is it possible to judge people?
● What is the source of the absolutes?

TASK

Can you think of anything that is intrinsically evil?
How does this question indicate an argument for a relativist or an absolutist ethical system?
Objective To understand the correct terminology

EXAM TIP

Use appropriate language where applicable. This demonstrates understanding through the use of correct language and terminology. (AO1)

? KEY QUESTIONS

- How can conflicting absolutes be resolved?
- Should circumstances be taken into account when making a moral decision?
- Is it morally defensible to claim that one's own moral views are superior to those of others?
- Are all actions beyond moral criticism?
- How does society change its views on morality?
- Is it true that there is a hierarchy of moral actions?

d) It is intolerant

It implies that only one view is correct and therefore all other views are in error. This seems an intolerant approach as it disregards approaches of different cultures.

3 Strengths of an ethical system that is relative and subjective

a) It reflects the postmodern age

One of the features of our postmodern age is the rejection of universal truths. The diversity of cultures and of world faiths has meant that there has been a growing awareness of a wide variety of world-views. This has resulted in the movement away from the idea that one culture or religion has all the answers. Indeed, the rejection, both of the big picture of the Universe and the idea of the truth, is a feature of our postmodern age.

Relativism sits comfortably against such a background, since it acknowledges this diversity.

b) It avoids judging one culture against another

Another feature of our age is tolerance. If it is accepted that there are no universal truths, then there are no objective standards by which one culture can judge another. No one culture is better than any other. Such a non-judgemental approach, that accepts all cultures as morally equal, is seen as furthering tolerance.

4 Weaknesses of an ethical system that is relative and subjective

a) Are all cultures morally equal?

If morality is relative, then that would suggest that no culture can criticise another. However, many people would be reluctant to say that a culture that practises genocide is acting morally. Thus, there do appear to be some actions that arouse criticism and judgement. This implies that there may be moral absolutes. Most would argue that apartheid in South Africa, and concentration camps under Nazism, do not suggest all cultures are morally equal.

b) Can moral choices be justified?

If no culture can be criticised for its moral actions, since they are all equally valid, then it is not clear how a person can value their own moral actions, knowing that another culture would act differently, and still be acting morally.

c) Can morality change?

If no culture can be criticised for its moral actions, then how does a culture change its views on morality?

d) Can morality progress?

If no culture can be criticised for its moral actions, then is it possible for morality to progress? Progression suggests some sort of hierarchy of moral actions but this would surely be contrary to relativism. However, many might argue that challenging both racial prejudice and the widespread use of torture were progressive steps.

e) What constitutes the group?

What is the boundary of the group of individuals who share the same ethical code? Is it a nation, a race, a state or a city?

5 Possible conclusions

When assessing the issues that arise from absolutist and relativist ethical systems, it is important to reflect upon the arguments previously discussed and arrive at some appropriate conclusion. It may be that you accept none of these listed here, or just one of them, or you may have a different conclusion that is not listed. However, what is important is the way that you have arrived at your conclusion – the reasoning process.

From the preceding discussions, here are some possible conclusions you could draw.

1   An absolutist ethical system has more strengths than weaknesses and has fewer weaknesses than does a relativist ethical system.

2   A relativist ethical system has more strengths than weaknesses and has fewer weaknesses than does an absolutist ethical system.

3   The strengths and weaknesses of a relativist ethical system are roughly equal. This is also true for an absolutist ethical system.

4   A relativist ethical system has as many weaknesses as an absolutist ethical system.

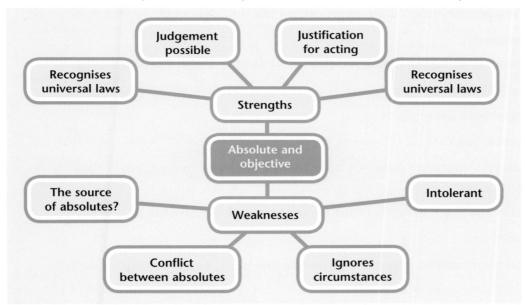

Summary diagram: Strengths and weaknesses of ethical theories

Reflection and assessment AO2

Earlier in this topic you considered the assessment objective AO1 focused on knowledge and understanding. The second way of being assessed is through assessment objective AO2. For this objective we need to be able to 'sustain a critical line of argument and justify a point of view'.

Use the writing frame provided to answer the question:

Critically assess the claim that the absolutist ethical system is the only one that is defensible.   (10 marks)

Key points

- Always point out the *case in support* of the concept and the *case against* the concept.
- Always *respond to* and *assess* each point as you proceed through the answer so you show critical analysis.
- *Avoid* just listing points.
- *Always juxtapose* and *integrate* the views so you show *engagement*.
- Keep relating the material back to the *focus* of the discussion.
- Always give a clear weighing up leading to an *appropriate conclusion*, even if the conclusion is that both sides are equal.
- Remember that the case against can include better *alternatives* as well as *weaknesses* of the case in support.

Writing frame

The term 'absolutist ethical system' means …

This is in contrast to the alternative ethical system, called 'relativist', because …

One reason given to support the absolutist approach as the only defensible approach is …

This is a strength because …

In contrast, the alternative approach of the relativist has serious flaws. For example …

This makes it indefensible because …

Another flaw of the relativist approach is …

This makes it indefensible because …

In contrast, the absolutist approach does not have these criticisms. Indeed, a strength of the absolutist approach is …

However, the absolutist approach is not without its problems. One weakness is …

This is a weakness because …

Likewise, many do find the relativist approach defensible and point to its strengths such as …

and …

The conclusion as to whether the absolutist approach is the only defensible one is …

Although quite basic, this writing frame does focus on critical analysis. It is better to deal with three or four criticisms in some detail than to compile a longer list with very brief comment. It is important also to make clear in what way your criticism challenges the argument or view.

Suggestion for further application of skills

Construct your own writing frame for the question:

Critically assess a relativist approach to ethics. (10 marks)

Part 1
Key facts and key issues

What am I required to study?

■ The issues of abortion, euthanasia, genetic engineering and war and peace

This means I am expected to know about:

■ key facts about abortion, euthanasia, genetic engineering and war and peace

■ the legal status of abortion, euthanasia, genetic engineering and war and peace

■ specific ethical issues related to each issue and key areas of debate.

This section is a brief introduction to **applied ethics**. It deals with key facts about the topics highlighted in the specification, including the legal status of each one. It also identifies the key issues for consideration and the key questions raised by the topics.

It would be helpful to write your notes using the headings listed under 'This means I am expected to know about', as it is from these areas that the exam questions will be derived.

Remember that your studies will include elements of the two basic assessment objectives of:

■ Knowledge and Understanding (AO1)
■ Evaluation (AO2).

See pages 7–8 in the Introduction to remind yourself of these objectives.

The evaluation material is set out in Part 2 of this topic (page 141) and can be studied either alongside the AO1 material, as you work through this topic, or as a discrete topic.

1 A general introduction to applied ethics

Applied ethics is the term used to describe the debates that arise when ethical issues are considered in practice. The study of applied ethics is complex and difficult because it is the point at which principles are tested in the real world. Applied ethics often involves the conflicting nature of principles and challenges a person to order and prioritise these principles.

An ethical dilemma arises when two or more causes of conduct may be justifiable in any given set of circumstances, possibly resulting in diametrically opposed outcomes.

(Mason and Laurie)

KEY WORD

Applied ethics debates that arise in discussion of ethical issues

KEY WORD

Value judgement an
assessment that reveals
more about the values
of the person making it
than about the reality of
what is assessed

66 **KEY QUOTES** **99**

Given that we want to
regard a newly born
baby as a person, and
to forbid the killing
of it as murder, it
seems arbitrary to
distinguish between
this and the killing of
an unborn child almost
at full term, and then
the argument can be
carried back step by
step until immediately
after conception.

(Mackie)

Abortion means
ending a pregnancy so
that it does not result
in the birth of a child.

(Brook Advisory)

EXAM TIP

It is important to be
able to describe and
explain the key facts
relating to ethical ideas.
However, it is even more
important to be able to
discuss the implications
and questions raised
by the ethical issues.
This would distinguish a
level 4 answer that has
'good understanding'
from a level 2 answer
that 'focuses on the
general topic'. (See level
descriptors on pages 7–8.)

When a person makes an ethical decision, it is often driven by deeply held convictions. This is especially the case when a **value judgement** is made to decide whether something is right or wrong. Such convictions are influenced by principles, emotions, different situations, a process of reasoning, cultural influences, the immediate environment and even upbringing. These are all issues to consider at a deeper level.

There is no one uniform approach to dealing with the ethical issues that face us. It is interesting to see that there are even slightly different perspectives and emphases when it comes to considering ethical issues. For example, in medical ethics the philosophical writer takes a slightly different approach from the medical stance and the approach of the legal scholar is different again. Compare, for example, the works of Singer, Vardy, Grosch and Wilcockson (philosophy) with those of the General Medical Council, the *British Medical Journal* and Hope (medical) and Mason and Laurie (legal).

We are considering matters of life and death. When it comes to these ethical issues, there are some important factors to recognise when debating the apparent rights and wrongs.

No one would argue that the act of abortion is a good thing to do *per se*. That is because there are universal principles to which all rational and sane people would agree. One such principle is that killing is not a good thing. However, it is when we ask the question: 'In what situation…' that the whole area explodes. What about war? What about respecting the rights of another individual? What about protecting another? The list is endless.

It is important to bear in mind that those people that compromise this principle, whether in times of war or in an argument for euthanasia or abortion, are doing so not because they reject the idea that killing is wrong but because they recognise two things:

■ the principle that 'killing is wrong…' is an ideal that, when applied to the real world, needs further qualification
■ sometimes one has to weigh up and prioritise the application of principles in a real situation where conflicts of ideology arise.

There is, therefore, a clear distinction between theory in itself and that same theory in terms of how it unfolds in practice. The classic case is euthanasia for which the complexities of situations give rise to a plethora of legal and ethical dilemmas.

Jesus is believed to have said, in response to violence: 'Turn the other cheek.' Mahatma Gandhi interpreted this literally and founded his ideology of passive resistance through non-violence (*ahimsa*) on such a principle. However, there are always limitations and even Gandhi could not make this a legal principle. Turning the other cheek and forgiveness would not be workable principles for society. The individual can be inspired and such principles are wonderful for people to follow as a guide. They are, however, directives addressed to the individual, not regulations for society, and only a fool would reject our legal and judicial system for such principles. Why? Ideally, they are splendid, but in practice regrettably unworkable as enforced rules or laws.

Applied ethics, then, can be seen as the pursuit of standards that can be applied and that work in practice. It is the search for a solution that offers the workability of a principle that recognises the rights of an individual, respect for deeply held values and principles and thus being able to institute the solution for the benefit of society as a whole.

It is here that things really get interesting as, once again, the principles and their varying application and prioritising give way to a complexity of debates.

2 Abortion and the right to a child

a) Introduction

The issue of abortion is complex and debate can be very passionate and emotive. Although there is some degree of consensus, there is vagueness and lack of clarity in crucial areas. The perceptions of rights and principles, viewed from medical, legal, ethical and religious perspectives, are often conflicting. Against this complex background is the additional factor of the continual advance of science and technology; for example, rapid progress has been made in supporting a **fetus** outside the womb. Abortion is an issue that involves conflicting rights of individuals, therefore it is vital to consider all angles and perspectives when considering a response.

Another issue related to that of abortion is the right to have a child, or whether a child is a 'gift from God'. This includes the issues of infertility treatment and surrogacy. Approximately ten per cent of marriages in the UK are infertile. There is a distinction between childlessness and infertility. Infertility is a medical condition and there are medical treatments available to assist with reproduction; childlessness, however, is a general term applied when such treatment has been unsuccessful. This introduces the concept of **surrogacy**.

b) Key facts

It is important to begin with the stages of development of a human being. The beginning of 'humanness' is debated in philosophical, ethical and legal circles but, biologically speaking, the beginning is at conception.

In its broadest terms, the development, that is, the actualisation of the potentiality to become fully human, takes the following course:

- **conception**
- **zygote** (pre-embryo, 0–5 days)
- **blastocyst** (a group of multiplying cells, pre-embryo, 5–14 days)
- **embryo** (14 days to 8 weeks)
- **fetus** (8 weeks onwards)
- **new born** (birth, usually between 38 and 42 weeks).

It is interesting that the stage of pregnancy is calculated from the first day of the woman's last period. Despite such accuracy of science and technology, even the stage of conception is arguably vague and the timings given above assume normal growth rates.

> **Personhood may be one thing and human life another; hence it is possible to argue that, while the zygote may not be a person, there is no logical alternative to regarding it as the first stage in human life.**
>
> **(Mason and Laurie)**

An abortion can be defined as the termination of a pregnancy before 24 weeks. Abortions are available on the NHS but women seeking them must be referred by a doctor. According to the Brook Advisory Service:

> **… although the normal legal limit for abortion is 24 weeks, it is usually easiest to get an abortion on the NHS if a woman is under 12 weeks pregnant.**

KEY WORDS

Fetus the unborn baby from the end of the eighth week after conception (when the major structures have formed) until birth

Surrogacy one woman carrying a baby for another woman who cannot do so herself

Zygote a cell formed by the union of a male sex cell (a sperm) and a female sex cell (an ovum), which develops into the embryo according to information encoded in its genetic material

Blastocyst a group of multiplying cells

Embryo an animal in the early stage of development before birth; in humans, the embryo stage is the first three months after conception

KEY WORDS

Medical abortion by means of the abortion pill

Surgical abortion by means of the suction method

There are two classifications of abortion: medical and surgical. The first, achieved by means of an abortion pill (*mifepristone*) and a tablet (*prostaglandin*) inserted into the vagina 36 to 48 hours later, is a **medical abortion**. It involves no surgery and, in effect, is like heavy menstruation; however, it is not available in all areas.

The second type involves surgery and is called a **surgical abortion**. Most commonly, it is achieved through vacuum aspiration or suction and is available up to the 13th week of pregnancy. Women usually recover within a few hours and can go home the same day. In later stages of pregnancy, a process of dilation and evacuation is used, which involves opening the cervix and entering the womb, then removing the contents by means of surgical instruments as well as suction.

The traditional Christian teaching is that a child is a blessing and a gift from God, recognised many times throughout both the Old and New Testaments. The more specific biblical teachings about sexual relationships, understood at a literal level, suggest that the purpose of sexual intercourse is procreation. Indeed, this is the line taken by both the Roman Catholic Church and the theory of natural law. A child should clearly be born within a marriage.

There are, however, definite disagreements within Christianity regarding the ideas of both infertility treatments and surrogacy. This tends to be related to how the biblical text should be interpreted and understood.

From a non-religious perspective, the *Universal Declaration of Human Rights*, Article 16, cites 'the right to marry and found a family'. The crucial question, however, depends upon how this right is understood. Does this extend to and mean that any government should provide opportunities for infertile couples as a basic human right? What about single women? What about homosexual relationships?

The *Human Fertility and Embryology Act 1990* (HFEA) provides regulations on infertility treatments. Surrogacy has a separate Act or Agreement from 1985; however, there are overlaps and qualifications with the HFEA.

Generally, treatments for infertility are partial and involve donor insemination (the insertion of semen from either the woman's partner or another donor) or IVF, in which the egg and sperm cells (gametes) are combined outside the woman's body and then inserted into her womb, to produce what are known as test-tube babies.

There is, however, another alternative to infertility treatment as described above. This involves the complete insertion of the gametes into a third party.

> **Surrogate motherhood requires the active cooperation of an otherwise uninvolved woman in the process of pregnancy and birth. It thus introduces a third party into the reproductive process.**
>
> (Mason and Laurie)

This is often referred to as womb-leasing.

c) The legal status

The history of the law against abortion begins with the *Offences Against the Person Act 1861*, which depicts procuring a miscarriage as a criminal act. The problem was that there was no option for therapeutic activity. In 1929 the *Infant Preservation Act* allowed the preservation of the mother's life as reason for a termination.

TASK

Try to identify the positive and the negative aspects in relation to abortion. Record your ideas in the form of a table. Look at factors such as *religious ideas, the law* and *practical implications.*

Objective To be able to 'select and demonstrate clearly relevant knowledge' (AO1 descriptor) and to work towards a 'good selection of material' (level 4 descriptor)

David Steel introduced the *Abortion Act 1967* that stated:

- two doctors must agree that an abortion is necessary.

It is deemed necessary if:

- the woman's physical health is threatened by having the baby
- any existing children would be harmed mentally or physically by the woman proceeding to have the baby
- there is a high risk the baby would be handicapped.

This was clarified by the *Embryology Act 1990* (section 37):

… it now states that a person is not guilty of an offence under the law of abortion when termination is performed by a registered practitioner and two registered medical practitioners have formed the opinion in good faith that the continuance of the pregnancy would involve risk, greater than if the pregnancy were terminated, of injury to the physical or mental health of the pregnant woman or any existing children of her family.'

(Mason and Laurie)

The legal limit was reduced from 28 weeks to 24 weeks but the 1990 Act, however, also removed time restrictions for a fetus aborted due to abnormality. This raises two issues.

What is to be done with a live fetus? The 1990 Act absolves the gynaecologist of destruction only and not the killing of a 'creature in being'.

(Mason and Laurie)

The dilemma of the gynaecologist who is there to relieve a woman of her fetus, however, is that 'there is now an infant who, on any interpretation, is entitled to a birth certificate, and, if necessary, a certificate as to the cause of death'.

(Mason and Laurie)

Infertility treatment is currently legal, although it is very difficult to access and is also expensive. Voluntary surrogacy is legal but, in line with the *1985 Surrogacy Agreement*, any form of surrogacy for financial gain is illegal. The illegal nature of payments relates directly to laws covering adoption, the only alternative prior to surrogacy:

… the rigid prohibition of commercialisation within adoption derives from a fear of exploitation of the woman concerned.

(Mason and Laurie)

Because 'both the ethics and the law relating to surrogacy are still in an uncertain state' (Mason and Laurie), a review was set up to evaluate the situation. The Brazier Review, as it was known, recommended that:

- genuine expenses and reasonable costs need to be defined by ministers for surrogacy
- agencies should be overseen and arrangements established and registered by health departments that also operate under a code of practice
- current legislation be improved by the addition of a consolidated and separate surrogacy act.

At present, costs incurred through surrogacy are estimated at £10–12 000. One final complication is that surrogacy arrangements cannot be enforced by law and either party can change its mind at any time.

> **" KEY QUOTE "**
> The basic argument against abortion, on which all others build, is that the unborn child is already a human being, a person, a bearer of rights, and that abortion is therefore murder.
>
> (Mackie)

> **" KEY QUOTE "**
> Whether or not abortion should be legal turns on the answer to the question of whether and at what point a fetus is a person. This is a question that cannot be answered logically or empirically. The concept of personhood is neither logical nor empirical: it is essentially a religious, or quasi-religious idea, based on one's fundamental (and therefore unverifiable) assumptions about the nature of the world.
>
> (Paul Campos, Professor of Law at the University of Colorado, 2002)

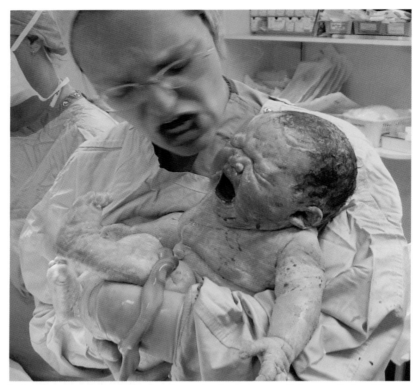

Is having a child a right, basic to the human condition, or is it a blessing or gift from God?

d) Specific ethical issues and key areas of the debate

These tend to be grouped into debates concerning key ideas, as discussed below.

Principles

The first issue involves the principles associated with abortion and hinges on the consideration of the act of killing and the ethical questions that this raises.

> **To kill a human adult is murder, and is unhesitatingly and universally condemned. Yet there is no obvious sharp line which marks the zygote from the adult. Hence the problem.**
>
> (Singer)

KEY WORD

Sanctity of life the belief that life is sacred or holy, given by God

The second and related issue involves the **sanctity of life**, which is the belief that life is in some way sacred or holy, traditionally understood as being given by God. Kant actually gives the idea of the sanctity of life a non-religious perspective based on purely ethical grounds, and philosophers such as Peter Singer have long called for a shift from talking about the sanctity of life towards a more universal discussion about the value of life.

> **We may take the doctrine of the sanctity of human life to be no more than a way of saying that human life has some very special value … The view that human life has unique value is deeply rooted in our society and is enshrined in our law.**
>
> (Singer)

The key debates then consider when an act can be classed as killing, or even murder, and at which point potential human life acquires such value as to make abortion an ethical injustice. This leads into more specific questions concerning the nature and status of the fetus, which is the second key area of debate.

The beginning of life and personhood

One of the major problems with the abortion debate is that there are blurred and inaccurate definitions for the terminology. For example, those campaigning against abortion (**pro-life**) and those campaigning for the rights of women to have abortions (**pro-choice**), interpret the terms *life* and *unborn* differently. For one group the idea of a human person includes the stage of an embryo, while the other considers only that stage beyond birth.

It is important, therefore, to establish what such interested parties actually mean when they refer to a baby, a person and a life. This is intrinsic to this aspect of the debate and therefore it is important to consider some different views.

There are several arguments concerning the application of the status of personhood to the embryo, fetus or child. These tend to be based on either biological stages or related to philosophical and religious principles or concepts.

Biological debates

Biological debates depend upon physical evidence to define the status of the fetus.

Birth: the status of personhood is only applied at actual physical birth. This is the first true point of independence and individuality.

Viability: the status of personhood is awarded at that time when the unborn can exist beyond any dependence on the mother. Obviously, with advancing technologies this stage is fluid. There is also debate about the appropriate meaning of viability. For example, how can a newly born child exist independently, in real terms?

Quickening: a traditional understanding that the status of personhood can be applied when the 'child' is first felt to move, although this varies from individual to individual. The ideas of viability and live birth 'both depend upon the medical support available' and 'the diagnosis can only be made after the event' (Mason and Laurie).

Potential (at conception): the possibility, from the point of fertilisation of the egg (conception), of becoming a human.

e) Philosophical and religious debates

Philosophical or religious arguments are based on concepts or principles beyond the physical evidence, that is, the metaphysical issues.

Consciousness: the status of personhood is applied at the first point of consciousness; however, is status of personhood dependent on the ability to think and reason?

Ensoulment: the status of personhood is deemed appropriate when the soul enters the body. Once again, this point is debated, proposals between 40 and 90 days have been offered, but the argument defies accuracy.

Continuity: life must begin when the potential life as an individual entity is recognisable, which is the zygote at conception. Any line drawn beyond this is arbitrary and has no justification, since life is one continuous and related process.

Relational factors: all arguments are based upon the meaning of words, or what Vardy calls relational factors. That is, there are different interpretations or understandings of the same words. This is where the argument began. Until accurate definitions of key terms are agreed, the stage at which personhood status is awarded can never be universal.

KEY WORDS

Pro-life against abortion
Pro-choice supporting women's rights to have abortions
Birth the point at which the child is separated from the mother and becomes a separate entity
Viability the ability to grow and develop into an adult, especially the ability of the child to exist without dependence on the mother
Quickening traditionally, when the child is first felt to move inside the mother
Potential the possibility, at conception, of becoming a human person
Consciousness awareness of self
Ensoulment the point when the soul enters the body
Continuity occurs at the first point at which potential life is recognisable
Relational factors different interpretations of the same words or terms, depending on the viewpoint of the observer

? KEY QUESTION

Is this status of personhood dependent on the ability to think and reason?

KEY QUOTES

The only absolute in the saga is that 'life' as it is generally understood begins with the formation of the zygote; on this view, the conservative Roman Catholic view represents the only tenable option – the difficulty is that it is also the least practical solution to the question.

(Mason and Laurie)

Definitions intended for statistical use are not, however, necessarily the same as those to be applied in practice.

(Mason and Laurie)

Finally, there is a clear disparity in the development of individuals. During life, although there are broad timescales at which people mature, develop and grow, there is, by the very nature of individuality, a blurring of the exact moment one moves from adolescence to adulthood, from childhood through puberty and so forth. Why are the early stages of development any different?

This leads to the last key issue: when the point of life is established and the status of personhood awarded, does it follow that the rights afforded to a person are already in place when this status is established?

Rights

The underlying question here is the right of all those involved to life. This must include both the established personhood and the woman involved. When the rights of both are in direct conflict, for example, when the mother's life is at risk, the law is clear – but is it ethically justified? When rights have been awarded it is then appropriate to consider the relative importance of different rights. Are those of the personhood limited and restricted or basic in any way? Does the woman's right to choice supersede the basic right to life of the personhood? Although these issues are difficult to consider, they are at the heart of the untidy nature of the debate.

Related to this, among physicians is the issue of adherence to the **Hippocratic Oath**, to preserve life at all costs, but also the right not to take part in abortion according to conscience.

> **KEY IDEA**
>
> **Hippocratic Oath – *Classical version***
> .... I will neither give a deadly drug to anybody who asked for it, nor will I make a suggestion to this effect. Similarly I will not give to a woman an abortive remedy. In purity and holiness I will guard my life and my art.
> ... What I may see or hear in the course of the treatment or even outside of the treatment in regard to the life of men, which on no account one must spread abroad, I will keep to myself, holding such things shameful to be spoken about.
> If I fulfil this oath and do not violate it, may it be granted to me to enjoy life and art, being honoured with fame among all men for all time to come; if I transgress it and swear falsely, may the opposite of all this be my lot.

This oath has been the basis of medicine for centuries. Although it has been updated for our times and transformed to suit the current aims of medicine, the principles of preservation of life still remain.

In such a consideration of rights, there is also the issue of infertility and the right to have a child. If a woman has established the right to decide how to treat and deal with her own body, this has implications for the manipulation and use of advancements in both medical science and technologies associated with infertility treatment. Should bearing a child be seen as a right? Or, as some would argue from religious perspectives, is a child a divine gift?

Several awkward questions remain.

- What exactly are the rights of the third party in surrogacy?
- What are, and who protects, the rights of the fetus?

■ What about the freedom to choose for non-medical reasons?

■ Do the infertility technologies invade a woman's life? Does a woman relinquish control over her own body?

Alternatively, is technology the opportunity to exercise the rights afforded to the status of womanhood? Are the infertility technologies an opportunity for women to have more power?

Practical implications

Finally, whatever conclusion is drawn or line of argument taken, it is vital to consider the opening observation regarding applied ethics. One of the most crucial stages and factors for arriving at a conclusion to an argument is its workability. Each line of argument will have practical implications that affect real people in the real world.

On the pro-life side there is the practical impact of cheapening what they regard as the specific status of life. It has often been said that the Abortion Act encourages in practice a lack of responsibility and hides the real issues concerned with sexual behaviour and individual responsibilities. The final practicality here would be the devaluation and undermining of the sexual act that, according to some, is for procreation.

The issue of a right to have a child raises many questions. With IVF comes the option of choosing the gender of the child. Although posing 'a negligible effect on the distribution and status of the sexes in the UK' (Mason and Laurie), this could have devastating effects in other areas of the world. Even if there were valid medical reasons for gender selection, what are the implications of selection for non-medical reasons? Infertility treatment is very costly and therefore its availability is restricted. The issue of infertility treatment being available, nationwide, has prompted the recent proposal to aim to offer three free cycles of treatment for all qualifying infertile couples. How far in the future is this and how is it prioritised?

On the issue of surrogacy, the right of singles or homosexuals to have a child has already been mentioned. Effectively, 'since there is no legal regulation of the matter, the practitioner acting in a private capacity will have to decide on ethical grounds alone whether or not to proceed in these circumstances'. Should such a crucial decision be made on personal ethical grounds alone? If the fetus is deformed, then can the surrogate mother request an abortion? Who actually owns the unborn child?

The whole nature of what it means to be a mother, whether in biological or social terms needs consideration.

> **Surrogacy could, however, be used for purely selfish reasons – for example, a desire to have a child without interference with a career – although the prospect may be given exaggerated importance.**
>
> **(Mason and Laurie)**

Indeed, the matter is even more complicated by the suggestion that to prohibit payments, despite preventing potential exploitation, could lead to another, equally unpleasant social scenario:

> **… the effect of prohibiting paid arrangements in the registered field must be to force the process onto the 'back streets', which would be to overturn the whole purpose of regulation.**
>
> **(Mason and Laurie)**

TASK

Try to identify the positive and the negative aspects in relation to the right to a child. Record your ideas in the form of a table. Look at factors such as *religious ideas, the law* and *practical implications*.
Objective To identify central key questions and arguments and to 'use a range of evidence to sustain an argument' (levels A02)

However, to tighten up on abortions or surrogacy and to restrict them would equally imply the curtailment of rights for which society has fought. There would be a clear feeling of oppression and lack of human freedom. This also leads to considerations of feminist issues.

3 Euthanasia

a) Introduction to euthanasia

KEY WORD

Euthanasia the ending of one person's life by another, usually to relieve suffering

The issue of **euthanasia** is equally as complex as abortion and for similar reasons. The context is the end, as opposed to the beginning, of life, yet some of the principles are the same. Certainly, the ethical issues identified progress under similar headings.

The first problem involves the technical difficulties surrounding the different definitions and types of euthanasia. There is a clear disparity in law both between countries and the ways in which legislation is applied. Euthanasia as an issue is as emotive as abortion, perhaps even more so, and involves a variety of principles and conflicts of interests. It is in the practicality and implementation of any decision where the most ferocious debate can be found.

b) Key facts about euthanasia

The meaning of the word derives from the Greek *eu thanatos*, interpretations of which include good, easy, gentle (*eu*) and death (*thanatos*). The key idea goes beyond the mere descriptive term and encompasses an idea of a death that is beneficial for the party involved. However, as with confusion over key terms in the debates about abortion, the actual understanding of the various types of euthanasia needs clarification.

Tony Hope, Professor for Medical Ethics at the University of Oxford and author of a key text for student doctors, *Medical Ethics and Law: The Core Curriculum*, offers the following distinctions.

Euthanasia	One person kills another with intention or allows another's death for the other's benefit
Active euthanasia	One person brings about another's death for the second person's benefit
Passive euthanasia	One person allows another to die, by withholding treatment or taking away vital life-prolonging support
Voluntary	A request to be allowed to die is made by the person who competently wishes it so
Non-voluntary	A decision is made by a second party on behalf of someone who is unable to make that decision
Involuntary	A decision is made by a second party to impose or permit the death of another, even though death is against the other's wishes
Suicide	One person intentionally takes their own life
Assisted suicide	One person helps another to commit suicide
Physician-assisted suicide	A qualified physician helps another person to commit suicide

c) The legal status of euthanasia

Having clarified and identified the key types of euthanasia, it is important to consider the legal status of euthanasia and again, as with applied ethics in general, to debate the workability of any change in law or viewpoint put forward.

The legal status of euthanasia varies according to geography. In the Netherlands and Belgium it is within the bounds of the law if specific criteria are met; in Switzerland physician-assisted suicide is allowed subject to specific criteria being met. In Britain, euthanasia is illegal.

In 1961 suicide was decriminalised. Despite this, the *Suicide Act 1961* was very explicit that to aid or assist suicide in any way was still a crime. Clearly this has implications for euthanasia.

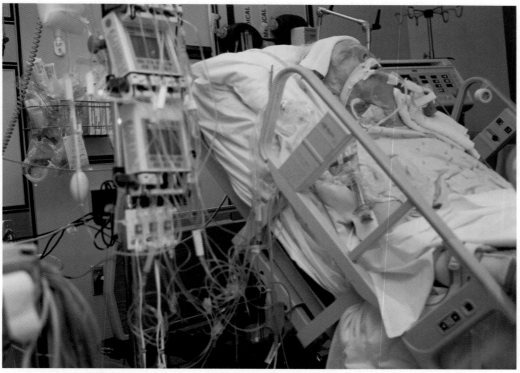

At what point should a person be afforded the right to decide to die?

d) Specific ethical issues and key areas of debate surrounding euthanasia

Principles

As with the debate surrounding abortion, there are two central principles at stake. The first is whether or not killing should be allowed in any circumstances. The second relates to the value that is given to life in respect of issues such as sanctity or quality, whether for religious, ethical or philosophical reasons.

Life and the quality of life: where does it finish?

In the consideration of abortion, the second area for debate was the point at which it could be said that life actually begins. The problems associated with establishing the start of a life could be deemed similar to those related to the end of life. Generally, a physical end of life can be determined medically. However, for a person in a

TASK

Try to identify the positive and the negative aspects in relation to euthanasia. Record your ideas in the form of a table. Look at factors such as *religious ideas, the law* and *practical implications*.
Objective To be able to 'select and demonstrate clearly relevant knowledge' (AO1 descriptor) and work towards a 'good selection of material' (level 4 descriptor)

❝ KEY QUOTE ❞

The massive technological advances of the last half century have increased our capabilities … we have become more and more aware that, occasionally, the preservation of life can be a negative blessing.

(Mason and Laurie)

KEY WORDS

Persistent vegetative state (PVS) a state in which body processes are maintained but the brain is functioning only at its lowest automatic levels
Double effect even if a good act has bad consequences, then it is still right to do it
Medical futility a situation in which treatment achieves no positive medical results, or is against the patient's best interests

❝ **KEY QUOTES** ❞

When suffering is the result of following an ethical principle then we need to look very carefully at our ethical principle and ask whether we are applying it too inflexibly.

(Hope)

It is perverse to seek a sense of ethical purity when this is gained at the expense of the suffering of others.

(Hope)

persistent vegetative state (PVS) there are issues surrounding the death of the consciousness. Such a situation again calls into question the definition of life and even whether a physical definition suffices. This is a key question in the euthanasia debate.

Related to this issue are also the philosophical questions about quality of life. Is there a point at which one can conclude that life has lost its value? If so, exactly when should this be and who is going to decide?

Human rights
It is interesting to note that:

> **patients have the right to decide how much weight to attach to the benefits, burdens, risks and the overall acceptability of any treatment. They have the right to refuse treatment even where refusal may result in harm to themselves or in their own death, and doctors are legally bound to respect their decision.**
>
> (General Medical Council)

This refers to those who are dying. They have the right not to prolong their life, by refusing treatment. They do not have the right, however, to hasten an end to their life by administering a different course of medication.

Does this pose a contradiction? If a person refuses treatment to prolong life then have they shortened their life? How, in principle, is this different from shortening life in another way?

Thus, humans have the legal right to the opportunity to extend life but not to shorten it. Where death is inevitable, humans can only stave it off and are not allowed to welcome it. (This relates to the idea of **double effect**, see page 149.)

There appears to be an uncomfortable inconsistency here. Consciously refusing treatment, knowing that the consequence is death, is seen as acceptable. Consciously willing medication of which the consequence is also death, only sooner and with less pain, is unacceptable. It is this delicate dilemma – if, indeed, it is one – that is at the very heart of the euthanasia debate: namely, just how far should a person's individual rights extend over their own body, fate and destiny?

This discussion of rights is further complicated when the affected party has lost the capacity to indicate preference, the physical ability to commit suicide or the ability to reason and make an informed decision regarding treatment.

Practical implications
The issue of **medical futility** is crucial here. That is:

> ... treatment may be contra-indicated on the grounds either that it is achieving no medical effect or that continued treatment can be seen as being against the patient's best interests ...
>
> (Mason and Laurie)

Who is to decide and how is this decision to be reached?

Is a law that allows euthanasia workable? Some countries legislate that, under strict conditions, it is. In support of euthanasia it could be pointed out that death might be for the person's benefit and that passive euthanasia is already widely accepted. Ethically, perhaps people should have a duty to prevent the prolonged and meaningless suffering of others. In addition, consideration should be given to the impact that a prolonged and painful death may have on others, such as close family and friends.

Arguments against the introduction of a law that allows euthanasia point to the very real risk of abuse. How could such a law be effectively monitored? Would it be in the best interests of society as a whole? Would it be a workable law?

Further, does euthanasia go against the Hippocratic Oath? Is it interfering with the natural or divinely ordained course of events?

For medical practitioners there is no clear legal guideline other than advice given by such bodies as the British Medical Association in 2001 or the Royal College of Paediatrics and Child Health. However, such guidelines are very vague with respect to active intervention and the withholding of curative medical treatment. Even doctors are unsure and clearly vulnerable, both legally and ethically.

4 Genetic engineering

a) Introduction to genetic engineering

Over the last thirty years, there have been enormous advances in science and technology.

The major question surrounding the issue of **genetic engineering** concerns the parameters, established by law, that control the allowable scope and extent of genetic manipulation. While the human race has developed the technology and ability for extensive manipulation, is it necessarily the case that they should automatically proceed? How far should they go, without careful monitoring and consideration?

Genetic engineering has many far-reaching implications. This makes the whole field an interesting and exciting challenge for the world today.

The complex nature of genetics raises similar questions to those raised about the threshold of life and death, already discussed. Several questions remain.

- How far should science and technology change the course of nature and, as some believe, the divine plan?
- There are practical issues regarding confidentiality of any personal information gleaned from genetic predictions, and how it is used. Who has the right to access of this information?
- Mistakes made in genetics can have widespread implications that do not simply affect the individual. Who decides and assesses the risks involved?
- The use and distribution of this technology has financial implications: is it just available to the wealthy, who can afford it?

At a more basic biological level, genetic modification could weaken resistance to disease, which could lead to drastic problems for the human race as a whole. Such important challenges to the use of genetics clearly need to be considered.

b) Key facts about genetic engineering

Humans
Genetic engineering is broadly divided into three main types.

- **Somatic cell** engineering involves changing the genetic codes of a cell, in other words, fixing cells so that they work in a desired way.
- **Germ-line** engineering involves only reproductive **germ cells** and all such alterations are hereditary, so could impact upon others.
- **Enhancement gene therapy**: commonly referred to as **eugenics**, this involves

KEY QUOTE

The doctor's dilemma is self-evident – is he or she practising truly 'good' medicine in keeping alive a neonate who will be unable to take a place in society or who will be subject to pain and suffering throughout life?

(Mason and Laurie)

KEY WORDS

Genetic engineering the artificial introduction of changes to the genes in a cell
Somatic cell any cell in the body that is not a sperm or egg cell
Germ-line the line or sequence of germ cells that have genetic material that may be passed to a child
Germ cells reproductive cells; the egg and sperm cells

KEY WORDS

Enhancement gene therapy attempts to make an already functional person better than they are

Eugenics the belief that information about heredity can be used to improve the human race

Cloning acquiring a group of genetically identical cells from a single cell; making identical copies of a gene

Reproductive cloning the cloning of an embryo for transplantation into a uterus with the intention of producing offspring genetically identical to the donor

Therapeutic cloning cloning an embryo for the purpose of deriving stem cells for therapeutic uses

the ability to manipulate and create cells and beings that have set characteristics and features and is sometimes associated with designer babies.

The area of eugenics has major implications for those who feel that they have the right to a child. Does this also extend to the right to design this child?

Animals

In 1997, Dolly, the **cloned** sheep, achieved international status. The ability to clone animals raised very many important ethical questions.

Selective breeding has been practised for generations. With the advancement of technology it was only a matter of time before the natural progression to genetically engineered breeding took place. Benefits for medical treatments are cited as justification. These include using animals for medical testing and as spare parts, such as valves and organs that are compatible with the human body.

Plants

The use of genetically modified ingredients has given rise to much concern. Genetically modified organisms such as fruits and vegetables have commercial benefits. Farmers of genetically modified products achieve increasing yields.

c) The legal status of genetic engineering

Using embryos for research purposes, as opposed to creating a child, inevitably raises all the questions that have been highlighted in relation to abortion. Since different countries have different cultures, beliefs and historical influences, each country has its own laws on genetic engineering. Science and technology are developing so rapidly that the laws cannot always keep pace with designating what is permissible, let alone considering the ethical implications.

So what is the law regarding genetic engineering?

The *Human Fertilisation and Embryology Act 1990* allows research on human embryos in the areas of miscarriage, infertility and genetic disease. In 2001, this was amended so that serious diseases and research into the development of human embryos themselves was allowed. In all cases, embryos must not be kept alive for more than 14 days.

If consent is given, donated sperm and eggs can be used to create an embryo for medical research.

The amended *Human Fertilisation and Embryology Act 2001* means that human embryos can be used to produce stem cells, subject to a licence being obtained. The 14-day rule also applies.

There are two type of human embryo cloning.

- **Reproductive cloning** is the cloning of an embryo and its development to produce identical offspring to the donor and it is illegal. Scientists breaking this law could spend up to ten years in prison. The *Human Reproductive Cloning Act* was passed in December 2001, making it an offence to place a cloned human embryo in the womb of a woman.
- **Therapeutic cloning** produces stems cells for medical research and therapeutic use and is not illegal, although it is still hotly debated. It has now been decided that human–animal hybrid embryos can also be used for this purpose.

Cloning to produce stem cells for research into curing serious diseases is covered by the 2001 amendment; however, questions have been raised about whether the human cloned embryo is different from an ordinary embryo and thus would not be covered under the *Human Fertilisation and Embryology Act 1990*.

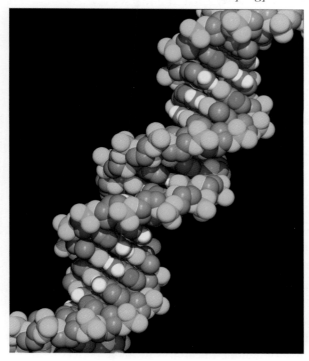

Deoxyribonucleic acid (DNA) provides all the instructions to enable living organisms to function properly. It is like a central memory bank that holds all the necessary information. Genetic engineering aims to reconstruct damaged DNA by using recombinant DNA technology. Engineered DNA can be used to create products that are useful for medical research.

d) Specific ethical issues and key areas of debate surrounding genetic engineering

Principles

If an embryo is classed as a human being, with personhood and rights, the issues are similar to those concerning abortion. Questions about violence and principles of killing also apply.

There are also added complications arising from the debate on how far science and technology should interfere and manipulate nature. Indeed, the whole relationship between the law, ethicality and science-technology needs to be examined. It has already been noted that the law always trails behind developments in science and technology and is often responding to ethical objections raised to scientific advancements. Is there any way of foreseeing developments and their implications?

In addition, how serious does the disease have to be to merit experimentation? Where is the line drawn? Why investigate some and not other conditions?

Life

It is always important to consider the principle of the value of human life in the light of medical ethics. Once again, the questions that are relevant to abortion regarding the sanctity, value or quality of life are raised here. Is life a gift or does it become something made?

However, there appears to be a much more global aspect to issues relating to genetic engineering than to those centred around abortion. This is because any advances in procedures or treatments that are developed have a much broader impact worldwide.

❝ KEY QUOTE ❞

You cannot explain the complexities of human personality and intelligence by simply looking at genes or neurons – there is much more going on than that. It is as if you tried to explain the beauty of a painting stored in a computer by the series of binary numbers in which it is stored. There is 'more' to a painting or to being human than any number of cells or genes.

(Vardy and Grolsch)

Human rights

The main issue here is one of patient confidentiality.

> **No specific legislation to regulate the control and use of genetic information has been introduced in the United Kingdom to date.**
>
> (Mason and Laurie)

There is debate about use of any genetic screening by interested parties such as insurers and employers. There are no specific laws against using genetic screening in making decisions, although in 2001 there was a five-year agreement among insurers that this information would not be sought.

Other issues that arise include those affecting the rights of the clones. Do they have any? Once again, what is the actual legal status of a clone, let alone its ethical or religio–philosophical status?

Practical implications

This is a particular minefield. Decisions have to be made carefully, on the theoretical and legal level, to avoid complications that arise in practice. For example, if potential employers and insurers are allowed to use predictions and calculations based on genetic information, does this mean that society is becoming too deterministic? This has obvious implications for how anyone is treated. There have been several recent science-fiction films that explore the nightmare scenarios associated with this. See, for example, the film *Gattaca*.

However, despite this, a rational context must be established for sensible debate. Several surveys carried out by The Human Genetic Commission suggest there is anxiety among the public that the goal of genetic research is to make perfect people; over a third of the public regard it as tampering with nature and therefore unethical. Until clarification and greater public awareness are achieved, the problem of misunderstanding of genetics will always be there to affect any debate.

A final practical dilemma is that of balancing the state's duty to reduce the financial burden on society while simultaneously eliminating harm to its citizens. The subjective nature of deciding what is for the public good will always be a factor in any debate.

5 War and peace

a) Introduction to war and peace

It is a regrettable fact that violence and murder are part of human history. The Old Testament is full of violence; the Mahabharata is based on family feuds and warfare; even the establishment of Islam, the religion of peace, was achieved through famous conflicts.

Indeed, it has often been observed that, of all creatures on Earth, the human being is by far the most ferocious and dangerous. For example, humans in recent history have developed **weapons of mass destruction** such as nuclear, biological and chemical weapons. It is interesting to note that, in shifting from medical ethics to war, we move from the idea that humanity is advancing towards improvement in the quality of life worldwide to the appalling fact that, over the last century, humanity is faced with the worst record of **genocide** and cruelty in its history.

TASK

Try to identify the positive and the negative aspects in relation to genetic engineering. Record your ideas in the form of a table. Look at factors such as *religious ideas, the law* and *practical implications*.
Objective To be able to 'select and demonstrate clearly relevant knowledge' (AO1 descriptor) and work towards a 'good selection of material (level 4 descriptor)

KEY WORDS

Weapons of mass destruction weapons capable of killing enormous numbers of people
Genocide mass killing, unlawful mass murder; the intentional destruction or eradication of an entire racial, political, cultural or religious group

---

*b) Key facts about war and peace (the **just war** and **pacifism**)*

The idea of a just war has been debated for centuries. It would be incorrect to identify the just war theory as a single theory. It is more fluid than this. It has developed from simple ideals to a complex range of proposals and even now is still being debated and re-evaluated.

> **Many credit Augustine with the founding of just war theory but in its origins just war theory is a synthesis of classical Greco-Roman, as well as Christian, values. If we have to 'name names', the founders of just war theory are probably the triad of Aristotle, Cicero and Augustine.**
>
> *(Stanford encyclopedia)*

The original questions of *when* it was right to go to war and *how* to fight in a war have developed into two main areas of the theory of a just war. In response to modern conflicts much of this has been re-evaluated and developed.

> **Many of the rules developed by the just war tradition have since been codified into contemporary international laws governing armed conflict, such as The United Nations Charter and The Hague and Geneva Conventions.**
>
> *(Stanford encyclopedia)*

There are three aspects of a just war to consider:

- ■ *jus ad bellum*: the just nature of the reasoning and decision to take part in a war
- ■ *jus in bello*: the just nature of conduct during the war once it begins
- ■ *jus post bello*: the just nature of how a war is ended.

Jus ad bellum

These are rules for state leaders and there are six requirements.

- ■ **Just cause**: war has to be for the right reason. The ideas of right reason and just cause cover self-defence, defending others from attack and protecting the innocent.
- ■ **Right intention**: even if a just cause can be established, the motive has to be pure. Power, finance, land or revenge are examples of wrong motives.
- ■ **Proper authority and public declaration**: the leader must declare war and do so publicly.
- ■ **Last resort**: all other diplomatic negotiations must have failed. Every attempt to resolve the matter peacefully has been unsuccessful.
- ■ **Probability of success**: some see this as biased against smaller countries, but in practice the principle of self-defence over-rides it.
- ■ **Proportionality**: it is only sensible to weigh up the probability that greater good is going to come from the war. The benefits need to be worth the devastating costs the war may bring.

KEY WORDS

Just war a specific concept of how warfare might be justified, typically in accordance with a particular situation or scenario

Pacifism the doctrine that all violence is unjustifiable; opposition to war or violence as a means of settling disputes

Jus ad bellum a set of criteria to be consulted before engaging in war, in order to determine whether entering into war is justifiable

Jus in bello law stating acceptable practices while engaged in war, such as the Geneva Conventions

Jus post bello suggested rules about justice after a war, including peace treaties, reconstruction, war crimes trials and war reparations

Jus in bello

It is the military that effectively bear the brunt of these responsibilities.

- **Obey all international laws on weapons prohibition**: chemical and biological weapons must not be used.
- **Discrimination and non-combatant immunity**: the military must distinguish between civilian life and legitimate military, political and industrial targets.
- **Proportionality**: once the end is achieved, no further force is needed. In reaching the end, excessive force is not to be used, only that which is necessary.
- **Benevolent quarantine for prisoners of war (POWs)**: all prisoners are to be given basic rights as they are no longer 'engaged in harm'.
- **No means that are *mala in se***: no methods or weapons that are 'evil in themselves' may be used. This covers a breadth of possibilities. Sadly, the reality of history tells us that these do happen. Crimes such as genocide, ethnic cleansing, biological weapons, rape campaigns, torture and poison fall into this category.
- **No reprisals**: this includes the ideas of revenge and retribution.

Jus post bellum

This is a relatively new aspect to the just war tradition and is continually being debated. The purpose is to restore peace and arrive at the most effective way of doing this in a controlled manner. Debated principles include:

- restoring human rights
- distinguishing between innocent civilians, who are to be free from post-war punishment, and those who have incurred penalties
- public agreement and proclamation
- giving war criminals fair trials: this applies both to leaders and any ordinary soldiers
- establishing financial compensation where necessary but so that civilians are not taxed and that the country can restore itself
- giving the country and its inhabitants the opportunity to reform.

c) Specific issues and key areas of debate surrounding war and peace

Principles

Waging of war contradicts principles such as peace, non-violence, that killing is wrong and that conflicts can be resolved through discussion. The compromise of such principles is seen as necessary by those who support the use of war. Essentially, the questions raised focus on whether such principles can be compromised at all and the consequential vagueness that ensues about when and why such compromises are made.

There are two main responses to the idea of war. The first considers war as lesser evil than the one that allows matters to continue unaddressed.

The other is the line taken by **ethical and religious pacifism**. Examples of who have consistently refused to support war in any way include the Quakers, **Gandhi** and **Bertrand Russell**.

Life

The main issue, once again, relates to the value, sanctity and quality of life. War devastates. As well as immediate destruction, the impact of war can be felt for years after. Another consideration is the impact upon individuals affected by the violence and poverty that war brings.

TASK

Try to identify the positive and the negative aspects in relation to war and peace. Record your ideas in the form of a table. Look at factors such as *religious ideas, the law* and *practical implications.*

Objective To be able to 'select and demonstrate clearly relevant knowledge' (AO1 descriptor) and working towards a 'good selection of material' (level 4 descriptor)

 **KEY TERM**

Ethical and religious pacifism belief that war cannot be condoned on any grounds

---

TASK

Find out when Russell's imprisonment occurred and the specific reasons why it happened.

KEY PERSON

Mohandas Karamchand Gandhi (1869–1948)
Also known as the Mahatma (great soul), Gandhi was
an inspirational spiritual and political leader in the drive
for Indian independence from the British, during last the
century. He inspired many people worldwide through his
principles of truth and active resistance to evil through
non-violent protest. His strong ideas of justice through
peaceful means influenced later civil rights leaders and those
in the fight for freedom, and are still respected by many
today. His birthday is a national holiday in India.

KEY PERSON

Bertrand Russell (1872–1970)
A famous British philosopher and mathematician,
Russell was renowned for his attitudes towards social
reform and pacifism. Russell was critical of war and
of the nuclear arms race and, in his early life, was
imprisoned for his beliefs.

Human rights

Debates about the violation of human rights before, during and after war continue.
The rights to life, freedom and protection are the first three that seem to be relevant.
The issues of such rights can be seen running through the just war theory and its
process of reasoning.

Practical implications

This is the most crucial area of debate and any decision for war must take it into
account. Many questions need to be asked, and many arguments debated, about the
consequences of war. Death, poverty, discrimination, suffering, disease and financial
ruin of a country are all potential areas for consideration. Is there ever a case for
justifying such horror? How can we learn from human history? How can war be
prevented? How can humanity ensure atrocities such as the Holocaust and the ethnic
conflicts in Rwanda and former Yugoslavia will never happen again?

EXAM TIP

Always point out the wide
variety of influences that
determine the issues for
debate. Make sure that
you explain clearly any
problems. This enables a
demonstration of 'use of
evidence and examples'
(AO1 descriptor) and also
builds up and will help any
following 'analysis' (AO2
descriptor).

TASK

**Try to find some
examples of how
Gandhi practised his
non-violent resistance.
In pairs, identify 5–10
important issues and
make a bulleted list of
points for each of the
applied ethics topics:
abortion, euthanasia,
genetic engineering and
war. Present your lists
to the rest of the group.
Following discussion,
add two or three more
points for each topic.
Now look at the
level 5 descriptor and
see how your selections
could be described
as demonstrating
'understanding and
engagement with the
material' and 'accurate
use of technical terms'.
Then, individually, use
these points to prepare
a summary that is
'well constructed and
organised'.**
Objective To prepare
a summary, using
collaborative learning
and peer assessment, to
aim for a level 5 answer

Abortion and the right to a child
- stages of development
- the laws
- medical procedures
- principles of taking life
- question of when life begins
- biological and philosophical or religious debates
- human rights
- practical implications of any decisions made

Euthanasia
- the law
- the dilemmas in defining euthanasia: different types
- principles of taking life and who decides
- human rights
- practical implications of any decision made

Genetic engineering
- human
- types of cell research
  - somatic
  - germ line
  - enhancement gene therapy
- animals: cloning; medical procedures
- plants: genetically modified crops
- legal status of genetic engineering
- idea of a person
- ideas about life
- human rights
- practical implications of any decisions

War and peace
- definitions of war and pacifism
- history of war
- the just war
- jus ad bello (before)
- jus in bello (during)
- jus post bello (after)
- principles of violence and peace
- the right to life
- practical implications of decisions about war

Summary diagram: Part 1: The issues

Reflection and assessment AO1

Below is an answer given in response to the question:

Outline the principles of a just war and examine its application. (25 marks)

It is not the best possible response and will probably be awarded level 2. There are some comments attached to suggest why.

Needs a context for how and why the just war theory developed.

Again, needs to explain how it 'developed' rather than just involve one thinker.

A just war is when a country decides that it has good reason to go to war. It is not just because of land or because they have disagreed with another country. Augustine said it had to be a proper authority that started it and it must be for a genuine reason. Over the years the just war has developed and there are many areas to consider. Many people have added rules and countries now generally agree as to what a just war is. It is usually split into two parts that deal with behaviour during the war but also considering reasons for going to war in the first place.

Reasons are not explored in a systematic manner – disorganised.

This is quite vague and the answer lacks examples of rules or applications to illustrate points made.

Suggestion for further application of skills

As a group, divide up the tasks to explain the principles, law and areas for debate for abortion, euthanasia and genetic engineering. In small groups or as individuals, take charge of one area. Spend 15 minutes on this and then swap with another group (or person) for them to add to or rework your initial outline. Keep going as a group until you are satisfied that you have a good enough description to present as an examination answer.

TASK

Try rewriting this response, using the following plan:
Principles: list reasons for war, conduct and termination
Application: explain the rules suggested for each.
Objective To develop awareness of what will constitute a very good answer (levels 4–5) by gradually building up a response

Part 2

A critical analysis of the issues

What are the issues that I am expected to consider and to analyse critically?

- Key strengths of the arguments about abortion, euthanasia, genetic engineering and war and peace
- Key weaknesses of the arguments about abortion, euthanasia, genetic engineering and war and peace
- Possible conclusions related to each issue

Introduction

When critically evaluating the ethical issues studied, it is always useful to identify the strengths and weaknesses of each of the arguments that are put forward.

Generally, this involves highlighting the crucial points that support an issue and those that challenge it. The next stage is to decide which arguments are effective and which can be challenged. However, in terms of standardised strengths and weaknesses, there is little that can be written here because of the subjective nature of argument. Remember that what one person views as a strength of an argument may well be seen as a weakness by another.

Therefore, no official judgements are made here regarding the quality of the points put forward. That is for you to decide, after study, reflection and debate. Each topic is presented with one or two points that support and one or two that challenge an issue. It is anticipated that classes will use these as a base for further thought, analysis and argument.

Since the section of the Specification that covers applied ethics involves four distinct issues, it would be unreasonable to group them all together under issues of life and death for evaluation purposes. Each issue will therefore be dealt with separately.

TASK

In groups, develop your tables to include extra arguments in support of and challenging the issues under debate. All four areas of the specification need addressing. Discuss some possible conclusions and devise a flow chart or thought process diagram for each area. Include key questions for discussion.

Objective To encourage the use of questions in answers for AO2 and also serve as information to use in 'sustaining an argument' (AO2) Questions facilitate more than one point of view (AO2 level 3 and above)

1 Abortion

In support	Challenges
The mother has a basic human right to choose the fate of her own body when it comes to abortion and this right supersedes the right of the fetus.	The fetus has an equal right for protection as the woman and should be protected.
The law is on the side of those that champion the right to abortion as a morally acceptable course of action.	Teachings concerning the sanctity of life are crucial for religious people. Even the non-religious appreciate the value of human life.
History suggests that if the law was abolished then greater suffering and injustice would result.	If the beginning of life can be established as conception then this has implications as to the lawfulness of abortion and the act would need rejecting.
Strict guidelines are there to prevent any misuse of the law and the abortion act is grounded in medical rationale.	It would be morally irresponsible in the light of technological advancements and the new possibilities of saving lives to continue with the law as it stands.

2 Euthanasia

In support	Challenges
Euthanasia can be considered humane. It is immoral and irresponsible to deny someone a gentle death and allow needless suffering simply because of a 'principle'.	It is against the principles of not killing and the Hippocratic Oath.
Euthanasia supports the rights of the individual.	Some have argued that a legalisation of euthanasia would set up a 'slippery slope', opening the situation up to abuse and sinister motives.
Euthanasia benefits both the individual and any persons involved with the individual, preventing needless physical suffering, emotional pain and mental anguish.	There is a strong argument that any legalisation for euthanasia is far too complex to manage in practical terms. It would be an unworkable law.
The laws as they stand do not assist medical practitioners. There is still vagueness and uncertainty that leads to a moral dilemma for doctors. Some forms of euthanasia need introducing.	Once again, if euthanasia is legalised it will be impossible to measure and maintain its use because the parameters are so blurred.

TASK

Now complete a similar table for the right to have a child.

Objective To identify central key questions and arguments and to 'use a range of evidence to sustain an argument' (level 5 AO2)

3 Genetic engineering

In support	Challenges
There is a historical justification in terms of advancement in technology and the practice of medicine.	The use of genetic engineering is open to abuse. Interested parties can take advantage and discriminate against people.
Governments are morally responsible for helping citizens.	Any technological, medical and scientific advancements need challenging in terms of their practicality and workability for society. Too many advancements are going unchallenged.
There will be a decrease in suffering.	The role of science is not to 'play God'. The idea of the sanctity of life is slowly being eroded.
The use of technology to improve the quality of life for all concerned is not just morally right but is linked to the basic human right of 'right to life'.	The practical side of genetic engineering will simply mean further inequality between rich and poor. Only the wealthy can afford treatment. Until equality can be secured, should we really advance in blatant inequality?

4 War

In support	Challenges
War is an absolutely necessary evil. It is not entered into lightly and, with close monitoring, is a means of protection and righting wrongs in the world.	War is totally against the principles of rights to life and freedom. It is destructive and any good at the end can never justify the catastrophic means used.
War is controlled by the principle of just war. We have advanced from the primitive approaches to conflict. War today is much more effective.	History demonstrates the evils of war and even now we have not learned sufficiently to justify its continuance.
We have to consider the reality of the situation and not just the ideals. The ideal is to have peace at all cost; the reality is that, in the face of aggressors, there is sometimes cause for self-defence and self-preservation.	The ideal of just war does not work and it is open to interpretation. Guidelines to a just war are vague and do not work in practice.
In the long term, war saves lives and alleviates suffering. It frees the oppressed and is a step towards a world in which peace can be established in real terms.	*An eye for an eye just makes the whole world blind.* **(Gandhi)** Very simply, two wrongs do not make a right. Non-violence and pacifism can work.

TASK

Carry out some research about weapons of mass destruction. Try to find arguments people have put forward, both in favour and in opposition to them.
Objective To identify contrasting arguments and to 'use a range of evidence to sustain an argument' (level 5 AO2)

Reflection and assessment AO2

The second way of being assessed is through assessment objective AO2. For this objective you need to be able to: sustain a critical line of argument and justify a point of view.

Use the writing frame provided to answer the question below.

As you work through each unit in this book, you will find that the amount of support in these sections will gradually be reduced, in order to encourage the development of your independence and the honing of your AO2 skills.

Assess the view that a just war is an effective means of solving conflicts.

(10 marks)

Writing frame

The issue for debate here is ...

There are different ways of looking at this and many key questions to ask such as ...

The just war theory involves a variety of thinkers, religious ideas, traditions and practices. We need to look at how people have reacted and used these principles throughout history. ...

Some ideas, however, are still debated today ...

Despite this, another point of view would be that there is clarity to the just war and an argument for its necessity ...

In light of all this, it could be argued that ...

Nevertheless, it is my view that ...

and I base this argument on the following reasons ...

Although quite basic, this writing frame does focus on critical analysis. It is better to deal with three or four criticisms in some detail, than to compile a longer list with very brief comment. It is important also to make clear in what way your criticism challenges the argument or view.

Suggestion for further application of skills

After completing the question, use the levels and AO descriptors to award marks out of 10. Identify strengths and areas for development in each answer. Now, as a group, collaborate to create an ideal answer that demonstrates and displays 'successful and clear analysis' (level 4) by 'using evidence to sustain an argument' (level 4). Discuss what could make this answer show 'understanding and critical analysis of different view points' (level 5 descriptor).

Part 1A
Natural law

What am I required to study?

- Natural law

This means I am expected to know about:

- the origins of Aquinas' natural law in Aristotle's idea of purpose
- Aquinas' ideas of purpose and perfection
- the use of reason to discover natural law
- the primary and secondary precepts
- application of natural law to abortion, euthanasia, genetic engineering, and war and peace.

This section explores the ethical theory of natural law. Then natural law will be applied to the issues of abortion, euthanasia, genetic engineering and war and peace. Refer back to Topic 2, page 121, for the background to the issues.

In Part 1B we shall assess the strengths and weaknesses of natural law, both as an ethical theory and in its approach to the above four issues. It would be helpful to write your notes under the headings listed in 'This means I am expected to know about', as it is from these areas that the exam questions will be derived.

Remember that your studies will include elements of the *two* basic assessment objectives of:

- Knowledge and Understanding (AO1)
- Evaluation (AO2).

See pages 7–8 in the Introduction to remind yourself of these objectives.

The evaluation material is set out in Part 1B of this topic (page 154) and can be studied either alongside the AO1 material, as you work through this topic, or as a discrete topic.

1 Aristotle and natural law

a) What is natural law?

Natural law is based on a particular view about nature and the Universe. That view is that the Universe has a natural order that works to achieve an end or purpose. The order, direction and purpose are determined by a supernatural power. Human beings are part of the natural world and so they, too, have a purpose or nature. It is a nature that is in all human beings. Natural law is therefore about acting in such ways that we consistently move towards this purpose.

KEY WORD

Natural law an ethical system based on the view that humans have a set of natural inclinations that, if followed, will lead to the perfection of our being

KEY WORDS

Eudaimonia a contented state of being happy, healthy and prosperous
Logos **fundamental principle**

KEY PEOPLE

The Stoics
For the Stoics, *Logos* could be thought of as the soul of the universe. It was the impersonal force of reason that formed the universe.

KEY QUESTION

What is natural law?

" KEY QUOTES "

The many, the most vulgar, seemingly conceive the good and happiness as pleasure, and hence they also like the life of gratification … the life they decide on is a life for grazing animals.

(Aristotle)

… from Socrates, through Plato to Aristotle. The faculty of reason is not merely one of understanding, but also one of action; ethics is reason put into practice …

(Mel Thompson)

For Aristotle, the result will be fulfillment and what he called **eudaimonia**, which is interpreted as flourishing or happiness. For Aquinas, the natural law was located in the activity of human reasoning. He thought that by applying reason to moral problems, we shall find that we act consistently with the natural law. Such acts are deemed good acts, since they are in line with our true human nature and purpose. For Aquinas, the natural law was created by God and designed to achieve the ultimate purpose, which is to enjoy fellowship with God, to be perfect in the image of God.

b) Origins of the concept of natural law

Many scholars regard the first clear explanation of the concept of natural law to be that of the **Stoics**. However, the idea did not originate with them. As early as the sixth century BCE there was the idea of *logos* or reason, which was thought to pervade the world. *Logos* was seen as that which gave order to the Universe. Human beings, as part of the natural world, were therefore seen as also reflecting the natural order. From this, there gradually developed the idea that living properly involved acting in accordance with our human nature.

c) Aristotle's idea of purpose

As already mentioned, Aristotle (384–322BCE) saw the goal or purpose of human life as eudaimonia – flourishing or happiness. He argued that we pursue other goals in order ultimately to achieve happiness. Confusion can arise because of the modern interpretation of happiness. For Aristotle, happiness was very different from pleasure, since he regarded the pursuit of pleasure for its own sake as mere gratification. In contrast, happiness was living well and being fulfilled, since it involved behaving rationally or consistently with human nature and the order of the natural world. Therefore, he thought that making reasoned choices would lead to happiness. There is more about Aristotle and final causes on pages 17–18 in Unit 1, *The philosophy of religion*.

 KEY PROFILE: ARISTOTLE (384–322BCE)

Aristotle was a student of Plato, at the Academy in Athens. He is credited with writing the first ever ethics book, *Nicomachean Ethics*. The book is more practical than philosophical, in that it aims to teach people to be virtuous rather than to discuss what virtue is.

Aristotle assumed that all our actions aim at some end or good, and that there is one ultimate end. The highest good is that to which all actions aim; it must be attainable and an end in itself. He argued that it is happiness that satisfies and concluded that happiness alone must be the highest good.

d) The Stoics

The Stoics made clear a link between the natural order and the concept of moral goodness. The fundamental principle, or *logos*, that underpinned and directed the Universe, which they called the *Logos*, was seen as morally good. This led them to reject Aristotle's view of the purpose of human beings as being happiness. For them, the goal was to be at one with the *logos* that guided the whole Universe. This involved making choices that were morally good and that brought about this goal. Morality became an end in itself.

2 Aquinas and natural law

a) Aquinas' ideas of purpose and perfection

For Aquinas, reason still played a key role in his development of natural law.

God was seen as the source of the natural law, which was rooted in the human mind. When reasoning about moral questions takes place, then good reasoning will coincide with the natural law. Aquinas saw God as having designed us for perfection. He believed that we were made in God's image and our purpose was to reflect this image perfectly. Unlike earlier philosophers such as Aristotle and the Stoics, Aquinas believed in a personal, creator God. He also saw the final purpose of human beings in terms of the eternal rather than the temporal.

Aquinas did not think that this perfection could be discovered by natural law alone. He also appealed to **eternal law** and **divine law**.

- Eternal law refers to the principles by which God governs the Universe, so we know or understand only partially.
- Divine law refers to the Bible, which guides us in reaching our goal of perfection. However, Aquinas believed that such perfection was not achievable in this life, but only after death.

Natural law is the part of the eternal law that applies to human choices and can be known by our natural reason.

KEY PROFILE: THOMAS AQUINAS (CE 1224–74)

Saint Thomas Aquinas is often regarded as the greatest medieval philosopher. He tried to show the harmony between faith and reason, and between Christianity and philosophy. The teaching of Thomas Aquinas has been particularly influential in the Roman Catholic Church. Hence natural law and the doctrine of double effect, see page 149, have become central tenets of Roman Catholic theology.

Although Aquinas is seen to be the father of natural law, some scholars challenge such a view, and argue that the role should be attributed to the Stoics.

b) The primary and secondary precepts

The primary precepts apply to all human beings without exception. They are good acts because they lead us towards the main human purpose or goal. The most fundamental one that underpins them all is:

- act in such a way as to achieve good and avoid evil.

KEY IDEA

Natural law is not the same as a law of nature. Natural law is about human actions and natural inclinations. However, laws of nature are about the laws that apply to material things, and include such laws as the universal law of gravitation, which explains gravity.

KEY WORDS

Eternal law order in the mind of God
Divine law God's law mediated through special revelation; the Bible and the Church

KEY IDEA

Natural law does not refer to action that is natural but rather to action that is based on reason, interpreting purpose within the world.

For Aquinas, obeying natural law meant doing actions that develop our image to reflect more closely the image of God.

Natural law is about the fulfilment of human potential, through actualisation.

" KEY QUOTES "

Natural law is the same for all men ... there is a single standard of truth and right for everyone ... which is known by everyone.

(Aquinas)

True law is right reason in agreement with Nature; it is of universal application. Unchanging and everlasting; it summons to duty by its commands and averts from wrongdoing by its prohibitions.

(Marcus Cicero)

This summary identifies the most basic natural inclination. From this, Aquinas then identified five more general inclinations or tendencies. In one sense they can be seen as fundamental principles that must be followed in order to achieve the required ends. These five principles are:

- preserve innocent life
- maintain orderly living in society
- worship God
- educate children
- reproduce to continue the species.

From these primary precepts, secondary ones can be deduced. The difference between the primary and secondary is that the primary precepts are always true and held universally, without exception. They are also self-evident. In contrast, the secondary precepts are not strictly universal since they may not hold in certain circumstances. They are also derived from reasoning from the primary precepts.

An example of a secondary precept would be: 'Do not steal.' This reflects the primary precept of 'orderly living in society'.

However, it is accepted that sometimes situations occur whereby the enactment of a secondary precept would go against a primary precept. In such a case the primary precept takes precedence. Natural law always demands that the primary precept is followed.

c) Apparent good

Natural law is within all of us but it is not like a physical law that has to be followed. It derives from reason and reason can sometimes be in error.

Reason should tell us what we should desire, since we have a natural inclination. This should lead us to our goal of reaching perfection, which is the image of God. However, Aquinas recognised that sometimes we do not do the things that we should. We reason wrongly.

One example of reasoning wrongly would be if a good were pursued that actually was not a good as understood by natural law: it did not develop perfection. It is what is referred to as an apparent good. Aquinas argued that our fallen nature can lead us astray, to choose things that we desire but that may not be contributing to our development into the image of God.

One way that correct reasoning can be developed is through the cultivation of certain virtues.

Natural virtues	prudence temperance fortitude justice
Theological virtues (revealed by the Bible)	faith hope charity

d) Double effect

Aquinas made a distinction between the intention of an act and the act itself. For those looking on, it may well be judged that an action was good; for instance, holding a large reception apparently to raise money for charity, but actually to promote a new product. However, if the onlooker knew the real motive or intention, then it may well be seen rather differently. Likewise it is not acceptable to do a bad act intentionally even if the aim is to bring about good outcomes, for example, stealing from the rich to give to the poor.

This approach to understanding intentions is important when applying natural law to moral dilemmas. It is at the heart of what is known as the **doctrine of double effect**. This states that even if a good act has bad consequences, it is still right to carry out that act. So, it is still right to perform an act, despite it being known that bad consequences would result. The important issue is the intention. If the intention was not to bring about these bad consequences, then the unfortunate side effects do not make the act morally wrong.

Classical formulations of the principle of double effect require four conditions to be met if the action is to be morally permissible:

- we do not wish the evil effects, but make all reasonable efforts to avoid them
- the immediate effect should be good in itself
- the evil is not made a means to obtain the good effect
- the good effect should be as important, proportionately at least, as the evil effect.

An example of this would be a bombing of an area in a war, where it was known that civilians lived and some would be killed. As long as killing civilians was not the intention, but rather an unfortunate side effect, then the act is deemed good and morally right, according to natural law ethics.

e) Deontological and absolutist

The principles of natural law ethics are usually regarded as being **deontological** and **absolutist**:

- deontological because what should be done is seen as being determined by fundamental principles that are not based on consequences
- absolutist because they identify the right action by means of the primary precepts.

Note, however, that scholars such as **John Finnis** challenge the view that natural law is deontological. They draw attention to the role of the adoption, by Aquinas, of the notion of final cause in the natural law theory.

KEY WORDS

Doctrine of double effect even if a good act has bad consequences, it is still right to do it
Deontological focusing on the rightness or wrongness of actions themselves, rather than the rightness or wrongness of the consequences
Absolutist the idea that actions are right or wrong, devoid of the context

KEY PERSON

John Finnis (1940–) an Australian philosopher, is professor of Law and legal philosophy at Oxford University.

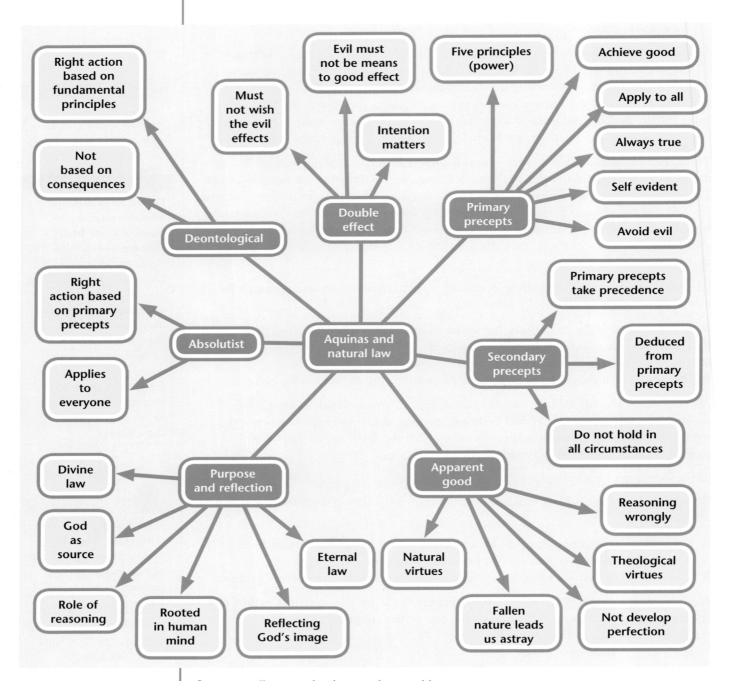

Summary diagram: Aquinas and natural law

3 What natural law says about the issue of abortion

a) Application of primary precepts

Those who accept Aquinas' doctrine of natural law, and seek to apply this to the issue of abortion, believe that the key primary precept involved here is that of preserving innocent life. Hence the act of abortion is seen as inherently evil because of the intentional and direct killing of an innocent human being. This would apply to all situations, including cases of rape or incest.

66 KEY QUOTE 99

Whether inflicted upon the mother or upon the child, [abortion] is against the precept of God and the law of nature: 'Thou shalt not kill'.

(Pope Pius XI)

The debate then focuses on when a fetus can be considered as a person. Opinions vary, from regarding it as the moment of conception to choosing the time of the appearance of a certain feature, such as neural activity.

b) The doctrine of double effect

The doctrine of double effect does permit the death of the fetus, but only as a by-product of another act. This means that the intention was not to kill the fetus. For instance, the use of chemotherapy, or the performance of a hysterectomy to remove a cancerous uterus, would lead to the death of the fetus. However, as that is not the intention of the act, but rather a by-product, the removal of the cancerous uterus is acceptable.

If there is any other reasonable medical treatment available to save the life of the mother, which would not entail harm or death to the fetus, then that action must be chosen instead.

4 What natural law says about the issue of euthanasia

a) Application of primary precepts

The primary precept of preserving innocent life is also the key principle when faced with the issue of euthanasia. It is often expressed in terms of the argument about sanctity of life. Sanctity is the quality of being sacred or holy. Natural law teaches that there is something special about human life that is above and beyond that of animals. Therefore it should be protected. The taking of another's life, even if they request it, is not therefore morally acceptable. By the same argument, the taking of one's own life (suicide) is equally an immoral act.

b) The doctrine of double effect

The rules of double effect are set out on page 149. Although administering drugs to end a life is unacceptable, it could be argued that it is morally acceptable, under natural law, to give a large dose of morphine to control the pain of a terminally ill patient, even if it was foreseen that the morphine would shorten the patient's life. Whatever the consequences, the intention was not to kill the person but to bring relief to their pain.

5 What natural law says about the issue of genetic engineering

Application of primary precepts

The preservation of innocent life is the key principle in the issue of embryo research. If the embryo is deemed to be a human life, then it would be immoral to use it for experimentation.

A recent development has been the use of the blastocyst as a source for embryonic stem cells. The blastocyst is the structure formed in early embryogenesis, before implantation. It possesses an inner cell mass, which subsequently forms the embryo, and an outer cell mass that forms the placenta. Blastocyst formation begins at day five. It is this inner cell mass that is the source of embryonic stem cells.

Using the blastocyst could be seen as adhering to the primary precept of preserving innocent life, since it may naturally stop developing after a few days and so lack potential to become a human being. Therefore, there is no conflict with the argument for the sanctity of life.

TASK

Using the case of the mother with the cancerous uterus, apply the four rules of double effect (page 149) and explain why the death of the fetus is allowed in this instance.
Objective To develop the skill of applying an ethical theory to an issue, to 'demonstrate clearly relevant knowledge and understanding' (A01)

EXAM TIP

When answering a question about an application of an ethical theory, make sure that you highlight the key principles and explain how they are applied to the issue debated, drawing out the resulting action or view. This ensures focus is on the reasons that determine a decision rather than simply on the general topic.

However, such a view has been rejected by the Roman Catholic Church on the grounds that these live cells could still contain a soul. Therefore, the Roman Catholic Church has judged that the use of these inner cells is morally wrong.

The only gene therapy that the Roman Catholic Church permits is genetic enhancement to remove genetic disorders. This clearly refers to serious illnesses and diseases rather than any cosmetic enhancement. Germ-line therapy is rejected since it has the potential to change the whole of humanity and what it means to be human.

6 What natural law says about the issue of war and peace

a) Application of primary precepts

The tradition of the just war (see page 137) rests on the primary precept of protecting innocent life and preserving conditions necessary for decent human existence. All the criteria – just cause, right authority, right intention, proportionality, reasonable hope of success, and last resort – must be met in order for the use of force to be morally justified.

b) The doctrine of double effect

This may include such situations as the killing of innocent lives by bombing, often referred to as collateral damage. The intention is not to kill innocent people. However, the bombing could result in some innocent people being killed. It would not be morally acceptable to bomb some non-combatants to break down the enemy's morale so that they would sue for peace. This would be using a bad means to achieve a good end.

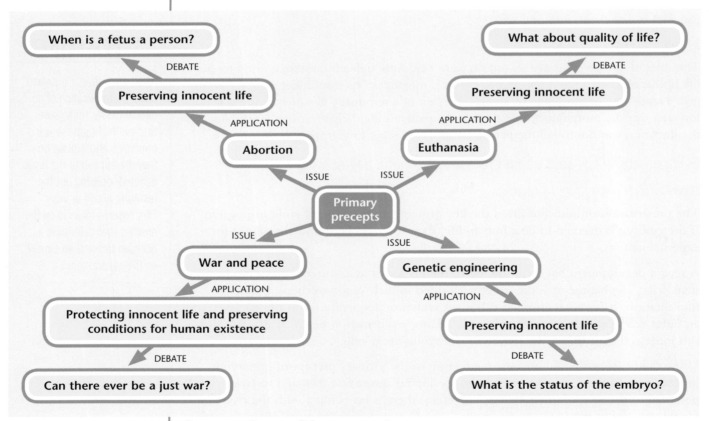

Summary diagram: Primary precepts

Reflection and assessment AO1

It is vital to bring together the information you have covered so far and recognise how it can be transformed into effective examination–style revision and answers. The best way to do this is to ask the question: 'How am I going to be assessed on my use of this information?'

The first way is through assessment objective 1 (AO1). For this objective you need to be able to 'select and clearly demonstrate the relevant knowledge and understanding through the use of evidence, examples and correct language and terminology'.

Look back to page 7 in the Introduction to review the level descriptors for AO1. There is a description of the character and features for each level. The exam is marked with reference to levels.

Look at the following sample level 2 answer, which is a response to the question:

What is the approach of natural law towards the issue of genetic engineering?

(25 marks)

> Genetic engineering involves our genes. It is about gene cloning, gene therapy and gene manipulation. Gene therapy can correct, alter or replace genes. The aim is to cure or prevent disease by changing the genes. Some gene engineering passes the changes to an offspring, while others only affect the one individual.
>
> Natural law is based on what it understands it means to be human. It has a number of primary precepts. The five principles are:
>
> preserve innocent life
>
> orderly living in society
>
> worship God
>
> educate children
>
> reproduce to continue the species.
>
> The precept of preserving innocent life means that gene therapy is allowed if it is used to remove genetic disorders rather than just cosmetic needs. However to change a future offspring is seen as changing what it is to be human and so would be disallowed and seen as immoral.

TASK

What makes this a level 2 answer?

Identify ways in which you could improve this answer.

Now write your own answer to the same question, aimed at level 4–5.

Objective To develop awareness of the characteristics of a good answer according to the level descriptors

Suggestion for further application of skills

Look again at the section on abortion, as viewed by natural law. As a class, read it through again. Then, without the support of the text or your notes, try answering this question, allowing yourself 15 minutes to do it.

What is the approach of natural law towards the issue of abortion?   (25 marks)

You should now have a basic answer, ready to develop. In pairs or groups, look at the answers and select one for development. Identify ways in which you could improve this answer. Complete your own comments analysis on this answer.

Finally, write your own answer to the same question, aiming at level 4–5.

Part 1B

A critical analysis of the issues

What are the issues that I am expected to consider and to analyse critically?

■ The strengths and weaknesses of natural law, both as an ethical system and in its application

1 Strengths of the natural law theory

a) Natural law is based on what it means to be human

Being human means acting in line with our true nature, when we follow our natural inclinations. When the theory is applied, it assumes the special status of human beings. For instance, when applying it to the issue of euthanasia, human life is always protected. It should be protected, because it is special.

b) It is a universal law, and not relative to culture or a religion

The primary precepts are common to all. Because it is about following natural inclinations, the application to a moral issue is always the same, wherever you are and whoever you are. For instance, germ-line therapy is seen as immoral, since it risks changing what is human. That view holds, no matter what your culture, as far as natural law theory is concerned.

c) It gives a clear basis for morality, with authority and justification

It is clear how natural law is applied. The primary precepts, for example, are precisely identified and justified. All can see why abortion is wrong.

d) Its application seems clear

Again, the application of the primary precepts is straightforward. It is clear how to apply them. For instance, euthanasia is seen as inherently evil because it involves the intentional and direct killing of an innocent human being.

e) It judges the intrinsic value of actions regardless of outcomes

It is the action itself, not the outcomes, that decides whether an act is moral. This avoids the problem of seemingly taking an action that appears good but has evil motives. In such cases the theory does not identify those acts as good. This seems a correct judgement.

f) The doctrine of double effect allows for possible conflicts of primary precepts

A possible problem is overcome by the doctrine of double effect. Return to the pregnant mother with a cancerous uterus. If nothing is done the mother will die, yet the fetus will not survive surgery. It seems that either action breaks the primary precept of preserving innocent life. However, the doctrine of double effect overcomes this by permitting the death of the fetus and saving the mother, as long as it was not the intention to harm the fetus.

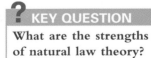

KEY QUESTION

What are the strengths of natural law theory?

2 Weaknesses of the natural law theory

a) Belief in God

It is unreasonable to expect someone who does not believe in the existence of a moral God to accept that what simply exists as human nature has moral authority. It is argued that describing the facts of any situation never leads to making a value judgement. What *is* (fact) does not imply what *ought to be* (value). Thus, there seems to be a fallacy or mistake in reasoning in identifying morality with another concept – nature. This is sometimes referred to as the **naturalistic fallacy**.

b) What does it mean to say an action is natural?

Does it just mean that it refers to the action that is common to a particular group? For instance, some people might argue that voluntary euthanasia is natural. Others do not.

c) Is there a common human nature?

Surely the fact that cultures have different values challenges the idea of a common nature? For instance, some people value love above everything else. However, that is not a focus within natural law theory.

d) Some would deny there was any such thing as a human nature

Darwinism sees natural selection as the source of human nature, rather than any divine or rational source and guidance. This damages the justification and authority of natural law theory.

e) Have we got it wrong?

If there is a constant unchanging human nature, and a natural law that stems from it, how is it that so many, through the centuries, have got human nature so wrong? How could slavery and apartheid be considered natural?

f) Changes in human nature

Human nature seems to change. For instance, the debate about homosexuality has raised questions about what is natural.

Natural law is a major component of Roman Catholic doctrine. However, its legalism might seem, to some, to be in conflict with a Christian stance. It is action-centred rather than people- and consequence-centred. This is particularly evident in natural law approaches to abortion and euthanasia.

g) Double effect

The doctrine of double effect assumes that a sharp distinction can be drawn between directly intending a result and merely foreseeing it. If a result can be foreseen then, in performing the action, the person must be intending the consequence, for instance, the acceptance of collateral damage from a bombing raid. If it is known that many innocent lives will be lost, then is the act moral?

It is difficult to see how those who accept the doctrine of fallen humanity, and therefore the moral imperfection of the human mind, can have such faith in human reasoning when applied to moral issues.

KEY WORD

Naturalistic fallacy when moral judgements are confused with factual judgements; it is an error in reasoning to conclude how the world ought to be from observing how the world actually is, goodness is not a property of nature

KEY QUESTIONS

- Is there a constant unchanging human nature?
- What is natural?
- Why should something that is natural be considered good?

3 Possible conclusions

When assessing the issues that arise from natural law, it is important to reflect upon the arguments previously discussed and arrive at some appropriate conclusion. It may be that you accept none of these listed here, or just one of them, or you may have a different conclusion that is not listed. However, what is important is the way that you have arrived at your conclusion – the reasoning process.

From the preceding discussions, here are some possible conclusions you could draw.

1   Natural law is the correct moral theory and so defines all moral action. Other ethical theories are therefore in error.

2   Natural law makes assumptions that may or may not be correct. Whether or not it is valid cannot be determined. However, its strengths outweigh its weaknesses.

3   Natural law makes assumptions that may or may not be correct. Whether or not it is valid cannot be determined. However, its weaknesses outweigh its strengths.

4   Natural law is one ethical system among others and has equal status with them.

5   Natural law is flawed and invalid.

> **EXAM TIP**
>
> Do not feel that you must reach a clear conclusion. Not being able to reach a clear conclusion is an acceptable answer. However, there has to be justification in your answer as to why no one particular conclusion could be fully supported. This demonstrates critical evaluation by reasoned argument. (AO2)

Reflection and assessment AO2

Earlier in this topic you considered the assessment objective AO1 focused on knowledge and understanding. The second way of being assessed is through assessment objective AO2. For this objective you need to be able to 'sustain a critical line of argument and justify a point of view'.

Look back to page 8 in the Introduction to review the level descriptors for AO2. There is a description of the character and features for each level. The exam is marked with reference to levels.

Look at the following sample answer, which is a response to the question:

To what extent is natural law theory a good approach to the issue of euthanasia?

(10 marks)

The remarks were made by an examiner.

The natural law theory is based on a view about nature. It is the view that nature works to an end. Human beings are part of the world so they too work towards a goal or purpose. This is what Aristotle called 'eudaimonia'. Aquinas gave the approach a more religious slant and saw the goal as being perfect in the image of God. Reason was also important for Aquinas. Aquinas was a medieval philosopher who applied Aristotelian philosophy to Christianity. His teaching has been influential in the Roman Catholic Church.

Material needs to help move the argument on. This is detail that is not relevant to the question.

You need to ask yourself what this adds to the argument. If the answer is 'nothing' then it is a clear signal that it should be omitted.

The focus of the question is on applying natural law theory to abortion. Therefore the answer should do the same. Here the theory is isolated from the issue of abortion.

The primary precepts underpin the fundamental principle 'act in such a way as to achieve good and avoid evil'.

Euthanasia means 'good death' and refers to the issues of quality of life and human dignity. It is argued by some that it is moral to uphold human dignity when the quality of life, through pain and illness, is so severe. The way that this is achieved is to bring an end to that life – euthanasia.

This is a very brief and poor exploration of natural law theory.

Essay starting to be on track.

Natural law rejects this view. It maintains that human dignity is not upheld by bringing an end to that life. The primary precept is to preserve innocent life. Therefore the life cannot be ended prematurely.

This needs explaining.

There is a case where euthanasia is acceptable unless it is the double effect example.

Is it a good approach to the issue? Well it does have some strengths. The law is clear. In addition, the fact that it is our natural inclination to obey this drive within us to do good and avoid evil, means we all agree that this is the moral action. However do we all agree? Some people don't accept we have this inbuilt nature. Hence, they argue that we should not preserve life at all costs. Indeed it is the consequence that matters not the action. Love should be the driving force.

The start of some evaluation but it is limited

A conclusion – but not consistent from what has been argued. Also a conclusion is more than just a statement of a position. It requires some justification.

An alternative view expressed. Promising but it is very brief.

Therefore I conclude it is the best approach.

So what does it score?

In the exam the answer will be marked according to levels (see page 8 in the Introduction). Certainly there is some basic reasoning. The candidate clearly has an understanding of the main debate and is aware that natural law does have some weaknesses as well as some strengths. However, the problem of applying the theory to euthanasia is not really developed. One alternative approach is mentioned, but there is no discussion about 'to what extent…'. There is a conclusion but it is not clear that it logically follows from what has been written. Also, it has not really explained why this is the case.

This would score a low 3 (some analysis which may be implicit).

TASK

Using this answer and the comments, write a level 4 answer.

Objective To transform unsuccessful analysis and identify asserted views that differentiate a level 2 response from higher levels

Suggestion for further application of skills

Consider the question:
To what extent is the natural law theory a good approach to the issue of genetic engineering? (10 marks)

Read pages 151–2 again.

Consider some key questions and the possible conclusions. As a group, building upon the experience of the earlier question above, see if you can directly attempt to create a plan for a higher level answer.

Write this up under timed conditions and then compare answers.

Finally, compare the standard with that of the previous question. Are there any ways in which you can learn from one to develop the other further. Ask yourselves which is the best answer and why.

Part 2A
Kantian ethics

What am I required to study?

- Kantian ethics

This means I am expected to know about:

- the difference between the categorical and the hypothetical imperatives
- the various formulations of the categorical imperative
- Kant's understanding of the universalisation of maxims
- Kant's theory of duty
- Kant's ideas of the moral law, good will and the *summum bonum*
- the application of Kantian ethics to abortion, euthanasia, genetic engineering, and war and peace.

This section explores the principles of Kantian ethics, then applies them to the issues of abortion, euthanasia, genetic engineering and war and peace. Refer back to Topic 2, page 121, for the background to the issues.

In Part 2B we shall assess the strengths and weaknesses of Kantian ethics, both as an ethical theory and in its approach to the above four issues. It would be helpful to write your notes using the headings listed under 'This means I am expected to know about', as it is from these areas that the exam questions will be derived.

In your studies, remember that have to bear in mind the *two* basic assessment objectives of:

- Knowledge and Understanding (AO1)
- Evaluation (AO2).

See pages 7–8 in the Introduction to remind yourself of these objectives.

The evaluation material is set out in Part 2B of this topic (page 166) and can be studied either alongside the AO1 material, as you work through this topic, or as a discrete topic.

1 Duty and good will

a) Kant's approach

Kant believed there was an objective moral law and that knowledge of this law could be gained through reason. He argued that human beings are rational and so are able to work out what is right and wrong. Acts are either morally right or wrong. According to Kant, moral value is not judged by the consequences of the act but by the actual act itself. Thus Kant has a deontological (see page 115) approach to ethics. If a certain act

KEY QUOTE

Two things fill the mind with ever new and increasing admiration and awe … the starry heavens above me and the moral law within me.

(Kant)

KEY WORD

Phenomenal composed of or relating to things that occupy space and can be perceived by the senses

was right, then it was right in all circumstances and in all conditions. Kant also believed that we were obligated to act morally and so obey the moral law.

 PROFILE: IMMANUEL KANT (1724–1804)

Kant is often regarded as one of the greatest philosophers of the Enlightenment. He argued that we are not entitled to make claims based on human reason about what is not **phenomenally** accessible, since they are unknowable to us. He therefore thought that the traditional attempts to prove God's existence failed. However, he saw that the idea of God was necessary if the moral world was to be intelligible.

In his essay, *Perpetual Peace: A Philosophical Sketch* (1795), Kant listed several conditions that he thought necessary for ending wars and creating lasting peace. They included a world of constitutional republics. He viewed the problem of war as one that only an international government could solve.

b) The moral law

Kant held that the categories by which we understand the world, such as space, time and causality, were *not* derived from experience. Rather, the mind imposes categories on all its experiences; for example, we cannot prove anything has a cause: we assume it and confirm by experience.

Thus, Kant argued that we cannot prove that we ought to do something by analysing it, since we shall never have enough evidence. For Kant, the idea of moral obligation comes from within ourselves and we experience it as the categorical imperative.

c) Kant's theory of duty

As seen above, Kant believed that moral laws were binding on human beings. This stemmed from his views about human beings as rational beings. He believed that there was an objective moral law that we can know by means of our reasoning. It is the consequences of our acts that confer moral value on them. Nevertheless, our duty is to act morally. When we act out of duty, we are acting out of a desire to be moral.

Kant also made clear that it is not our duty to do things that we are unable to do. The obligation (ought) of moral actions is only applicable when it implies they are possible (can be done). In summary, it is only meaningful to say I ought to do something if, in fact, I can do it.

d) Kant's theory of the good will

KEY WORD

Good will the highest form of good, not concerned with consequences or self-interest

When we are driven by a desire to act always to do right – to do our duty – then we are said to act with a **good will**. Good will is an innate human capacity and is the highest form of good. This is because it is not concerned about consequences or self-interest. When we act with a good will, we act with the intention of being moral. The key element is the intention behind the act.

Kant distinguished between behaviour and intention. It is the inner motive that is the vital element, since outward behaviour, however good it seems, does not necessarily reveal a good will. A good will is the one that does the right thing with the right intention.

e) The importance of freedom

Kant also argued that the will is free and independent. This is necessary for morality to be meaningful. To make rational choices we must be free; to do our duty we must be free. If our actions are not the result of free choices, then they cannot be regarded as the acts of a moral agent.

2 Imperative

a) Hypothetical imperative

An imperative is something that must be done. If you want to achieve a particular goal, then there is usually something you must do in order to achieve it. If your goal is to get fit, then you must exercise more and eat less. The **hypothetical imperative** informs us of a factual relation between a particular goal and how to achieve it. There is no concept of obligation attached to it. Kant did not see this type of imperative as referring to morality. For Kant, morality was not about achieving goals; morality was an end in itself.

b) Categorical imperative

In contrast to the hypothetical imperative, the categorical imperative has a binding force on people, irrespective of their interests. Kant saw moral principles as commands that have a truth value and are obligatory. Kant devised various formulations of the categorical imperative that act as general rules to gauge whether an act is moral. Morality was about categorical imperatives.

i) Universal law

- **Act only according to that maxim by which you can at the same time will that it should become a universal law.**

Kant argued that the only actions that are moral are those that can be universalised – applied in all situations and to all rational beings, without exception.

ii) Treat human beings as ends not as means to an end

- **So act that you treat humanity, both in your own person and in the person of every other human being, never merely as a means, but always at the same time as an end.**

Kant held human beings as the pinnacle of creation. Therefore, it can never be moral to exploit people, to use them as a means to an end. Each person is unique and of equal value so cannot be sacrificed, even if it would result in some overall greater good.

iii) Act on the assumption all will act in the same way

- **So act as if you were through your maxim a law-making member of a kingdom of ends.**

Kant argued that our actions had to based on the assumption that others would also act morally and treat everyone as ends, not means.

iv) Examples

An example of a moral rule, derived from the above principles of the categorical imperative, would be: 'Do not lie.' Kant argues that this rule applies universally. He applied the following reasoning. Is it moral to lie? He would apply the first law

KEY QUOTE

It is impossible to conceive of anything at all in the world, ... which can be taken as good without qualification, except a good will.

(Kant)

KEY WORDS

Hypothetical imperative a moral command that is conditional on personal motive or desire

Categorical imperative an unconditional moral law that applies to all rational beings and is independent of any personal motive or desire (For Kant, *the* categorical imperative was the principle that one should act on a maxim only if one can will that it becomes a universal law.)

KEY QUOTES

... if the action is represented as good in itself ... then the imperative is categorical.

(Kant)

There is ... only one categorical imperative. It is: Act only according to that maxim by which you can at the same time will that it should become a universal law.

(Kant)

and reason what would happen if it were universalised. Such action – lying – would clearly harm society. It would also involve treating people as means to an end rather than an end in themselves. The conclusion is that lying is immoral.

3 The *summum bonum*

Kant referred to the highest good as the *summum bonum*. This was the best possible good and he saw it as comprising virtue and happiness. His argument went like this.

- Our moral experience shows that we are under an obligation to achieve goodness or virtue, and not merely an average level of morality but the highest standard possible. We recognise an obligation to achieve what is best, which is real virtue.
- Beyond this, we recognise also that true virtue should be rewarded by happiness, for it would not be a rationally satisfying state of affairs if happiness came to the non-virtuous, or unhappiness to the virtuous. If people were virtuous but were also in pain and misery, their virtue would still be valuable but nevertheless, the total situation would not be the best possible.
- The desired state of affairs in which human beings are both virtuous and happy is called the *summum bonum* or highest good. This we recognise to be what ought to happen.
- Now, in Kant's famous argument, *ought* implies *can*: an obligation to achieve something implies the possibility that the goal can be achieved, otherwise there can be no obligation. It has to be possible, therefore, for the *summum bonum* to be achieved.
- However, while humans can achieve virtue, it is clearly outside their power to ensure that virtue is rewarded or coincides with happiness.
- Thus, there is a need to postulate the existence of God as the one who has the power to bring virtue and happiness into harmony. Such proportioning clearly does not take place before death, so Kant also argued that there must be survival after death.

Note that Kant was not arguing that morality is invalid if God's existence is denied. For Kant, the fact that it is a duty or obligation is sufficient reason to do it. However, he thought that the existence of God was demanded if the goal of morality was to be realised.

4 What Kantian ethics says about abortion

In general, Kantian ethics argues against abortion on the grounds that we have a duty to preserve life. It does raise questions about the status of the fetus and the timing of the abortion. It could be argued that, whatever its status, the fetus potentially develops into a rational free human being. It is unlikely that the developed human being would later support the view that they should have been aborted rather than allowed to develop.

a) Universal law

The universalisation of the rule that everyone should have an abortion is clearly unacceptable. One good reason is that the human race would become extinct! Again, it might be possible to reformulate by limiting it to when the woman's life is in danger.

Another reformulation might concern the future mental state of the developed fetus.

TASK

Draw a diagram to show the stages of the argument for *summum bonum*.

Objective To use a different learning style, to help understand the reasoning of the argument

---

Some Kantians might argue that, if the mental state was so limited that the person would be unable to reason or make choices, then abortion could be seen as permissible. This could be argued on the grounds that the fetus and the resulting human being had no intrinsic value.

b) Treat human beings as ends not as means to an end

If the fetus is regarded as a person, then an abortion would mean that the person was treated as a means rather than an end. This implies that the fetus, as a person, was exploited. It was used, by being destroyed, to get the mother something.

5 What Kantian ethics says about euthanasia

In general, Kantian ethics argues against euthanasia on the grounds that we have a duty to preserve life and not to murder.

a) Universal law

Often the justification for euthanasia focuses on issues such as the level of suffering being endured and the quality of life experienced. A universal law stating that 'everyone should help people die if they are suffering' is unacceptable. By universalising the rule, it would include those who did not choose to die. However, it might be possible to reformulate by limiting it to people who have freely chosen to die. Kant himself stated that he was against suicide and so would not have agreed with voluntary euthanasia.

b) Treat human beings as ends not as means to an end

Involving someone else in the act of ending a human life could be understood to deny the Kantian rule that human beings must be treated as ends, not as means.

6 What Kantian ethics says about genetic engineering

One of the difficulties in applying Kantian ethics to this issue is not knowing Kant's view of the status of embryos. However, it could be argued that, whatever its status, the embryo potentially develops into a rational free human being. It is unlikely that the developed human being would later support the view that they should have been used for genetic engineering rather than allowed to develop.

If animals rather than humans were the source, then there would be no problem since animals are not seen to have intrinsic value.

a) Universal law

It would seem contrary to Kantian ethics to have any universal law involving the creation of embryos that were later destroyed, for whatever reason. This is because all embryos would then have to be created for that purpose. As a result, no embryo would develop into a normal human being. This would mean that eventually the human race would cease to exist.

Perhaps a universal law is possible if it includes the clause that it applies only to embryos that are artificially produced for the specific purpose of genetic engineering or research.

KEY IDEA

The kingdom of ends Kant believed that all people have absolute value because they have the capacity to be autonomous and rational. Therefore, they should be treated in ways that acknowledge these capacities. Kant thought that the ideal moral community would be a community that held such views. It would be a community in which people are used as ends and never used by others as a means to an end. This ideal moral community is a kingdom of ends.

❝ KEY QUOTE ❞

… war is the source of the greatest evils which oppress civilised nations.

(Kant)

b) Treat human beings as ends, not as means to an end

The embryo is used as a means to an end and is clearly not able to make any choices itself. Therefore, using embryos in genetic engineering would not be a moral act. The weak must be protected and generally an embryo will develop into a normal human being. However, it could equally be argued that since it is unable to make choices it has no intrinsic value. This would imply that it is moral to use the embryo.

c) Act on the assumption all will act in the same way

This maxim is about the kingdom of ends. However, it could be argued that the embryo is not part of that kingdom because of its undeveloped state. Therefore, it is acceptable to use embryos for research and genetic engineering.

7 What Kantian ethics says about war and peace

At face value, Kantian ethics seems to rule out war as an acceptable moral action, since it involves the killing of human beings. However, Kant wrote a pamphlet in 1795 called *Perpetual Peace: A Philosophical Sketch*, in which he argued that war for self-defence was morally justified. However, he ruled out any support for a pre-emptive strike.

a) Universal law

Although the universalisation of killing is unacceptable, it might be possible to reformulate it to focus on self-defence and self-preservation. It is imaginable that this could involve some degree of violence, even including killing.

b) Treat human beings as ends, not as means to an end

Kantian ethics raises questions about the role of soldiers. Some might argue that they are a means to an end, and in that case are exploited. Such a view would mean that war was morally unacceptable. However, if the role of the soldier is seen in terms of fighting for self-preservation, then it might be argued that it is morally acceptable.

Reflection and assessment AO1

It is vital to bring together the information you have covered so far and recognise how it can be transformed into effective examination-style revision and answers. The best way to do this is to ask the question: 'How am I going to be assessed on my use of this information?'

Look back to page 7 in the Introduction to review the level descriptors for AO1. There is a description of the character and features for each level. The exam is marked with reference to levels.

Look at the key points, below, in answer to the question:

Explain the approach of Kantian ethics towards the issue of abortion? (25 marks)

You will need to refer to these points, which are not presented in any particular order, to complete the task.

- The universalisation of the rule that everyone should have an abortion shows that abortion is unacceptable and therefore immoral.
- The doctor is exploited since he is involved in the abortion.
- Whatever the status of the fetus, it still develops into a rational free human being.
- Kantian ethics argues that preserving life is a duty.
- Kantian ethics teaches that we should treat human beings as ends, not as means to an end.
- Kant believed that the idea of moral obligation comes from within ourselves.
- Kant's categorical imperative of a universal law can be applied to the issue of abortion.
- The status of the fetus is an issue.

Suggestion for further application of skills

Look again at the section on genetic engineering. Make a list of five key points to explain it in the light of Kantian ethics. With a partner, add further points to make it more comprehensive. Try, as well, to find relevant quotes from scholars or text or further sources of information, to add at suitable places to use as examples or illustrations or to support for a point.

Now use your lists to develop an answer to this question.

Explain the approach of Kantian ethics towards the issue of genetic engineering.

(25 marks)

TASK

Use the key points as a basis for a writing frame to answer the question:

What is the approach of Kantian ethics towards the issue of abortion?

(25 marks)

Put the points in order and add three more relevant points at suitable places.

Objective To practise good 'selection and demonstration of clearly relevant knowledge' (AO1) and aiming at an answer that is demonstrating 'understanding and engagement with the material' (level 5) through use of quotes or examples as evidence (AO1)

Part 2B

A critical analysis of the issues

What are the issues that I am expected to consider and to analyse critically?

■ The strengths and weaknesses of Kantian ethics as an ethical system and when applied to the issues

1 Strengths of Kantian ethics

■ The system states clear rules. For instance, it is generally against abortion on the grounds that we have a duty to preserve life and, whatever the status of the fetus, it will develop into a rational human being.

■ It emphasises the importance of each person. Everyone is equally valued in their own right. Therefore, euthanasia and suicide are not morally defensible according to Kantian ethics.

■ It is applied universally and therefore impartial. If a certain act is right, then it is right in all circumstances.

■ It treats people as ends rather than means to an end. Therefore it is against exploitation of people. For example, using embryos for genetic engineering is morally unacceptable, on the grounds that the embryo is a means to an end. This approach gives high value to human beings.

■ It emphasises motive and intention rather than just the outward behaviour. This avoids the problem of doing an act that appears outwardly good, but was, in fact, carried out for immoral reasons. In such a case, Kantian ethics would deem such an act as immoral.

2 Weaknesses of Kantian ethics

■ Kant put obligation as the reason for acting morally. However, it is not clear why that motive is superior to motives such as love and compassion. Many may feel that it is difficult to defend keeping someone alive on the grounds of obligation, when that person is suffering acutely with terminal illness. The appeal to love and compassion, which sound like higher motives, seems to be ignored.

■ Kant claimed that there was only one categorical imperative and the other maxims were just stating the same in different ways. However, it is disputed whether the three forms of the categorical imperative are equivalent. For instance, the universalisation of the rule that everyone should have an abortion is clearly unacceptable, since the human race would become extinct. However, the imperative about the kingdom of ends seems to allow for abortion, since it could be argued that the embryo is not part of that kingdom because of its undeveloped state. Equally, the universal law can be expressed in different ways so that contradictory actions are both seen as moral. For instance, war is unacceptable since it involves the killing of human life, which cannot be in accordance with a universal law. However, the universal law could be written as: 'Self-defence is right.' This might then include killing.

■ Fundamental to Kant's theory are freewill and rationality. However, both of these have been challenged. Modern science looks to nurture and nature to explain the cause of our actions, while experience of life seems to suggest that people do not always act rationally.

■ Applying reason to actions has led many to argue for self-interest as a motive.

■ It does not accept exceptions. What happens if two duties conflict? For instance, the duty to preserve life can conflict with the duty to protect life, as in the case of war. Surely the rephrasing of the universal law, to include self-defence, is really an example of an exception to killing if it is allowed in the case of self-defence?

■ Is universalisability feasible? Many would claim that no two moral dilemmas are the same and the strict, no exception approach does not allow for the variety of situations that arise. It seems to count as nothing the acute suffering of someone who has a terminal illness.

■ Kant argued that ought implies can. If he meant that it is logically possible to bring about the *summum bonum*, then he is merely saying it is not a logical contradiction. But just because it is not a logical contradiction does not therefore mean that it factually happens. If he means that it factually happens, we can ask the questions: 'Why must it? How can anyone know?' In other words, we can question his assumption.

■ Why make the assumption that only God can bring about the highest good?

■ Why make the assumption that virtue must be rewarded with happiness?

■ Sense of duty can be explained by other means, such as socialisation.

3 Possible conclusions

When assessing the issues that arise from Kantian ethics, it is important to reflect upon the arguments previously discussed and arrive at some appropriate conclusion. It may be that you accept none of these listed here, or just one of them, or you may have a different conclusion that is not listed. However, what is important is the way that you have arrived at your conclusion – the reasoning process.

From the preceding discussions, here are some possible conclusions you could draw.

1 Kantian ethics is the correct moral theory and so defines all moral action. Other ethical theories are therefore in error.

2 Kantian ethics makes assumptions that may or may not be correct. Whether it is valid or not cannot be determined. However, its strengths outweigh its weaknesses.

3 Kantian ethics makes assumptions that may or may not be correct. Whether it is valid or not cannot be determined. However, its weaknesses outweigh its strengths.

4 Kantian ethics is one ethical system among others and has equal status with them.

5 Kantian ethics is flawed and invalid.

> ### EXAM TIP
>
> If you are asked to assess a view, do not merely give your opinion. Opinions that lack any justification or reasoning do not qualify as evaluation, they are merely an expression of a personal view. Evaluation must give evidence of a reasoning process. Avoiding mere statements of opinion demonstrates justifying a point of view by means of a reasoned argument. (AO2)

TASK

Look at the basic answer opposite. Try to work out how a developed answer would deal with the question, by adding two or three more bullet points.

Now develop this answer to indicate how a higher-level answer would deal with the question, by adding further bullet points. Remember to keep the bullet points focused on the question. For higher-level answers the evaluation should show reasoning, with a range of evidence to sustain an argument and show understanding of critical analysis of different viewpoints, for a well-constructed and organised answer.

Objective To develop awareness of what will constitute a very good answer by gradually building up a response that is 'an excellent attempt to address the question, showing understanding and engagement with the material' (level 5 descriptor)

Reflection and assessment AO2

Look back to page 8 in the Introduction to review the level descriptors for AO2. There is a description of the character and features for each level. The exam is marked with reference to levels.

Look at the following notes for a sample basic level 1–2 answer, which is a response to the question:

To what extent is Kant's ethical theory a useful method of making decisions about issues of war and peace? (10 marks)

A basic answer might deal with the question by:

■ stating Kant's categorical imperative
■ applying the categorical imperative to the issue of war and peace by stating the universal law that killing is unacceptable
■ drawing a simple conclusion that Kantian ethics is not a useful method of making decisions since it ignores the importance of self-defence.

Suggestion for further application of skills

Using a flow chart or some other diagrammatical form, list:

■ some key weaknesses of Kantian ethical theory
■ some possible responses
■ any possible counters to those responses.

Part 3A

Utilitarianism

What am I required to study?

■ The classical forms of utilitarianism from Bentham and Mill

This means I am expected to know about:

■ the classical forms of utilitarianism from Bentham and Mill

■ the principle of utility

■ the difference between the utilitarianism of Bentham and of Mill

■ the hedonic calculus, higher and lower pleasures, quantity versus quality, and act and rule utilitarianism

■ the preference utilitarianism of Peter Singer

■ application of utilitarianism to abortion, euthanasia, genetic engineering, and war and peace.

This part of the ethics unit explores **utilitarianism**. This ethical theory will then be applied to the issues of abortion, euthanasia, genetic engineering, and war and peace. Refer back to Topic 2, page 121, for the background to the issues.

In Part 3B we shall assess the strengths and weaknesses of utilitarianism, both as an ethical theory and in its approach to the above four issues. It would be helpful to write your notes using the headings listed under 'This means I am expected to know about', as it is from these areas that the exam questions will be derived.

In your studies, remember to bear in mind the *two* basic assessment objectives of:

■ Knowledge and Understanding (AO1)
■ Evaluation (AO2).

See pages 7–8 in the Introduction to remind yourself of these objectives.

The evaluation material is set out in Part 3B of this topic (page 176) and can be studied either alongside the AO1 material, as you work through this topic, or as a discrete topic.

1 Bentham's utilitarianism

a) Why is it called utilitarianism?

Utilitarianism derives its name from utility, which means usefulness. In particular it concerns the usefulness of the results of actions. Utilitarians argue that everyone should do the most useful thing. The most useful thing is seen as action or actions that result in maximum levels of happiness or pleasure. Therefore, actions that produce the most happiness are seen as good and right actions or moral actions.

KEY WORD

Utilitarianism an ethical theory that maintains that an action is right if it produces the greatest balance of good over evil; morality of actions is therefore based on consequences for human happiness

KEY QUESTION

What is the most useful act?

Because utilitarianism is concerned about the outcome of an action, it is a consequential and teleological ethical theory (see page 115).

b) Bentham's principle of utility

Jeremy Bentham (1748–1832) is usually accepted as the originator of utilitarianism. He was a social reformer and sought to develop an ethical theory that promoted actions that would benefit the majority of people. For him, happiness was the only ethical value. Actions are good or useful if they produce happiness. Bentham argued that we are motivated by pleasure and pain so that we pursue pleasure and avoid pain. This view of happiness being linked to pleasure owes something to an earlier ethical theory called **hedonism**, in which the only thing that is right is pleasure.

Although utilitarianism is a teleological ethical theory, there is a rule or guiding principle underpinning this approach. This guiding principle, known as the **principle of utility**, states that people should act to bring about the greatest balance of good over evil. Bentham expressed this as the greatest happiness for the greatest number. This is a slightly misleading summary of the principle, since the greatest happiness did not necessarily involve the greatest number of people. The emphasis is more on the action that produces the greatest amount of happiness overall. In other words, what is right is what maximises happiness.

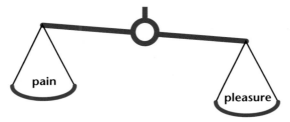

c) The hedonic calculus

Having established that the measure of happiness is the criterion for a right act, there arises the problem of how to calculate that measurement. For Bentham, happiness consisted of pleasure minus pain. The principle of utility centred on the act delivering the greatest amount of pleasure and the least amount of pain. Bentham's solution to measuring this balance was his **hedonic calculus**, also called the pleasure calculus.

He thought there were seven different elements that should be taken into account when calculating the amount of happiness. They are:

- the intensity of the pleasure – the more intense, the better
- the duration of the pleasure – the longer-lasting, the better
- the certainty of the pleasure – the more certain that pleasure will result, the better
- the fecundity, fertility or fruitfulness of the pleasure – the more chance the pleasure will be repeated or will result in other pleasures, the better
- the propinquity or nearness of the pleasure – the nearer the pleasure is to you, the better
- the purity of the pleasure – the least amount of pain it involves, the better
- the extent of the pleasure – the more people who experience it, the better.

Using these criteria, Bentham argued that it was possible to work out the right course of action in any situation. The balance of pain and pleasure created by one choice of action could be compared with those created by other available choices.

KEY WORDS

Hedonism an ethical theory that defines what is right in terms of pleasure

Principle of utility an action is right if it maximises happiness

Hedonic calculus a method of calculating the degree or amount of pleasure that a specific action is likely to cause

? KEY QUESTION

What is happiness?

❝ KEY QUOTES ❞

Nature has placed mankind under the governance of two sovereign masters, pain and pleasure. It is for them alone to point out what we ought to do, as well as to determine what we shall do.

(Jeremy Bentham)

By the principle of utility is meant that principle which approves of every action whatsoever, according to the tendency which it appears to have to augment or diminish the happiness of the party whose interest is in question.

(Jeremy Bentham)

KEY PROFILE: JEREMY BENTHAM (1748–1832)

As a barrister, Bentham became aware of widespread social injustice. This prompted him to become concerned with issues of public morality. He was instrumental in reforming prisons and advocated that the penalties imposed for crimes should be sufficient to deter but not cause unnecessary suffering. He also advocated such things as censorship and laws governing sexual activity, in an attempt to improve public morality. His guiding principle for public policy was 'the greatest happiness for the greatest number'. He then developed this into a moral philosophy.

In 1826, Bentham founded University College. Rather strangely, his embalmed body, wearing his usual clothes, sits in the entrance hall in a glass case! Only his head was replaced by a wax model.

2 Mill's utilitarianism

a) Bentham's approach revisited

The ethical theory of utilitarianism proposed by Bentham soon started to raise some strong criticisms. Not least amongst the critics was his former pupil, **John Stuart Mill**. The main criticism against Bentham was that he tried to measure pleasure in quantitative terms. It appeared to allow for some actions to be called right and good when they seemed, to others, to be wrong. For instance, Bentham's approach appeared to conclude that a gang rape would be a right action if the pleasure gained by the group of rapists exceeded that of the pain experienced by the person raped. This also raised questions about the exact nature of pleasure.

As a result, Mill revised Bentham's form of utilitarianism.

b) Mill's alterations to Bentham's utilitarianism

i) The definition of happiness (pleasure)
This equating of happiness with good is a view that can be found in the writings of Aristotle. He referred to it as eudaimonia (see page 146). Aristotle argued that pleasure was not mere gratification but rather includes the idea of well-being, living well, being fulfilled. This is much closer to the view that Mill took.

 KEY PROFILE: JOHN STUART MILL (1806–73)

John Stuart Mill went to neither school nor university. He was educated by his father, assisted by Jeremy Bentham. He followed in his father's footsteps and worked at the East India Company, where his father held a high position. However, during the period 1865–68 Mill was elected as a member of Parliament and became famous for being the first MP to propose votes for women. Another claim to fame is the writing of his book, *On Liberty*, in which he argued that a person should be free to do whatever they want as long as it does not bring any significant harm to anyone else.

The theory of utilitarianism affected all of Mill's thinking, possibly because of his home education in his early years. Both his father, James Mill, and Bentham were adherents to the theory. However, John Mill deepened the understanding of happiness and advocated a weak rule utilitarianism.

> **❝ KEY QUOTES ❞**
>
> **It is better to be a human being dissatisfied than a pig satisfied; better to be Socrates dissatisfied than a fool satisfied.**
> (John Stuart Mill)
>
> **Over himself, over his own body and mind, the individual is sovereign.**
> (John Stuart Mill)

EXAM TIP

Be careful when using quotations. Always make sure that they relate to the focus that is being examined. To make sure of this, always explain the relevance of the quotation in your answer. This makes the difference between 'not successful' (level 1–2) and 'successful' (level 3–5) analysis.

KEY WORDS

Rule utilitarianism a form of utilitarianism in which general rules rather than acts are assessed for utility
Act utilitarianism a form of utilitarianism in people are to act in the way that will produce the best actual overall consequences

ii) Higher and lower pleasures

Mill distinguished between pleasure that stimulated the mind, which he called higher pleasure, and pleasure that was merely physical or lower pleasure. He claimed that human beings alone could achieve the higher pleasure and it was the higher pleasure that was more satisfying. However, Mill was aware that often people did not choose the higher pleasure in preference to the lower pleasure. He felt that this was because they had not experienced both. Had they done so, they would have known that higher pleasure was more satisfying than the lower pleasures.

iii) Quantity versus quality

By making a distinction between higher and lower pleasures, Mill moved the calculation of pleasure away from quantity towards quality. No longer was it simply how much pleasure an action caused. Now it was also a matter of the quality of the pleasure.

iv) Universalisability

This is a form of Bentham's principle of utility. Mill wanted to show that what is right and wrong for one person in a situation is right or wrong for all. He argued that:

■ happiness is desirable, since we all desire it
■ happiness is the only thing desirable as an end, since things are only desirable because they bring about happiness.

Therefore, everyone ought to aim at the happiness of everyone, as increasing the general happiness will increase my happiness.

This argument supports the idea that people should put the interests of the group before their own interests. Bentham's principle of utility had focused much more on the individual and had no concept of protecting the common good.

v) Act versus rule

There are two different forms of utilitarianism – **rule utilitarianism** and **act utilitarianism**. In its strong form, rule utilitarianism claims that an action is right if, and only if, it follows the rules: the rules should never be disobeyed. These rules are universal in nature and, if applied in any situation, would lead to the greatest happiness for the greatest number. They would maximise happiness.

In contrast, act utilitarianism treats each new situation as different from all the others, thus requiring a fresh calculation. The rule utilitarian would notice the similarities between the present case and the previous ones and draw on those previous calculations.

Many would argue that the two types of utilitarianism are not mutually exclusive. For instance, Bentham is said to be an act utilitarian; however, he did not claim that it was necessary to calculate the rightness and wrongness of every act from first principles. Likewise, Mill is said to be a rule utilitarian; however, it is doubtful whether he advocated the strong form. He viewed the rules more as helpful guidance than obligatory. They were necessary as a means of saving time and addressing the distribution problem. This view, known as weak rule utilitarianism, states that, on certain occasions, the rules can be disobeyed if a greater amount of happiness will result.

3 Singer's utilitarianism

a) Preference utilitarianism

As for the utilitarianism theories discussed above, **preference utilitarians** claim that the right thing to do is that which produces the best consequences. However, instead of specifying the end to be pursued in terms of pleasure, they define the best consequences in terms of preference. This is based on the questions: 'What outcome do I prefer? What is in the best interests of those concerned?' The principle of utility is still followed, so preference utilitarianism considers the preferences of all sentient beings. The more preferences satisfied in the world, the better. **Peter Singer** argues that it is preferences, rather than human life, that we ought to value, and this means that animals fall within our sphere of moral obligations since certain animals show preferences, such as to be with others of the same species and to avoid pain. It also means that killing a person who wanted to be killed could be seen as a morally right action.

 KEY PROFILE: PETER SINGER (1946–)

Peter Singer is an Australian philosopher who continues to be an influential figure in the area of ethics. He specialises in practical ethics, approaching ethical issues from a preference utilitarian and atheistic perspective. His views, such as those on the welfare of animals, are often regarded as controversial. In his book, *Animal Liberation*, he questioned the idea of discrimination based on species, arguing that it should be on grounds of ability to experience suffering. This would mean that some animals should be accorded equal considerations to human beings, in certain circumstances. His views about abortion are coloured by his view that a fetus is not a person. He defines personhood as 'a self-conscious being that sees itself over time'. He is also outspoken on the issue of poverty, supporting the ethical view that the rich should help the poor.

4 What utilitarianism says about the issue of abortion

In one sense, utilitarianism is always difficult to apply to any moral issue, because there are never any absolutes. It is the situation that will affect the decision, and no two situations are identical. However, the key principle in utilitarianism is 'the greatest happiness of the greatest number'. When applied to abortion, it seems that there is a strong case to allow abortion, if the mother requests it. It is assumed that the mother would be happier, given she requested the abortion. Any number of reasons could apply, such as work or other family members' needs. Balanced against this would be considerations such as possible guilt and regret at the loss of the child.

However, the mother is not the only one involved and utilitarianism demands that we measure the extent of the happiness. What about the father? What about the fetus itself (if it is regarded as a sentient being)? Not only may the future happiness of the fetus be lost, but there may also be pain and suffering felt in the actual process of the abortion. What about relatives? All these consequences could outweigh the happiness of the mother. In such cases it seems that utilitarianism would deny a woman the right to choose to have an abortion.

 KEY WORD

Preference utilitarianism an ethical theory that sees actions as right when they allow the greatest number to live according to their own preferences, even if those preferences are not those that will make them experience the most pleasure

❝ KEY QUOTES ❞

… an action contrary to the preference of any being is, unless this preference is outweighed by contrary preferences, wrong.

(Peter Singer)

The life of a fetus is of no greater value than the life of a non-human animal at a similar level of rationality, self-consciousness, awareness, capacity to feel, …

(Peter Singer)

KEY QUOTE

... killing a disabled infant is not morally equivalent to killing a person. Very often it is not wrong at all.

(Peter Singer)

Preference utilitarianism takes into account the preferences of people affected. This would include not just the mother, but also the fetus. On grounds of quality of life, Singer questions bringing unwanted children into the world. He also questions the value of life of a severely disabled fetus. Hence, preference utilitarianism sees abortion, in certain circumstances, as a possibly right action.

5 What utilitarianism says about the issue of euthanasia

Whereas many ethical theories focus on the sanctity of life, utilitarianism focuses on the quality of life. This is because Bentham's principle of utility involved calculating the happiness by means of the hedonic calculus. The important measure was happiness or quality of life. Mill made a distinction between higher and lower pleasures, so his understanding of happiness might focus more on the person's dignity and their right to make decisions about their own life. Therefore, those who have some kind of brain damage or disease would not be able to experience higher-level pleasures and thus quality of life would be less.

The measurement of happiness extends to the relatives and to the greater community. In terms of the community, issues such as the effect on the value of human life would need to be taken into account, as might also the consideration of better use of resources. For instance, could the money that would be used on keeping the individual alive not be used to create more happiness, if it were spent in a different way?

Preference utilitarianism would see both suicide and voluntary euthanasia as morally acceptable actions, since the person is enacting their preference and not harming anyone else.

6 What utilitarianism says about the issue of genetic engineering

The consequential approach to ethics that utilitarianism uses is always problematic when the possible outcomes are unknown. This is especially true when considering the issue of genetic engineering. The use of embryos raises issues about applying the hedonic calculus. The debate relates to the status of the embryo and the extent to which this should feature in the calculations about happiness. Weighed against this are the possible breakthroughs in curing certain common but crippling illnesses. The unknown element here is the success rate.

A different unknown is involved in genetically modified crops. Concern has been raised about the long-term effects.

Utilitarianism generally supports embryo research on the grounds that the good that results outweighs the loss of the embryo.

Because of its views that embryos, and especially pre-embryos, have limited value, preference utilitarianism sees embryo research and genetic engineering as morally acceptable.

7 What utilitarianism says about the issue of war and peace

As with most moral issues, the outcomes are difficult to predict with any certainty. This is certainly true of war. The criterion used by utilitarians is 'the greatest happiness for the greatest number'. However, the calculation of happiness seems impossible where a war is involved. One of the key considerations would be the peace that is gained as a result of

EXAM TIP

Remember that there are different forms of utilitarianism. What utilitarianism says about the different issues might vary depending on the form of utilitarianism to which you are referring. Make clear which form it is and explain why it responds to that issue in that particular way. This demonstrates clear relevant knowledge and understanding. (AO1)

the war. Put simply: 'Does the end justify the means?' The idea of a just war (see pages 136–9) may be applicable as it is concerned with just causes and the likelihood of success.

Preference utilitarianism focuses on the preferences of those involved. This is very difficult to assess, given the complexities of war and the numbers that could be involved.

Reflection and assessment AO1

It is vital to bring together the information you have covered so far and recognise how it can be transformed into effective examination-style revision and answers. The best way to do this is to ask the question: 'How am I going to be assessed on my use of this information?'

Look at the following sample answer, which is a response to the question:

Explain Bentham's hedonic calculus. (25 marks)

1 Spelling errors

2 Irrelevant material

3 Inaccurate material

4 Needs an example to illustrate.

5 Illustration needs to be explained, as it is not clear why it demonstrates the point

6 Not enough to demonstrate the point

7 No religious references

8 Repetition of same point

9 Not answering the question

Bentham believes in utilitarianism. This is to act in a good way to bring happiness to a great number of people. He takes his view from the Principle of Utility which is about the consequences of the situation or action creating more good than pain. To do this he calculates the good (happiness) through his hedonic calculus. Hedonic means pleasure. The calculation has 7 stages. Three of them are intensity, duration and proximity. These measure happiness and if the happiness is greatest for the greatest number of people then the action is seen as morally right. If a different action would cause more happiness to more people then this action rather then the previous one would be the one considered morally right. The first would be morally wrong.

Suggestion for further application of skills

Look at an essay that you have recently completed.

1 Underline in green what could have been omitted or is repeated.
2 Underline in blue any evaluation words.
3 Underline in red key phrases.
4 Identify strengths and weaknesses.
5 Identify how the essay could be improved.

TASK

Connect the comments with the appropriate parts of the essay. Start by drawing a chart with two columns. Write the word or phrase from the essay in one column and the number of the appropriate comment alongside it, in the other column. Note that not all the comments are appropriate for this essay answer.

What do you think about this style of writing? How would you improve it? Do you think it explains the hedonic calculus? If not, how would you improve the answer? Why would this answer not score a level 4?

Using this structure, write a level 4–5 answer.

Objective To develop an awareness of what will constitute a very good answer (levels 4–5) by gradually building up a response

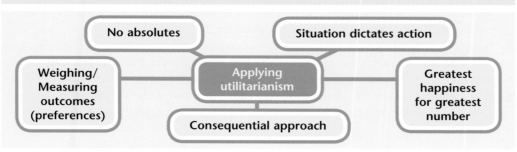

Summary diagram: Applying utilitarianism

Part 3B
A critical analysis of the issues

What are the issues that I am expected to consider and to analyse critically?

- The strengths and weaknesses of utilitarianism as an ethical system and its application to the issues of abortion, euthanasia, genetic engineering and war and peace

1 Strengths of utilitarianism

- It has aims that are attractive – happiness and avoidance of pain. It does seem that we are motivated by pleasure and motivated to avoid pain.
- It seems straightforward to apply to most situations and concurs with common sense.
- It takes into account consequences of our actions. Looking just at intentions, with no regard to their consequence, seems impersonal. For instance, keeping alive someone who is terminally ill and suffering great pain ignores the consequences for that person.
- It considers others and not just the individual. It is concerned with the common good. It takes into account all who are affected by the action. It even goes wider in that it can consider society as a whole. For instance, does allowing abortion have a detrimental effect on society as a whole, in terms of devaluing human life?

2 Weaknesses of utilitarianism

- It seems to ignore intentions and an individual's motive. The means by which the greatest good is achieved seems incidental and of no moral relevance. Indeed, it could allow an innocent person to be punished if the consequences resulted in an overall greater happiness – greater than if the person was justly found innocent. In other words, injustice could be seen as the right action, which seems contrary to common sense.
- It rejects any theory of moral rights. Rights get in the way of utility.
- Because it is concerned with the happiness of the greater number, the happiness of minorities may not be protected.
- It is not clear how the hedonic calculus resolves the problem of assessing the quantity of pleasure. For instance, how is it possible to quantify and compare intensity of pleasure with duration of pleasure? Listing elements of pleasure does not resolve the problem of quantifying the pleasure.
- Is happiness or pleasure a valid aim? Does it seem rather self-indulgent? Is Mill right when he argued that higher pleasures are better than lower pleasures?
- Are there not instances where pain is a good thing?
- In deciding whether an action is morally right, it requires the outcomes of the action to be known. However, outcomes may not be accurately predictable.

? KEY QUESTIONS

- Is it possible to quantify pleasure?
- Is discussing philosophy (higher pleasure) more desirable than having sex (lower pleasure)?
- What about the rights of individuals?
- What about the happiness of the minorities?
- Are pleasure and happiness valid aims? Are they not rather self-indulgent?
- Is pain always a bad thing?

Indeed, the consequences of our actions persist for an almost indefinite time, and may well affect a large number of people. This is certainly true in the case of a war. It is also true with some forms of genetic engineering.

■ To decide what action will produce the greatest good, the alternative actions also have to be considered and their possible outcomes predicted. This seems an impossible task.

■ Utilitarianism seems too demanding since we ought always to do that which gives greatest good for the greatest number. However, there may always be an act, other than what we choose, that would give greater good.

3 Possible conclusions

When assessing the issues that arise from utilitarianism, it is important to reflect upon the arguments previously discussed and arrive at some appropriate conclusion. It may be that you accept none of these listed here, or just one of them, or you may have a different conclusion that is not listed. However, what is important is the way that you have arrived at your conclusion – the reasoning process.

From the preceding discussions, here are some possible conclusions you could draw.

1 Utilitarianism is the correct moral theory and so defines all moral action. Other ethical theories are therefore in error.

2 Utilitarianism makes assumptions that may or may not be correct. Whether it is valid or not cannot be determined. However, its strengths outweigh its weaknesses.

3 Utilitarianism makes assumptions that may or may not be correct. Whether it is valid or not cannot be determined. However, its weaknesses outweigh its strengths.

4 Utilitarianism is one ethical system among others and has equal status with them.

5 Utilitarianism is flawed and invalid.

Reflection and assessment AO2

Earlier in this topic you considered the assessment objective AO1 focused on knowledge and understanding. The second way of being assessed is through assessment objective AO2. For this objective you need to be able to 'sustain a critical line of argument and justify a point of view'.

Look back to page 8 in the Introduction to review the level descriptors for AO2. There is a description of the character and features for each level. The exam is marked with reference to levels.

Read the following question and the sample answer below it. Read the examiner's comments.

'A utilitarian could never agree that abortion is morally acceptable.' Discuss.

(10 marks)

TASK

Study the answer on page 178, given to the question about utilitarianism and abortion. Although it is a very good answer, it could be improved. In groups, mark this answer by adding your comments on sticky notes around it. Use one colour to indicate the strong points. Use a different colour to suggest ways in which this answer could be made perfect! You have been given one or two boxes already to start you off. As a group, rewrite the answer so that it can score maximum marks according to the levels of response.

Objective To apply critical analysis and application of the mark scheme to create a top level answer

Development: Need only to include information that is relevant.

Bentham devised his teleological ethical theory from a phrase he came across whilst reading Priestly's essay on Government. This essay contained the phrase 'greatest good of the greatest number'. From this he devised his principle of utility which in summary is 'what is right is what maximises good.' To help decide whether an action produces the greatest good for the greatest number, he devised the Hedonic Calculus. This weighed up a number of factors and could be applied to all moral issues.

Development: Need to indicate some aspects of the hedonic calculus and then relate them specifically to the issue of abortion.

When abortion is examined by these criteria, they suggest that abortion could be judged 'right', that is, morally acceptable and so implies that the claim in the question is not true. For instance, if the woman already has a large family and the pregnancy was unplanned, utilitarians might argue that an additional family member would cause unhappiness to the whole family and if the child was unwanted, may also result in unhappiness for the child. In such a case the principle of utility points to abortion as being the morally right action.

However, if all the consequences have to be considered, then it involves more people than just the mother. What about the wishes of the father? What if it would cause him pain if the fetus was aborted? What of relatives? Might they not feel unhappiness about the loss of the child? There is also the mother herself – it is possible that she may feel grief and remorse at the action she took which is irreversible. The weighing up of consequences is so wide ranging that it is difficult to come to any clear conclusion. For instance, would it cause society in general to be saddened that potential life is so easily killed off? Indeed Mill spoke about higher and lower levels of pleasure. Would not the effect of cheapness of life be detrimental to the dignity of human life and society as a whole?

Strength: Good to pick up the focus of the essay. Keeps material relevant.

So is it morally acceptable to utilitarians? Well certainly a case can be made out for it and in that sense it is acceptable. However, it also raises questions whether the issue is that clear cut and some utilitarians may feel the greatest happiness for the greatest number is not actually served by carrying out an abortion. In such instances, using the principle of Utility, the utilitarian would have to conclude it was not morally acceptable. As with all ethical theories that deny absolutes and appeal to consequences instead, the conclusion remains in dispute.

Strength: A good conclusion that is supported by the rest of the essay.

Suggestion for further application of skills

Using some of the strengths and weaknesses of utilitarianism listed on pages 176–7, write a counter argument to each. Then write a reply to that counter. This will develop your evaluative skills as it will help move you away from just listing points. Instead, you will start to show a process of reasoning by responding to arguments.

Part 4A

Buddhist ethics

What am I required to study?

- A religious ethical system: Buddhism

This means I am expected to know about:

- the main ethical principles of Buddhism and how the followers of Buddhism make ethical decisions

- the ways in which religion and morality may seem to be linked or be seen as separate from each other

- how far religious ethics may be seen as absolutist or relativist

- Buddhist responses to the ethical issues of abortion, euthanasia, genetic engineering, war and peace.

The Specification content relating to theoretical approaches to ethics tends naturally towards Christianity, for example, natural moral law, absolute morality and Kantian ethics. Thus, as most schools will illustrate these theories in terms of Christianity, to include a Christian approach here will not present anything new in terms of content or approach. It is useful, therefore, to present a different system as a contrasting or independent approach. Buddhism, with its practical approach centred on the individual, is an ideal alternative.

Refer back to Topic 2, page 121, for the background to the issues.

It would be helpful to write your notes under the headings listed in 'This means I am expected to know about', as it is from these areas that the exam questions will be derived.

Remember that your studies will include elements of the *two* basic assessment objectives of:

- Knowledge and Understanding (AO1)
- Evaluation (AO2).

See pages 7–8 in the Introduction to remind yourself of these objectives.

The evaluation material is set out in Part 4B of this topic (page 190) and can be studied either alongside the AO1 material, as you work through this topic, or as a discrete topic.

1 Introduction to Buddhist ethics

Buddhism is often described as a philosophy or way of life rather than a religion. The emphasis in Buddhism is on practice. Questions about belief are relatively unimportant in the sense that the way of life is driven by the goal of diminishing suffering, both mental and physical. This is not dependent on any external agency or creator God. The Buddhist path is **empirical**; it involves scientific testing and a practical solution.

KEY WORD

Empirical based on evidence and experience

KEY WORD

Divine command theory a system of ideas or commandments given by a supreme being

❝ KEY QUOTES ❞

Morality in Buddhism is not founded on any doubtful revelation nor is it the ingenious invention of an exceptional mind, but it is a rational and practical code based on verifiable facts and individual experience.

(Thera)

A Buddhist is aware of future consequences, but he refrains from evil because it retards, does good because it aids progress to Enlightenment (bodhi).

(Thera)

KEY WORDS

Sadhu an itinerant holy man
Yoga *literally* union; in Hinduism, a method for becoming one with the Universal spirit
Bodhi the wisdom by which one attains enlightenment
Suffering the idea that life involves dissatisfaction
Impermanence the idea that the universe is in an unstable state of flux
Selflessness the idea that there is not a permanent essence within a person as all is impermanent

What does this mean for Buddhist ethics? Is there a clear ethical system? Clearly, if there is, it is not one 'given by God'. There is no **divine command theory** in Buddhism.

> It should be mentioned that any external supernatural agency plays no part whatever in the moulding of the character of a Buddhist ... there is no one to reward or punish. Pain or happiness are the inevitable results of one's actions.
>
> (Thera)

However, while morality is not dependent upon God it would be wrong to say that religion and morality are not intertwined.

> Buddhism is much more than an ordinary moral teaching. Morality is only the preliminary stage on the Path of Purity, and is a means to an end, but not an end in itself. Conduct, though essential, is itself insufficient to gain one's emancipation. It should be coupled with wisdom or knowledge. The base of Buddhism is morality, and wisdom is its apex.
>
> (Thera)

The Buddhist ethical system, then, is driven by the ideas of eliminating suffering through a proactive, empirical approach to the problem and also by developing wisdom to help a person deal with suffering.

Ethical practice is the start of the Buddhist path. This relates to the ancient Indian ideal of the **sadhu** or wandering holy man and **yoga**, the practice of meditation. In order to practise meditation one's conduct has to be moral. The idea of morality as a foundation to spiritual progress and practice is not new and is certainly not unique to Buddhism.

The ideas of conducting oneself appropriately, spiritual development, the cultivation of wisdom and the elimination of suffering are all inextricably linked. That is, one must behave ethically in order to eliminate suffering and be able to focus on becoming wise. More than this, ethical conduct actually reduces the incidence of suffering and also benefits other beings.

Buddhist ethics are derived from basic observations about the world in which we live. Buddhist ethics have been referred to as a common-sense 'morality from within'. Central to this are the basic observations of the three marks of existence or characteristics of being (see page 329 in Unit 4, *Buddhism*):

- **suffering**: a person who has a true understanding of the nature of suffering would appreciate that it is not the best course of action to inflict suffering upon another.
- **impermanence**: things change and do not last; this means a person can change and develop for the better, no matter what has been done. There is a famous Buddhist tale of a detestable character called Angulimala who changed for the better in response to an encounter with the Buddha.
- **selflessness**: while Buddhists hold to this principle literally by denying the existence of a permanent entity known as a soul, it does encourage giving up any idea of self in terms of attachment. Therefore, the idea of selflessness and an ultimate concern for others who suffer follows from this.

2 Buddhist ethical theory

The Buddhist teaching about **kamma** has been called the Buddhist absolute ethic. Kammic influence is described as **wholesome** or unwholesome, **fruitful** or unfruitful or even **skilful** or unskilful, rather than as good and bad. In everyday use, good and bad tend to have more personal value judgements attached to them. Thus, an action is either beneficial to oneself and to others or it is not beneficial.

The whole idea of Buddhist kamma is related to motive. Actions are measured by the intention associated with them, and may be:

- intentional actions
- accidental or neutral actions
- ignorant actions.

Each action has different consequences based upon the seriousness of intention. For example, an intentional action that does not benefit others is worse than an accidental or neutral action. An ignorant action that does not benefit others can sometimes be the worst type!

Peter Harvey outlines five such principles of kammic formations, graded from least damaging to most damaging:

- an unintentional action
- an action done in a state of passion, diminished responsibility or lack of self-control
- an action of which the outcome is uncertain in terms of its beneficial nature, or about which one is genuinely mistaken with regard to its effects
- an action that is done in full knowledge that it is wrong
- an action that is done when one is in full control and intends to perform it and yet is unaware that it is wrong through ignorance or a lack of compunction.

To find out more about kamma refer to Unit 4, *Buddhism*, pages 273–362.

3 Compassion and skilful means

Two other principles that impact upon Buddhist ethics are:

- **karuna** or compassion: the idea that concern and understanding for others demonstrates an attitude of not-self, that is, selflessness
- **skilful means**: basically the application of wisdom to a given situation so that the kammic benefits are maximised, both for others and self.

Skilful means is a flexible approach to ethics, involving the prioritising of principles. For example, killing a violent murderer in self-defence, or defending another, is contrary to the principle of not killing but in the long term the outcome is skilful because it saves more lives and prevents further killing. A calculated decision may appear contrary to ethical principles in the short term, but is more in line with ethical principles in the long term.

In Mahayana Buddhism, this principle has been used widely, even to justify 'compassionate killings' and to arrive at the conclusion that:

> **… where the motive is to help people, there is no fault in an action.**

> (Harvey)

KEY WORDS

Kamma (Sanskrit: karma) intentional actions, good or bad, bringing consequences and affecting this and future lives

Wholesome description of positive and beneficial actions

Fruitful description of actions that will yield positive results

Skilful description of intelligent or wise actions

Karuna compassion; sometimes interpreted as the idea that concern for others demonstrates selflessness

Skilful means the application of wisdom so that kammic benefits are maximised

TASK

Turn to Unit 4, *Buddhism*, to find out some more information about kamma and the three marks.
Objective To develop the 'use of evidence and examples' to 'demonstrate clearly relevant knowledge and understanding' (AO1)

❝ KEY QUOTES ❞

As a moral teaching it excels all other ethical systems, but morality is only the beginning and not the end of Buddhism.

(Thera)

The law of karma is seen as a natural law inherent in things, like a law of physics.

(Harvey)

EXAM TIP

When answering a question on Buddhist ethics, make sure that you pick out the key principles and explain why they are important in relation to the issue debated. This ensures focus is on the reasons that determine a decision rather than simply on the general topic (level 2).

 KEY WORDS

Pancasila the five moral precepts
Vows personal undertakings rather than rules

" KEY QUOTE "

For Buddhism, a good society is one in which individuals act correctly together – not a society that is coerced into obedience by a set of laws or regulations.

(Vardy and Grosch)

In practice, the principles of kamma, as determined by intention when combined with the ideas of compassion and skilful means, encourage a relativist or situationist approach to ethics. While the absolute principle once again appears to be kamma, in practice it is much more complex than this.

4 Buddhist ethical precepts

As discussed above, Buddhists tend not to describe actions as being good or bad but rather in terms of being (un)skilful, (in)appropriate and (un)fruitful. This may be because there are no rules or 'oughts' in Buddhism that can dictate whether something is good or bad.

a) Precepts as vows

Buddhists do have some basic ethical principles to guide them, known as the **pancasila** or five precepts. They are, however, forms of guidance for moral behaviour and are taken as **vows**. The precepts are not commandments given by an outside agency or God. They encourage personal ethical responsibility. The precepts are, broadly, abstaining from:

- killing any living being
- stealing
- unlawful sexual intercourse
- lying
- the use of intoxicants.

The idea that the precepts are guidelines implies that they are not absolute. Indeed, although Buddhists are encouraged to take all vows, it is entirely a personal decision based upon individual spiritual and moral development.

The precepts are interpreted and applied in different ways. Some Buddhists take them very literally. For example, there is a warning from Thanissaro Bhikkhu that altering the implications and understanding of the precepts too much sets impossible standards that defeat the whole basis and idea of the precepts.

Others, for example Harvey, give great thought and consideration to analysing each one and considering its broader implications and applications.

For the first precept, Harvey includes the idea of injury as 'clearly against the spirit of the precept' and also says that 'fraud, cheating, forgery and falsely denying that one is in debt' are embraced by the second precept.

According to Harvey, 'The third precept relates primarily to the avoidance of causing suffering by one's sexual behaviour.' In addition, 'any form of lying, deception or exaggeration, either for one's own benefit or that of another' is precluded by the fourth precept.

Finally, the fifth precept is really to do with states of unmindfulness. This means that anything that causes such a lack of focus should be avoided. The full implications of this precept are often debated, but its essential relationship to the other four can be stressed by a story of a Thai monk who was challenged to break a precept. Seeing the fifth as having the least direct impact, he became drunk, only to break the other four precepts while in this state!

Whatever the case may be, it can be concluded that the precepts form the basis of moral behaviour and, whichever way they are interpreted, they can be applied to real-life situations and ethical dilemmas.

b) Breaking the precepts

In relation to the workings of the principles of kamma, there are also different levels of demerit (or negative kammic influence) involved in breaking a precept. This depends upon intention. Therefore breaking a precept cannot be described as a bad action but is better described as unskilful.

> **Buddhist ethics are not codified into a rigid moral code; nor are they about making judgements and arousing sin and guilt.**
>
> (Snelling)

The role of conscience in Buddhism is played by mindfulness; that is, a person is aware of their actions and the intentions or motives behind them. This ideal of complete awareness is referred to as **ottappa**.

The term **hiri** is used when breaking a precept. It means shame rather than guilt and reflects the idea of self-responsibility and, essentially, encourages self-respect and a positive approach to life. To dwell too much on oneself would be too indulgent, so Buddhists are encouraged to learn from mistakes and move on.

Therefore a Buddhist is to develop from the stage of hiri or self-indulgence to that of ottappa, where there is a complete regard for consequences.

c) Emphasis on the positive side of the precepts

According to Thanissaro Bhikkhu, the precepts are part of a course of therapy for wounded minds and are aimed at curing the ailments that underlie low self-esteem.

> **Healthy self-esteem comes from living up to a set of standards that are practical, clear-cut, humane, and worthy of respect; the five precepts are formulated in such a way that they provide just such a set of standards.**
>
> (Thanissaro Bhikkhu)

Thanissaro Bhikkhu sees the precepts as practical. If they become over complicated or their interpretation is widened, they become complex and unmanageable. Kept simple, they are workable principles. Actions are also clear-cut and either fit a precept or not. The precepts are humane in their treatment of others and their regard for self and they also command respect and are vindicated as principles in themselves. The precepts are, therefore, totally positive and set an aspiration that is reachable.

5 The relationship between morality and religion

The relationship between morality and religion can clearly be seen in Buddhism through both kamma and the moral principles discussed so far. Indeed, Nyanatiloka's *Buddhist Dictionary* states that morality is 'the acting out of positive kamma'.

This becomes more evident when the ultimate teaching of Buddhism is considered; this is the **eight-fold path** (see Unit 4, *Buddhism*, for more information on this). In Buddhism, to follow the path is to aim towards enlightenment. On the path there is a clear section that deals with morality. One has to be ethically pure in one's actions if **nibbana** or enlightenment is to be reached. One who is unethical cannot be enlightened.

KEY IDEA

The five precepts
Without killing or causing injury to any living creature, man should be kind and compassionate towards all, even to the tiniest creature that crawls at his feet. Refraining from stealing, he should be upright and honest in all his dealings. Abstaining from sexual misconduct which debases the exalted nature of man, he should be pure. Shunning false speech, he should be truthful. Avoiding pernicious drinks that promote heedlessness, he should be sober and diligent.

(Thera)

KEY WORDS

Ottappa complete awareness of intentions and motives behind moral actions
Hiri shame, reflecting the idea of self-responsibility and encouraging self-respect
Eight-fold path the ultimate teaching of Buddhism
Nibbana enlightenment

 KEY QUOTE

The Buddha was like a doctor, treating the spiritual ills of the human race. The path of practice he taught was like a course of therapy for suffering hearts and minds.

(Thanissaro Bhikkhu)

TASK

Draw up a table with the three headings 'precept', 'meaning' and 'further meanings'. Use the information here to complete the table.

Objective To develop an understanding of the literal meanings of the precepts but also the wider application of these meanings. To demonstrate a deeper understanding of the precepts, using examples to support explanation, and demonstrating 'selection and deployment of relevant material' (level 5)

KEY WORDS

Concentration employment of all one's powers or attention
Wisdom ability to apply knowledge and experience critically
Panna wisdom
Sila morality, moral living or moral virtue; one of the three aspects of the eight-fold path comprising right speech, action and livelihood
Samadhi meditation
Transmigration the passing over of one consciousness stream into another

❝ KEY QUOTE ❞

Meditation helps the individual to pay close attention to whatever he or she is doing without being distracted – it therefore has an ethical value.

(Vardy and Grosch)

It is the foundation of the whole Buddhist practice, and therewith the first of the three kinds of training that form the three-fold division of the eight-fold path – morality, concentration and wisdom.

(Nyanatiloka)

Morality involves right speech, action and livelihood. Speech and action are integral to the idea of kamma at a generic level. In terms of application of these principles, once again, kamma comes into play:

This is making one's living in a way that does not involve the habitual breaking of the precepts by bringing harm to other beings, but which hopefully aids others and helps cultivate one's faculties and abilities.

(Harvey)

All these aspects are driven by intention and thus directly related to the principle of kamma. The parts of the eight-fold path are:

- **panna** – wisdom
- **sila** – morality
- **samadhi** – meditation.

It is the case, however, that the whole of the eight-fold path, and not just the section designated as morality, is driven by the idea of mindfulness or awareness of intentions. The morality section is overtly ethical; the other two sections covertly link themselves to ethics.

These eight factors are the key to Buddhist ethics...

(Vardy and Grosch)

Directly related to the whole idea of religion and morality is the idea of rebirth (see Unit 4, *Buddhism*, for further information). The ethical actions of an individual have consequences, not just in this life but also beyond it. Ethical activity, then, is inextricably linked to the idea of liberation, enlightenment or the Buddhist religious goal beyond this life.

6 Buddhist attitudes to abortion

As with the issue of abortion itself, the debate in Buddhism begins with the question: 'At what point does life, or consciousness, begin?' Given that the idea of kamma and rebirth imply a continuous cycle of existence (see Unit 4, *Buddhism*), this is by no means a clear decision.

Most Buddhists have adopted the later classical Indian teachings that the **transmigration** of consciousness happens at conception. This includes the acceptance that this passing over of one consciousness stream into another is a sudden and not a gradual event. The true nature of this passing over, however, is still debated.

Harvey and Keown suggest that the accepted Buddhist view is that life, or consciousness, begins at fertilisation. Abortion is therefore a serious act.

It must be noted again that the language of right and wrong in Buddhism is replaced by degrees of kammic consequences. These impact upon individual access to, or regress from, the spiritual path.

The serious nature of abortion demands that if a monk is involved he can be permanently expelled from the **sangha**. Indeed, **jataka** tales refer to abortion-mongers in hell, once again reflecting the kammic seriousness of the act.

So is abortion ever an acceptable course of action for Buddhists? Harvey identifies several grounds for abortion in Buddhism and grades them accordingly in terms of order of priority for consideration:

- the threat to mother's physical or mental health
- the threat to the health of the fetus
- socio-economic factors
- the woman's rights
- the needs of society.

Despite the apparent absolute that life or consciousness begins at conception, there is also the relative, **utilitarian** or **situationist** aspect to kamma that accounts for all the complexities embracing intentions, age and development of being. In practice, as Ling has demonstrated through research in **Theravada** Buddhist countries, the seriousness of the act of abortion increases with the age of the embryo. This relates to the Buddhist ideal that destroying a more developed being generates greater consequences.

Given the above, one could argue that, in practice, the nature of kamma and intention can justify different routes and therefore transforms the Buddhist approach from an absolutist one to a casuistic, relativist approach.

For example, Suwanbubbha argues that therapeutic abortion 'may be considered as unsevere kamma as long as this action is not based on the roots of unwholesome or bad intention'. In addition, regarding the socio-economic view, Suwanbubbha writes: '… it is very difficult to determine absolutely what one should do … the doers … will know best what their real intentions and states of mind are.'

In terms of applying karuna or compassion and skilful means, a Buddhist can argue that the kammic benefit in the long term can certainly outweigh the immediate seriousness.

However, in counter-argument to this approach, one should bear in mind the words of Damien Keown:

> **The doctrine of rebirth, moreover, sees the new conceptus as not just a 'potential person' evolving from the first time from nothing, but as a continuing entity bearing the complete karmic encoding of a recently deceased individual. If we rewind the karmic tape a short way … we would typically find an adult man or woman fulfilling all the requirements of 'personhood'.**

Despite Keown's words, it is still the case that this entity is a product of previous kammic activity and should not necessarily be seen as a storehouse of kammic consequences in the same way as in the previous guise of a fully developed being.

All in all, abortion is to be avoided. If it is performed there are serious kammic consequences. The relative seriousness of these consequences is the area of debate today among Buddhists.

KEY WORDS

Sangha the Buddhist monastic community
Jataka sutras narrating the birth stories of the Buddha in past lives, and effects related to the past and the present lives
Utilitarian ethical doctrine that the moral worth of an action is solely determined by its contribution to overall utility
Situationist individual circumstances rather than sets of rules determine the outcome of any ethical dilemma
Theravada *literally* the way of the elders, it focuses on the devotion to and support of the sangha as the primary source of teaching and example

EXAM TIP

Remember to explain each point that you make in an exam answer to the full. Think carefully about each sentence and how it relates to the question and the previous sentence. Aim for at least three sentences to explain a point. For example, state what the teaching is, how it is applied to an ethical issue and then give an example. This demonstrates 'understanding and engagement with the material' (level 5), 'good and successful selection of material' (level 3–4) and 'clearly relevant understanding' (AO1 descriptor).

" KEY QUOTES "

KEY QUOTES

It is clear that
Buddhism sees
abortion as akin
to killing an adult
human, but that does
not mean that all
such acts are equally
as bad.

(Harvey)

Buddhist literature
emphasises the
importance of
meeting death
mindfully since
the last moment
of one life can be
particularly influential
in determining the
quality of the next
rebirth.

(Keown)

Whoever, O monks,
would nurse me, he
should nurse the sick.

(Buddha)

7 Buddhist attitudes to euthanasia

The Buddhist view of suicide is straightforward enough:

> **... suicide is an act which will bring grief to friends and relatives, and so, if for no other reason, is to be avoided.**
>
> **(Harvey)**

Despite this, remember the nature of applied ethics – sometimes the ideal is not always a workable principle. In his book, *Buddhist Ethics: A Very Short Introduction*, Damien Keown presents the powerful image of the suicide of Buddhist monk, Thich Quang Duc, in Saigon in 1963, which had a profound impact on the world. The monk calmly sat while his body was destroyed by flames in protest against the policies of a dictator. It can be seen, then, once again that questions are raised concerning the theoretical principles and the conflicts of actual situations.

The key issue, according to Peter Harvey, is whether or not euthanasia breaks the first precept. The Buddhist stance, if there is a single approach, is very complicated. The criteria of kamma, the precepts, compassion and skilful means can all have various possible responses. Generally, however, the Buddhist stance resists the idea of euthanasia, based upon the following principles.

- Killing is to be avoided.
- Compassion is to be encouraged and there is greater merit in supporting the dying than helping them to die early.
- Euthanasia could have a negative impact upon rebirth.
- Life is suffering and killing is not an effective way to end suffering because life continues through rebirth.

One might think that compassion would permit euthanasia; however, this must be weighed against the principles of kamma and the consequences of actions for a better rebirth in the long term.

Indeed, unlike the issue of abortion, where a life is rudimentary and kammic accumulation minimal, the ending of a fully developed human life seriously impacts upon the balance of kammic accumulation incurred by that life.

This, then, is the biggest problem for a Buddhist. The main question appears to be: 'Can killing ever be effective enough to end suffering in the ultimate context of rebirth?'

It is for this reason that most Buddhist writers advise against euthanasia as a preferred course of action. Indeed, in Theravada countries, monasteries have been used as hospices, reflecting Buddhism's practical approach to dealing with the problem of suffering.

8 Buddhist attitudes to genetic engineering

The Buddhist aim of eliminating suffering is identical to the objectives of medicine. Indeed, the Buddha's teaching is often referred to in terms of a medical diagnosis (see Unit 4, *Buddhism*).

There is a strong Buddhist tradition of working with the sick. It has already been noted in relation to euthanasia that this extends to hospices.

The Buddhist King Asoka introduced many social reforms, placing great emphasis on caring for others (see Unit 4, *Buddhism*).

Genetic engineering, and specifically the creation and use of embryos for medical research, in the widest sense, has as its aim the prevention of massive future suffering. This would certainly be in keeping with the Buddhist ideal. It could be seen as a genuine application of the principle of skilful means to justify genetic engineering.

For some Buddhists scholars, the question of the nature and role of DNA as it relates to kamma is crucial:

> **The belief in karma introduces many conundrums and complexities of this kind, since both karma and DNA may be thought to account for how people come to be born with specific physical and mental characteristics.**
>
> (Keown)

Keown rejects the link between kamma and DNA for the following reasons.

- The process of enlightenment, with regard to development of consciousness, is not a function of DNA.
- During the course of life from one rebirth to another, the DNA may be modified by kamma for the next life.

Therefore, the actual idea of cloning is 'not to be seen as theologically improper or immoral' (Keown). It is not possible to create a clone that has the absolute identity and personality of another, due to the influences of kamma.

Despite this, reservations remain among Buddhists as to the kammic benefits of creating life to destroy it. Again, this is where this discussion began and, as with abortion, similar principles of the value of rudimentary forms of life, the use of skilful means and the role of intention are all major factors.

9 Buddhist attitudes to war

In his book, *An Introduction to Buddhist Ethics*, Peter Harvey spends a great deal of time outlining the Buddhist analysis of the causes of conflict. Indeed, in the Buddhist path much emphasis is placed on preventing conflicts from arising in the first place. Identifying the causes at an early stage can help defuse a potentially awkward situation.

The great Buddhist ruler, King Asoka (see Unit 4, *Buddhism*) is the ideal convert from the horrors of war. Asoka promoted peace and non-violence at all costs.

The idea of a life as a soldier clearly breaks with the first precept and also the aspect of the eight-fold path that indicates right livelihood. There are, though, several justifications for a Buddhist to be involved with war and it has been argued that there is a great history of the just war that has evolved in Buddhism.

Typical of this is the association of the Japanese *bushido* or warriors within Zen Buddhism. Military practices were modelled upon Zen monastic practices to create in the soldier an indifference to death and suffering:

> **This hardness to life and death made Zen the preferred form of Buddhism for the medieval Samurai. Combat and war were not contradictory to enlightenment but could become avenues to it if done responsively without attachment, desire, or hatred.**
>
> (*Journal of Military Ethics*)

❝ KEY QUOTES ❞

Buddhas … are thought to have a profound insight … a deep understanding of important truths … as far as I am aware, no geneticist would suggest that specific concepts, truths or propositions of this kind are encoded in the structure of DNA.

(Keown)

I have had this Dhamma edict written so that my sons and great-grandsons may not consider making new conquests, or that if military conquests are made, that they be done with forbearance and light punishment, or better still, that they consider making conquest by Dhamma only, for that bears fruit in this world and the next.

(From Asoka, 13th Rock Edict)

In her book, *In Defense of Dharma: Just-War Ideology in Buddhist Sri Lanka*, Tessa Bartholomeusz explores the apparent disparity between the ideal and the real in Buddhism in relation to war. The ideal that one should cultivate compassion, respect and reverence for all life implies that war cannot be justified. To use violence is to betray the Buddha's teachings.

As always with applied ethics, there are noticeable exceptions. Theravada monks and followers have been implicated in persecution and violence in the Sri Lankan ethnic conflict and civil war. Buddhist literature may also suggest that war is sometimes necessary, for example, in post-canonical narratives such as the *Mahavamsa*, which describe the Buddha's legendary Sri Lankan visits and the victories of Buddhist warrior kings.

Bartholomeusz points out that, while Buddhism has a heritage of peace, compassion and non-violence, it also has a long history of responding thoughtfully to war, including the occasional justification of it as a last resort.

Essential to this approach to practical, applied ethics, when faced with such absolutes as non-violence, are once again the casuistic, relativist computations regarding kammic consequences, benefits combined with the application of such principles as skilful means. Buddhism's use of skilful means encourages the use of practical judgement in applying moral principles to any situation. For example, the precept against violence is not absolute because it can be suspended in favour of defending another.

In practice, in Buddhism there is certainly a tradition that parallels the Christian and western criteria for a just war.

Nonetheless, as within any religious tradition, there remains a group of thinkers who could not justify violence in any shape or form. The Buddhist precepts are deontological in nature and, no matter how the situation is justified through the use of kammic calculations, emotional pleas through compassion or by the use of skilful means, the cold facts are that violence met with violence only produces more violence.

In the words of the Buddha: 'Conquest begets enmity; the conquered live in misery; the peaceful live happily having renounced conquest and defeat.' (Dhammapada, verse 201)

Harvey takes a similar view to that expressed in the quote, suggesting that in Buddhism there are 'strong resources to draw on for conflict resolution, but that these resources and ideals must sometimes become better known and applied more fully.'

Harvey cites the examples of the work of the Dalai Lama and that of the Cambodian peace-activist, Maha-Ghosananda, to support the ideals of the great King Asoka.

> **KEY QUOTE**
>
> **Although the Buddha's precepts are unconditional, conflicts between precepts require contextual reasoning that employs utilitarian (maximising compassion and minimising suffering) and virtue ethical (the effects actions have on one's condition) considerations.**
>
> *(Journal of Military Ethics)*

Reflection and assessment AO1

It is vital to bring together the information you have covered so far and recognise how it can be transformed into effective examination-style revision and answers. The best way to do this is to ask the question: 'How am I going to be assessed on my use of this information?'

In the examination you will be assessed by levels of response (see page 7 in the Introduction). Below is an examination-style question about Buddhist responses to abortion. Beneath it are three sets of bullet points under the headings 'basic', 'developed' and 'higher'. A basic answer relates to levels 1 and 2. The developed answer can score level 3 or possibly the lower requirements for level 4. The higher level scores from level 4 up to the maximum.

Explain Buddhist teachings about abortion.

(25 marks)

Basic	Developed	Higher
• Precept of non-harming • Kammic consequences • Life begins at conception	• Kamma is flexible • Some situations allow for abortion • Application of skilful means	• Complexity of the teaching of kamma • In practice Buddhist societies accept it • Idea of rebirth implies that the embryo is more developed than it may appear

Suggestion for further application of skills

Look again at the question above, applied to abortion and euthanasia. Use the notes you made to create a plan for each topic and then write them up, under timed conditions. After grading it would be beneficial to copy the best of your answers (one for each essay) and, as a group, consider what makes them good. Use this time of reflection to revisit your own work and improve it through redrafting it.

TASK

Consider the question:

Explain Buddhist teachings about euthanasia. (25 marks)

Study the examples of responses that could be given for 'basic', 'developed' and 'higher' for the question about abortion, opposite. As a group, add to this list. Now, in small groups, work out what could be included for 'basic', 'developed' and 'higher' for the question about euthanasia. You could swap ideas between groups, to finalise your notes, or each group could take the 'basic', 'developed' and 'higher' sections in turn and discuss your notes.
Objective To develop awareness of what will constitute a very good answer (level 4–5) by gradually building up a response

Part 4B

A critical analysis of the issues

What are the issues that I am expected to consider and to analyse critically?

- Key strengths of the Buddhist ethical system in relation to the arguments about abortion, euthanasia, genetic engineering and war and peace
- Key weaknesses of the Buddhist ethical system in relation to the arguments about abortion, euthanasia, genetic engineering and war and peace
- Possible conclusions related to each issue

? KEY QUESTIONS

- How do we define Buddhist ethics?
- Are the principles of Buddhist ethics more absolutist or more relativist?
- Are the principles of Buddhist ethics 'user friendly and flexible' or 'too complex and impractical'?
- Is the promotion of virtues more important than the establishment of absolute principles?
- Can the impact of kamma according to Buddhist ethics ever really be measured?

It is very difficult to define Buddhist ethics as a system.

In terms of the precepts and the guidance offered by the eight-fold path it can be argued to be absolutist.

In terms of the absolute principle of kamma that underpins the whole ethical system, however, the approach can be argued to be more relativist.

Adding to this the flexible principles of intention, compassion and skilful means, one could argue that most actions could be in some way ethically justified.

Mel Thompson regards Buddhism as situationist; that is, individual circumstance rather than a set of rules determine the outcome or any ethical dilemma. Damien Keown prefers to see it as a mixture of alternatives. It is both egotistical and altruistic, mainly absolutistic but not exclusively so, and objective in principle in that it is related to universal impersonal laws of kamma. Overall, Keown sees it as a form of virtue ethics as opposed to a deontological or teleological approach.

Whatever the case may be, it is important to bear in mind that there is diversity of opinion in Buddhism, just as in any other world religion, as to what precisely the Buddhist perspective entails.

1 Strengths of Buddhist ethics

The first key strength of Buddhist ethics is that it is clear and simple to apply. For example, the precepts are very explicit as to what should be avoided, the morality section of the eight-fold path is precise as to how to live and the ideal of selflessness combined with compassion for others can consistently be applied.

The Buddhist ethical system also has the attraction of being empirical in its approach and offers analysis of life without divine influence. It is based upon the very simple observation: things that do not cause suffering are wholesome acts; things that bring suffering are to be avoided. Where suffering cannot be avoided, the least suffering for all, a utilitarian perspective, is, in most cases, the most appropriate course of action. It moves beyond what is right and wrong. It eliminates the idea of self-indulgence through self-pity, guilt and remorse. It frees the consciousness to speak a new language of what is appropriate and universally conducive to enlightenment for all.

The principle of kamma in Buddhist ethics is easily applied at a personal level. In this sense it is accessible to all. It is almost like an individualised learning plan that equips a person to cope with the complexities of life, with reference to a few basic principles.

Positive virtues of compassion, wisdom through skilful means, selflessness and empathy with others are promoted through Buddhist ethics.

Possibly the greatest strength of Buddhist ethics is the provision of a flexible framework that can be applied to different situations, at the same time following the few central principles offered as guidance.

2 Weaknesses of Buddhist ethics

There are weaknesses to the Buddhist system. The first observation is that it is not really a universal system but much more an individualised programme. In this sense it can never be workable as a system of ethics for society as a whole. In decisions concerning matters of life and death, ethical principles need to be clearly defined and applied for the good of society as a whole.

Buddhist ethics may be seen as vague. There is clearly debate and indecision as to the applications and interpretations of the precepts. In addition, the role of kamma is unclear in that it is based entirely on the subjective nature of intention, which is really self-governing and not means-testable by an outside absolute or objective view.

Principles of Buddhist ethics are too open to interpretation and subjective views and decisions. This is the case with the precepts and their application, the role of intention behind kamma, the application of skilful means and an understanding of compassion.

At best, Buddhist ethics can offer a useful guide for the individual but would be useless for society as a whole in arriving at decisions. Rather than making decisions when ethical principles conflict, the Buddhist ethical system has the beauty of avoiding the conflicts by recognising a variety of applications. This cannot, however, be considered a strength.

3 Possible conclusions

When assessing the Buddhist ethical system, it is important to reflect upon the arguments previously discussed and arrive at some appropriate conclusion. It may be that you accept none of these listed here, or just one of them, or you may have a different conclusion that is not listed. However, what is important is the way that you have arrived at your conclusion – the reasoning process.

From the preceding discussions, here are some possible conclusions you could draw.

? KEY QUESTIONS

- How simple are the principles of Buddhist ethics?
- Are the principles of Buddhist ethics a precise science?
- How flexible is the principle of kamma?

TASK

Think of the questions you would like to ask about each of the teachings. Is there anything that is not clear? What needs further explanation? Objective To develop an awareness of areas in knowledge and understanding where there are gaps to be filled. Aids self-reflection and development, creating 'clear analysis' expected for responses at level 4 and above

EXAM TIP

Be careful when using quotes in critical assessments. Always make sure that they relate to the argument that is presented. To make sure of this, always explain the relevance of the quote in your answer. This is the difference between 'not successful' (level 1–2) and 'successful' (level 3–5) analysis.

TASK

Look at the basic answer opposite. Try to work out how a developed answer (level 3) would deal with the question, by adding two or three more bullet points. Now develop this answer to indicate how a higher answer (level 4–5) would deal with the question, by adding further bullet points. Remember to keep the bullet points focused on the question.

Objective To develop awareness of what will constitute a very good answer, by gradually building up a response that is 'an excellent attempt to address the question, showing understanding and engagement with the material' (level 5 descriptor)

1. The Buddhist ethical system reflects the very complex nature of the practical aspects of the dilemmas involved in applied ethics. In this sense it is one of the most realistic systems available.

2. When the Buddhist ethical system is kept simple and the precepts are prioritised in their purest form, it is a clear and effective guide to the dilemmas presented by applied ethics.

3. Due to the potential computations and complexities of kamma, skilful means and interpretation of the precepts, the Buddhist ethical system becomes so flexible that it serves no useful purpose in establishing ethical parameters. It is too vague and subjective.

4. The Buddhist ethical system is simply too complicated. Might this mean that only those capable of working out the appropriate course of action would be the intelligentsia of society? In this case is it in danger of becoming an elitist and authoritarian system?

Reflection and assessment AO2

It is vital to bring together the information you have covered so far and recognise how it can be transformed into effective examination-style revision and answers. The best way to do this is to ask the question: 'How am I going to be assessed on my use of this information?'

Look back to page 8 in the Introduction to review the level descriptors for AO2. There is a description of the character and features for each level. The exam is marked with reference to levels.

Look at the following sample basic answer, which is a response to the question:

'Buddhist ethics has an effective response to war.' Discuss. (25 marks)

A basic answer might deal with the question by:

- stating the basic definition of first precept – non-violence
- giving some basic evidence or reasoning why Buddhism promotes peace
- drawing a simple conclusion about actions bearing consequences, referring to kamma.

Suggestions for further application of skills

Now try this technique of building an ideal answer for a question such as:

- 'Buddhist ethics offers an effective solution for genetic engineering' Discuss.
- 'Buddhist ethics is an effective way of dealing with the issue of abortion.' Discuss.

Then try creating a few questions about Buddhist ethics and the ways in which it deals with the issues from applied ethics.

Part 1
Background

What am I required to study?

- Common Judaism
- Religious groups
- Impact of Roman occupation

This means I am expected to know about:

- common Judaism, monotheism, law and covenant, Jerusalem temple, sacrifice and synagogue
- the influence and distinctive ideas of the Pharisees, Sadducees, Zealots and Essenes
- the Roman occupation of first-century Palestine and its impact on Jewish life and religion.

This section is a brief introduction to the background of the times of Jesus. The people and the way of life form the setting of many of the events recorded in the Gospels. Jesus lived at a particular time in history (first century CE) and in a particular place (Palestine). Therefore, to understand fully the account of his life, it is important to know about the religious and political background of those times. Jesus was a Jew who lived in a country in which the religion and way of life were dominated by Judaism. The country was occupied by the Romans who oversaw the administration and government of the people.

It would be helpful to write your notes using the headings listed under 'This means I am expected to know about', as it is from these areas that the exam questions will be derived.

Remember that your studies will include elements of the *two* basic assessment objectives of:

- Knowledge and Understanding (AO1)
- Evaluation (AO2).

See pages 7–8 in the Introduction to remind yourself of these objectives.

The evaluation material is set out in Part 3 of this topic (page 212) and can be studied either alongside the AO1 material, as you work through this topic, or as a discrete topic.

KEY WORDS

Monotheism the belief or doctrine that there is only one God
Covenant God bestows his favour on the people
Torah usually refers to the first five books (the law books) of the Hebrew Bible
Tanakh a word formed from the initial letters of the three parts that make up the Hebrew Bible (Torah/Nevi'im/Ketuvim) as a collective term for what Christians call the Old Testament
Talmud a record of rabbinic discussions about Jewish law, ethics, customs and history
Shema the first word of Deuteronomy 6: 4
Rabbi from the Hebrew meaning great in knowledge, refers to a Jewish religious teacher
Rabbinic relating to the rabbis

❝ KEY QUOTES ❞

Hear, O Israel: the Lord our God is one Lord.

(Deuteronomy 6: 4)

Do not make any gods to be alongside me; do not make for yourselves gods of silver or gods of gold.

(Exodus 20: 23)

1 The gospel setting – common Judaism

The gospels recount the life of Jesus, set in Palestine in the first century CE. The majority of the population were followers of Judaism, and were referred to as Jews. It is not certain exactly when Jesus was born but most scholars agree that it was towards the end of Herod the Great's reign (4BCE) and that Jesus died around CE29.

Scholars such as E.P. Saunders and James Dunn have argued that Judaism, in the centuries either side of the Common Era, exhibited common features and reflect a world of thought that makes it possible to refer to it as common Judaism. Dunn identified four common themes that ran through all the wide wealth of writings during this period:

- **monotheism** – there is only one God
- election – God has chosen the people of Israel alone and given them the Promised Land
- **covenant** and **Torah** – the covenant between God and Israel is focused on their keeping the Torah
- the Temple – the Temple in Jerusalem was at the centre of national worship of God.

However, some scholars have argued that such an overview is too simplistic. They point to literature in that period that seems hostile to the Temple and shows little interest in the Mosaic Torah. Perhaps it would be more accurate to say that there was a common Judaism, as outlined by Dunn, that shared some – if not, at times, all – of the four features.

a) Monotheism

Monotheism is belief in only one God or deity. Judaism, Christianity and Islam are the three main monotheistic religions. Judaism is based on principles and ethics found in the **Tanakh** and the **Talmud**. The Tanakh corresponds to the books in the Old Testament of the Bible, though in a different order. The Jewish belief in one God is most clearly expressed in the **Shema**, which is the first word of Deuteronomy 6: 4, in Hebrew, and translated as hear. This is part of Jewish daily prayers and declares a very clear monotheistic belief.

Hear, O Israel: the Lord our God is one Lord.

(Deuteronomy 6: 4)

The term is applied by extension to the whole of the daily prayers and comprises Deuteronomy 6: 4–9 and 11: 13–21, and Numbers 15: 37–41. The Ten Commandments also contain very explicit statements of monotheism. For instance, the first commandments prohibit having other gods and the making and worshipping of idols (Exodus 20: 1–6).

The Talmud is a record of **rabbinic** discussions about Jewish law, ethics, customs and history. The Talmud has two components: the Mishnah (c CE200), and the Gemara (circa CE500). The Mishma contains Judaism's Oral Law.

b) Law and covenant

At the heart of Judaism is the Torah which derives its name from a root word meaning guidance or instruction, though often it is translated as law. Although it is not always clear, the Torah probably refers to the scrolls containing the first five books of the Bible, namely Genesis, Exodus, Leviticus, Numbers and Deuteronomy. The Jews believed that Moses was the author of these writings. Within these accounts is the story of God's dealing with the Jewish people, of how he brought them out of slavery from Egypt and into the Promised Land of Israel. However, the same word, Torah, can also refer to specific sections of law contained within these first five books.

The laws gained their authority from the belief that they had divine origin. They were not seen as negative, but rather as evidence of God's favour to his chosen people.

> **He has revealed his word to Jacob,**
> **His laws and decrees to Israel.**
> **He has done this for no other nation;**
> **They do not know his laws.**

(Psalm 147: 19–20)

The Torah gave Israel its distinctiveness. The sense of being chosen by God, and the various laws and rituals, marked the Jews as being different from others. In particular, the Torah law about circumcision, **Sabbath** laws and food laws meant that Jews stood apart from non-Jews.

Inseparable from the law was the idea of covenant, often taken to mean an agreement but a much more accurate idea is that God bestows his favour on the people. The condition for them to enjoy this was obedience. It was not that God required the people's agreement, but rather that they could enjoy the results of God's blessings only if they were obedient.

This idea of God favouring the Jews in some special way, by making covenants, occurs throughout the Torah. God made covenants through Noah (Genesis 6: 18), Abraham (Genesis 17: 6–8) and Moses (Exodus 6: 6–8). Other parts of the Hebrew scriptures mention a covenant through David and a new covenant (Jeremiah 31) to which Jesus makes reference at the Last Supper.

The history of the Jews was a story of how the people strayed from obedience to God's covenant and suffered the consequences of disobedience. Given the importance of the law, it is easy to see why the religious authorities saw Jesus as a threat to their commitment to God's law, for example, in his attitude towards the Sabbath.

c) The Temple

The First Temple was built by King Solomon during the tenth century BCE, but 400 years later it was destroyed by the Babylonians (586BCE). In 536BCE Cyrus the Great authorised the Temple to be rebuilt and, under the leadership of Zerubbabel, the Temple was completed by 516BCE.

By the time of Jesus, the Temple had been renovated by Herod the Great. The work, having begun in about 20BCE, took about ten years to complete. In fact, other minor work continued right up until its eventual destruction by the Romans in CE70. Because of its position, the Temple could be seen from a great distance away. In addition, the entire façade was covered with gold plate and the upper parts are thought to have been made of white marble, so that when the sun rose the reflection was almost blinding. The Temple dominated as a building but it also played a major part in the life of the Jews in Palestine. It is mentioned a number of times in the gospels. It was considered to be the very dwelling place of God and a sign to the Jews that they were his special people. Jerusalem and the Temple became the heart of Judaism for the Jews.

❝ KEY QUOTE ❞

'The time is coming,' declares the Lord, 'when I will make a new covenant with the house of Israel and with the house of Judah.
… I will put my law in their minds and write it on their hearts.
I will be their God, and they will be my people …'

(Jeremiah 31: 31, 33)

KEY WORD

Sabbath the seventh day of creation when God rested; in Judaism, it is observed from sundown on Friday until sundown on Saturday

---

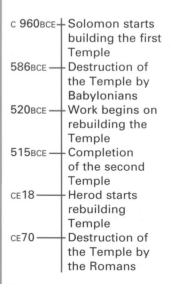

c 960BCE — Solomon starts building the first Temple

586BCE — Destruction of the Temple by Babylonians

520BCE — Work begins on rebuilding the Temple

515BCE — Completion of the second Temple

CE18 — Herod starts rebuilding Temple

CE70 — Destruction of the Temple by the Romans

The history of the Temple

KEY WORDS

Holy of Holies the inner sanctuary of the Temple, only the High Priest could enter and then only on the Day of Atonement

Day of Atonement also known as Yom Kippur, the most solemn of the Jewish festivals where the theme is repentance (Leviticus 23: 26–32)

Eschatology a study of the last things and final events; often linked to the arrival of the Messianic Age

Messiah in Jewish tradition, a future Jewish king from the line of David, who will rule the Jewish people during the Messianic Age; the Messiah is associated with events of the end times

66 KEY QUOTE 99

Once, when Zechariah's division was on duty and he was serving as priest before God, he was chosen by lot, according to the custom of the priesthood, to go into the temple of the Lord and burn incense.

(Luke 1: 8–9)

KEY WORD

Passover a Jewish festival commemorating the liberation of the Israelites from Egypt

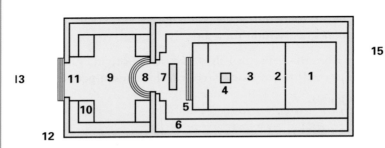

1 Holy of Holies
2 Veil (curtain)
3 Holy place
4 Altar of Incense
5 Court of the Priests
6 Court of Israel
7 Altar of Sacrifice
8 Nicanor Gate
9 Court of Women
10 Temple of the Treasury
11 Gate Beautiful
12 Court of the Gentiles
13 Solomon's Porch
14 Royal Porticos
15 Western Wall

The layout of the Temple in Jerusalem

The Temple consisted of a series of courts, which eventually led to the **Holy of Holies**. This was the innermost room of the Temple, the inner sanctuary. Only the High Priest could enter, and that was only on one day in the year, the **Day of Atonement.** The entrance to the Holy of Holies was covered by a double veil. The inner room was windowless. It was an exact cube and was empty apart from a small rock where the High Priest made his annual offering of incense on the one and only time in the year when he was allowed in the Holy of Holies. No one else was ever allowed in.

The Court of Women was the nearest women could get to the sanctuary, and it functioned as a meeting place. The 13 chests of the Temple treasury were kept there and offerings were put in to pay for the sacrifices. In each of the four corners of the court was a separate walled enclosure. One was reserved for lepers who believed themselves cured. They could be inspected by priests. If found to be cured they would be pronounced clean, but only after suitable rituals had been carried out. The Court of the Israelites could only be entered by Jewish men, and the Court of the Priests only by priests. A priest was allowed to offer incense on the altar of incense once only in a lifetime. Luke 1: 8–22 records what happened when it came to the turn of a priest named Zechariah. (Do not confuse this with the High Priest going into the Holy of Holies once a year.)

The role of the Temple has always been a feature of Jewish **eschatological** beliefs. Orthodox Judaism believes in the rebuilding of the Temple and the resumption of sacrificial worship. Most orthodox scholarship links the rebuilding to the time when the Jewish **Messiah** appears. A prayer for the reconstruction of the Temple is part of every orthodox Jewish prayer service.

d) Sacrifice

The Temple was central to animal sacrifices, which were a major part of the religious rituals. Each day there was a burnt offering of two lambs. In addition, people made their own private sacrifices, which ranged from pigeons to bulls. On the Sabbath no private offerings were made but the priests sacrificed two additional lambs.

At various festival times and new moons, extra sacrifices were performed, many following the regulations laid out in the Torah. One of the busiest occasions at the Temple was **Passover**. This Jewish festival commemorates the liberation of the Israelites from Egyptian slavery, and their protection from the tenth plague by the smearing of blood on the doorposts of their homes. On the afternoon preceding the

Passover feast, people brought unblemished lambs to the Temple where they killed their own lambs in sacrifice. A small portion of the internal organs were then burned on the altar. Then each lamb was taken home to be cooked for the Passover meal. On this day, thousands of lambs were killed (see also page 250).

The most solemn occasion in the Temple was the Day of Atonement. This was when the High Priest played the lead role in the rituals and the one time in the year when he entered the Holy of Holies. The purpose was to offer sacrifice to cleanse the people from sin. A goat, referred to as a scapegoat, was driven into the wilderness and pushed down a cliff to its death. This goat symbolically carried with it the sins of the people.

Maintaining such a complex organisation required vast numbers of administrators and priests. They were assisted by **Levites**, members of the tribe of Levi, one of the twelve sons of Jacob, who became responsible for many of the duties in the Temple. It has been estimated that up to 17 000 priests and Levites were required at the Temple at Passover. The majority of these, however, were not in Jerusalem all the time but came to assist on special occasions. The High Priest was supported by about 200 chief priests, but it was the High Priest who had the most authority. He was leader of the people and head of the **Sanhedrin**, a Jewish judicial body who, in Jesus' time, ruled mostly over religious and legal issues as the Romans occupied and governed the country.

e) The synagogue – a place of gathering

The **synagogue** was in marked contrast to the Temple. There were no priests and no sacrifices were offered. Prayer and reading of the Torah took the place of sacrifices. According to Jewish religious law, men must pray three times a day, ideally in a group of ten or more. The synagogue's primary purpose was to assist this public prayer. Synagogue worship kept alive the religious traditions after the Jews were taken into captivity (586BCE) and when they were away from the Temple. It seems that they found this so worthwhile that they continued synagogue worship even when they returned to Palestine and rebuilt the Temple. The gospels make various references to their existence and indicate that synagogues became the focus of religious and community life.

The synagogue was also the place of education and transmission of knowledge of the Torah. Some who benefited from this went on to more formal training to become **scribes** or **doctors of the law**. These students studied the interpretation of the Torah.

The synagogues were administered by a council of **elders** or respected counsellors of the Jewish community, who appointed a ruler whose duty it was to prepare for the daily worship.

2 The Jewish setting – the religious groups

Jesus lived between two periods where the Jews struggled to gain political freedom. In 165BCE, the Jews defeated the Syrians and gained independence in Judea. However, by 63BCE, the Romans had invaded and became the occupying force. An attempt to revolt against the Romans took place in CE66–70, but the outcome was defeat for the Jews and the destruction of Jerusalem and the Temple. It was during this earlier period of independence that various religious groups emerged, in particular the Pharisees, the Sadducees and the Essenes.

KEY WORDS

Levites members of the tribe of Levi, responsible for many of the duties in the Temple

Sanhedrin a Jewish judicial body who ruled mostly over religious issues

Synagogue place of meeting for prayer and reading the Torah

Scribes the interpreters, preservers and teachers of the law; scribes of the Pharisees (Mark 2: 16) may have been Pharisees who were learned in law

Doctors of the law mostly Pharisees, more associated with giving teaching through speaking rather than written opinions

Elders often from aristocratic families, they served in local councils and also in the Sanhedrin; senior and respected members of the community

TASK

Read Exodus 28 and 39 and research the symbolism contained in the High Priest's garments.

Objective To develop understanding of the importance and significance of the office of High Priest

KEY WORD

Oral law law passed down, by word of mouth

TASK

Use a concordance to research Jesus' attitude towards the Pharisees as recorded in the synoptic gospels.

Objective To develop knowledge and understanding of the Pharisees

KEY PERSON

Josephus was a first-century Jewish historian who wrote an account of the Fall of Jerusalem (CE70); his writings are also a source about first-century Judaism, including mention of the main religious groups, such as the Pharisees and Sadducees.

a) The Pharisees

i) Their origin

The struggles and difficulties suffered by the Jews were seen by many as a result of their failure to keep the law, thus forfeiting God's blessings and protection. In response to this, there arose a group who wanted to maintain the purity of the Jewish faith and return to keeping the strict laws of the Torah. They wanted to separate themselves from the pagan world and, in particular, the effects of Greek and Roman influences. This group became known as the Pharisees. The root of the word is thought to mean separated ones.

ii) Their distinctive ideas

Their desire for purity and keeping of the law led the Pharisees to develop extra laws to make sure people did not break the Torah by accident or through ignorance. This was done to bring back God's blessing on his chosen people. They regarded the keeping of the Torah as an individual as well as a national duty. The Pharisees themselves were meticulous about the keeping of the law, particularly in matters of ritual purity and tithing. They claimed that the law contained 613 commandments of which 248 were positive and 365 were negative. The hedge they built around them became part of the **oral law**, which was passed down, by word of mouth. Thus they gained such authority, since they claimed they had the correct interpretation of the Torah, that it became attributed to Moses. These additions became known as the traditions of the elders and included such things as the list of 39 tasks that could not be done on the Sabbath because they would count as work.

The Pharisees also had distinctive beliefs about the end of the world. They believed in:

- the resurrection of the dead and a world to come
- the soul as being immortal
- angels and demons who surrounded human life and were concerned with human beings
- human beings having free choices about whether or not to follow God
- piety being rewarded in the afterlife
- punishment in the afterlife for evildoers
- a day of judgement
- the messiah, who would bring in a new age where the righteous would reign.

iii) Their influence

According to **Josephus**, at the time of Jesus they numbered about 6000. Their influence far outweighed their number. They feature numerous times in the gospels, particularly in clashes with Jesus about his actions on the Sabbath and his mixing with sinners. Though they supported the Temple, they mostly worked in synagogues, instructing the people. They were not particularly political but there were internal disputes amongst them. The most notable dispute was between two pharisaic teachers, Shammai, who was conservative, and Hillel, who was more liberal. The Pharisees did have some political influence in that they formed part of the Sanhedrin.

b) The Sadducees

i) Their origin

The Sadducees formed as a group at about the same time as the Pharisees. They rejected oral tradition and sided more with the ruling class. The origin of their name is unclear, though a popular suggestion is that it derived from Zadok, chief priest during

Solomon's reign. Certainly this would be consistent with the fact that the majority of Sadducees were priests. Alternatively, their name may derive from the Greek for fiscal controllers. Again, this would be consistent with them being a political party and also with the fact that they belonged to influential aristocratic families.

ii) Their distinctive ideas

The Sadducees contrasted markedly with the Pharisees. They were nearly all priests and were based in Jerusalem around the Temple. Very conservative, in terms of beliefs, they:

- only accepted the written Torah and rejected the additions of the oral law and traditions of the elders
- believed that correct worship at the Temple would bring material prosperity
- did not believe in the resurrection of the dead
- did not believe in the later doctrines of the immortality of the soul
- did not believe in rewards or punishments in the afterlife
- did not believe in the doctrines about angels and demons
- believed people had a free choice of good and evil.

iii) Their influence

Their influence, like that of the Pharisees, far outweighed their numbers. They were from influential aristocratic families. They controlled the Sanhedrin and the position of High Priest, which gave them dominant religious power in Jerusalem. Politically, they adopted a pragmatic attitude towards the Roman occupation.

However, they did not enjoy support from the people and Josephus records that for fear of the people they were sometimes forced to side with the Pharisees.

After the fall of Jerusalem and the destruction of the Temple in CE70, the role of the Sadducees was obsolete and they ceased to exist as a recognisable group.

TASK
Draw a table with two columns – one headed 'Pharisees' and one 'Sadducees'. Then list the differences between them. An example is given below.

Pharisees	Sadducees
Believed in resurrection of the dead	Did not believe in resurrection of the dead

Objective To develop better understanding of the beliefs of the Pharisees and Sadducees

Destruction of the Temple of Jerusalem, Francesco Hayez

TASK

Find out about the events surrounding the fall of Jerusalem. There is an excellent account in *The Jewish War* by Josephus.
Objectives To understand the significance of this event for the Jews To understand Roman attitudes to the Jews during the first century CE

KEY PERSON

Philo (20BCE–CE50), also known as Philo of Alexandria, a Jewish philosopher and biblical commentator

KEY WORD

Apocalyptic a type of literature with a narrative framework, containing certain features such as obscure symbolism and mysterious revelations; often, but not always, about the end times

c) The Zealots

i) Their origin

The beginnings of this group may possibly be traced back to Judas the Galilean who led a revolt against Rome in CE6. The revolt was sparked off by the demand for tribute to a pagan emperor. Their zealousness for the keeping of the Torah and opposition to any attempt to suppress the Jewish religion earned them the name of Zealots.

ii) Their distinctive ideas

The Zealots:

- were zealous for the keeping of the Torah
- believed that the invasion of Israel by Rome and the exacting of tribute was an affront to God, and had to be resisted
- because of the covenant relationship, believed that Israel was assured that God would protect their possession of the land of Israel.

iii) Their influence

When the revolt of CE6 was crushed, the Zealots tended to become disorganised. They resorted to guerrilla warfare and avoided capture by living in the hills. It is possible that Barabbas, as well as the two thieves crucified beside Jesus, were Zealots.

d) The Essenes

i) Their origins

Like the Pharisees, this group were separatists who sought strict religious purity. Often, they withdrew from normal life altogether. They are not mentioned in the gospels. We have become aware of them through discoveries of remains of what are thought to be their community at Qumran by the Dead Sea. See page 213 for further discussion of links between the Essenes and the Qumran community.

ii) Their distinctive ideas

Their beliefs included:

- rejection of the Temple ritual because it disagreed with their interpretation of the Torah
- that they were living in the last days and awaited an apocalyptic war where they would triumph
- the result of this war would enable them to take control of the Temple and Jerusalem
- there would be two Messiahs – one of Israel and one of Aaron
- property should be held in common
- practice of celibacy
- their own system of purity and water initiation
- their own calendar.

iii) Their influence

Philo estimated their number to be about 4000. They were of little influence, because they withdrew from the ordinary life of the people and set up isolated communities.

However, their writings do reveal some insight into Jewish **apocalyptic** ideas in first-century Judaism. One of the scrolls found, the *War Scroll*, refers to the Sons of Light who will be involved in the final eschatological war. In this war they would be opposed to the Sons of Darkness. Other texts discovered are commentaries on the Jewish scriptures and, again, provide new understandings of how these scriptures were interpreted, especially in relation to events at the end of days. The scrolls also reveal discontent with the Temple authorities and a desire for a Jewish religious revival.

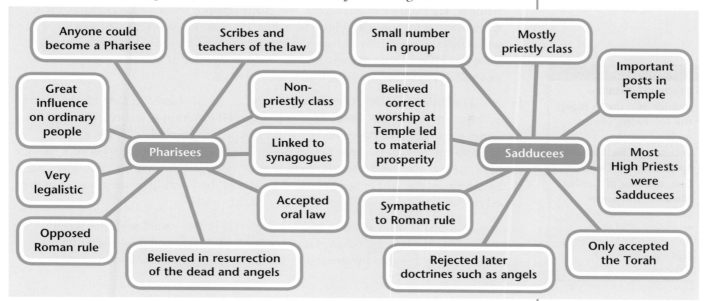

Summary diagram: Pharisees and Sadducees

3 The Roman influence

Palestine is about the size of Wales but was on the main routes from Egypt in the south to Syria and Mesopotamia in the north. As a result of its strategic position, it was much fought over in the power struggles between the major powers of the north and south.

a) Occupation

In 66–63BCE, the Roman general Pompey was engaged in campaigns in the Mediterranean. In 63BCE, he took advantage of a dispute between two brothers over the High Priest's office and entered Jerusalem. To the horror of the Jews, Pompey entered the Holy of Holies in the Temple, a place that only the High Priest entered and certainly where no Gentile was allowed. Nothing was looted but the trespass was an act that the Jews never forgave.

At the time of Jesus' birth, **Herod the Great** was ruling over the Jews from his royal palace in Jerusalem. He began the reconstruction of the Temple, as well as many other building projects. The latter part of his reign was marked by illness and paranoia. He murdered many of his family, believing they were plotting against him. At his death, the kingdom was split into three areas, in accordance with his will, and divided between three of his remaining sons.

- Archelaus was made ethnarch (ruler of a large area of conquered lands) of Judea, Samaria and Idumea, with a promise that he would be made king if he proved himself a good ruler. However, he was as brutal as his father. After deep unrest among the Jews, he was removed by Rome in CE6. A series of regional governors called procurators administered the area. The most well known of these was the sixth one, Pontius Pilate (see page 246).

KEY PERSON

Herod the Great (74BCE–CE3) Matthew's Gospel records that Herod killed all the children in Bethlehem who were up to two years old. This was because he feared a prophecy of the birth of a king in Bethlehem and thought this might threaten his own position. He had 10 marriages and at least 15 children.

- Philip was made tetrarch (ruler of a relatively small area) over the north-eastern part of Herod the Great's kingdom. In contrast to his half-brother Archelaus, he was a moderate ruler, with Greeks and Syrians, rather than Jews, forming the majority of the population.
- Antipas, the brother of Archelaus, was made tetrarch of Galilee and Perea. He built a new capital for himself, which he called Tiberias. He was regarded as a good ruler and Rome allowed him to have the dynastic title of Herod. During his reign he divorced his first wife and married the wife of another of Herod's sons, who was also called Philip but was not Philip the Tetrarch.

In CE34 Philip died and the Roman emperor, Caligula, appointed as king Herod Agrippa, the grandson of Herod the Great. Five years later, Herod Antipas was removed and his territories were added to the realm of Herod Agrippa. In January CE41, the emperor Caligula was murdered. Because Herod Agrippa had helped Claudius to become the new emperor, he was rewarded with the territories of Judea and Samaria. He was now king of all the territories that had once been ruled by Herod the Great. Jerusalem was again the capital of Palestine as a whole and received new city walls.

His son, Agrippa II, later ruled as king, though real power rested with the Roman governor. However, in CE66, religious tensions boiled over and there was a Jewish revolt. This ended with Titus besieging and destroying Jerusalem, and burning the Temple.

b) Impact on Jewish life and religion

Palestine was occupied by the Romans but the Jews were allowed much freedom in private matters, as long as they paid their taxes. There was freedom of worship and belief. The Romans intervened if there was public disorder or some threat to their political power. The Romans allowed the Jews to control certain religious and civil matters, even to the extent of allowing them to decide and administer punishments. This was done through the Sanhedrin which, according to Josephus, had 71 members presided over by the High Priest. Both Pharisees and Sadducees were members during the lifetime of Jesus, though the Sadducees were in the majority. It is debatable whether the Sanhedrin could pass the death sentence and it seems more likely that for this punishment they required the authority of the Roman administrator.

The Romans were well aware of the zealousness of the Jews for their religion, and so Herod the Great built the fortress of Antonia on the north side of the Temple courtyard. It had a staircase and an underground passage that connected with the Court of Gentiles. At festival times, when swelling crowds caused fear that a revolt may arise, the fortress contained up to 600 soldiers. The Roman authorities made the appointment of the High Priest subject to Roman consent. As a token of Roman power, the precious ceremonial robes of the High Priest were kept in one of the guard towers and released only on important religious occasions.

The purity of Judaism was also threatened by the spread of Hellenisation, which was the spread of Greek culture wherever the Romans occupied territories. The Greek language became widely spoken and aspects of Greek culture seeped into everyday life.

TASK

Study the satellite picture and try to locate the following places on it.

Jerusalem, Bethlehem, Nazareth, the Dead Sea, the Sea of Galilee, Masada, Caesarea

Objective To develop knowledge of the geography of incidents and events in the Gospels

The region of Palestine, a satellite image, 2003

The Torah provided the basis of belief and conduct for the Jews. The elders in the synagogue tried to show Jews how they could remain faithful to the Torah while being under Roman occupation. In the main, the Sadducees were pro-Roman. The Pharisees, on the other hand, were anti-Roman and looked for a messianic kingdom that would replace the rule of Rome. The Zealots tried to bring in that new kingdom by guerrilla warfare against the Roman occupation. In contrast, the Essenes withdrew to isolated communities to await the new kingdom.

Reflection and assessment AO1

It is now time to channel the information you have considered in a more focused way. In order to do this, once again you need to ask yourself the question: 'How am I going to be assessed on my use of this information?'

The first way is through assessment objective 1 (AO1). For this objective we need to be able to 'select and clearly demonstrate the relevant knowledge and understanding through the use of evidence, examples and correct language and terminology'.

Use the writing frame provided to answer the question:

Describe and explain the distinctive beliefs of the Pharisees.   (25 marks)

As you work through each unit in this book, you will find that the amount of support in these sections will gradually be reduced, in order to encourage the development of your independence and the honing of your AO1 skills.

Writing frame

The Pharisees were concerned about purity and the keeping of ...

They developed extra laws because ...

These extra laws became part of the oral law and gained authority. These laws gained authority because ...

The Pharisees belief about the soul was ...

Their beliefs about life after death and angels were different from the Sadducees in that the Pharisees ...

Another distinctive belief was ...

This belief is seen as distinctive because ...

Remember to use correct technical language where appropriate. The distinctive beliefs would be demonstrated by showing how certain beliefs of the Pharisees differed, compared to other groups of the time.

Suggestion for further applications of skills

Construct your own writing frame for the question:

Explain similarities and differences between the Sadducees and the Pharisees.

(25 marks)

Part 2

Source criticism

What am I required to study?
- Source criticism of the Gospels

This means I am expected to know about:
- source criticism
- the aims of source criticism
- the synoptic problem
- the one-source solution
- the two-source solution
- Markan priority
- the debate about Q
- the four-source solution.

You will be expected to be able to explain and illustrate the synoptic problem and be able to assess critically some solutions for source criticism that have been proposed.

It would be helpful to write your notes under the headings listed under 'This means I am expected to know about', as it is from these areas that the exam questions will be derived.

Remember that your studies will include elements of the *two* basic assessment objectives of:

- Knowledge and Understanding (AO1)
- Evaluation (AO2).

See pages 7–8 in the Introduction to remind yourself of these objectives.

The evaluation material is set out in Part 3 of this topic (page 212) and can be studied either alongside the AO1 material, as you work through this topic, or as a discrete topic.

1 The aim of source criticism

The first few verses of Luke's Gospel (Luke 1: 1–4) record the process by which it came finally to be written. First, he mentions 'eye witnesses and servants of the word' who handed down information about the life of Jesus. Then he mentions that 'many had undertaken to draw up an account'. Finally, Luke himself claims that he 'investigated everything from the beginning' and 'wrote an orderly account'. So Luke's Gospel is a researched document in which Luke consulted other material and information before finally writing his Gospel.

" KEY QUOTE "

So when you see the desolating sacrilege spoken of by the prophet Daniel, standing in the holy place (let the reader understand), then let those who are in Judea flee to the mountains …

(Matthew 24: 15 RSV)

Identifying the **sources** used in a document like Luke's Gospel is a difficult process. The attempted identification of the sources of documents, including such documents as the four Gospels, is referred to as **source criticism**.

2 The synoptic problem

a) The word synoptic

Prior to the eighteenth century, the tendency was to study the gospels together, as one harmonised story, rather than individually. Then, in the 1770s, the scholar **Johann J. Griesbach** printed the gospels of Matthew, Mark and Luke in three parallel columns, with common material placed adjacently. He called his work a synopsis, which literally means seeing together. From this the term **synoptic** became a popular way of referring to the first three gospels. John's Gospel was not included because the material in it was very different from that of the other three in the **synoptic gospels**. The result of Griesbach's synopsis was to view the gospels as separate works.

b) The synoptic problem

The fact that, prior to Griesbach, the gospels were harmonised shows that the similarities and the differences between the accounts were well known. However, no attempt had been made to investigate the relationship between the gospels. It is not surprising that the gospels share similar outlines of Jesus' life but the close correlation of detail, even to the extent of phraseology, does seem to require an explanation. This close wording is even more striking when it is realised that the agreement is in Greek and Jesus probably spoke in Aramaic, which is the language that replaced Hebrew and was largely spoken by the Jews. There are examples where the gospel-writers have exactly the same phrase in the middle of a narrative (Matthew 9: 6; Mark 2: 10; Luke 5: 24).

Equally, there are some marked differences. Order changes in some places and each gospel has material that is unique to itself. For instance, only Luke has the parable of the good Samaritan.

The synoptic problem is that of determining the inter-relationship between the first three gospels that explains both their similarities and their differences. The similarities are:

- in order, for example, Matthew 12: 46–13: 58; Mark 3: 31–6: 6; Luke 8: 19–56
- in wording, for example, Matthew 24: 4–8; Mark 13: 5–8; Luke 21: 8–11
- in edited or explanatory asides, for example, Matthew 24: 15, Mark 13: 14.

It is a useful process as it enables us to see how the gospel-writers manipulated their written sources.

3 Possible solutions to the synoptic problem

a) One-source solution

Early attempts at explaining the nature of the literary relationship focused on an oral rather than written source. For example, J.G. von Herder (1796) argued for a common oral tradition used by all three synoptic gospel-writers. However, many felt that this did not adequately explain the close wording, which implied some sort of written link between the gospels.

It was not until the eighteenth century that Griesbach proposed a more popular solution. He argued for a simple interdependence, where one gospel was copied by the

KEY WORDS

Source non-specific term that does not make clear whether it is written or oral; in contrast, a document is a written source
Source criticism the attempted identification of the sources of documents
Synoptic *literally* seeing together, identifying similarities between the first three gospels set out in parallel
Synoptic gospels the first three gospels: Matthew, Mark and Luke

KEY PERSON

Johann J. Griesbach (1745–1812), professor of New Testament Studies at the university of Halle and later of Jena, created the first synopsis of the gospels and forwarded the one-source hypothesis as a solution to the synoptic problem.

❝ KEY QUOTE ❞

'But that you may know that the Son of man has authority on earth to forgive sins' – he then said to the paralytic – 'Rise, take up your bed and go home.'

(Matthew 9: 6 RSV)

TASK

How do these passages illustrate the synoptic problem?

- Mark 9: 2–8; Matthew 17: 1–8; Luke 9: 28–36
- Matthew 7: 7–11; Luke 11: 9–13
- Matthew 14: 28–31
- Luke 10: 25–37

Objective To understand the various aspects that make up the synoptic problem

KEY WORDS

Church tradition writings and oral traditions passed down and accepted by the Church
Q source of common sayings

66 KEY QUOTE 99

That evening, at sundown …

(Mark 1: 32 RSV)

KEY PERSON

Heinrich Holtzmann (1832–1910), professor of New Testament Studies in Heidelberg and later of Strassburg, is credited with establishing the two-source theory of the synoptic gospels.

other two. Griesbach suggested that Matthew's Gospel was written first, that Luke used Matthew, and that Mark used both Matthew and Luke. The theory had a number of persuasive arguments.

- **Church tradition**, which endorses writings and oral traditions in the Church, claimed Matthew's Gospel was the first to be written.
- Matthew, being an apostle, would not have used non-apostolic sources such as Mark and Luke.
- Where Matthew and Luke have different versions, Mark includes both, for example, Matthew 8: 16; Luke 4: 40; Mark 1: 32.
- No other unknown sources are necessary to explain the literary interdependence.

However, the theory is not without flaws.

- It disagrees with Church tradition that speaks of Matthew's Gospel being written in Aramaic.
- It disagrees with Church tradition that Mark used Peter's memoirs as his source.
- There is good evidence that Mark's Gospel was the first to be written.
- It does not explain the agreements of Mark and Luke against Matthew.

As a result, this approach has largely been rejected though there has been recent renewed interest in the view that Matthew's Gospel was the first to be written.

b) Two-source solution

The most widely accepted solution to the synoptic problem is the two-source hypothesis. Central to this solution are two claims.

- Mark's Gospel was written first.
- A common sayings source exists or existed.

The theory states that Mark's Gospel was written first and was used independently by Matthew and Luke. In addition, Matthew and Luke used another common source, often referred to as the Lost Sayings Gospel Q or, more simply, **Q**. The scholar **Heinrich Holtzmann** was the first to suggest this solution, in 1863.

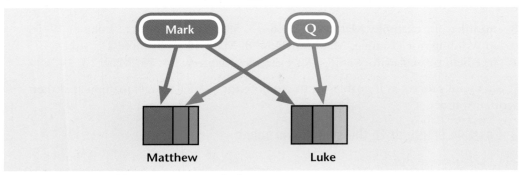

Summary diagram: The two-source solution

i) The priority of Mark

There are a number of reasons why Mark's Gospel is thought to be the first to have been written.

Content

Mark's is the shortest gospel and most of what is in Mark can be found in Matthew and Luke. Mark has 661 verses, Matthew has 1068 and Luke has 1149. Matthew reproduces 97.2% of Mark, and Luke reproduces 88.4% of Mark. That means only 31 verses of Mark are unique. It is usually argued that the shortest gospel is the most likely to be the earliest. It is hard to see why Mark would omit material and then write those stories that are similar in a more wordy form. Also it is possible to explain why Matthew and Luke omitted those 31 verses included by Mark, but it is not clear why Mark should have added them in.

Style

Mark has the poorest command of Greek, which suggests that Matthew and Luke improved on Mark. It is difficult to understand why this should be, if Mark's was not the first gospel. Also, Mark's vocabulary is improved by Matthew and Luke. For example, in Mark's account of the story of the healing of the paralytic who was let down into the room through the roof, the word for bed is a slang word. Both Matthew and Luke use a different word.

Theology

Sayings that create theological difficulty appear in Mark's Gospel but not in Matthew's or Luke's. For example, Mark 6: 6 states that Jesus could do no mighty work in Nazareth. In contrast, Matthew simply says that Jesus did no mighty work there, while Luke omits the observation altogether.

In Mark, Jesus is referred to as Lord only once. Instead, he is almost always referred to as Rabbi. However, the word Lord is used 19 times by Matthew and 16 by Luke.

Order

As far as order is concerned, Matthew and Luke generally follow Mark. When one departs from Mark's order, the other supports it. Luke and Matthew rarely agree against Mark. This suggests that Matthew and Luke have independently relied on Mark.

Editing

A notable characteristic of Mark's Gospel is the use of the word 'immediately', which occurs 41 times in the text. There are 18 occurrences of this word in Matthew's Gospel. However, 14 of them are in the Mark-parallel material, leaving only four occurrences in Matthew's own material. This suggests Matthew has retained that particular usage from Mark's material. It is not a word that Matthew uses himself in the rest of his gospel.

Although one argument by itself may not be convincing, the weight of the argument is in the cumulative effect. Many believe that assuming Matthew and Luke did indeed use Mark's Gospel provides the best solution to the synoptic problem.

ii) Debates about Q

The existence of a source that we do not now have is usually seen as the best explanation for the common material that is found in Matthew and Luke but not in Mark. This consists mainly of sayings and teachings of Jesus. It amounts to about 250 verses and there is often similarity of style. For instance, compare Matthew 23: 37–39 with Luke 13: 34–35.

The label Q is thought to have come from the German *Quelle,* meaning source. Many support the view that Q was a written source, as the agreement in wording between Matthew and Luke is so exact. However, there are always exceptions to this and other scholars are reluctant to accept Q as a single document. These scholars believe that Q may have been a blend of written and oral material.

TASK

The 31 unique verses in Mark consist of the story of Jesus' friends calling him mad, the youth running away in Gethsemane, the parable of the seed growing, healing of the deaf stammerer and a blind man.

What reasons can you think of to explain why Matthew and Luke may have omitted these verses?

Objective To develop understanding of the case for Mark's priority

---

KEY WORD

Quelle (Q) the material common to Matthew and Luke, but not found in Mark, consisting mostly of sayings

KEY WORDS

Gospel of Thomas found in 1945 in Egypt and thought to date back to 200CE, it contains 114 sayings attributed to Jesus

Early Church an ambiguous term used to denote the Church at its inception or through its development in the first five years

Doublets sayings that occur twice in Matthew and twice in Luke, seeming to support the existence of Q since, in both gospels, one of the sayings could be from Mark and one could be from Q

However, it is true to say that a common feature in the material of Q is that it consists of sayings and teaching rather than events. The **Gospel of Thomas**, discovered in Egypt in 1945 and thought to date back to CE200, consists of a collection of sayings of Jesus. Therefore, it seems that it was not unusual for the **Early Church** to make such collections.

Another argument for the existence of Q as an actual document is the existence of **doublets**. These are sayings that occur twice in Matthew and Luke. It is argued that one is from Mark and the second is from Q. For example, the saying: 'He who has, to him will be given,' appears in the Mark parallels (Matthew 13: 12; Mark 4: 25; Luke 8: 18) which suggests the source was Mark. However, it also recurs in Matthew 25: 29 and Luke 19: 26, suggesting a common source to Matthew and Luke, which might be Q.

Though most scholars do not think Matthew and Luke knew each other, they disagree about the nature of the independent source that they shared (Q). Q could be a single written source, or several written sources, or even common oral tradition.

c) The four-source solution

The four-source solution was proposed by **Burnett H. Streeter** in 1924. It assumes that the unique material in Matthew and in Luke comes from two additional written sources called M and L respectively. Streeter argued that M and L were independent sources representing the traditions of the Christian community in Jerusalem (M) and in Caesarea (L). He thought the origins of the M material were traditions preserved by Jewish Christians associated with James, the brother of Jesus. The M material includes the parables of the labourers in the vineyard and the pearl of great price. Streeter did not include the birth narratives (Matthew 1–2). He thought they were from a different source.

The L material includes the parables of the good Samaritan and the prodigal son but again excludes Luke's birth narratives (Chapters 1–2).

d) Criticisms of the four-source solution

There are several issues that the theory does not resolve.

KEY PERSON

Burnett H. Streeter (1874–1937), a Fellow of Queen's College, Oxford, contributed to biblical scholarship by his work on textual criticism and his four-source theory.

- **Agreements of Matthew and Luke against Mark** – There are some 272 agreements. Matthew and Luke are said to have been independent and have both used Mark. It seems unlikely that they would both agree against Mark.
- **Omissions in Matthew and Luke from Mark** – The theory does not explain why there are sections of Mark missing from either Matthew or Luke. This implies that Mark was not their source
- **The Q hypothesis is doubtful** – The fact that Matthew and Luke have common material, not found in Mark, could be explained away with equal ease if, instead, Matthew had copied Luke or Luke had copied Matthew. There are no historical traces of an actual document such as Q, nor are there any ancient references to it. This seems strange.

- **Mark's being the first gospel is doubtful** – Tradition has always favoured Matthew's Gospel as being the first and renewed interest has arisen in this view through the work of B. Butler and W. Farmer.

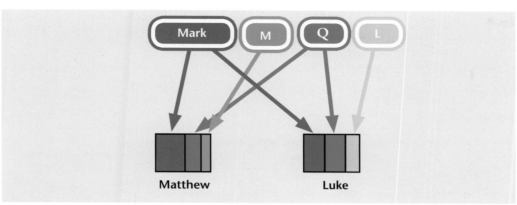

Summary diagram: The four-source solution

Reflection and assessment AO1

It is vital to bring together the information you have covered so far and recognise how it can be transformed into effective examination-style revision and answers. The best way to do this is to ask the question: 'How am I going to be assessed on this information?'

The first way is through assessment objective 1 (AO1). For this objective we need to be able to 'select and clearly demonstrate the relevant knowledge and understanding through the use of evidence, examples and correct language and terminology'.

Look back to page 7 in the Introduction to review the level descriptors for AO1. There is a description of the character and features for each level. The exam is marked with reference to levels.

Look at the following sample answer (overleaf), which is a response to the question:

Explain the case for Markan priority. (25 marks)

The remarks were made by an examiner.

KEY QUOTE

... while there is nothing improbable in the desire to write a shorter gospel, only a lunatic would leave out Matthew's account of the infancy, the sermon on the mount and practically all the parables in order to get room for purely verbal expansion of what was retained.

(B.H. Streeter)

EXAM TIP

When you illustrate a point, make sure that you explain the illustration and, in particular, how it does illustrate or support the point you are making. This demonstrates selection of clear, relevant knowledge and understanding through use of example (AO1).

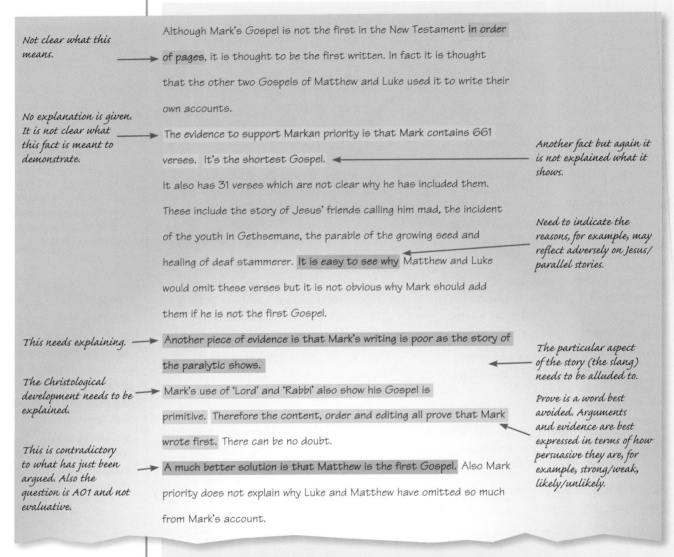

Not clear what this means.

Although Mark's Gospel is not the first in the New Testament in order of pages, it is thought to be the first written. In fact it is thought that the other two Gospels of Matthew and Luke used it to write their own accounts.

No explanation is given. It is not clear what this fact is meant to demonstrate.

The evidence to support Markan priority is that Mark contains 661 verses. It's the shortest Gospel.

Another fact but again it is not explained what it shows.

It also has 31 verses which are not clear why he has included them. These include the story of Jesus' friends calling him mad, the incident of the youth in Gethsemane, the parable of the growing seed and healing of deaf stammerer. It is easy to see why Matthew and Luke would omit these verses but it is not obvious why Mark should add them if he is not the first Gospel.

Need to indicate the reasons, for example, may reflect adversely on Jesus/ parallel stories.

This needs explaining.

Another piece of evidence is that Mark's writing is poor as the story of the paralytic shows.

The particular aspect of the story (the slang) needs to be alluded to.

The Christological development needs to be explained.

Mark's use of 'Lord' and 'Rabbi' also show his Gospel is primitive. Therefore the content, order and editing all prove that Mark wrote first. There can be no doubt.

Prove is a word best avoided. Arguments and evidence are best expressed in terms of how persuasive they are, for example, strong/weak, likely/unlikely.

This is contradictory to what has just been argued. Also the question is AO1 and not evaluative.

A much better solution is that Matthew is the first Gospel. Also Mark priority does not explain why Luke and Matthew have omitted so much from Mark's account.

TASK

Using this structure, now write a level 4 answer.

Objective To be able to 'select and demonstrate clearly relevant knowledge' (AO1 descriptor) and working towards a 'good selection of material' (level 4 descriptor)

So what does it score?

In the exam the answer will be marked according to levels (see page 7 in the Introduction). Certainly, the candidate has some knowledge and understanding but it is only partial since the response lacks explanation. Examiners cannot award marks for material that the candidate may well know, and even hint at knowing but does not include. The essay lacks clear order, given that the question demands a systematic coverage of the evidence. It is typical of a bordering level 1.

It would not take much to develop this essay into a level 4 response. The problem is that, as it stands, the candidate has left it to the examiner to work out what the stated facts demonstrate.

As with most topics for AO1, there is a risk that candidates will launch into more depth than is required, when the question is not aimed at AO2. This question asked only for the evidence in support. No marks are awarded in this case for challenges to that evidence.

Suggestion for further application of skills

As a group, explain:

- the one-source solution
- the two-source solution
- debates about Q
- the four-source solution.

Working individually or in small groups, divide up the tasks and take charge of one area. Spend 15 minutes on this and then swap notes with another group (or person) for them to add or rework your initial outline. Continue swapping notes and reworking until you are all satisfied that you have a sufficiently good description to present as an examination answer for each area.

Part 3

A critical analysis of the issues

What are the issues that I am expected to consider and to analyse critically?

- The issues arising from a study of the setting of the gospels
- The issues arising from the findings of source criticism of the synoptic gospels

1 Issues arising from a study of the setting of the gospels

a) Monotheism or henotheism?

It has been argued that the Torah takes a position not of **monotheism** but of **henotheism**. This worship of one special god of one's tribe or clan does not deny the existence of other gods of other tribes. God reveals himself not as the only God, but rather as the god whom Abraham knows (Gen 15: 7). This portrays the God who was worshipped by Abraham as more of a tribal deity. The fact that he alone was worshipped did not explicitly exclude the existence of other gods. A similar idea could be read into such passages as Exodus 18: 11 and 2 Chronicles 2: 5, where Israel claims that their God is the greatest. However, by the time of the prophet Isaiah, monotheism seems to have been accepted explicitly.

> **This is what the Lord says – Israel's King and Redeemer, the Lord Almighty: 'I am the first and I am the last; apart from me there is no God'.**
>
> (Isaiah 44: 6)

Thus, the movement of the people of Israel towards monotheism appears to be a gradual process.

Contradicting this view of a gradual acceptance of monotheism are texts such as Genesis 1: 1 where God is depicted as sole creator of the universe. Similarly, in Deuteronomy 4: 39 there seems an unequivocal claim that there is only one God: 'Acknowledge and take heart this day that the Lord is God in heaven above and on the earth below. There is no other.'

b) Pharisees – unfairly depicted?

In the gospels there are some strong criticisms of the Pharisees by Jesus. In particular, Matthew 23 lists a succession of woes (seven in all) against the Pharisees, which culminate in:

> **Therefore you are witnesses against yourselves that you are sons of those who murdered the prophets. Fill up, then, the measure of your fathers' guilt. Serpents, brood of vipers! How can you escape the condemnation of hell?**
>
> (Matthew 23: 31–33)

KEY WORDS

Monotheism the belief or doctrine that there is only one god
Henotheism the worship of one god as the special god of one's tribe or clan

KEY QUESTIONS

- Did the Jews believe in more than one God?
- Was the move to monotheism by the Jews a gradual step?

❝ KEY QUOTE ❞

In the beginning God created the heavens and the Earth.

(Genesis 1: 1)

Jesus' accusations centred on the areas of teaching and practice. Jesus accused them of hypocrisy and pretentiousness. The gospels also present some positive aspects of Pharisaism. For instance, the Pharisee Nicodemus features positively. There were also various occasions when Pharisees showed Jesus hospitality.

What Pharisaism attempted to do was to bring every area of life into subjection to the law. They had a longing for a righteous Israel and the hope of the coming Messianic kingdom. They felt God was about to do a great work and so they sought to turn the people back to the law as the means by which the kingdom would come. However, they became self-righteous and self-satisfied and proud of their law-keeping, but lost the spirit of the law, getting too caught up in its minute detail. It is not surprising that the Pharisees saw Jesus as a threat.

c) Zealots – wrongly identified?

There has been a tendency in the past to equate the Zealots with a group that Josephus referred to as 'holding a fourth philosophy'. Josephus commented that this group had, as its founder, the teacher Judas the Galilean who led a revolt in CE6.

Such an identification of the Zealots as a separate fourth party, who continually led rebellions against the Romans, has been challenged. Josephus only mentions the Zealots by name when describing the Jewish revolt (CE66). Their formation seems more a reaction to pilfering from the Temple treasury by the Roman Procurator Florus. The response of the priests and people to this pilfering was to terminate the sacrifices offered twice each day on behalf of Rome and the Roman Emperor. In political terms, such action amounted to a declaration of war on the Romans. The Zealots became a recognisable group during the course of this action. They were not so much a separate party but consisted of anyone who believed in fighting against the Romans, in the name of Israel's God and of his law. If they are seen in this light, then members of other Jewish parties could be labelled Zealots if they took to arms in this cause.

Masada, a city on a hill

d) Essenes – Qumran community?

Much that is written about the Essenes is based on the findings about the community that lived beside the Dead Sea at Qumran. **Pliny the younger** states that there was a group of Essenes at the Dead Sea. The Qumran excavations are the only evidence that has been found of a community existing in that area. Scrolls found at Qumran, and other remains such as baptismal pools, indicate that whoever lived there held beliefs that were similar to those of the Essenes. This is why some link the Essenes to Qumran.

KEY QUESTIONS
- Were the Pharisees hypocrites?
- Was Jesus unfair to condemn the Pharisees?
- Why did the Pharisees see Jesus as a threat?
- Were the Zealots the fourth party?
- Were the Zealots a separate party?

TASK

Find out what Masada has to do with Zealots and why members of the present-day Israeli army go there to be sworn in.
Objective To develop understanding of the Roman occupation

KEY PERSON

Pliny the younger (CE61–113), a Roman official and writer famous for his letters, which are an important source for Roman history. His letters also contain the earliest external account of Christian worship and reasons for the execution of Christians.

KEY QUESTION

Were the Qumran community Essenes?

However, not all the evidence is consistent with the Qumran community being an Essene community. It is possible that the Sadducean party based in Jerusalem was responsible for the writing of the scrolls. In addition to this, Pliny, who referred to the Essenes in the Dead Sea area, is thought to have been citing a community that post-dated the Jewish revolt, whereas the Qumran excavations suggest a date prior to the Jewish revolt. If our only evidence for the existence of Essenes at Qumran is from Pliny, then we have to accept that the evidence is far from conclusive.

TASK

Do some research about the finding of the Dead Sea Scrolls at Qumran.

Find out about the archaeological findings at Qumran and assess whether you think they indicate that an Essene community lived there.

Objective To gain further background understanding to the New Testament and the significance of the discovery of the Dead Sea Scrolls

The caves at Qumran where the Dead Sea Scrolls were discovered

2 Possible conclusions

When assessing the issues that arise in New Testament gospel background, it is important to reflect upon the arguments previously discussed and arrive at some appropriate conclusion. It may be that you accept none of these listed here, or just one of them, or you may have a different conclusion that is not listed. However, what is important is the way that you have arrived at your conclusion – the reasoning process.

From the preceding discussions, here are some possible conclusions you could draw.

1 The traditional New Testament gospel background picture of Jewish monotheism and the four major religious groups is correct and accurate. The evidence is reliable.

2 The traditional New Testament gospel background picture of Jewish monotheism and the four major religious groups is not accurate in all its details.

3 We simply do not possess enough reliable information to make a judgement about whether the traditional New Testament gospel background picture of Jewish monotheism and the four major religious groups is accurate.

3 Critical assessment of the findings of source criticism of synoptic Gospels

a) Alternatives to the four-source theory

i) Matthew's Gospel was the first
The majority of scholarship has favoured Mark's as the first gospel to have been written. However, there has been renewed interest in the theory that Matthew's Gospel was the

first. The debate was reopened in 1951 by Chapman and Butler, two Roman Catholic scholars, and has gained support, particularly through the writings of William Farmer. Butler suggested that Matthew wrote his gospel in Aramaic. This was then used by Peter in his preaching and Mark wrote down Peter's preaching, including his eye-witness touches. Matthew's Gospel was then translated into Greek and Luke used both Matthew and Mark.

It is argued that just because Matthew's parallels to Mark are shorter, it does not demand that Matthew therefore abbreviated Mark. It could be that Mark embellished the account with eye-witness touches.

It is also claimed that Mark shows knowledge of Matthew and so must have been written after Matthew. For example, Mark's reference to 'in the house' (Mark 9: 33) only makes sense if you look at the Matthew parallel (Matthew 17: 24–27), where the house is identified in a passage not paralleled in Mark.

It was also the Early Church tradition that Matthew's was the first gospel. Such a view is consistent with the fact that Matthew's Gospel seems written for Jews whereas Mark's seems written for Gentiles. Given that it was Jews who formed the bulk of the Early Church membership, it seems more likely that the first gospel would be written for them.

ii) A more fluid inter-relationship

Source criticism has tended to take the view that one gospel simply used another. However, such a view has been challenged, notably by **John Robinson**. He argued that, within a short space of time after the death of Jesus, there would have been a multitude of information circulating about him. As well as oral information there would be a growing body of written material. The gospel-writers would have been part of the developing situation and the writings would have passed through a number of different stages. In other words, it may be impossible to disentangle the sources of any of the synoptic gospels as they were collecting from a vast array of data. Hence John Robinson argued for a less sequential view of the inter-relationship of the gospels and, instead, favoured a more fluid inter-relationship.

4 Possible conclusions

When assessing the issues that arise from source criticism, it is important to reflect upon the arguments previously discussed and arrive at some appropriate conclusion. It may be that you accept none of these listed here, or just one of them, or you may have a different conclusion that is not listed. However, what is important is the way that you have arrived at your conclusion – the reasoning process.

From the preceding discussions, here are some possible conclusions you could draw.

1   The three gospel-writers collaborated. They shared sources and they shared information.

2   Two of the gospel-writers relied, at least partly, on the first gospel-writer.

3   One or more of the gospel-writers relied not only on the first gospel-writer but also on another source or sources as well.

4   The third gospel-writer wrote a summary of the other two gospels.

5   The gospel-writers wrote more or less independently of each other, using first- or second-hand information.

6   The gospel-writers wrote more or less independently but relied on oral tradition.

 KEY QUESTION

Was Matthew's Gospel the first?

 KEY PERSON

John Robinson (1919–83), Bishop of Woolwich, became famous for his controversial book, *Honest to God,* which challenged traditional views about God. His book, *Redating the New Testament* was, in contrast, very conservative and argued that John's Gospel was the earliest.

EXAM TIP

Remember that evaluation involves the process of reasoning. Good answers will display a sustained argument rather than just presenting a list of points. This demonstrates justifying a point of view through reasoned argument (AO2).

Reflection and assessment AO2

Earlier in this topic you considered the assessment objective AO1 focused on knowledge and understanding. The second way of being assessed is through assessment objective AO2. For this objective you need to be able to sustain a critical line of argument and justify a point of view.

As you work through each unit in this book, you will find that the amount of support in these sections will gradually be reduced, in order to encourage your independence and the perfecting of your AO2 skills.

Use the writing frame provided below to help you answer the question:

'The synoptic problem remains unsolved.' Discuss. (10 marks)

Key points

Always point out the case in support of the concept and the case against the concept.

■ Always respond to and assess each point as you proceed through the answer so you show critical analysis.
■ Avoid just listing points.
■ Always use juxtaposition and integrate the views so you show engagement.
■ Keep relating the material back to the focus of the discussion.
■ Always give a clear weighing up leading to an appropriate conclusion, even if the conclusion is that both sides are equal.
■ Remember that the case against can include better alternatives as well as weaknesses of the case in support.

Writing frame

The synoptic problem is the problem of ...

The most popular solution is the four-source theory. This theory states ...

It solves the problem by ...

There is good evidence to support it, for instance ...

However, it is not without its critics. Possibly the strongest challenge to this solution is ...

As a result other solutions have been suggested. One such suggestion is ...

This solves the problem by ...

It also addresses the challenge raised to the four-source theory because it ...

However, it also is not without its challenges. For instance ...

John Robinson has drawn attention to this narrow approach of linear sources. He suggested that the relationship between the gospels is ...

Therefore, to say that the synoptic problem remains unsolved is ...

Although quite basic, this writing frame does focus on critical analysis. It is better to deal with three or four criticisms in some detail, than to compile a longer list with very brief comment. It is important also to make clear in what way your criticism challenges the argument or view.

Suggestion for further application of skills

Construct your own writing frame for the question:

'The gospels do not give an accurate portrayal of the Pharisees.' Discuss.

(10 marks)

Part 1

The writer

> **What am I required to study?**
> ■ Mark's Gospel
>
> **This means I am expected to know about:**
> ■ the authorship of this gospel
> ■ the date of Mark's Gospel
> ■ the historical accuracy of Mark's Gospel.

This section studies areas about the writer of Mark's Gospel and considers the questions of authorship, date and historical accuracy. It is expected that you will have first-hand knowledge of Mark's Gospel, where relevant to these issues. The introductory issues in Part 1 and Part 2 of this topic are inter-related. Hence there is some overlap with the material. Often this involves looking at the external evidence. This is evidence drawn from sources other than the gospel itself. It usually includes quotations from Early Church writings. Internal evidence is derived from the contents of the gospel itself.

It would be helpful to write your notes under the headings listed under 'This means I am expected to know about', as it is from these areas that the exam questions will be derived.

Remember that your studies will include elements of the *two* basic assessment objectives of:

■ Knowledge and Understanding (AO1)
■ Evaluation (AO2).

See pages 7–8 in the Introduction to remind yourself of these objectives.

The evaluation material is set out in Part 3 of this topic (page 230) and can be studied either alongside the AO1 material, as you work through this topic, or as a discrete topic.

1 Who wrote Mark's Gospel?

The gospel itself is anonymous. We know that early in the second century it was already being linked to Mark.

a) Who did the Early Church think wrote it?

Early Christian testimony has been unanimous in claiming that a person called Mark was the author, and also connects this Mark with Peter in the production of the gospel. The earliest document supporting Mark's authorship is found in the writings of **Papias**, who wrote around CE120. Although we no longer have Papias' writings, they are cited

KEY PERSON

Papias (CE70/75–163), Bishop of Hierapolis, has become well known because of fragments of his writings that are quoted by later writers and relate to the Apostolic Age.

KEY WORD

Apostolic Age the time of the twelve apostles, from the time of Jesus' death and resurrection to the Fall of Jerusalem in CE70; the period is detailed, in part, in the book of the Acts of the Apostles

by **Eusebius** and claim that Papias had been informed of Peter's connection with Mark's Gospel by an Elder:

> **And this is what the Elder said, 'Mark, who became Peter's interpreter, accurately wrote, though not in order, as many of the things said and done by the Lord as he had noted.'**

It is not clear who the Elder is but, if the citing from Papias is correct, it would mean that this tradition probably dates from the first century.

Given that Peter is also connected to the production of this gospel, it is interesting that it was not attributed to Peter, since Peter would be a highly respected authority. This adds weight to the argument that Mark is the author.

The link with Peter is said to be supported in this gospel. Peter is the first disciple to be mentioned and is portrayed as a member of Jesus' inner circle. Bearing in mind the different lengths of the gospels, proportionately Peter is mentioned more times in Mark than in Matthew or Luke. Peter's house is mentioned five times in Mark, and Andrew is identified as Simon's brother.

The inclusion of eye-witness touches in Mark's Gospel, including incidental details and characters, as in Mark 6: 39, again supports the link with Peter.

b) Who is this Mark?

If the Papias citation is accepted as reliable, and Mark is seen as the author, then it is generally agreed that this Mark is the same person as the John Mark mentioned in Acts 12: 12, 25; 13: 5, 13; 15: 37–39.

It is true that Mark was a common name, but it is unlikely that the Early Church would assign a gospel to a minor figure such as John Mark, unless he was the actual author.

c) Problems with the traditional view

- Many scholars do not accept the Papias citation as a reliable representation of the gospel's authorship.
- It is possible that Papias was referring to Q rather than Mark's Gospel.
- Tradition has argued that Matthew's Gospel was the first to be written. If this is so, we have to ask why Mark would use both Matthew and Peter as sources.
- It is argued that there is no distinctive **Petrine** tradition in Mark.
- The material in Mark is composed of units that received their form in the life of the community (see page 222), not from Peter.
- John Mark lived in Palestine. However, it is claimed that there are passages in Mark's Gospel that suggest it was written by someone who did not have a good knowledge of the geography of Palestine.
- The first identification of Mark with John Mark as the author does not appear until **Jerome** (CE350–420).

KEY PERSON

Eusebius (CE265–339?), Bishop of Caesarea, whose writings quote the works of Papias.

❝ KEY QUOTE ❞

Then Jesus directed them to have all the people sit down in groups on the green grass.

(Mark 6: 39)

TASK

What can we learn about John Mark from the New Testament? Acts 12: 12, 25; 13: 13; 15: 37–39; 2 Timothy 4: 11; Colossians 4: 10; Philemon 2: 4; 1 Peter 5: 13
Only Mark includes the incident recorded in Mark 14: 51–52. Can you suggest reasons why?
Objective To investigate further the question of the authorship identification with John Mark

KEY WORD

Petrine of or relating to Peter

KEY PERSON

Jerome (CE347–420), was a biblical scholar who translated the Bible into Latin. This translation is known as the *Vulgate*.

d) Alternatives to the traditional view

Suggestions include:

- Mark, the companion of Peter (1 Peter 5: 13) who, it is argued, is a different person from John Mark
- an unknown person whom was referred to as Mark in later tradition.

Summary diagram: how external evidence traces the author as Mark
Now show, in a diagram, the internal evidence, which is evidence drawn from the contents of Mark's Gospel.

External evidence is evidence drawn from sources other than Mark's Gospel itself. Often, as here, it is fragments from the writings of the Early Church fathers, who were the leaders of the Early Church.

2 When was the gospel written?

a) When did the Early Church think it was written?

According to earliest tradition, which is the writings of **Irenaeus** (CE160/180), Mark wrote after Peter's death in Rome. This would place the date of the gospel as some time after CE64–65.

Another early tradition from **Clement of Alexandria**, cited by Eusebius, states that the writing of the gospel took place during Peter's time in Rome. This would put the date somewhere between CE45 and CE65.

Most scholars tend to favour the earlier tradition of Irenaeus, placing the date of writing of the gospel after CE65. The debate then moves to the question of whether the writing was before or after the fall of Jerusalem (CE70). To answer this question, scholars turn their attention to the gospel itself.

b) The abomination of desolation

In Mark 13: 14 there is a reference to the 'abomination of desolation', being set up where it ought not to be. This is taken to refer to the defilement of the Temple at the fall of Jerusalem in CE70. Some scholars see it as a prophecy inserted by Mark during the time of the siege, when Mark guessed that the Temple would be defiled. Such a view would place the dating of the gospel somewhere in the period CE65–70.

Further support for dating the gospel just prior to the fall of Jerusalem is in the references to suffering and persecution (see page 226). These are seen to depict events during CE60–70.

c) The traditional date questioned

Many scholars question the evidence for a date of CE65–70.

- The Early Church traditions disagree with each other.
- The reference to the destruction of the Temple in CE70 in Mark 13 is too obscure to be of any relevance.
- Jesus could have made the prediction, rather than what is claimed: that Mark made it and added it in. In this case the reference tells us nothing about the date the gospel was written.

KEY PERSON

Irenaeus (born circa CE130), Bishop of Lyons, wrote extensively opposing heretical doctrines and teachings.

KEY PERSON

Clement of Alexandria (CE150–215?), united Greek philosophical traditions with Christian doctrine. He wanted to demonstrate that Christianity was intellectually respectable.

d) Alternative dates

i) Earlier date

■ The evidence here rests on the findings of source criticism. If Acts was written by CE63 and Luke's Gospel was written earlier than that (Luke and Acts are seen as a two-volume work, see Luke 1: 1–4 and Acts 1: 1–2), then, according to the two- or four-source theory, Luke used Mark's Gospel. This would put the date of Mark before CE60.

■ Recent evidence from the scrolls of Qumran has added support for an early date. It is claimed that a fragment from Mark 6: 52–53, found at Qumran, would imply that a copy of Mark's Gospel existed and had circulated by, at the latest, CE68 (when Qumran was destroyed). This would seem to require a date earlier than CE65 for the writing of Mark.

ii) Later date

■ This has very little support from scholars. One scholar who has argued for a date after CE70 is S. Brandon, in *The Date of the Markan Gospel*. He saw the reason for the writing of the Gospel as the need for Roman Christians to have a version that dissociated Jesus from the Jerusalem Jews. Brandon argued that there was a need to separate Christianity from Judaism in the light of Rome's attitude about Jews after their revolt in Jerusalem.

■ A later date is also possible according to the findings of source criticism. If Mark was used by Matthew and Luke, this would still allow a date for Mark before CE80, since the dating of Matthew and Luke are usually placed later than that.

3 Historical accuracy

If source criticism is correct and Mark's is the gospel that the other gospel-writers used as a source, then it would have been important to such writers that Mark's account was reliable and accurate. If John Mark was the author of Mark's Gospel then, as someone who lived in Palestine, he would have known the geography of Palestine and the Jewish rituals very well. However, doubts have been raised about Mark's accuracy on three different grounds.

a) Geographical errors

■ Mark 5: 1 – The city of Gerasa was 30 miles away from the traditional location where Jesus healed Legion. Hence, the reference to the 'region of the Gerasenes' is said to be inaccurate. Alternative place names appear in manuscripts, none of which can be identified with present-day sites that might fit in with the location of the story of the miracle healing in which pigs fall down the cliffs into the Sea of Galilee.

■ Mark 6: 45 – There is no known place called Bethsaida on the shores of the Sea of Galilee.

■ Mark 7: 31 – Sidon is not on a direct route from Tyre to the Sea of Galilee. Nineham, in his commentary on Mark's Gospel, likens the route to a man travelling from Cornwall to London via Manchester.

■ Mark 11: 1 – Bethphage and Bethany are given in the reverse order to that in which travellers from Jericho would reach them. It could be argued that Mark did not know the positions of the two villages on the Jericho road.

" KEY QUOTES "

When you see 'the abomination that causes desolation' standing where it does not belong – let the reader understand – then let those who are in Judea flee to the mountains.

(Mark 13: 14)

They went across the lake to the region of the Gerasenes.

(Mark 5: 1)

Immediately Jesus made his disciples get into the boat and go on ahead of him to Bethsaida, while he dismissed the crowds.

(Mark 6: 45)

Then Jesus left the vicinity of Tyre and went through Sidon, down to the Sea of Galilee, and into the region of Decapolis.

(Mark 7: 31)

As they approached Jerusalem and came to Bethphage and Bethany at the Mount of Olives ...

(Mark 11: 1)

KEY QUOTES

> The Pharisees and all the Jews do not eat unless they give their hands a ceremonial washing, holding to the traditions of the elders.
>
> (Mark 7: 3)
>
> On the first day of the Feast of Unleavened Bread, when it was customary to sacrifice the Passover lamb ...
>
> (Mark 14: 12)

b) Jewish ritual errors

Again, if John Mark was the author he would have known about Jewish ritual customs. Commentators highlight two possible errors in the gospel.

- Mark 7: 3 – It is argued that ceremonial washing was only obligatory for the priests. The Pharisee was only concerned about defilement when entering the Temple or making a sacrifice. Not until about CE100 did ritual washing become obligatory for all.
- Mark 14: 12 – Some have argued that this shows some confusion about the dates. The lamb was slaughtered during the afternoon of the Passover meal. Technically speaking, this was the day before, since Jews reckoned that the day ended at 6pm. Mark seems unaware of this and refers to it as the same day.

c) Chronological errors

Biblical criticism portrays Mark's Gospel as a collection of stories and sayings of Jesus that seem artificially linked, without much regard for chronological accuracy. It is claimed that the Early Church selected and shaped oral material to meet the needs and situations within their community. The gospel-writer merely collected these units and strung them together. However, the historical setting and chronology have been dropped, so the links and placements are artificial. The writer himself was responsible for the ordering of the units in the gospel.

The view that the events in the gospel are not in chronological order is supported by the Papias extract, in which he claims that Mark wrote accurately what Peter remembered, but not in order. Papias explains that Mark's method of composition was to collect the traditions used by Peter in his preaching. The order did not matter.

 KEY WORDS

Sitz im leben literally life situation; the Early Church used particular material to meet particular needs and situations within their community, often taking the material out of its original context; refers to these possible Early Church circumstances
Oral period the period when the stories and sayings were passed around only by word of mouth; the period of verbal transmission, before the words were written down

 KEY IDEA

The Early Church shaping material

Jesus is recorded as saying and doing many things, but not all that he said and did is written down. Some things were passed on and some things were not. Those that were passed on were passed on for a reason. They were used in and for particular situations. For instance, maybe the story or words were passed on because they could be used to convince people to become Christian.

When something has a particular audience, situation or purpose it is called a *sitz im leben* – literally a life situation. Thus, this book has a life situation – to help students studying for the OCR religious studies New Testament exam at AS level.

Similarly, Jesus' words had an original *sitz im leben*: the circumstances for – and in which – he spoke them. Those words were then used again by the Early Church, sometimes in a different situation and for a different purpose. This was known as the oral period, before the words were written down. This is now the second *sitz im leben*. A third *sitz im leben* was when the writers incorporated these stories and teachings into their gospels and used them to address yet another situation and purpose, for example, Luke writing to non-Jews.

So modern biblical criticism has identified three stages of transmission through which the words and events of Jesus may have passed. One of the debates about this view concerns the extent to which the stories changed (either deliberately or accidentally) as they were transmitted.

CE30		CE60+	CE70+
Jesus	Oral period	Mark's Gospel	Matthew and Luke's gospels
Speaks to crowds or individuals	Word of mouth Unconnected units Shaped by usage	Units collected	Used Mark and special sources
1st *sitz im leben*	2nd *sitz im leben*	3rd *sitz im leben*	

A timeline showing the growth of the Early Church

d) Conclusions

Many scholars question these claims of errors in Mark's Gospel, pointing out that we know very little about Palestine during the time of Jesus. The supposed errors may actually be due to our lack of knowledge. They will have to be weighed against the conclusions about authorship and date. It should also be remembered that the other gospels follow Mark's Gospel. If we are to believe Luke's claims in Luke 1: 1–4, then it would suggest they independently supported Mark's general outline and order of events.

Reflection and assessment AO1

It is vital to bring together the information you have covered so far and recognise how it can be transformed into effective examination-style revision and answers. The best way to do this is to ask the question: 'How am I going to be assessed on this information?'

The first way is through assessment objective 1 (AO1). For this objective you need to be able to 'select and clearly demonstrate the relevant knowledge and understanding through the use of evidence, examples and correct language and terminology'.

Look back to page 7 in the Introduction to review the level descriptors for AO1. There is a description of the character and features for each level. The exam is marked with reference to levels.

Look at the following sample level 2 answer, which is a response to the question:

Explain the problems of the authorship of Mark's Gospel. (25 marks)

> The traditional author for Mark's Gospel is John Mark. The problem is that Mark was a common name so it is not clear which Mark is being identified. External evidence links the author to a Mark who was Peter's interpreter. Certainly this seems to fit as there are many eye-witness touches in the gospel.
>
> But who is this Mark? The reference to John Mark in the New Testament appears in the Acts of the Apostles. He is a minor figure. Some identify him in the story of the boy in the garden of Gethsemane who flees (only recorded in Mark's Gospel). However, there were other Marks, such as the one mentioned in 1 Peter, who is a companion of Peter.
>
> The title of the gospel is 'Gospel according to Mark', which supports the view that someone called Mark is the author. This title dates from the end of the first century. Hence there is another problem of the time gap.

Now complete the task on the next page.

TASK

Read Mark chapters 2–3. Examine the links between the different stories. Do you think Mark's Gospel is unreliable? How does this issue affect other areas discussed in this unit?

Objective To bring together the various sections of this topic and appreciate their inter-relationship

TASK

What makes this a level 2 answer?

Identify ways in which you could improve this answer.

Now write your own answer to the same question, aimed at level 4–5.

Objective To develop awareness of the characteristics of a good answer by gradually building up a response

Suggestion for further application of skills

Look again at the discussion about when Mark's Gospel was written. Without support of notes or text, allow yourself about 15 minutes to try answering the question:

Explain the problems of dating Mark's Gospel. (25 marks)

You should now have a basic answer that you can develop. In pairs or groups, share answers and select one to use for development. Identify ways in which you could improve this answer. Then write your own comments analysis to the question you did. Write up your answer, aiming at level 4–5.

Part 2
The readers

> **What am I required to study?**
> - Mark's Gospel
>
> **This means I am expected to know about:**
> - the setting of Mark's Gospel
> - the intended readership
> - the purpose of Mark's Gospel.

This section looks at questions about the readership of Mark's Gospel. It considers the circumstances of the writing of Mark's Gospel. For whom did Mark write his gospel? Why did he write it? You will be expected to have first-hand knowledge of Mark's Gospel where passages are relevant to these issues. The introductory issues in Part 1 and Part 2 of this topic are inter-related. Hence, there is some overlap with the material. Often this involves looking at external evidence, which is evidence drawn from sources other than the gospel itself. This usually includes quotations from Early Church writings. Internal evidence is evidence derived from the contents of the gospel itself.

It would be helpful to write your notes under the headings listed under 'This means I am expected to know about', as it is from these areas that the exam questions will be derived.

Remember that your studies will include elements of the *two* basic assessment objectives of:

- Knowledge and Understanding (AO1)
- Evaluation (AO2).

See pages 7–8 in the Introduction to remind yourself of these objectives.

The evaluation material is set out in Part 3 of this topic (page 230) and can be studied either alongside the AO1 material, as you work through this topic, or as a discrete topic.

1 The setting of Mark's Gospel

a) Where, according to the Early Church, did Mark write his gospel?

Papias claims that Mark was Peter's interpreter. Tradition claims that Peter was martyred in Rome, so this implies a Roman location.

Another Early Church source, the *Anti-Marcionite Prologue* (CE180) is very specific and says that Mark wrote in Italy. Indeed, there seems to be general agreement among other Early Church sources that Rome was the place of writing.

KEY IDEA

Marcionites were a heretical sect founded by Marcion in CE144 in Rome. They rejected the writings of the Old Testament. They taught that Christ was the Son of the good God, who was different from the God of the Jews.

KEY QUOTE

She who is in Babylon, chosen together with you, sends you her greetings, and so does my son Mark.

(1 Peter 5: 13)

KEY WORDS

Latinisms Latin words that have been transliterated into Greek characters; transliteration refers to transcribing words written in one alphabet or writing system into another. Aramaic a semitic language, spoken by Jesus, that is closely related to Hebrew and gradually replaced it amongst the Jews

KEY QUOTES

He took her by the hand and said to her: 'Taltha Koum!' (which means 'Little girl! I say to you, get up!').

(Mark 5: 41)

But a poor widow came and put in two very small copper coins, worth only a fraction of a penny.

(Mark 12: 42)

A certain man from Cyrene, Simon, the father of Alexander and Rufus, was passing by on his way from the country, and they forced him to carry the cross.

(Mark 15: 21)

The reference to Mark in 1 Peter 5: 13 suggests Mark is connected with Rome, if the reference to Babylon is understood to relate to Rome.

b) Does Mark's Gospel itself suggest Rome as its place of origin?

Scholars supporting the place of origin as Rome argue that there is some evidence in the gospel itself that is consistent with such a view.

- There are several references to suffering and persecution, for example, in Mark 8: 34–38, 10: 38f, 13: 9–13. Many see these as referring to Nero's persecutions that took place in Rome.
- Mark's Gospel, like all the New Testament, is written in Greek. Mark has some **latinisms**, which are Latin words that have been transferred into Greek characters. Some scholars see this as evidence of a Roman origin since the gospel appears to be addressed to Latin speakers and these were found mostly in Italy. It is difficult to appreciate this argument because it is based on the subtlety of the Greek language. An example would be the word for centurion. The Latin is *centurio* and Mark uses that root word, written in Greek characters. Matthew and Luke, however, use a different Greek word.
- Mark's Gospel appears to have gained authority quickly. If it was associated with the Roman Church, this would explain why.

c) Alternative places of origin

Various alternative places have been suggested, but there is little evidence to support any of them. Some scholars have pointed out that the evidence for a Roman origin is also weak. The references to persecution are very general and could refer to any persecution. Latinisms were used in various parts of the Roman Empire.

It is important to remember that this issue is related to questions about authorship and date and readership. If Roman origin is rejected, then the question of its place of writing remains unclear.

2 The intended readers of Mark's Gospel

The task of identifying the intended readership is inter-related with other questions discussed above and in Part 1 of this topic. However, if Mark's Gospel was written in Rome it seems likely, though not certain, that its readers lived in Rome.

There is some support for this in the gospel itself.

- **Aramaic** expressions are explained, for example, in Mark 5: 41, which implies that the readers would not have understood them. This fits in with a Roman audience who would not have understood Aramaic.
- The readers seem to have been Gentiles, since Mark often explains Jewish terms and customs, for example in Mark 7: 3 and 12: 42.
- Things that Jews in Jerusalem would have known are assumed to be unknown. For instance, the location of the Mount of Olives in relation to the Temple is pointed out for the readers (Mark 13: 3). This is consistent with the readers being in Rome.
- The references to suffering and persecution would be consistent with a readership that may have been undergoing persecution from Nero, in Rome.
- There is a mention of Rufus in Mark 15: 21 and also in Romans 16: 13. If the readers were in Rome then they would know Rufus. The reference to Rufus seems otherwise pointless.

- Mark gives reference to the Jewish scriptures only once (Mark 1: 2–3). This would have suited his readership if they were in Rome, since they would have little or no knowledge of the Jewish scriptures.

3 The purpose of Mark's Gospel

a) A gospel

Mark's Gospel should not be thought of as a biography. It does not attempt to record the life of Jesus. The majority of the events recorded in Mark in total cover only a period of about four weeks.

At the start of his gospel, Mark indicates what his purpose is in writing. Mark quotes from the Old Testament prophet Isaiah, who tells of Jesus' coming to bring in God's rule or Kingdom. A summary is then given in Mark 1: 15 of Jesus' mission. It involves the coming of the Kingdom of God, and the pressing invitation to 'repent and believe the good news'. In Isaiah 52: 7 the **good news** – the gospel – is explained in terms of salvation and God's rule. Likewise in Romans 1: 16, the substance of the gospel is declared to be God's power to salvation to all who believe. The good news had been foretold in Old Testament times. What Mark does is to show that Jesus is the one who brings the good news of God's kingdom into being. Right at the start, Mark proclaims that Jesus is the Messiah. Christ is the Greek form of the Hebrew word *messiah*, meaning anointed one.

Mark gives reminders throughout his gospel that Jesus is the Christ, the Messiah, the Son of God. Jesus is depicted as the one who defeats Satan, forgives sinners, heals the sick, feeds the hungry and raises the dead. In particular, two-thirds of the Gospel are taken up with the final weeks of Jesus' life (the **Passion narrative**). Mark seems to be emphasising that God had decisively acted in history in the person of Jesus and that Jesus' death was victory, not failure. Whereas Paul tends to make statements about what God has done through the person of Jesus, Mark expresses it through narrative and story. This use of narrative is similar to Peter's usage in his sermons.

If the above conclusions about readership and situation are correct, and Mark was writing to persecuted Christians, then his emphasis on the future kingdom and the harvest to come would be an encouragement to them to keep their faith.

b) Theological purposes

The development of biblical criticism has led to Mark being depicted not just as a collector of material but also as a theologian. Mark has put his material together in a particular way. In 1901, **William Wrede** wrote his book, *The Messianic Secret*, which was a study of Mark's Gospel and concluded that Mark had deliberately introduced into the gospel story a demand by Jesus for secrecy about who he was. Wrede argued that this fabrication attempted to explain why no one recognised Jesus as Messiah during his lifetime. Although most scholars reject this view, the idea of a theological purpose has remained popular. For instance:

- J.H. Ropes (1934) proposed that Mark was written to answer the problem: 'Why should the Messiah die a criminal's death?' This is seen to explain Mark's emphasis on the Passion as a self-chosen sacrifice by Jesus, in accordance with scripture and the will of God.

66 KEY QUOTES 99

The beginning of the Gospel about Jesus Christ, the Son of God.
(Mark 1: 1)

How beautiful on the mountains are the feet of those who bring good news, who proclaim peace, who bring good tidings, who proclaim salvation, who say to Zion, 'Your God reigns!'
(Isaiah 52: 7)

I am not ashamed of the Gospel, because it is the power of God for the salvation of everyone who believes ...
(Romans 1: 16)

 KEY WORDS

Good news literal meaning gospel
Passion narrative the description of the events leading up to the death of Jesus

 KEY PERSON

William Wrede (1859–1906), argued that Mark's Gospel had a theological structure and so challenged its historical reliability.

■ P. Carrington (1952) argues that the structure of Mark's Gospel, especially the occurrence of two accounts in which large numbers are fed miraculously, suggests that it was designed for liturgical use. He claims that the sequence of narrative is dictated by the sequence of festivals in the Jewish calendar.

■ D. Nineham (1963) claims that the structure of Mark's Gospel is determined by specific intentions, in particular:

1 to show that Jesus as Messiah was innocent of Jewish charges and that his sufferings were part of God's purpose

2 to explain why Christians have to suffer

3 to explain why Jesus did not publicly declare himself as Messiah

4 to show Jesus' triumph over evil.

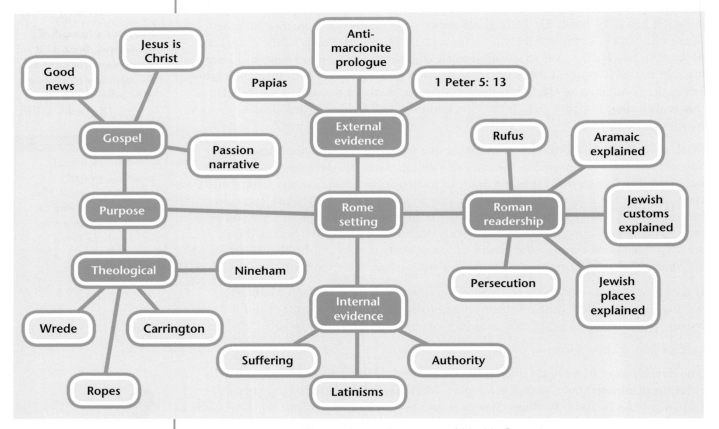

Summary diagram: The setting and purpose of Mark's Gospel

Reflection and assessment AO1

It is vital to bring together the information you have covered so far and recognise how it can be transformed into effective examination-style revision and answers. The best way to do this is to ask the question: 'How am I going to be assessed on this information?'

The first way is through assessment objective 1 (AO1). For this objective you need to be able to 'select and clearly demonstrate the relevant knowledge and understanding through the use of evidence, examples and correct language and terminology'.

Look back to page 7 in the Introduction to review the level descriptors for AO1. There is a description of the character and features for each level. The exam is marked with reference to levels.

Look at the key points, below, in answer to the question:

Explain the setting of Mark's Gospel.   (25 marks)

You will need to refer to these points, which are not presented in any particular order, to complete the task.

- There are lots of references to suffering and persecution.
- Mark's Gospel was written in Rome.
- The readers seem to be Gentiles.
- Mark's Gospel contains Latinisms.
- 1 Peter 5: 13 suggests Mark is connected with Rome.
- Mark's Gospel gained authority quickly. If it was connected with the Church in Rome then this would explain it.
- Equally, if Mark's Gospel was connected with Peter it would explain why it was accepted.

Suggestion for further application of skills

Turn to the discussion about the purpose of Mark's Gospel. Make a list of five key points to summarise it. With a partner, add further points to make it more comprehensive. Try to find relevant quotes from scholars, texts or further sources of information, to add at suitable places to use as examples, illustrations or support for a point.

Now use your points to write an answer to the question:

Explain the purpose of Mark's Gospel.   (25 marks)

TASK

Use these key points as a basis for a writing frame to answer the question:
Explain the setting of Mark's Gospel.
(25 marks AO1)
Put the points in order and add two relevant quotes at suitable places.
Objective To practise good 'selection and demonstration of clearly relevant knowledge' (AO1) and aiming for an answer demonstrating 'understanding and engagement with the material' (level 5) through use of quotes or examples as evidence (AO1)

Part 3
A critical analysis of the issues

What are the issues that I am expected to consider and to analyse critically?

- The introductory areas of Mark's Gospel

1 Issues arising

a) Does it matter who wrote Mark's Gospel?

The debate about authorship is complex and perhaps no conclusion can be reached with any certainty. However, many scholars comment that the author's identity may not be a vital issue. The conclusion has little bearing on the reading of the gospel. Even if we knew for certain who wrote it, it would not help our understanding of its content. Hence the issue may be historically interesting but of no significant consequence.

b) Does it matter if we cannot be certain about the dating of Mark's Gospel?

Many scholars would argue that the account of Jesus' life and death is not affected by the date at which Mark's Gospel was written. The account stands alone and can be understood irrespective of whether we know that date.

c) Does history matter?

The gospel–writers did seem to be interested in recording accurate history; for example, see Luke 1: 1–4. Likewise, Paul emphasised the fact that Christianity rests on an historic event, namely the Resurrection (1 Corinthians 15). The sermons of Peter and Paul in the Acts of the Apostles also focused on events in Jesus' life, death and resurrection. Many scholars argue the importance of the historical basis of the gospel. Hunter commented: 'if early Christian faith created the gospel record, what created Christian faith?'

There seem to be two main general views about the historicity of the gospels. One accepts the gospel narratives as presenting a basically accurate account of the historical Jesus. The other emphasises the role of the Early Church community and sees the gospels more as products of the faith of this community (see page 222). This means that the historical value of the gospels is questionable since they are seen as creations of a slightly later community.

However, the assumption of inaccurate transmission has been questioned.

- Was the oral period too short for stories to be changed by the Early Church?
- Was the oral period exclusively oral?
- Would the Church create material and then attribute it to Jesus?
- What of the testimonies of eye witnesses?
- Was it not the Jewish cultural tradition to transmit material accurately?

? KEY QUESTIONS

- **What difference would it make if we did know who the author was?**
- **Is the date of writing a vital issue?**

❝ KEY QUOTE ❞

If early Christian faith created the Gospel record, what created Christian faith?

(A.M. Hunter)

d) Does the place of writing or the target readership of Mark's Gospel matter?

As with the question of authorship and date, the conclusions about place of writing and target readership do not radically affect the way we read the text. Many would argue that the message of 'repent and believe' remains the same 2000 years on.

e) How can we determine the purpose of Mark's Gospel?

Some of the purposes suggested earlier, on page 227, focus on a variety of ways of understanding Mark's Gospel in a cryptic fashion. Many would argue that such a view seems unnecessarily complex. The type of literature in Mark's Gospel seems very different from that of, for example, the Book of Revelation. Ralph Martin commented: 'Whatever Mark's deep meaning is … it does not lie in the solving of a conundrum or the unravelling of a tangled skein of scattered hints or mysterious allusions.'

As mentioned previously, conclusions about readership and date may well contribute towards reaching a conclusion about the purpose of Mark's Gospel.

2 Possible conclusions

When assessing the issues that arise with introductory areas of Mark's Gospel, it is important to reflect upon the arguments previously discussed and arrive at some appropriate conclusion. It may be that you accept none of these listed here, or just one of them, or you may have a different conclusion that is not listed. However, what is important is the way that you have arrived at your conclusion – the reasoning process.

From the preceding discussions, here are some possible conclusions you could draw.

1 The problems of the introductory areas can be resolved with confidence. There is a level of certainty about conclusions to questions such as authorship and date. They are consistent with one another.

2 Some of the problems of the introductory areas can be resolved with confidence, while others remain unclear through lack of evidence.

3 None of the problems of the introductory areas can be resolved with any confidence. There is a contradiction of evidence.

4 None of the problems of the introductory areas can be resolved with any confidence. The evidence is too scant or unclear to reach any firm conclusions.

5 None of the problems of the introductory areas can be resolved with any confidence. However, this is irrelevant because Mark's Gospel stands in its own right. These problems of the introductory areas do not affect our understanding of the gospel.

6 None of the problems of the introductory areas can be resolved with any confidence. This uncertainty affects the value of Mark's Gospel and our understanding of it.

? KEY QUESTIONS

- Is Mark's Gospel historically reliable?
- Is Mark's Gospel a community invention?
- To what extent are the introductory questions, such as place of writing and destination, important to understanding Mark's Gospel?
- How is the purpose of a writing to be decided?

❝ KEY QUOTE ❞

Whatever Mark's deep meaning is … it does not lie in the solving of a conundrum or the unravelling of a tangled skein of scattered hints or mysterious allusions.

(Ralph Martin)

Reflection and assessment AO2

Earlier in this topic you considered the assessment objective AO1 focused on knowledge and understanding. The second way of being assessed is through assessment objective AO2. For this objective you need to be able to sustain a critical line of argument and justify a point of view.

Look back to page 8 in the Introduction to review the level descriptors for AO2. There is a description of the character and features for each level. The exam is marked with reference to levels.

Read the following question and the sample answer below it. Read the examiner's comments.

'Mark's Gospel is not historically accurate.' Discuss. (10 marks)

Some reference to what it says is needed.

Scholars have often appealed to the beginning of Luke's Gospel as evidence that the gospels are historically reliable and accurate accounts. However in more recent times this view has been challenged and in particular Mark's Gospel has been seen as unreliable and inaccurate.

The significance of this to the debate of reliability needs discussion.

An illustration from the text needed to develop this point.

Need to analyse this a little more.

Needs an example to illustrate it.

This challenge has come from a variety of arguments. Firstly the questions of authorship and date of writing have been unresolved. It still is not certain who wrote the Gospel or when it was written. Furthermore our knowledge of the New Testament period has improved and we now know that Mark's Gospel contains some glaring inaccuracies such as geography and Jewish rituals. Furthermore biblical criticism has drawn attention to the transmission of the material and the likelihood that it was changed by the early church and at times even created and attributed to Jesus. This clearly shows that the Gospel of Mark is unreliable. In addition theological purposes have been discovered that explain the framework of the gospel. This again suggests that the gospel is fabricated and unreliable. In fact the mere fact that the gospels recount supernatural events shows that it is not a trustworthy document.

The reply is very brief and stated in one sentence. As it stands it is very one-sided debate.

There are replies to these arguments such as the view that the Early Church would not change the words of Jesus.

There is an attempt at some sort of conclusion though it needs more development.

However it does not really matter if it is accurate or not. What matters is not the historical detail. It is spiritual truth not literal truth that is important.

So what does it score?

In the exam the answer will be marked according to levels (see page 8 in the Introduction). Certainly there is some basic reasoning. The candidate clearly has an understanding of the main debate and is aware of arguments on both sides. However, the discussion is one-sided and lacks illustrations to support the arguments. There is no real evidence of critical analysis and views are just stated rather than analysed. This would score a top level 2.

Suggestion for further application of skills

Look at an essay that you have recently completed.

1 Underline in green what could have been omitted or is repeated.
2 Underline in blue any evaluation words.
3 Underline in red key phrases.
4 Identify strengths and weaknesses.
5 Identify how the essay could be improved.

TASK

Using this framework and the comments, write a level 4 answer.
Objectives To identify the weaknesses of a poor answer and know how to improve it.
To be able to 'select and demonstrate clearly relevant knowledge' (AO1 descriptor) and working towards a 'good selection of material' (level 4 descriptor)

Part 1
The texts

What am I required to study?

- The Passion story, trial and death of Jesus, Mark 11; 14: 1–15: 41

This means I am expected to know about:

- the event of the triumphal entry into Jerusalem
- the significance of the triumphal entry into Jerusalem for Jesus
- the significance of the triumphal entry into Jerusalem for the gospel-writer
- the event of the Temple cleansing
- the significance of the Temple cleansing for Jesus
- the significance of the Temple cleansing for the gospel-writer
- the event of the Last Supper
- the link of the Last Supper to Passover
- the meaning of the Last Supper
- comparison with Luke 22: 7–23 and 1 Corinthians 11: 17–26.

Explicit reference is made in the Specification to the set passages in Mark that are to be studied. You are expected to have first-hand knowledge of these texts, and so the actual narrative has not been reproduced in this topic. Answers will need to show knowledge of the text but not in narration form. Rather, it is important that you focus on the particular aspects referred to in the list given above, for example, their significance and meaning.

It would be helpful to write your notes under the headings listed under 'This means I am expected to know about', as it is from these areas that the exam questions will be derived.

Remember that your studies will include elements of the *two* basic assessment objectives of:

- Knowledge and Understanding (AO1)
- Evaluation (AO2).

See pages 7–8 in the Introduction to remind yourself of these objectives.

The evaluation material is set out in Part 3 of this topic (page 255) and can be studied either alongside the AO1 material, as you work through this topic, or as a discrete topic.

EXAM TIP

Good knowledge of the text is vital. However, at AS level you will not be asked to describe the event, the focus will be on its significance or meaning. Therefore, allude to the account by commenting on the aspects and features relevant to the focus of the question.
This demonstrates clearly relevant knowledge and understanding (AO1).

1 The triumphal entry into Jerusalem

a) The event (Mark 11: 1–11)

The authorities were hostile to Jesus, but Jesus chose to enter Jerusalem publicly and triumphantly. The crowd spontaneously expressed respect by spreading garments on the road.

b) The significance for Jesus

The significance for Jesus can be identified by studying the deliberate actions that he made and by considering the meaning of these actions.

It was not usual for a pilgrim to ride into Jerusalem. His choice of riding on a donkey is seen to signify that Jesus was a man of peace or a priest. A king would be expected to ride on a warhorse.

Riding a donkey could be seen as fulfilling the words of the prophet Zechariah, in Zechariah 9: 9. This links the ideas of kingship, righteousness, salvation and gentleness with riding on a donkey into Jerusalem.

Jesus was making clear that he was not the sort of messiah that many of the Jews were expecting; he was not a messiah who would bring them military liberation from Roman rule.

Jesus may have deliberately made a veiled assertion of his messiahship, which would not have been recognised at the time.

c) The significance for the gospel-writer

Because it is difficult to know what Mark's source was, we cannot be sure how he adapted his material or what he chose to omit. We can see what he chose to include. Presumably, it was this material that Mark thought was important for his readers.

- Mark's description of the event is shorter, compared to those of the other gospel-writers. There appear to be hints of the supernatural in the arrangements made to find the donkey. Nothing seems to have been previously arranged. Possibly, Mark is hinting to his readers that something extraordinary is taking place.
- Mark draws attention to the fact that the colt had not been ridden before. Again, this could be an allusion to the use of animals that had never been yoked for sacred purposes as, for example, in the carrying the Ark of the Lord, in 1 Samuel 6: 7.
- Mark records how the crowd spontaneously expressed respect by spreading garments on the road. There is an interesting parallel to this in 2 Kings 9: 13, where the people proclaim Jehu as king. Hence, the writer may be implying Jesus is King. Only Luke and John state that the people called Jesus 'King' as he entered Jerusalem, but Mark certainly implies it with his reference to kingdom in verse 10.
- Jesus appears to be fulfilling the Zechariah prophecy (see above). Mark seems to want to show that the crowd is hailing Jesus as the long-awaited Messiah. The people quote Psalm 118: 26. Although the psalm was sung at various feasts, it may well be that Mark wants the reader to see more meaning in it than a mere blessing of the pilgrims who had come to the feast. It was a welcoming of the Lord.
- Mark links this shout of 'Hosanna' with the expected coming of David's messianic kingdom. Although the sentence: 'Blessed is the coming kingdom of our father David,' is not from the Old Testament, the reference to David's kingdom would remind the readers of words from Isaiah 9 about the Prince of Peace reigning over David's kingdom for ever.

❝ KEY QUOTES ❞

Rejoice greatly, O daughter of Zion! Shout, Daughter of Jerusalem!
See. Your king comes to you,
Righteous and having salvation,
Gentle and riding on a donkey,
On a colt, the foal of a donkey.
(Zechariah 9: 9)

They hurried and took their cloaks and spread them under him on the bare steps. Then they blew the trumpet and shouted 'Jehu is King'.
(2 Kings 9: 13)

Now then, get a new cart ready, with two cows that have been calved and have never been yoked.
(1 Samuel 6: 7)

Blessed is he who comes in the name of the Lord …
(Psalm 118: 26)

EXAM TIP

Do not use a Bible quotation just to repeat what you have just written. You need either to allude to the quotation or to use it to draw out some further comment.
This demonstrates relevant knowledge and understanding through the use of evidence and examples (AO1).

KEY QUOTES

... He will reign on David's throne and over his kingdom, establishing and upholding it with justice and righteousness from that time on and for ever.

(Isaiah 9: 7)

Their burnt offerings and sacrifices will be accepted on my altar; for my house will be called a house of prayer for all nations.

(Isaiah 56: 7)

Has this house, which bears my Name, become a den of robbers to you? But I have been watching! declares the Lord.

(Jeremiah 7: 11)

'See, I will send my messenger, who will prepare the way before me. Then suddenly the Lord you are seeking will come to his temple; the messenger of the covenant, whom you desire, will come.' says the Lord Almighty.

(Malachi 3: 1)

2 The cleansing of the Temple

a) The event (Mark 11: 15–19)

Mark places this event on the day after the triumphal entry into Jerusalem. Several events were taking place in the Court of Gentiles.

The sale of animals for sacrifice was an established institution of the Temple (see page 196). It was more convenient for pilgrims to be able to buy suitable animals for sacrifice within the Temple area. The area for this trading was in the Court of the Gentiles.

Some were changing money. Only Tyrian coinage was accepted in the Temple offerings, and other coins had to be changed into this currency.

There seems to be a direct link between the actions of Jesus in the Temple and the hardening of opposition on the part of some of the Jerusalem authorities. Refer again to the discussion about the Temple in Topic 1, Part 1 (page 195), paying particular attention to the messianic and eschatological role of the new Temple.

b) The significance for Jesus

Again, the significance for Jesus is seen in the actions he chose to take and the words he chose to say.

Many commentators identify the driving out of those who were buying and selling, the overturning of tables and the stopping of anyone carrying merchandise through the Temple as an acted parable. It is interpreted as a prophetic declaration of God's judgement on the Temple and Israel as a whole. In addition to this, it could be seen as a sign that God would soon replace the Temple with some form of purified new temple.

A more traditional interpretation is that Jesus was protesting against the actions of the money-changers. Their trade should not have been taking place within the precincts of the Temple. Jesus is seen as attempting to restore pure worship of God.

Another view is that Jesus was making clear that the Temple – and worship there – were for everyone. The use of the Court of Gentiles to set up trading areas prevented the one area of the Temple that was open to the Gentiles from being used for prayer. The reference in verse 17 to 'a house of prayer for all nations' adds support to such an interpretation. The quotation comes from Isaiah 56: 7.

The last part of the verse is similar to Jeremiah 7: 11. Again, this seems to focus on the protest against abuse of the Temple area.

c) The significance for the gospel-writer

Given that we do not know Mark's sources, it is difficult to determine whether he has inserted any special emphasis. He does seem to see the cleansing of the Temple as a messianic declaration by Jesus. This is shown by Mark's comments about the hostility that then arose. It seems that the chief priests and the teachers of the law began looking for a way to kill Jesus. However, the messianic nature of the event was veiled.

Some commentators see a reference to Malachi 3: 1, supporting a messianic understanding of the event. Jesus is seen as both King and High Priest.

Only Mark has the reference to ' ... for all nations'. Some see this as indicating Mark's understanding of the event. For him, the significance of the event was that it showed that Jesus was concerned that the Gentiles should be incorporated into the life of the people of God. Mark may have regarded this as part of Jesus' messianic role.

3 The fig tree (Mark 11:12–14, 20–25)

The account of the cleansing of the Temple is sandwiched between the two parts of the story of the fig tree. It seems clear that Mark linked it to the actions of Jesus in the area of the Temple. The fate of the fig tree symbolised the fate that awaited Jerusalem and the Jewish people and religion. The fig tree promised much fruit with its fine leaves, just as the Temple promised much righteousness with all its outward ritual and ceremony. However, the fig tree failed to produce fruit despite its outward appearance of fine leaves. In a similar way, Judaism failed to produce fruits of righteousness despite the fine trappings of ceremony and observance. The implication by Mark is that the fate awaiting the Temple and Judaism would be the same as that of the fig tree. There will be judgement.

4 The Last Supper

a) The event (Mark 14: 12–26)

The account in Mark's Gospel includes the preparation for the Passover (verses 12–16) and an account of the Last Supper itself (verses 17–26).

The disciples were sent to prepare a room in Jerusalem for the celebration of the Passover meal, for that evening.

Many commentators suggest that the instructions for finding the room imply some supernatural foresight on the part of Jesus. Others argue that there was a prior arrangement made by Jesus in order to keep the place of meeting secret from the authorities.

The sight of a man carrying a water jar would have been unusual so the person would have been easy to identify.

The emphasis, in the account of the actual meal, is of:

- the foretelling of the betrayal by Judas
- the words of institution of the Lord's Supper.

Mark makes clear that Judas' betrayal did not take Jesus by surprise. Jesus knew it would happen and freely accepted it. It was all part of God's plan rather than some meaningless tragedy. However, Mark also makes clear that Judas is to be held responsible and is guilty. Interestingly, Mark makes no specific mention of Judas. It is not clear that the disciples were aware of who the traitor was.

The words used by Jesus at the meal are those that the Christian Churches repeat in their **liturgy** when they celebrate the Last Supper. This celebration is known by various names such as the **Eucharist**, **Holy Communion**, **Mass** or the **Lord's Supper**.

Mark's account is very brief and many commentators argue that he was interested only in establishing that the practice in the Early Church of celebrating the Last Supper, had its origins in the actions of Jesus himself.

KEY QUOTES

So they prepared the Passover.

(Mark 14: 16b)

The Son of Man will go just as it is written about him. But woe to that man who betrays the Son of Man! It would be better for him if he had not been born.

(Mark 14: 21)

KEY WORDS

Liturgy a particular order or form of public service prescribed by a Church

Eucharist an alternative name for the celebration of the Last Supper, from the Greek word for thanksgiving

Holy Communion an alternative name for the celebration of the Last Supper

Mass from the Latin *missa*, meaning dismissal, a word used in the final sentence of the service celebrating the Last Supper

Lord's Supper an alternative name for the celebration of Eucharist

KEY QUOTES

The blood will be a sign for you on the houses where you are, and when I see the blood, I will pass over you.

(Exodus 12: 13)

For I received from the Lord what I also passed on to you: The Lord Jesus, on the night he was betrayed, took bread, and when he had given thanks, he broke it and said, 'This is my body, which is for you; do this in remembrance of me.'

(1 Corinthians 11: 23)

For Christ, our Passover Lamb, has been sacrificed.

(1 Corinthians 5: 7)

The next day John saw Jesus coming towards him and said, 'Look, the Lamb of God, who takes away the sin of the world!'

(John 1: 29)

TASK

Read Jeremiah 31: 31–34 and list the features of the new covenant.

How do these features link to the Last Supper?

Objective To understand the meaning of the Last Supper and how it relates to the new covenant

 KEY IDEA

The Passover

At the time of Moses the Israelites were captive in Egypt. God sent ten plagues against Egypt to force the Pharaoh to free the Israelites. The tenth plague was an angel of death who would go from house to house, killing every first-born son. Israelite children would not be killed and thus God would show that they were his chosen people. So that the angel would know which houses were Israelite homes, the Israelites were to follow very specific instructions.

- Each household was to take an unblemished, male lamb.
- Four days later they were to slaughter it.
- Blood from the lamb was to be brushed on the door-frames.

This would tell the angel of death that it was an Israelite home and to 'pass over'.

The families roasted the lamb and ate it with bitter herbs and unleavened bread.

The resulting deaths of the first-born of the Egyptians forced the Pharaoh to send the Israelites out of Egypt and he even gave them silver and gold to encourage them to leave.

The Passover became a symbol of God's deliverance from slavery. This event was remembered in a festival each year that culminated in the Passover meal, where each family ate together, remembering the events of this escape.

The origin of the word Passover is thought by some to come from this brushing of the door-frame with blood. The blood was smeared on or passed over the door-frame to cover and protect the Israelites. A more common explanation is simply that the angel of death passed over those houses where blood had been smeared (Exodus 12: 13).

b) The links with the Passover

Mark implies that the Last Supper was a Passover meal (Mark 14: 16b). However, he does not develop this connection. Indeed, it is not at all clear whether the Early Church attached any importance to the Passover format of the meal, with respect to the significance and meaning of Jesus' actions at the Last Supper. Had the Passover meal link been important, it might have been expected that Paul would have made reference to it being Passover night when he referred to 'the night Jesus was betrayed …' (1 Corinthians 11: 23). Neither is there any mention of the Passover lamb as being part of the meal.

However, there are other texts in the New Testament, for example, 1 Corinthians 57 and John 12: 9, 35, that do seem to make a link between the Last Supper and the Passover. Certainly, many commentators draw some parallels between the two events. These have been recognised as clues to understanding the meaning of the words and actions of Jesus at the Last Supper. It could be interpreted that Jesus was giving the symbols of the Passover meal new meanings. The Passover celebrated liberation from slavery into freedom by the shedding of blood. So, in a similar way, the Last Supper celebrated liberation from slavery of sin into freedom by the shedding of Jesus' blood (his death).

KEY IDEA

Covenant

A covenant is a divinely imposed agreement between God and human beings, and states the conditions of their relationship. The Bible often uses the words testament and will, which reflect the idea that the provisions of the covenant were laid down by one of the parties only (similar to a will, which decides the distribution of goods at death). Several covenants are described in the Bible, for example, with Abraham, Noah and David, but the only one that is referred to as the old covenant is that made through Moses. This depicts a series of detailed laws to restrain the sins of the people. However, the people did not keep these laws. Jeremiah 31 makes reference to a new covenant yet to come. This new covenant speaks of God writing his laws on our hearts and remembering our sins no more.

Look back to page 195 for further information about covenants.

Passover	Last Supper
God remembered his covenant	A new covenant is enacted
The covenant was ratified by the sprinkling of sacrificial blood	The new covenant is established by Jesus' death
In slavery in Egypt	In slavery to sin
Freed from slavery of Egypt	Freed from slavery of sin
Power of Egyptian Pharaoh broken	Power of evil broken (forgiveness of sins)
Begin journey to Promised Land	Begin journey to heaven
Saved from physical death	Saved from spiritual death
Saved by the blood of the Passover lamb	Saved by the blood of the Lamb (Jesus)
Saved by faith in the shedding of the blood	Saved by faith in the death of Jesus
Elements in meal interpreted	Elements in meal interpreted
God calls for Passover to go on being celebrated	Jesus calls for Last Supper to go on being celebrated
Looked back to the redemptive act of the Old Testament and forward to the messianic age	Looked back to the redemptive act of the New Testament and forwards to Jesus' return and the messianic banquet with his followers

Summary diagram: Links between the Passover and the Last Supper

c) The meaning of the Last Supper

There is much debate as to the degree to which the Passover meal and the Last Supper are linked. However, at the very least, it does seem that Jesus was giving the elements of the bread and the wine new meanings, centred on liberation being achieved through his death. Theologians point to a number of symbolic aspects of the Last Supper.

" KEY QUOTE "

He has made us competent as ministers of a new covenant – not of the letter but of the Spirit; for the letter kills, but the Spirit gives life.

(2 Corinthians 3: 6)

TASK

Draw a chart showing the *differences* between the Passover meal and the Last Supper.

Objectives To know and understand the details of the two events

To understand the degree to which the two events are linked

" KEY QUOTES "

While they were eating, Jesus took bread, gave thanks and broke it, and gave it to his disciples, saying, 'Take it; this is my body.'

(Mark 14: 22)

For whenever you eat this bread and drink this cup, you proclaim the Lord's death until he comes.

(1 Corinthians 11: 26)

Then he took the cup, gave thanks and offered it to them, and they all drank from it. 'This is my blood of the [new] covenant, which is poured out for many,' he said to them.

(Mark 14: 23)

KEY IDEA

Identification

Poppies – evocative of the carnage that once took place

❝ KEY QUOTES ❞

A man ought to examine himself before he eats of the bread and drinks of the cup.

(1 Corinthians 11: 28)

Whoever eats my flesh and drinks my blood remains in me, and I in him.

(John 6: 56)

I tell you the truth, I will not drink again of the fruit of the vine until that day when I drink it anew in the Kingdom of God.

(Mark 14: 25)

KEY WORD

Messianic banquet a celebration when the Messiah brings in the Kingdom of God

i) Proclaiming Christ's death

When Christians celebrate the Last Supper, the actions portray Christ's death. The bread being broken symbolises the breaking of Christ's body. The cup poured out symbolises the pouring out of Christ's blood for humankind. Hence, it can be seen that the act is a form of proclamation. This is made clear in the account in 1 Corinthians 11: 26.

ii) Identification

The Christian understanding is that we are the beneficiaries of what Jesus has achieved. We identify with that liberation in the same way that the Jews identified with their liberation from slavery when they celebrated the Passover. Christians are claiming that they want to be associated with the event. Christians are identifying themselves with Christ's death for them.

The celebration of the Last Supper in the Christian Church involves the token acts of eating bread and drinking wine. The point of eating and drinking is identification. An illustration of this idea is wearing a poppy on Remembrance Sunday.

> **The poppy is a moving emblem of men's bodies broken in battle. It grew in profusion on the battlefields of the Western front. The poppy is fragile, like human flesh, and is easily broken and bruised. Its colour is vividly crimson like blood, and stains the earth when crushed. So the poppy is a potent emblem of the body and blood of a human being brutally broken in warfare. When we wear a poppy, we wear it on our person to be identified with the suffering of those who died and so acknowledge that it was for us. We also wear it in our hearts and say thank you for their sacrifice.**
> **So it is with the bread and the wine. Christians take it to identify themselves openly with Christ's death – with his broken body and shed blood, and in their hearts they say 'thank you' to him for dying for them. They do so with others, so that their identification is open and public.**
>
> (*A Second Adam*, G. Ratcliffe)

iii) Affirming faith

Part of the identification with the benefits of Christ's death is the affirmation of faith in what Christ has achieved. Christians are acknowledging that they accept the need to be freed from sin. Hence Paul, in 1 Corinthians 11, warns the partakers that they should approach the Lord's Supper in a serious manner.

iv) Spiritual nourishment

Many believe that the words of Jesus about the body and blood are to be taken literally. Others take the words to be symbolic. Nonetheless, even among the second group some believe that the symbolism includes the idea of feeding on Christ. There is a serious debate about whether John 6 contains teaching about the Last Supper. If it does, then this would support the view that spiritual nourishment is at the heart of the symbolism. Others think that the idea of feeding on Christ is not part of the intended meaning and doubt that John 6 is connected with the Last Supper. All seem to believe that the effect of focusing on the death of Christ is in itself a means of nourishment.

v) Messianic banquet

Jesus points his disciples to the future with the arrival of the Kingdom of God and the **messianic banquet**, a celebration when the Messiah brings in the Kingdom of God. Therefore, his forthcoming death is not seen as a tragedy but a victory. It secures redemption and ensures the future.

The Last Supper, Leonardo Da Vinci

TASK

The Last Supper, painted by Leonardo Da Vinci, specifically portrays the reaction of each apostle when Jesus said that one of them would betray him. Do some research about the various characters, symbols and speculations about the painting, as well as its history.
Objective To understand interpretations of the events of the Last Supper

d) The two traditions of the Last Supper

There are four accounts of the Last Supper in the New Testament. Most commentators agree that they derive from two main sources:

- Mark and Matthew
- Paul (1 Corinthians) and Luke.

The similarities and differences are set out below, in parallel columns.

The Lukan account is the most unusual since it alone mentions the cup before the bread.

Mark 14	Luke 22	1 Corinthians 11
	After taking the cup Gave thanks Take this and divide it among you Will not drink again … until … in the kingdom of God	
Take it	Took bread Gave thanks Broke it	Took bread Gave thanks Broke it
This is my body	This is my body	This is my body
	Given for you	Which is for you
	Do this in remembrance of me	Do this in remembrance of me
Took cup Gave thanks Offered it to them They all drank from it	After supper, took cup	After supper, took cup
This is my blood Of the [new] covenant	This cup is the new covenant in my blood	This cup is the new covenant in my blood
Which is poured out for many	Which is poured out for you	
Will not drink again … until … in the kingdom of God		
	But the hand of him who is going to betray me is with mine on the table …	
		Whenever you drink it, in remembrance of me For whenever you eat this cup, you proclaim the Lord's death until he comes

TASK

From what you have so far learned about levels of response, create a list of points to go in a developed-level answer (level 3).
Improve this further for a higher-level answer.
Then create writing frames and fully drafted answers for each level.
Objectives Gradually to build up and improve on an answer
To develop appreciation of the difference between a level 3 answer and a level 4–5 answer

Reflection and assessment AO1

It is vital to bring together the information you have covered so far and recognise how it can be transformed into effective examination-style revision and answers. The best way to do this is to ask the question: 'How am I going to be assessed on this information?'

The first way is through assessment objective 1 (AO1). For this objective you need to be able to 'select and clearly demonstrate the relevant knowledge and understanding through the use of evidence, examples and correct language and terminology'.

Read the following question and complete the task. To do the task you will need to look back at the level descriptors given in the Introduction on page 7.

Explain the significance of the triumphal entry into Jerusalem for Mark. (25 marks)

Suggestion for further application of skills

Produce a spider diagram for the following question:

Compare Mark's account of the Last Supper with that recorded in Luke's Gospel.
(25 marks)

Your spider diagram will need to break down the essay title into its component parts, identifying the relevant material required in each part.

Part 2
The themes

> **What am I required to study?**
> - The Passion story, trial and death of Jesus, Mark 11; 14: 1–15: 41
>
> **This means I am expected to know about:**
> - the presentation and accuracy of women, Judas, Peter, Pilate
> - the presentation of Jesus as Son of God, Son of Man, righteous martyr
> - Jesus' death as atonement and sacrifice
> - the idea of ransom
> - the idea of covenant and new covenant
> - the role of Romans and Jews
> - the use of the Old Testament.

You are expected to have first-hand knowledge of the text of Mark's narrative of the Passion. The texts given for study are Mark 11; 14: 1–15: 41. This part of the topic looks at the way in which Mark has presented various characters and themes. It is vital that you know and understand the material in Mark, particularly those parts of the given study text that were not covered in Part 1 of this topic, for example, the trial and death of Jesus. It would be helpful to write your notes under the headings listed under 'This means I am expected to know about', as it is from these areas that the exam questions will be derived.

Remember that your studies will include elements of the *two* basic assessment objectives of:

- Knowledge and Understanding (AO1)
- Evaluation (AO2).

See pages 7–8 in the Introduction to remind yourself of these objectives.

The evaluation material is set out in Part 3 of this topic (page 255) and can be studied either alongside the AO1 material, as you work through this topic, or as a discrete topic.

1 Presentation of characters

a) Women

The socio-cultural background of the times of Jesus is the Jewish context. Because the country was occupied by the Romans, the attitudes of Greco-Roman society were also influential. As far as women were concerned, the male perspective of them was mainly as

KEY PERSON

Philo (20BCE – CE50), also known as Philo of Alexandria, was a Jewish philosopher and biblical commentator.

KEY WORD

Tosefta *literally* supplement, a supplement to the oral law in Judaism

❝ KEY QUOTES ❞

There was a prophetess, Anna … she gave thanks to God and spoke about the child to all who were looking forward to the redemption of Jerusalem.

(Luke 2: 36–38)

Daughter, your faith has healed you. Go in peace and be freed from your suffering.

(Mark 5: 34)

Why are you bothering her? She has done a beautiful thing to me.

(Mark 14: 6)

In Galilee these women had followed him and cared for his needs. Many other women who had come up with him to Jerusalem were also there.

(Mark 15: 41)

KEY WORD

Garden of Gethsemane *literally* garden of the oil press, the quiet garden area at the foot of the Mount of Olives where Jesus prayed after the Last Supper

wife and mother. Writings from the first century CE reflect a rather negative view, with women being depicted as inferior and submissive to men. For instance, **Philo** regarded female traits as weaknesses. The **Tosefta**, a supplement to the Jewish oral law, includes a statement that a Jew should thank God that he was not made a woman.

In contrast, Jesus treated women with respect and dignity. For instance, Luke's birth narratives refer to three women (Elizabeth, Mary, Anna) who, through God's power, interpret the significance of Jesus' birth. Jesus also healed many women. In the parable of the lost coin, the woman is portrayed in the same role as the shepherd and the father (Luke 15). The imagery in Luke 15 is of God.

In the set text of this unit, women also appear in positive roles.

i) Mark 14: 3–9

There are similar accounts to Mark's account in the other gospels, but they are placed differently. It was usual to anoint the body with oil for refreshment or before a meal. However, despite the fact that the oil was expensive, the woman used the entire contents of the flask. She was criticised by the other guests for wasting the oil, but Jesus saw her action as a spontaneous expression of her love and devotion to him. He defended her and referred to her act as an anointing in preparation for his burial. He also stated that her act would be remembered.

Some commentators see links with this story and the claim that Jesus was the Messiah (the anointed). As Jesus' body was never properly anointed at his death, some commentators argue that this is why Mark has placed the story at this point in his Passion narrative.

The story is placed between those of the plotting of the Jewish leaders and the betrayal by Judas. It seems that Mark is making the contrast between her love and the actions of the others.

ii) Mark 15: 40–41

This again is an illustration of women as disciples of Jesus. The implication is that some women accompanied Jesus during his ministry and helped to support him. The very people who were regarded as inferior show more perseverance than the disciples.

The story is important for the Early Church in that it shows that the women were not mistaken about the tomb when, later on, they found it empty. They clearly knew the tomb into which the body of Jesus had been placed.

b) Judas Iscariot

Judas Iscariot is named as one of the twelve disciples, known collectively as the Twelve. Although his name always appears last in any list, for example, Mark 39, he played an important role as treasurer (John 12: 6).

i) Mark 14: 1–2, 10–11

Mark recounts how Judas plotted with the Jewish leaders so that they could arrest Jesus when he was away from the crowds, for fear of starting a riot. The **Garden of Gethsemane** was on the Mount of Olives and outside the city of Jerusalem. As noted above, it is interesting that Mark has put this statement about betrayal immediately after the account of the woman's anointing of Jesus, thus making a sharp contrast.

ii) Mark 14: 17–21

During the Last Supper, Jesus declared that one of those eating with him at the table would betray him. The statement in Mark 14: 21 suggests the paradox of Judas being used for the fulfillment of God's purposes, and yet being responsible for the betrayal. Jesus' death was inevitable but Judas was still guilty. Mark does not suggest that the other disciples realised the identity of the betrayer.

Mark gives no clear indication why Judas betrayed Jesus. In contrast, John's Gospel implies it was for money; see John 12: 1–6. Some commentators have suggested an alternative explanation. The gospels make clear that the disciples interpreted the Kingdom of God as an earthly kingdom. They were expecting the Messiah to free them from the Romans and establish God's kingdom. It has been suggested that perhaps Judas realised that Jesus was not going to challenge and overthrow the Roman authorities. Therefore, either he tried to manipulate circumstances so that Jesus would have a confrontation with the authorities, or, feeling that Jesus had failed, he was content to help the Jewish authorities kill him.

iii) Mark 14: 43–51

An interesting word-play appears in verse 41, before the description of the arrival of the arresting party. Jesus rebukes the disciples a third time for sleeping and says: 'Enough'. Some commentators point out that the Greek word used is the commercial term for a receipt, and may have the implication: 'He's got his money.'

Judas selected the garden of Gethsemane as the best place for the Jewish authorities to arrest Jesus. It was away from the city and the crowds and would attract little or no attention. Although it was light, as there was a full moon, Judas arranged to give a sign so that the correct person, Jesus, would be arrested. The sign was a kiss, the customary greeting among the rabbis and their disciples. After this event, Judas is not mentioned again by Mark.

A station of the Cross at the Church of Our Lady at Ta'Pinu in Gozo

KEY QUOTES

The Son of Man will go just as it is written about him. But woe to that man who betrays the Son of Man! It would be better for him if he had not been born.

(Mark 14: 21)

Returning the third time, he said to them, 'Are you still sleeping and resting? Enough! The hour has come. Look the Son of Man is betrayed into the hands of sinners.'

(Mark 14: 41)

KEY QUESTION

Why did Judas betray Jesus?

TASK

There are several versions of the 14 stations of the Cross. Carry out some research and find out which one the picture opposite shows. Find out what was different about the list of the stations of the Cross that Pope Paul II created in the year 2000.

Objectives To reinforce understanding of the events of the Passion account

To be aware of those aspects of the account that are biblical and those that have been added by tradition

KEY QUOTES

Strike the shepherd, and the sheep will be scattered.

(Zechariah 13: 7)

Again the High Priest asked him, 'Are you the Christ, the Son of the Blessed One?' 'I am' said Jesus. 'And you will see the Son of Man sitting at the right hand of the Mighty One and coming on the clouds of heaven.'

(Mark 14: 61-2)

c) Peter

In all the lists of the disciples Simon Peter always appears first, which may reflect his importance. He seems to be portrayed in the gospels as the main spokesperson who often responded impulsively, without thinking.

i) Mark 14: 27–31

At the end of the Last Supper, Jesus predicts that they will all fall away. He quotes from Zechariah 13: 7. Peter impetuously promises never to fall and, in response, Jesus predicted that Peter would deny him. The Old Testament quotation shows that what happened was in accordance with God's plans and prophecy. Some commentators argue that it would help to explain to the Early Church why Peter and the other disciples denied Jesus, despite their fearlessness on other occasions.

ii) Mark 14: 32–42

Peter is specifically rebuked for his lack of vigilance when he falls asleep in the Garden of Gethsemane. Jesus addresses him as Simon rather than Peter, which some commentators see as a reference back to his old character before he knew Jesus.

iii) Mark 14: 53–54, 66–72

Mark has placed the story of Peter's denial within the account of the trial of Jesus in front of the Sanhedrin. The effect is to highlight the contrast between the responses made by Jesus to his questioners and that of Peter to his questioners. Jesus, for the first and only time in public, proclaimed his heavenly status and the glory that awaited him. In contrast, Peter denies Jesus. Mark shows the irony of the event, since just as the Sanhedrin mock Jesus as a false prophet, his prophecy concerning Peter's denial is fulfilled.

Again, this account would have been encouraging to the Early Church as they knew, despite this failure, that Peter was later successful in his ministry and displayed great courage in the persecutions that he experienced.

d) Pilate

Pontius Pilate was the Roman governor of Judea in the period CE26–36/37 (see page 201). Information about him comes from a number of sources, besides the gospels, including three non-Christian writers:

- Josephus (*Antiquities of the Jews, The Jewish Wars*)
- Philo (*Letters of Gaius*)
- Tacitus (*Annals*).

In general, these writers depict Pilate as a brutal governor who showed little regard for Jewish customs. There is a hint of this in the gospels, in Luke 13: 1, where there is reference to an incident involving Pilate. On becoming Prefect, one of the first things Pilate did was to move the headquarters of the army from Caesarea to Jerusalem.

In CE36/37, Pilate was deposed after a complaint from the Samaritans about his treatment of them. He went to Rome to appear before Tiberius to account for his actions, but Tiberius died before Pilate arrived. Tradition says that Pilate was exiled to France and later committed suicide.

i) Mark 15: 1–15

The Jewish authorities were seeking the death penalty but, according to John 18: 31, the Jews had no authority to carry out such an act without the agreement of the Roman authorities. Hence the charge brought against Jesus was political, one that Pilate would be concerned about. Instead of the charge of blasphemy, they accused Jesus of claiming to be a king and thus guilty of anti-Roman activities.

Pilate was faced with a choice. He could execute Jesus and avoid the anger and possible stirrings that the Jewish authorities might cause if Jesus went free, or free Jesus and risk the consequences. He tried to escape the choice by using a custom at the Feast of the Passover to release one prisoner. He tried to get the people to choose. The people could free either Jesus or Barabbas, a Zealot leader. The crowd, incited by the priests, chose Barabbas. When Pilate asked the crowd what he should do to Jesus, they shouted: 'Crucify him.' Mark comments that, because Pilate wanted to satisfy the crowd, he released Barabbas, had Jesus flogged and then handed him over to be crucified.

Hence, Pilate is depicted as a weak person who was persuaded to execute an innocent person to pacify the Jewish authorities. He clearly thought Jesus was innocent, as Mark tells us that he knew it was out of envy that the chief priests handed Jesus over to him.

The phrase 'handed over' (delivered) is used 12 times in the Passion narrative. Some commentators see this as Mark telling his readers that Jesus' death is fulfilling prophecy, and so Pilate is an agent of God's plans. However, this does not absolve him from responsibility of his actions, just as Judas was responsible for his actions.

Inscription about Pilate

From an inscription found at Caesarea it seems that the correct title of his office was *praefectus*, which is more a military title than the financial title of procurator.

The name of Pilate, inscribed on a stone found in Caesarea

Although the inscription is not easy to read, the following letters and words can be identified:

> ... S TIBERIEVM
> ... NTIVS PILATVS
> ... ECTVS IVDAE

The inscription was probably attached to a building dedicated to Tiberius, referred to in the top line.

The second line contains part of the name of Pontius Pilate.

The third line refers to Pilate being *praefectus* (prefect).

KEY QUOTE

Now there were some present at that time who told Jesus about the Galileans whose blood Pilate had mixed with their sacrifices.

(Luke 13: 1)

TASK

Carry out some research into the incident referred to in Luke 13: 1. Find out what Josephus says about Pilate in his book, *The Jewish Wars*. What do these accounts reveal about the character of Pilate?

Objective To compare these accounts of Pilate's behaviour with those found in the gospel accounts

KEY IDEA

Messiah is the Hebrew form of the Greek word Christ. It has the meaning of 'the anointed one' and referred to one approved by God. Often linked to kings, it later became associated with the hope of an ideal king, the one sent by God to restore Israel.

66 KEY QUOTES 99

Again the High Priest asked him. 'Are you the Christ, the Son of the Blessed One?'

(Mark 14: 61)

… I will raise up your offspring … I will establish the throne of his Kingdom for ever … he shall be my son.

(2 Samuel 7: 12–14)

'Abba, Father,' he said, 'everything is possible for you.'

(Mark 14: 36)

And when the centurion, who stood there in front of Jesus, heard his cry and saw how he died, he said, 'Surely this man was the Son of God!'

(Mark 15: 39)

The beginning of the Gospel about Jesus Christ, the Son of God.

(Mark 1: 1)

ii) Mark 15: 42–45

Pilate's final appearance in the narrative occurs when Joseph of Arimathea asked him for Jesus' body in order to carry out the burial. It seems that Roman custom allowed friends to claim the body. Pilate is portrayed as a person whom Joseph was frightened to approach, to request Jesus' body.

Some commentators see this event as important, as the authorities were satisfied that Jesus was really dead.

2 Presentation of Jesus

a) As Son of God

There is no clear evidence that Palestinian Judaism associated the term 'Son of God' with the **messiah** (see page 227). Nevertheless, Mark clearly sees some connection (Mark 14: 61), which suggests that the idea was not totally unknown. The Dead Sea Scrolls (see page 213) seem to connect the two ideas. For instance, one fragment gives 2 Samuel 7: 14 a messianic interpretation.

There is much debate about the use by Jesus of Abba to refer to God, for example, in Mark 14: 36. In the past, some commentators have argued that it was a unique usage and not something that Jews would do. They claimed it showed that Jesus had a special awareness of God as his father. However, more recent studies, especially by Vermes, show that others used Abba to refer to God. Therefore, it is doubtful whether this usage by Jesus can be used as evidence of his sonship.

In the set texts for this exam, there is only one reference to the Son of God in Mark's Gospel.

Although the Greek does not demand the definite article (the), most commentators argue to include it. If this is correct then the importance for Mark might be that this is a Gentile who becomes a believer, and the Gentile makes that confession in response to the death of Jesus. Thus, the message of the Cross is the heart of the gospel.

Some commentators interpret it in two ways – what it meant for the centurion and what Mark intended it to mean for his readers. For the centurion it could be understood to refer to a martyr or divine man and be translated without the definite article (a son of God). However, for Mark's readers it was a confession of Christ's status. He was the Son of God.

Mark starts his Gospel with the title Son of God (Mark 1: 1) and concludes Jesus' death with the same claim.

b) As Son of Man

This title seems to be a self-designation, since the phrase is only ever applied to Jesus by Jesus himself. It occurs 82 times in the gospels.

Commentators tend to divide the occurrences of the term into three types:

1 the work of the Son of Man on Earth (Mark 2: 10, Luke 19: 10)
2 the suffering of the Son of Man (Mark 9: 12, 14: 41)
3 the future glorification of the Son of Man (Mark 14: 26, 62).

In the texts to be studied for the exam, there are no occurrences of the first type, the work of the Son of Man on Earth.

i) The background

The background to this term is thought to be Daniel 7 where Daniel prophesies that a figure would appear as God's agent to gather his people and act as judge.

ii) Mark's approach

In Mark's Gospel, Jesus seems to avoid referring to himself as Messiah or Son of God. In contrast, he uses Son of Man quite freely in public and on many occasions. Commentators suggest that this was deliberate. The title Messiah had particular connotations in the public mind that Jesus wanted to avoid. Referring to himself as the Son of Man allowed Jesus to fill it with his own meaning. The context in Daniel is of a redeemer figure with overtones of supernatural character and origin. However, it is sufficiently ambiguous to allow Jesus to link with it the idea of suffering. Only after the disciples were convinced that he was Messiah could he instruct them in the idea that he would suffer and die and come again in glory.

iii) Occurrences in Mark's Gospel

There are three Son of Man sayings in the texts set in this exam.

Mark 14: 21 and **Mark 14: 41** – Both of these are of type 2, as they relate to the betrayal of Jesus. They predict the betrayal and express woe to the betrayer. Other sayings within Mark's Gospel refer to Jesus' suffering.

Mark 14: 62 – This is a saying of type 3 as it refers to future glorification. It is said by Jesus to the High Priest, who then claims that blasphemy has been committed. However, the claim of messiahship is not blasphemy. It seems, therefore, that is was his claim to fulfil Daniel 7, as being the one who sits at God's right hand, that was regarded as blasphemous.

c) As righteous martyr

i) Righteous

Righteous means free from sin and guilt. The innocence of Jesus is a feature of all the gospel accounts. In Mark 11: 27–33, the Jewish authorities could not reply when he was challenged about his authority. At his trial, the Sanhedrin could find no evidence against him, so they persuaded people to give false testimony. Yet even then their testimonies did not agree (Mark 14: 55–59). Likewise, Pilate could find no guilt in Jesus and only handed him over to be crucified because of fear of the crowd. He was aware that the envy of the chief priests was the reason why Jesus had been handed over to him.

As has already been discussed (see page 247), Mark emphasises the phrase 'handed over' (delivered), which occurs 12 times in the narrative, showing that events were the fulfillment of prophecy. Mark sees the culmination in the centurion's recognition of Jesus as the Son of God.

ii) Martyr

A martyr is someone who witnesses to their religious belief and as a result endures suffering and death. It also incorporates the idea that they witness, knowing that the result will almost certainly be death. The martyr makes no attempt to avoid the consequences.

These features can be seen in Mark's narrative of the Passion of Jesus. The allusions to Old Testament passages (see page 227) link the righteous sufferer of the Psalms with the suffering servant of Isaiah.

66 KEY QUOTES 99

But that you may know that the Son of Man has authority on earth to forgive sins …

(Mark 2: 10)

Look, the Son of Man is betrayed into the hands of sinners.

(Mark 14: 41)

And you will see the Son of Man sitting at the right hand of the Mighty One and coming on the clouds of heaven.

(Mark 14: 62)

The chief priests and the whole Sanhedrin were looking for evidence against Jesus so they could put him to death, but they did not find any.

(Mark 14: 55)

" KEY QUOTES "

Take this cup from me.
Yet not what I will, but
what you will.

(Mark 14: 36)

In the hand of the Lord
is a cup … he pours it
out, and all the wicked
of the earth drink it
down to its very dregs.

(Psalm 75: 8)

… you who have
drunk from the hand
of the Lord the cup
of his wrath … the
goblet that makes men
stagger.

(Isaiah 51: 17)

… he, too, will drink of
the wine of God's fury,
which has been poured
full strength into the
cup of his wrath.

(Revelation 14: 10)

We are ready to die
rather than transgress
the laws of our
ancestors.

(2 Maccabees 7: 2)

In my vision at night
I looked, and there
before me was one like
a son of man, coming
with the clouds of
heaven. He approached
the Ancient of Days
and was led into his
presence. He was given
authority, glory and
sovereign power …

(Daniel 7: 13–14)

The lack of any attempt to avoid death is demonstrated in Jesus' knowledge of his betrayal and arrest, in his silence at the trial before the Sanhedrin and his silence before Pilate.

Perhaps it is in the garden of Gethsemane that Mark gives us the clearest picture of Jesus' willingness to suffer even to death, when he says: 'Take this cup from me. Yet not what I will, but what you will,' (Mark 14: 36). The cup is a symbol used in the Old Testament by the prophets and the psalmists and refers to God's judgement, for example, in Psalm 75 and Isaiah 51. It is also referred to in Revelation 14, which speaks of the cup of God's wrath. Hence Jesus was aware that he was facing suffering and a death that was so terrifying that he asked God if there was any way to avoid it. Yet if it was necessary, then he was willing to suffer.

Such steadfastness is reflected in the classic accounts of the martyrdoms of Eleazer and of a mother with her seven sons (2 Maccabees 6: 18–7: 42). The Wisdom of Solomon is another text that refers to a righteous one who was persecuted but, to the dismay of his persecutors, becomes a heavenly being at the final judgement. At one level, Jesus can be seen to be in this tradition of righteous martyrs.

3 Presentation of Jesus' death

a) As sacrifice and atonement

The idea that Jesus' death should be understood as a sacrifice is not stated, as such, in the set passages for this exam. However, it is a theme that recurs in the gospels. In particular, John's Gospel refers to Jesus as 'The lamb of God who takes away the sins of the world' (John 12: 9). It is even more developed in the rest of the New Testament.

Commentators disagree about what, exactly, John was referring to. Suggestions include:

- the lamb of daily sacrifice at the Temple
- the scapegoat that was banished in the desert, symbolically bearing away the sins of the people (Leviticus 16)
- the guilt offering, which was a sacrifice that dealt with sin (Leviticus 14)
- the Passover lamb
- the lamb led to the slaughter, whose death deals with transgressions (Isaiah 53).

The symbolism of the Last Supper also has hints at sacrifice. The bread represents the broken body and the wine, the spilt blood.

Certainly there are links with the suffering servant passages in Isaiah 52–53. Perhaps the clearest statement of this idea of sacrifice is found in the letter to Hebrews. However, the very idea of a suffering messiah was contradictory to the popular messianic expectations. It would not be until his resurrection that the true messianic role could be understood.

Literally, atonement means made at one with. This understanding of Jesus' death is found in Mark 15: 38, where there is reference to the Temple curtain tearing from top to bottom. This is thought to be the curtain that divided the Holy of Holies (where God was regarded as being present) from the rest of the Temple. It emphasised the gap between human beings and God – the gap caused by sin. Only the High Priest could go into the Holy of Holies. The fact that the curtain was split from top to bottom might indicate that the barrier between God and humankind had been removed (now all could go into the presence of God) and that God had been the initiator. That this happened at the moment of Jesus' death indicates that Mark saw the two events, the death of Jesus and the curtain being torn, as linked. Hence, Jesus' death dealt with the barrier between God and humankind, namely sin. In some way, through his death, Jesus absorbed the penalty of sin and made us at one with God. The fact that Mark has the centurion, a Gentile, recognising Jesus as the Son of God indicates that this atonement is universal, for all people.

Again, the suffering servant passages from Isaiah 52–53 are a possible background.

b) As the idea of ransom

Again, this idea is not specifically stated in the set texts. However, Mark does make a clear reference to Jesus' death as a ransom in Mark 10: 45.

A ransom could refer to the price paid for a life that would otherwise be forfeit (Exodus 21: 30). In the Roman world, a ransom was the price paid to set a slave free. The payment was made to the slave owner in a religious ceremony. This indicated that the slave was now no longer owned by men since he now was owned by the god.

Certainly both references have the idea of Jesus paying the price for sin in order to set people free.

Some commentators note that the translation 'for many' (Mark 10: 45) is better translated 'in place of'. Hence it contains the idea of substitution. The many receive what they cannot effect. Also the common usage of the word many does not necessarily demand that some are excluded.

Again, the suffering servant passage from Isaiah 53 is a possible background to the idea of ransom in Mark's Gospel.

c) As the idea of covenant and new covenant

For background to the idea of a covenant see page 194. The reference to a new covenant is from the passage in Jeremiah 31. God was performing a new act of deliverance. Just as the old covenant had been sealed by the sprinkling of sacrificial blood, so the new covenant is established by Jesus' death. Drinking from the cup is equivalent to the sprinkling of the blood.

4 Features in the stories

a) Use of Old Testament

Mark clearly saw Jesus' death as a fulfilment of scripture. As has already been stated, the major influence on the Passion narrative was the suffering servant passages in Isaiah, and Psalm 22. The Early Church saw these passages as messianic, so linking the messiah with suffering.

1. There are several quotes or allusions to the Old Testament within the set texts for this exam. For example:
   - the entry into Jerusalem – the crowds shout to Jesus with quotes from the Psalms
   - the cleansing of the Temple – Jesus quotes from Isaiah 56: 7 and Jeremiah 7: 11
   - on the Mount of Olives after the Last Supper – Jesus quotes from Zechariah 13: 7 to show how his arrest and the disciples' flight was fulfilment of prophecy.

2. In some instances it is claimed that prophecy is fulfilled but the Old Testament is not quoted. For example:
   - the arrest – references in general state that 'the scriptures must be fulfilled'.

TASK

Read Psalm 22 and Isaiah 52: 13–53: 12. What parallels can you find between Jesus and his death, and these Old Testament passages?
Objective To develop understanding of how the Old Testament passages form an important background to the New Testament view of Jesus

KEY QUOTES

Yet it was the Lord's will to crush him and cause him to suffer, and though the Lord makes his life a guilt offering …
(Isaiah 53: 10)

He [Jesus] sacrificed for their sins once for all when he offered himself.
(Hebrews 7: 27)

At the sixth hour darkness came over the whole land until the ninth hour … The curtain of the temple was torn in two from top to bottom.
(Mark 15: 33, 38)

KEY WORD

Symbolism the use of one thing to represent another, generally important ideas or beliefs

❝ KEY QUOTES ❞

For even the Son of Man did not come to be served, but to serve, and to give his life as a ransom for many.

(Mark 10: 45)

However, if payment is demanded of him, he may redeem his life by paying what is demanded.

(Exodus 21: 30)

'The time is coming', declares the Lord, 'when I will make a new covenant … I will put my law in their minds and write it on their hearts … they will all know me … for I will forgive their wickedness and will remember their sins no more.'

(Jeremiah 31: 31–34)

Moses then took the blood, sprinkled it on the people and said, 'This is the blood of the covenant that the Lord has made with you in accordance with all these words.'

(Exodus 24: 8)

3 In several instances, although no Old Testament is quoted, the idea or **symbolism** being expressed is rooted there. For example:

■ Garden of Gethsemane – the reference to the cup, which was an Old Testament symbol of God's wrath and judgement
■ Garden of Gethsemane – the Son of Man sayings were based on Daniel
■ the crucifixion of Jesus – the dividing and casting of lots, the cry of abandonment, the giving of drink are all reflected in Psalms 22 and 69
■ on the Cross – the link with Elijah, who was the recognised forerunner and helper of the messiah.

Christianity is presented as the fulfilment of the promises in Judaism. Jesus is seen as the Christ, the righteous sufferer, the fulfiller of the Old Testament, the long-awaited king.

b) The role of Romans

Nowhere in the gospels does Jesus denounce the Romans or appear to do anything that could be seen as subversive. Indeed, it is the Roman centurion who is the first to recognise, in Jesus' death, his status as Son of God.

The Romans were directly concerned with the trial of Jesus and his execution. Roman authority had to be obtained for any execution, so the Sanhedrin changed the religious charge of blasphemy to a political charge of Jesus claiming to be King of the Jews. Luke's Gospel comments that the specific charges were subversion, opposing taxes and claiming to be Christ, a king.

Crucifixion was a Roman form of punishment, which the Jews did not generally use.

Roman soldiers are also presented as mocking Jesus. However, Pilate is depicted as regarding Jesus as innocent but fearing the Jewish authorities and so found Jesus guilty (see page 247).

c) The role of the Jews

In fact, all the characters in Mark's Passion narrative are Jewish, apart from Pilate and the Roman soldiers.

In the set texts for this exam, there are several comments by Mark that seem to imply that the Jewish authorities were responsible for Jesus' death. At the cleansing of the Temple, Mark records that the chief priests and the teachers of the law began looking for a way to kill Jesus. They feared him because the crowds were amazed at his teaching. Again, the fear of the people silenced those who questioned Jesus' authority (Mark 11: 27–33). The start of Chapter 14 picks up the same theme, with the chief priests and teachers of the law looking for ways to arrest Jesus and kill him. The offer of help from Judas delighted them.

The trial before the Sanhedrin showed that there was no evidence against Jesus, but false witnesses spoke against him. The charge of blasphemy arose from Jesus' statement at the trial itself. The deliberate change, from a religious charge to a political one, was an attempt to secure the death sentence from Pilate. However, Mark comments that Pilate knew that it was envy that made the chief priests hand Jesus over, although the actual choice to save Barabbas and crucify Jesus is presented as coming from the crowd.

Reflection and assessment AO1

It is vital to bring together the information you have covered so far and recognise how it can be transformed into effective examination-style revision and answers. The best way to do this is to ask the question: 'How am I going to be assessed on this information?'

The first way is through assessment objective 1 (AO1). For this objective you need to be able to: 'select and clearly demonstrate the relevant knowledge and understanding through the use of evidence, examples and correct language and terminology'.

Look back to page 7 in the Introduction to review the level descriptors for AO1. There is a description of the character and features for each level. The exam is marked with reference to levels.

Look at the following sample answer, which is a response to the question:

Explain and illustrate how Mark presents Jesus as a righteous martyr.   (25 marks)

> Mark presents Jesus as Son of Man and Son of God as well as righteous martyr. There are three types of 'Son of Man' sayings and Mark has all three types in his gospel. In the Passion narrative is the eschatological type.
>
> Jesus is also portrayed by Mark as an innocent man. Even the centurion, a Gentile, agreed. Pilate, the Sanhedrin, the chief priests — none could find fault with Jesus yet still he was executed. Mark shows that there was no alternative. It was prophesied — it had to happen.
>
> He knew he would die and did nothing to stop it. He could have avoided death but he chose not to.
>
> Mark portrays him as a character in Isaiah. He is silent like Psalm 22 says. Yet he knew what was going to happen. Jesus shows this in the Garden of Gethsemane when he talks about the cup and asks it to be taken from him. Yet still he bows down to God's way of suffering.
>
> Jesus is in line with the martyrs of 2 Maccabees. Standing up for his faith even unto death. Nothing would tempt him to give way and avoid death.

An examiner made the following comments.

> References are not illustrated or explained.
> This is not in Mark's Gospel.
> Needs an example to show the evidence.
> Not enough to demonstrate the point.
> Material is irrelevant.
> Material is inaccurate.
> The illustration needs to be explained, as it is not clear why it demonstrates the point.
> The biblical reference is wrong.

Now complete the task on page 254.

TASK

Draw a table with two columns and use it to connect the comments with the appropriate parts of the essay. Write the word or phrase from the essay in one column and the appropriate comment alongside it, in the other column.

Note that not all the comments are appropriate for this essay answer.

Try to add further comments of your own.

What do you think about this style of writing? How would you improve it?

Do you think it is clear which material refers to 'righteous' and which to 'martyr'?

Do you think the two aspects have been adequately covered? If not, how would you improve the answer?

Why would this answer not score level 4?

Using this structure, write a level 4–5 answer.

Objective Examination focus on AO1 with a particular aim of developing the level 5 expectations of a 'very high level of ability to select and deploy relevant information' (level 5 descriptor)

Suggestion for further application of skills

Use what you have done to create the ideal essay plan for this question. Using the above answer and analysis, try doing this under timed conditions and then use the plan to carry out some peer assessment. Mark each other's work, identifying the strengths and the areas for development.

Part 3
A critical analysis of the issues

What are the issues that I am expected to consider and to analyse critically?

■ The issues arising from the themes in Mark's Passion narrative

1 Problems of interpreting the text

a) Significance for whom?

It is not always clear how to distinguish between the significance of the events as seen by the writer, and the significance of the event for Jesus. In the main, the words and actions that Jesus said and did are the focus of what was significant, since they were his words and actions.

In contrast, the placing of the story in a particular context and the way the event is recounted may reflect more the writers' understanding of what was significant.

b) Too much examination?

Another difficulty involves trying to avoid reading too much into the text. For instance, in Mark 11: 3 there is the sentence: 'The Lord needs it.' It is not clear to whom this refers. Is it Jesus? If so, is it a special title in which he reveals his Lordship? Or is it just a title of respect meaning Sir or teacher? Some commentators argue that it refers to God.

The New Testament has been examined and commented on in such detail that there is a risk of every word and nuance being studied to such a point that more is read into the account than the writer ever intended.

c) Was Jesus' entry into Jerusalem messianic?

Many commentators regard Jesus' entry on a donkey as a statement about his messiahship, and believe that the crowd recognised this claim in his actions. However, this has been questioned.

■ No mention is made of this incident at Jesus' trial.
■ The Romans would have arrested Jesus if it had been clearly messianic in nature.
■ John's account (John 12: 6) states that the disciples did not understand, implying that they saw no particular significance in the action of Jesus riding on a donkey into Jerusalem.
■ The events that followed seem to provide a very low-key end to this claim.

It is therefore possible that neither the disciples nor the crowds viewed this event as a messianic claim. However, it does not mean that it had no messianic significance. Rather, it may be that the disciples and crowd just did not recognise it.

? KEY QUESTIONS
- **What is the difference between the significance for Jesus and the significance for the gospel-writer?**
- **Is there a danger that scholars read too much into the accounts?**

d) The Son of Man

Perhaps a more significant debate is that of Jesus' use of the term Son of Man (see page 248). Some commentators argue that the term just means man or I and has no special significance. A few commentators have gone even further and claim that Jesus could not have used that phrase since it does not exist in Aramaic (the language in which Jesus would have spoken).

e) Possible conclusions

When assessing the issues that arise from the Son of Man sayings, it is important to reflect upon the arguments previously discussed and arrive at some appropriate conclusion. It may be that you accept none of these listed here, or just one of them, or you may have a different conclusion that is not listed. However, what is important is the way that you have arrived at your conclusion – the reasoning process.

From the preceding discussions, here are some possible conclusions you could draw.

1   The Son of Man sayings in all three categories are authentic.

2   Only the Son of Man sayings about the future are authentic.

3   The Son of Man sayings about the future are authentic but they refer to someone else.

4   The Son of Man sayings about his earthly life are the only authentic ones.

5   All the Son of Man sayings are creations of the Early Church.

2 Is the understanding of the cultural background to the New Testament accurate?

The New Testament recounts and describes events that occurred about 2000 years ago. Our knowledge of those times is not comprehensive. For instance, some commentators challenge the traditional view about the role and status of women in the time of the New Testament. Hence, Jesus' views may not have been so radical at the time as was first thought.

3 Issues about the Last Supper

a) Is Mark's account accurate?

Certainly there are differences between the accounts (see pages 237–8). There do appear to be two strands. Some scholars have tried to harmonise the accounts, others have tended to regard one strand as more trustworthy than the other, while yet others have challenged both strands as fabrication.

EXAM TIP

If you are asked to assess a view, do not merely give your opinion. Opinions that are unjustified do not qualify as evaluation. They are merely an expression of a personal view. Evaluation must give evidence of a reasoning process.

Avoiding mere statements of opinion demonstrates justifying a point of view through the use of reasoned argument (AO2).

? KEY QUESTIONS

- **Do we really know the cultural background to the New Testament?**
- **Was it just too long ago for us to be certain about anything?**
- **Is Mark's account of the Last Supper historically reliable?**

b) Was the Last Supper a Passover meal?

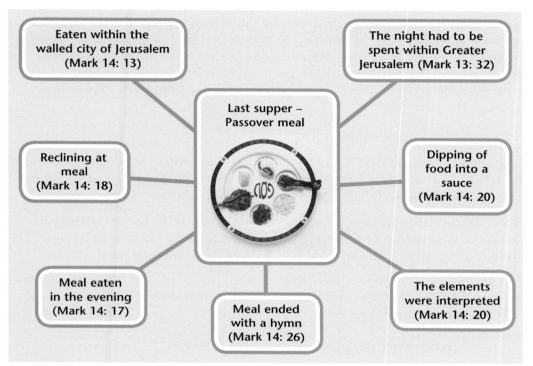

Eaten within the walled city of Jerusalem (Mark 14: 13)

The night had to be spent within Greater Jerusalem (Mark 13: 32)

Last supper – Passover meal

Reclining at meal (Mark 14: 18)

Dipping of food into a sauce (Mark 14: 20)

Meal eaten in the evening (Mark 14: 17)

Meal ended with a hymn (Mark 14: 26)

The elements were interpreted (Mark 14: 20)

Conditions for a Passover meal

Scholarly opinion as to whether Jesus was celebrating the Passover meal, at the Last Supper, is divided between two main conclusions:

- the Last Supper was the Passover meal
- the Last Supper was not the Passover meal but was a Kiddush, a feast celebrated at the beginning of the weekly Sabbath.

c) Was Jesus indicating he was present in the bread and the wine at the Last Supper?

There is also debate about exactly what happens at the Lord's Supper. Does anything happen to the bread and the wine? There are a number of different views about this.

i) Roman Catholic view: transubstantiation
According to Roman Catholic teaching (Council of Trent), during the mass, when the priest says: 'This is my body,' the bread and wine actually become the body and blood of Christ. Such an action can only be performed by a priest.

Every time the mass is celebrated, the sacrifice of Christ is offered. **Grace** is imparted to those present.

ii) The Lutheran view: Consubstantiation
Martin Luther did not accept transubstantiation. However, he did think the statement: 'This is my body,' had to be taken in some literal sense. He argued that the physical body of Christ is co-existent with the bread. Some commentators use the illustration of a sponge filled with water. The water is not part of the sponge but is present in it. Luther taught that it was a means by which Christ communicated grace to believers.

? KEY QUESTIONS

- Was the Last Supper a Passover meal?
- Is Jesus present in the bread and wine at the Eucharist?

TASK

The diagram shows the similarities between the Last Supper and the Passover meal.
Draw your own diagram to show the differences between the Last Supper and the Passover meal.
Objective To show understanding of the debate about whether the Last Supper was a Passover meal

 KEY WORDS

Transubstantiation the bread and wine change in substance but not in outward appearance
Grace a state of sanctification by God

 KEY PERSON

Martin Luther (1483–1546), was a German monk and theologian whose ideas inspired the Reformation.

KEY PEOPLE

Ulrich Zwingli (1484–1531), worked to spread the ideas of the Reformation in Switzerland.

John Calvin (1509–64), a French theologian, developed a reformed theology that became known as Calvinism. This emphasised the rule of God over all things.

Thomas Cranmer (1489–1556), Archbishop of Canterbury during the reign of Henry VIII, wrote and compiled the *Book of Common Prayer*.

TASK

Use the key points opposite as a basis for a writing frame to answer the question. Remember to add relevant quotes and questions at suitable places. The final product should show evidence of a sustained argument and critical analysis of more than one point of view. Critical evaluation means reasoning and responding to a point of view, rather than just stating a view.

Objective To develop awareness of what will constitute a very good answer by gradually building up a response that 'uses a range of evidence to sustain an argument' (level 5 descriptor)

iii) The Zwinglian–Calvinist view

Ulrich Zwingli and **John Calvin** both rejected any notion of the body and blood of Christ being locally present in the bread and the wine. They regarded the bread and the wine as symbols only, of Christ's broken body and shed blood. Whereas Zwingli regarded the supper as a Christ-given memorial, Calvin believed that Christ's body and blood were received spiritually in a person's heart by faith. Calvin's view is reflected in the service of the Lord's Supper in **Thomas Cranmer's** English *Book of Common Prayer*.

4 Strengths and weaknesses of these positions

The strength or weakness of each position depends partly upon whether Jesus intended his words to be taken literally or whether the bread and wine were intended by Jesus to be symbols of his body and blood.

It also depends upon whether eating and drinking represent feeding on Christ, either literally or symbolically, or they represent identification with Christ and his saving work. There may well be a very thin line dividing these two latter interpretations.

It further depends on whether there is an intended priestly offering of Christ's sacrifice of himself at the Last Supper or whether the sacrifice on the cross is so complete and sufficient that no further kind of offering of that sacrifice can now be made.

Reflection and assessment AO2

It is vital to bring together the information you have covered so far and recognise how it can be transformed into effective examination-style revision and answers. The best way to do this is to ask the question: 'How am I going to be assessed on this information?'

Look back to page 8 in the Introduction to review the level descriptors for AO2. There is a description of the character and features for each level. The exam is marked with reference to levels.

Look at the key points, below, in answer to the question:

'The Last Supper was a Passover meal.' Discuss. (10 marks)

You will need to refer to these points, which are not presented in any particular order, to complete the task.

- Mark's Gospel says it was a Passover meal.
- There is no mention of the Passover lamb.
- The bread was not unleavened.
- They were reclining, which was normal only at the Passover meal.
- The early Christians celebrated the Last Supper once a week, not once a year (like Passover).

The list is deliberately basic. At this stage you should be able to identify the fact that it contains the general issues but does not have the detail of development. You will need to add this.

Suggestion for further application of skills

Read the possible conclusions about the Son of Man sayings again. In groups, design a flow chart that clearly provides the evidence for each conclusion.

Part 1
The texts

What am I required to study?

■ The Resurrection narratives in the synoptic gospels

This means I am expected to know about:

■ how each gospel-writer understands the meaning of the Resurrection.

The Specification makes explicit reference to the set passages that are to be studied from the three synoptic gospels. You are expected to have first-hand knowledge of these texts, and it is important that you focus on the particular aspects referred to in the topic given above. It would be helpful to write your notes under the heading listed under 'This means I am expected to know about', as it is from these areas that the exam questions will be derived.

Remember that your studies will include elements of the *two* basic assessment objectives of:

■ Knowledge and Understanding (AO1)
■ Evaluation (AO2).

See pages 7–8 in the Introduction to remind yourself of these objectives.

The evaluation material is set out in Part 3 of this topic (page 268) and can be studied either alongside the AO1 material, as you work through this topic, or as a discrete topic.

1 The meaning of the Resurrection

The Resurrection meant that Jesus was now able to proclaim that which had not been clearly explained before. It was an announcement of his full glory, his status and position, and his power that had conquered death and overcome suffering.

Now the apparent defeat had been shown to be total victory and his saving message would be triumphantly spread throughout the whole world, with power.

Christ declares who he really is and that he is able to be with his followers even when he is not physically present.

The synoptic gospel accounts have both similarities and differences. For a comparison between the three accounts, see page 264. One explanation that accounts for these differences concerns the gospel-writers' aims and readership. The emphasis of each gospel is discussed below.

KEY WORD

Apologetic concerned with defensive arguments, particularly in Christianity

❝ KEY QUOTES ❞

'You are to say, "His disciples came during the night and stole him away while we were asleep." …' And this story has been widely circulated among the Jews to this very day.

(Matthew 28: 13, 15)

The tombs broke open and the bodies of many holy people who had died were raised to life.

(Matthew 27: 52)

When they saw him they worshipped him.

(Matthew 28: 17)

Therefore go and make disciples of all nations, baptising them in the name of the Father and of the Son and of the Holy Spirit …

(Matthew 28: 19)

KEY WORD

Great commission the last recorded personal instruction given by Jesus to his disciples, emphasising mission work, evangelism, and baptism

2 The Resurrection account in Matthew

Matthew was writing for Jewish Christians and therefore had a Jewish interest in the way he recounted the Resurrection. He clearly had an **apologetic** aim, seeking to answer many questions that people may have posed about Jesus. He wanted to provide evidence that Jesus was truly resurrected, with a physical body, and that this was in fulfilment of prophecy. In addition, commentators suggest that Matthew wanted to show the role and importance of the Church. Certainly, both these aims can be supported from the text, in terms of what Matthew has chosen to include in his Resurrection account.

a) Apologetic focus

The apologetic focus could explain Matthew's inclusion of the story of the guards at the tomb. He is the only gospel-writer to mention this. The text (Matthew 28: 11–15) answers the charge that the disciples stole the body. The guards themselves witnessed the supernatural removal of the body. The fact that the tomb was empty is made clear by the story of the guards. The physical body is emphasised as Matthew records how the women clasped the risen Jesus' feet (verse 9).

Matthew wants to make clear that these events are far beyond normal events. It is an event in which heaven comes down to Earth in power and declaration.

Matthew also emphasises the physical reality of the Resurrection. Jesus speaks to the women near the tomb. They see him in physical form and clasp his feet (verse 9). Likewise, the disciples see Jesus and hear him speak (verses 16–20).

b) The status of Jesus

Jesus is no ordinary prophet or man. His true identity is clearly revealed by his resurrection. Matthew portrays Jesus as the Messiah, who would bring in the Kingdom of God and a New Age. Part of these eschatological events would be the raising of the dead. Matthew is the only gospel-writer to mention the tombs breaking open and the dead being raised to life (Matthew 27: 52).

There are also references to angels. Angels were God's messengers, so this guaranteed that the proclamation was truth from God.

The fulfilment of prophecy also confirms Jesus' status. The angel, as God's messenger, announces: 'He is risen, just as he said.' (verse 6).

His status as divine is demonstrated as he is treated as a heavenly being.

He is worshipped (verses 8–9, 17) and he accepts it. In verse 18 he claims that all authority in heaven and Earth is given to him.

His heavenly status is also declared when he claims they are to teach all nations everything he has commanded them. Then he makes the claim that he would be with them always, to the very end of the age (verse 20). This **great commission** is a reflection of Daniel 7: 13–14, which depicts the Son of Man in similar terms, thereby showing Jesus as fulfilling this role.

c) Church focus

Matthew shows that the roles of Jesus are now passed to the Church. The Church is given authority to act as Christ on Earth. This is seen in the final section of Matthew where Jesus gives the disciples the great commission. Jesus tells them to make other disciples. The Church's mission is clearly stated: to teach and convert and baptise. However, the Church will not be doing these things in its own strength, but his. Jesus promises to be in the midst of the Church community.

d) Literary devices

Matthew has constructed his retelling of the events, using two sets of contrasting scenes to bring out the significance of the story.

Firstly, he contrasts the priests' demands to have the tomb guarded, to stop any possibility of something happening to the body of Jesus, with the intervening act of God raising Jesus from the dead.

Within this, there is the contrast of the women's simple reverence and the priestly intrigue.

The second contrast is between the plot to spread lies about what happened to the body and the great commission to spread truth.

3 The Resurrection account in Luke

Luke is writing to a non-Christian world, to present to them an historical account of the origins of Christianity. Therefore it is apologetic in its purpose. Luke is also thought to have written the Acts of the Apostles, as both are dedicated to Theophilus. The resurrection appearances recounted in Luke's Gospel occur in or around Jerusalem, rather than in Galilee. This focus on Jerusalem links with the start of Acts (where the Church began in Jerusalem at Pentecost – Acts 2).

Luke's Resurrection narrative makes clear how Jesus fulfils prophecy and is the Messiah. The reality of his physical resurrection is also emphasised.

a) God's salvation plan

Luke shows that God is at work in all the events. All these things are part of God's salvation plan. In Luke 24: 7, the word 'must' is used to emphasise how all these things were deliberate and planned rather than the result of some tragic accident. The use of the passive 'has been raised' points to the fact that God raised Jesus from the dead. Jesus did not resurrect himself.

The divine plan is explained to the two disciples on the road to Emmaus. Jesus tells them that 'the Christ must suffer' and explains to them all the prophecies in the scriptures concerning the event.

When Jesus appears to his disciples in the upper room, further appeals to fulfilled prophecy are mentioned and explained. The deliberateness of the happenings is made clear, especially in verses 44–46.

The doctrine of salvation is summed up in Jesus' words spoken to his disciples (Luke 24: 46–49). The message speaks of Christ's death and resurrection, of repentance for the forgiveness of sins, of preaching in Jesus' name to all nations, of being witnesses and of power from the Holy Spirit.

The gospel ends with the risen Lord becoming the exalted Lord, ascending to heaven.

❝ KEY QUOTES ❞

In my vision at night I looked, and there before me was one like a son of man, coming with the clouds of heaven. … He was given authority, glory and sovereign power; all peoples, nations and men of every language worshipped him. His dominion is everlasting dominion that will never pass away, and his kingdom is one that will never be destroyed.

(Daniel 7: 13–14)

The Son of Man must be delivered into the hands of sinful men, be crucified and on the third day be raised again.

(Luke 24: 7)

Everything must be fulfilled that is written about me in the Law of Moses, the Prophets and the Psalms.

(Luke 24: 44)

Did not the Christ have to suffer these things and then enter his glory?

(Luke 24: 26)

66 **KEY QUOTES** 99

They found the stone rolled away from the tomb, but when they entered, they did not find the body of the Lord Jesus Christ.

(Luke 24: 3)

Look at my hands and feet. It is I myself. Touch me and see; a ghost does not have flesh and bones, as you see I have.

(Luke 24: 39)

And we eagerly await a Saviour from there, the Lord Jesus Christ, who … will transform our lowly bodies so that they will be like his glorious body.

(Philippians 3: 20–21)

EXAM TIP

Do not use a Bible quotation just to repeat what you have written. Either you need to allude to the quotation or you need to use it to draw out some further comment. This demonstrates relevant knowledge and understanding through the use of evidence and examples (AO1).

TASK

Read Luke's Birth narrative (Luke 1–2) and draw a chart showing any parallels between Luke's birth narratives and his resurrection narratives.

b) The reality of the Resurrection

Luke makes clear that the women knew where the tomb of Jesus was. They followed Joseph and saw the tomb and how his body was laid in it. The women are presented as witnesses and there is no way they could later be mistaken and go to the wrong tomb. When they do go to the tomb, the stone has been rolled away and they are witnesses to the empty tomb.

When Peter ran to the tomb, after hearing the women's account, he saw the strips of linen by themselves. This observation again underlines the fact of the empty tomb, and that something marvellous had happened.

The reaction of the Eleven shows that these disciples were very sceptical. Even the women's account did not convince them. It would need strong evidence to convince such sceptics.

Jesus' physical presence is made clear in the story of the road to Emmaus. Jesus was visible. He walked, talked, broke bread. Later, when he appeared in the room with the disciples, it is made clear that he is not a ghost. They could touch him. He had flesh and bones. He ate broiled fish. Luke wanted the reader to have no doubt that Jesus was in physical form, even though he also possessed supernatural properties such as the ability to appear and disappear suddenly. His glorification meant that his body was somehow different. Paul makes reference to this in Philippians 3 and 1 Corinthians 15.

One of the characteristics of Luke's Resurrection narrative is the unbelief of the various characters (see below). This doubt was overcome by the direct presence of the resurrected Christ. It is the reality of the Resurrection that changed the unbelievers to believers.

c) The status of Jesus

When the women arrived and saw the tomb empty, Luke referred to the missing body of Jesus as the 'body of the Lord Jesus Christ'. His true status is revealed. His glory is revealed – we see who he really is. He is described as Lord and Messiah.

Again the presence of the angels made clear that God's truth was being proclaimed. The angels reminded the women of the prophecy by Jesus that he would be crucified and on the third day be raised again. Jesus is referred to as the Son of Man. (For notes on this title see pages 248–9.)

In the story of the road to Emmaus, it is clear that, initially, the two travellers had the wrong view of Jesus. He was *not* just a powerful prophet but the fulfilment of prophecy, the true Messiah who suffered and was glorified. The Resurrection was a demonstration of this.

d) Growth in faith

There is a theme of wondering that eventually moves to belief and faith. The women at first wonder (Luke 24: 4) when they see the empty tomb. By verse 8 Luke recounts that the women remembered the prophecy that Jesus had made about his death and resurrection. However, the Eleven did not believe the women because 'their words seemed to them like nonsense' (Luke 24: 11). In contrast, Peter goes to the tomb and sees the strips of linen. Luke characteristically comments: 'he went away, wondering to himself what had happened' (Luke 24: 12).

The two travellers on the road to Emmaus were kept from recognising Jesus (verse 16). As the story develops, they gradually come to understanding and belief. Luke parallels the lack of recognition at the start of the story with the ending: 'Then their eyes were opened and they recognised him.' (Luke 24: 31). By the time they return to Jerusalem to tell the disciples, they are able to proclaim: 'It is true! The Lord has risen … ' (Luke 24: 34).

Finally, Luke records the appearance of Jesus to the disciples. At first they are frightened and think they are seeing a ghost. Even after being shown the hands and feet of Jesus, they still did not believe. However, the last verse records: 'They worshipped him and returned to Jerusalem with great joy. And they stayed continually at the temple, praising God.' (Luke 24: 52–3).

4 The Resurrection account in Mark

The exact text of Mark 16 has long been a matter of debate (see pages 265-7). The best manuscripts end at verse 8 with the words: 'for they were afraid'. The focus of Mark's account is described below.

a) Discipleship

The trio of women, Mary Magdalene, Mary and Salome, are mentioned by name and are witnesses of the crucifixion, the burial and the empty tomb. They are described as 'those who followed and served' (Mark 15: 41). According to Mark, these are the very characteristics of the true disciple. In contrast, the Eleven are absent from these events.

The women also display the characteristics of confusion and misunderstanding.

Misunderstanding by the disciples is a feature of Mark's Gospel. The women bring spices to anoint Jesus but he has risen and is not dead. The women are very confused about what has really happened. The final verses of the gospel (Mark 16: 5–8) depict divine intervention – the only way the misunderstandings will be corrected. Despite the devotion and courage of the women, it still requires God to open their eyes so they can understand. As in the other gospels, the appearance of the angel signifies God's proclamation.

The mention of Peter reaffirms the fact that, despite his denials, he has not been cast off.

b) Awe

The Greek word used in verse 5 and verse 6, and often translated as alarmed, is used in the New Testament only by Mark. It has the sense of awe and describes the reaction of being in the presence of the majesty of God.

c) ' … because they were afraid.'

This is the end of the gospel (unless the original ending has been lost – see page 266). The event of the Resurrection renders the women speechless. Some commentators see the abrupt ending as deliberate, to emphasise the supernatural character of the event the women had witnessed: an event to which the only response is amazement and godly fear. R.H. Lightfoot commented that Mark's purpose may have been: 'to emphasise human inadequacy, lack of understanding, and weakness in the presence of supreme divine action and its meaning'.

> **❝ KEY QUOTE ❞**
>
> … to emphasise human inadequacy, lack of understanding, and weakness in the presence of supreme divine action and its meaning.
>
> (Lightfoot commenting on the ending of Mark's Gospel)

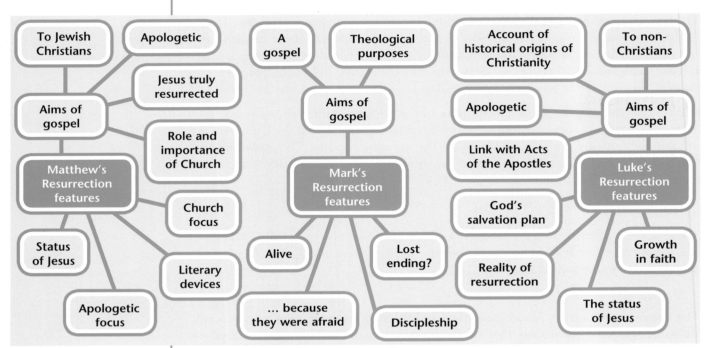

Summary diagram: Features of the Resurrection accounts

TASK

Look at the basic answer opposite. Try to work out what a developed answer would deal with by adding two or three more bullet points. Then develop this answer by adding further bullet points, to indicate how a higher answer would address the question. Remember to keep the bullet points focused on the question.

Objective To develop awareness of what constitutes a very good answer, by gradually building up a response that is 'an excellent attempt to address the question, showing understanding and engagement with the material' (level 5 descriptor)

Reflection and assessment AO1

It is vital to bring together the information you have covered so far and recognise how it can be transformed into effective examination-style revision and answers. The best way to do this is to ask the question: 'How am I going to be assessed on this information?'

Look back to page 7 in the Introduction to review the level descriptors for AO1. There is a description of the character and features for each level. The exam is marked with reference to levels.

Look at the following sample basic answer, which is a response to the question:

Explain how Luke presents Jesus' resurrection.   (25 marks)

The basic answer might deal with the question by:

■ stating the main purpose of Luke's Gospel – apologetic aim
■ giving some basic indication of how this aim is illustrated in the Resurrection account
■ giving some example of how Luke shows the reality of the Resurrection.

Suggestion for further application of skills

Now try the same technique to build a level 5 answer for the question:

Explain how Matthew presents the resurrection of Jesus.   (25 marks)

Part 2
Themes

> **What am I required to study?**
> - The Resurrection narrative in the synoptic gospels
>
> **This means I am expected to know about:**
> - the long ending of Mark (Mark 16: 9–20)
> - the short ending of Mark (Mark 16: 9)
> - debates about the lost ending of Mark.

You are expected to have first-hand knowledge of the various additional verses of the end of Mark's Gospel – what follows Mark 16: 8. You should be able to discuss which, if any, are the most likely to be the original ending to Mark's Gospel.

It would be helpful to write your notes under the headings listed in 'This means I am expected to know about', as it is from these areas that the exam questions will be derived.

Remember that your studies will include elements of the *two* basic assessment objectives of:

- Knowledge and Understanding (AO1)
- Evaluation (AO2).

See pages 7–8 in the Introduction to remind yourself of these objectives.

The evaluation material is set out in Part 3 of this topic (page 268) and can be studied either alongside the AO1 material, as you work through this topic, or as a discrete topic.

1 The ending of Mark

a) The end is at verse 8

Mark's Gospel has traditionally been regarded as the first and earliest. The section on the sources of the synoptic gospels (pages 205–9) offers the arguments that support the idea that Mark's Gospel was used by both Matthew and Luke. If such a relationship between the first three gospels is correct, this suggests that it is important that Mark's Gospel is seen as reliable. However, Mark 16 ends very abruptly at a crucial point in the story of Easter Sunday, when the empty tomb was discovered. Mark does not seem to record any resurrection appearances. Instead, he mentions the appearance of the young man dressed in a white robe, telling the women that Jesus had risen from the dead and that the disciples would see Jesus in Galilee.

Some arguments have been proposed to support the view that this was the intended end of the gospel (see page 263). However, most commentators do not agree. It does seem strange that a book about good news ends on a note of fear. It also seems highly unlikely that Mark would not have included any accounts of Jesus' resurrection appearances.

> **❝ KEY QUOTE ❞**
> **Trembling and bewildered, the women went out and fled from the tomb. They said nothing to anyone, because they were afraid.**
>
> **(Mark 16: 8)**

TASK

Carry out some research on the connection of the *Freer Logion* with the problem of identifying the ending of Mark's Gospel.

Objective To reinforce understanding of the problems of the ending of Mark's Gospel

KEY QUESTION

Are the verses beyond verse 8 to be regarded as scripture and therefore having authority as part of God's revelation?

KEY WORDS

Codex in the form of a book where the pages are bound together, as against a scroll

Codex Vaticanus the most famous manuscript, in the possession of the Vatican library, believed to be fourth century; thought to be the oldest and most complete copy of the Greek Bible in existence

Codex Sinaiticus a fourth-century manuscript housed in the British Museum; contains part of the Old Testament and the complete New Testament in Greek **Minuscules** early texts were all written in capital letters; manuscripts written in lower-case letters that went below base line (minuscules) appeared later

Some scholars, such as Bultmann, argue that the transfiguration (Mark 9: 2–8) is Mark's Resurrection account.

b) The end is now lost

It may well be that the end was lost and so we do not know how it ended.

Reasons to account for its loss include:

- it was damaged (presumably the original, before it was copied)
- it was never finished – something happened that stopped Mark completing it
- Mark intended to write another volume that would continue on from verse 8.

c) The ending is Mark 16: 9–20

Certainly this seems a more natural end as it contains a series of accounts of Jesus' resurrection appearances. Irenaeus, a second-century bishop, used these verses as part of the gospel. Tatian, who produced the first harmony of the four gospels into one narrative, also includes these verses. However, this material is not generally accepted as original, but rather composed from material drawn from the other three gospels (see pages 268–70). Thus, all the resurrection appearances in these verses can be found in the other gospels.

Moreover, there are other reasons for concluding that it is not part of the original Mark text.

- There is a difference in Greek style between these verses and the rest of Mark's Gospel.
- Mary Magdalene is introduced, even though she appears in the verses just prior to this ending.
- The best manuscripts, such as **Codex Vaticanus** and **Codex Sinaiticus**, do not have this ending. They stop at verse 8.
- Some manuscripts have both this ending and the shorter one (see below), implying that they are both additions to the original.
- Some **minuscules** mark it with an asterisk to indicate that it did not belong to the original.

KEY IDEA

Textual criticism seeks to identify and correct texts, to get back to the original text. Ancient texts, that were copied by hand, would often have scribal errors that would be carried over into later copies. The task of the text critic is to identify such errors and trace back through the branches of families of texts to recover the words of the original. Often, it requires trying to identify which manuscripts belong to the same family, having been copied from each other.

Various guidelines are used to identify errors, such as 'the more difficult reading is probably the correct one' and 'the shorter reading is more likely to be the original'. Clearly, these guidelines need to be applied with critical judgement.

The New Testament has been preserved in more manuscripts than any other ancient work, having over 5300 Greek manuscripts, 10 000 Latin manuscripts and 9300 manuscripts in various other ancient languages.

The earliest manuscript of a New Testament text is a small fragment from the Gospel of John, Rylands Library Papyrus P52, which dates to the first half of the second century.

d) The ending is the shorter version

This is found in some manuscripts and comprises:

But they reported briefly to Peter and those with him all that they had been told. And after this, Jesus himself sent out by means of them, from east to west, the sacred and imperishable proclamation of eternal salvation.

This ending is found in a number of manuscripts. Sometimes it is given as a preface to the longer ending. This ending takes the last words of verse 8 to mean that the women made no public announcement but went instead to relate to the disciples what had happened.

The reference to the gospel being spread to the west is seen to indicate a late date of writing, since it implies it had spread over a large part of the Roman Empire.

TASK

Find out about the connection between Mark 16: 9–20 and C. Conybeare, Ariston the Presbyter, Aristion and Papias.

Objective To reinforce understanding of the problems about the ending of Mark's Gospel

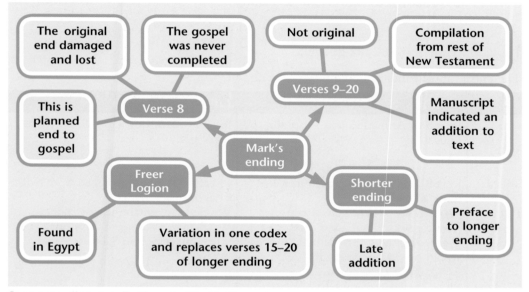

Summary diagram: Endings to Mark's Gospel

Reflection and assessment (AO1)

It is now time to channel the information you have considered in a more focused way. In order to do this, once again you need to ask yourself the question: 'How am I going to be assessed on my use of this information?'

Look back to page 7 in the Introduction to review the level descriptors for AO1. There is a description of the character and features for each level. The exam is marked with reference to levels.

Read the following question and complete the task.

Explain the reasons why the longer ending is regarded by many as an addition to the end of Mark's Gospel. (25 marks)

Suggestion for further application of skills

In your revision sessions, use this approach as a basis for revisiting the other topics. This not only applies to specific focuses on questions but is also a way of creating some good-quality summaries that demonstrate the skills relevant to AO1.

TASK

Use what you have learned so far about levels of response, writing frames and essay plans to do this task.

1 Work in small groups
2 For the question opposite, use bullet-point lists to create levelled responses.
3 Now let each person take one set of points and write up their answer.
4 Within the group, swap answers and use the OCR levels to mark and comment on the answer you have received.
5 Return each other's work and develop the suggestions made to improve your own answer.

Objective Collaborative learning and peer assessment for examination focus on AO1, with a particular aim of developing the level 5 expectations of 'a very high level of ability to select and deploy relevant information' (level 5 descriptor)

Part 3

A critical analysis of the issues

What are the issues that I am expected to consider and to analyse critically?

- Comparison between the three gospels
- The question of historical reliability

1 Comparison between the gospels

The entries in **red** indicate differences.

Mark 15: 42–16: 20	Matthew 27: 57–28: 20	Luke 23: 50–24: 53
Joseph of Arimathea asks Pilate for Jesus' body	Joseph of Arimathea asks Pilate for Jesus' body	Joseph of Arimathea asks Pilate for Jesus' body
Pilate surprised to hear Jesus was already dead		
Joseph took body, wrapped it, rolled stone across entrance	Joseph took body, wrapped it, rolled stone across entrance	Joseph took body, wrapped it, rolled stone across entrance
Women saw where he was laid	Women saw where he was laid	Women saw where he was laid
	Jewish authorities request tomb be guarded because Jesus had said he would rise in three days.	Women went home and prepared spices but rested on Sabbath
	Afraid disciples would steal body	
	Pilate agreed and stone had seal and guarded	
Sabbath over, women go to tomb with spices	Sabbath over, women go to look at tomb	Sabbath over, women go to tomb with spices
Who will roll stone away?	Violent earthquake, angel rolled stone and sat on it	
Stone already rolled away		Stone already rolled away
Enter tomb	His appearance is like lightning	Enter tomb, no body
Young man dressed in white robe sitting on right side	Guards afraid, became like dead men	Two men, appearance like lightning
		Women bowed down
Don't be alarmed – He has risen	Don't be afraid – He has risen	Why look for living among dead?
Tell disciples and Peter	Tell disciples	Son of Man must be delivered … and third day rise again
		Told all things to the Eleven
He is going ahead to Galilee	He is going ahead to Galilee	Not believed
		Peter ran to tomb, saw strips of linen lying by themselves
Women fled, said nothing		
They were afraid		
(Mark 16: 9–11)		
Jesus appears to Mary Magdalene	As they hurry away, Jesus meets them	
The disciples do not believe her	They clasped his feet and worshipped him	
	Tell my brothers to go to Galilee, there they will see him	

Mark 15: 42–16: 20	Matthew 27: 57–28: 20	Luke 23: 50–24: 53
(Mark 16: 12–13) Jesus appears in another form **to two** of them as they walk in the country	Guards report what happened Given money to say disciples stole body while guards asleep	The Road to Emmaus story and Jesus recognised in the breaking of the bread
(Mark 16: 14–18) Appears to the Eleven as they were eating ... rebukes them for lack of faith		Appears to the disciples Why are you troubled? Shows hands and feet ... not ghost ... eats fish Opened their minds to understand the scriptures Repentance and forgiveness ... preached to all nations ... My witnesses ... sending what Father promised ... stay in city until clothed with power
Go into world, preach good news Whoever believes and baptised is saved. Whoever does not is condemned Signs accompany them ... drive put demons ... speak new tongues ... pick up snakes ... drink poison ... heal		
(Mark 16: 19–20) Taken up into heaven and sat at right hand of God Disciples went out and preached Confirmed words by signs	With Eleven on mountain, worship him Great commission to make disciples of all nations With you until end of the age	Led them to Bethany Taken up into heaven Disciples returned to Jerusalem with great joy

2 Historical reliability

To say that the texts are historically reliable is to claim that the accounts are trustworthy and portray an accurate record of events. If the Resurrection accounts are historically reliable, then the disciples saw Jesus alive from the dead, as an objective reality. It was a physical resurrection. What they describe is what actually happened.

a) Difficulties with the Resurrection accounts

The gospel accounts raise a number of key issues relevant to the debate of the historical reliability of the Resurrection.

i) Apparent contradictions

There seem to be differences between the accounts concerning the number of women who went to the tomb, the number of angels at the tomb and the words Jesus is quoted as saying.

One response to this involves harmonisation. All the accounts have to be put together to get a complete account of what happened, since each gospel only gives a small part of the whole.

Another response is to accept that the accounts do contain small errors of detail, of the sort that you may get from witnesses giving accounts of a road accident. However,

? KEY QUESTIONS
- Are the gospel accounts of the Resurrection historically trustworthy?
- Do the accounts contradict each other?
- Can the accounts be harmonised?

❝ ▐ KEY QUOTE ▌ ❞

God has raised this Jesus to life, and we are all witnesses of the fact.

(Acts 2: 32)

❓ KEY QUESTION

The story of the road to Emmaus only appears in Luke's Gospel. Therefore, is it reliable?

❝ ▐ KEY QUOTE ▌ ❞

For what I received I passed on to you as of first importance; that Christ died for our sins according to the scriptures, that he was buried, that he was raised on the third day according to the scriptures, and that he appeared to Peter, and then to the Twelve. After that, he appeared to more than five hundred of the brothers at the same time, most of whom are still living, though some have fallen asleep. Then he appeared to James, then to all the Apostles, and last of all he appeared to me also, as to one abnormally born.

(1 Corinthians 15: 3–8)

this does not fundamentally undermine the thrust of the account of the Resurrection. Getting the details wrong about the driver of a car involved in an accident does not show that the accident never happened.

ii) Different accounts in different gospels

This is not about contradictions so much as to question why some events occur only in one gospel. For instance, only Luke has the story of the road to Emmaus. The implication is that if a story only appears in one source then it may not be regarded as reliable. Clearly, the debate will centre on assessment of the individual sources, including questions of authorship and date.

Form criticism argues that changes have been made to the text in its oral transmission. **Redaction criticism** argues that the gospel-writers themselves have made changes to their sources. For instance, some commentators draw attention to the apparent progressive embellishments of the number of angels at the empty tomb.

In response, attention is drawn to the fact that the earliest account of the Resurrection is thought to be 1 Corinthians 15, dated soon after CE50. Many regard this as a source too near the time of the Resurrection for the story to be fabricated, since eye-witnesses would still be alive. In addition, the Acts of the Apostles (Acts 2: 14–36) makes clear that the belief in the Resurrection was a basic claim of the Christians from the beginning.

KEY IDEAS

Form criticism
The conclusion of source criticism, namely the two-source solution, meant that scholars could not get back beyond Mark and Q. This drew attention to the oral period. Scholars noticed that Mark's Gospel was a collection of stories and sayings of Jesus that seemed artificially linked, without much regard for chronological accuracy. When the artificial links were removed the units stood out clearly.
By examining their form (or structure) similarities could be seen and groupings were devised. How and why these structures developed in the way they did is the essence of form criticism. Form criticism concluded that the Early Church used the material to meet particular needs and situations within their community. Some form critics argued that not only did the Early Church adapt the oral material but sometimes they actually created material. This would not be to accuse the Early Church of deceit but rather that they spoke in the spirit of Jesus.
Redaction criticism
While form criticism concentrated on the synoptic writers' role as collectors of units of tradition, redaction criticism looks at the synoptic writers as theologians who selected their material with particular themes in mind for a particular purpose.

iii) The supernatural

The events described involve supernatural happenings. Views about the possibility or non-possibility of the supernatural will be a major feature in deciding about historical reliability.

iv) The ending of Mark's Gospel

The doubt about the ending of Mark's Gospel raises questions as to whether the writer of the earliest gospel knew the traditions of the Resurrection appearances. Hence it could support the view that the Resurrection was a later fabrication by the Church.

In response, it is argued that 1 Corinthians is thought to be of an earlier date and this document contains a detailed account of the Resurrection appearances.

b) Alternative theories

Alternative theories have been suggested to explain how the belief in the Resurrection arose. These assume that the gospel accounts are not true.

i) Hallucinations

The appearances of the resurrected Jesus were actually hallucinations. The resurrected body of Jesus was not an objective reality.

ii) Wrong tomb

The women who reported that the body was missing had mistakenly gone to the wrong tomb. Hence the spread of the rumour that Jesus had risen from the dead.

iii) Jesus not dead

Jesus swooned and appeared dead. However, he never really died. It was a resuscitation, not a resurrection.

iv) Pagan myths

The Resurrection was adapted from pre-existing religious myths and tradition in pagan religions. Therefore there was no resurrection.

v) Conspiracy theory

The disciples stole the body and fabricated the stories to give power to their dogma.

3 Possible conclusions

When assessing the reliability of the Resurrection accounts, it is important to reflect upon the arguments previously discussed and arrive at some appropriate conclusion. It may be that you accept none of these listed here, or just one of them, or you may have a different conclusion that is not listed. However, what is important is the way that you have arrived at your conclusion – the reasoning process.

From the preceding discussions, here are some possible conclusions you could draw.

1   The Resurrection accounts are reliable and accurate. Jesus' resurrection was physical and had an objective reality. It was exactly as the gospels recorded.

2   The Resurrection accounts are basically reliable though there have been some embellishments by the writers. Jesus' resurrection was physical and had an objective reality.

3   The Resurrection accounts are basically reliable, though there have been some embellishments by the writers. The appearances of Jesus were hallucinations, not an objective reality.

4   The Resurrection accounts are unreliable. They have been fabricated to convince people that Jesus had risen from the dead.

5   The Resurrection accounts are myths and were never intended to be read as accounts of historical events.

TASK

Consider how you might refute each of the alternative theories listed.

Objective To develop evaluative skills

EXAM TIP

Critical evaluation means reasoning and responding to a point of view, rather than just stating a view. This demonstrates critical evaluation and reasoned argument (AO2).

TASK

From what you have so far learned about levels of response, create a list of points for a developed-level answer.

Improve this further for a higher-level answer.

Then create writing frames and fully drafted answers for each.

Objective To build an argument that uses a 'range of evidence to sustain an argument' (AO2 level 5)

Reflection and assessment AO2

It is now time to channel the information you have considered in a more focused way. To do this, once again you need to ask the question 'How am I going to be assessed on my use of this information?'

Look back at the level descriptors in the introduction on page 8. Then read the following question and complete the task.

'The accounts of the Resurrection in the gospels are historically unreliable.' Discuss.   (10 marks)

Suggestion for further application of skills

You will now be focusing on revision skills and, more importantly, past questions. Now you have developed your skills in essay preparation to this stage, return to other topics of critical analysis (Part 3 in each topic in this unit) and consider some key questions. Aim to build up some responses to these key questions.

Part 1

The historical, sociological, economic and religious background

What am I required to study?

- What society was like at the time of the Buddha

This means I am expected to know about:

- Hindu beliefs and practices
- contemporary religious ferment
- challenges to the traditional caste system
- conflict between the Kshatriya and the Brahmin castes.

The study of Buddhism begins with the religious, social and historical context of the life and work of the **Buddha**, which has a wide range of implications for study. If you search on the internet for Indian religious life and belief at the time of the Buddha you will find a wealth of material. Such a vast task is clearly too challenging for AS level. It is important, therefore, to stay close to the unit content listed above. It may be helpful to use the headings in this book for your notes as the examination questions will be derived from these topic areas.

Remember that, in your studies for AS, you will need to be constantly aware of the *two* vital parts of the basic assessment objectives:

- Knowledge and understanding (AO1)
- Evaluation (AO2).

Everything you will study in the following sections and, indeed, throughout this book has to be based on these principles. In this book the evidence and examples given are relevant and appropriate because this material focuses only on the context for AO1 that is given by the OCR Specification. The evaluation materials for AO2 will be aimed at helping you 'sustain a critical line of argument', and also to 'justify a point of view'.

See pages 7–8 in the Introduction to remind yourself of the key assessment objectives at AS level.

The evaluation material is set out in Part 3 of this topic (page 292) and can be studied either alongside the AO1 material, as you work through this topic, or as a discrete topic.

KEY WORD

Buddha enlightened one; one who possesses insight into ultimate and perfect wisdom

❝ KEY QUOTES ❞

Hinduism is a way
of life, a collection of
religions, a complex
culture, one yet
many.

(Lipner)

When the terms
'Hindu' and
'Hinduism' are used
... they are taken
to include the Jains,
along with the Sikhs
and Buddhists.

(Article 25 of the
Indian Constitution)

Because of the
wide range of
traditions and ideas
incorporated by the
term 'Hindu', it is a
problem arriving at
a definition ... It has
fuzzy edges. Some
forms of religion are
central to Hinduism,
while others are
less clearly central
but still within the
category.

(Flood)

Hinduism is all
things to all men.

(Jawaharlal Nehru,
First Prime Minister
of India)

KEY WORDS

Karma (Sanskrit)
intentional actions,
good or bad, bringing
consequences and
affecting this and future
lives
Kamma (Pali) karma
Brahminism religion
based upon priestly
rituals and sacrifices
Brahmin priest

1 Introduction to Buddhism

India at the time of the Buddha was very different from the India we know today. Modern India has a complex mixture of religious traditions with very different world-views. Within these world-views is a wide variety of cultural and regional differences that produce a diversity of religious expression.

At the time of the Buddha (c480–400BCE), the religious and philosophical ideas were no less complicated. Although Christianity, Islam and Sikhism were not yet founded, there were other religions and philosophies. Some of these do not exist in their original forms today. There would have been much questioning and debate both within and between these groups.

2 Hindu beliefs and practices

The first religious idea to consider is Hinduism itself. What is Hinduism? Many scholars have disagreed about the answer to this question. Gavin Flood admits that any definition has 'fuzzy edges', Julius Lipner presents a variety of definitions from scholars and Paul Dundas quotes the Indian Constitution (article 25) to indicate that today we define Hinduism in its broadest sense.

Hinduism was originally a term used to identify the peoples, cultures and religions of the Indus Valley, as it was known. In this sense, it did not really describe a set of beliefs or practices. However, with the development in its meaning, very many attempts have been made to define what Hinduism is now.

Without exploring all possibilities, here are two very different working definitions.

1　The religion of popular Hinduism as we know it today, includes all varieties of religious expression surrounding popular Hindu deities. This type of Hinduism is different from Jainism, Buddhism and Sikhism. Popular Hindu practices all share ideas about reincarnation, the eternal soul, the importance of daily worship, meditation and the idea that a wandering holy person can achieve liberation.

2　A religious tradition that originates from within India, it shares the principles of reincarnation and **karma**, which is the belief that actions, good or bad, bring consequences and affect future lives, thus including Buddhism, Jainism and Sikhism.

The first is more appropriate for the purpose of this book, but it is important to recognise that this is not the only definition. Scholars still debate its appropriateness. The Pali version of the word is **kamma**.

Brahminism

One particular expression of Hinduism from the time of the Buddha is often referred to as **Brahminism**. To the north-east of India, in the area surrounding the Ganges basin, is the area where Siddhartha Gotama, the Buddha, was active. Born around 480BCE to wealthy parents, sometimes referred to as the local royalty, Siddhartha (a local prince) would have been very familiar with the religious ideas of Brahminism.

What did Brahminism teach and how was it practised?
Brahminism was based on both written holy books and complicated rituals. These holy books (Vedas) were used to guide and give instructions for the performance of sacrificial rites that involved animals, and where the role of the **Brahmin** or priest

was vital. It was believed that prayers offered during the performance of the sacrifice satisfied the gods, so achieving the underlying purpose of retaining order in the Universe.

In early Indian religion, it was broadly assumed that there were three levels of existence, namely:

- the physical
- the spiritual
- the phonic (sound).

The physical was represented by the sacrifice, the spiritual by the role of the priest and the phonic by the chanting of a prayer. It was believed that such a combination, together, had the power needed to influence the Universe and maintain order.

Meditation was also a feature of Brahminism. At first, meditation was a preparation for the sacrifice. As Brahminism developed, meditation became a substitute for the sacrifice and was used as a means of mental focus or internalisation. The idea of the **Brahman**, the universal spirit, and the **atman**, the individual soul, became dominant in Indian thought, as did the notion of a continual round or cycle of reincarnations, known as **samsara**. The goal of practising religion was to advance through complex rituals and through meditation to achieve liberation from this round of reincarnation. It was believed that the soul then became united with Brahman.

Finally, in Brahminism, there is the basic idea of karma, as developed in later Indian thought. Although early Brahminism taught that all areas of spiritual influence were restricted to religious ritual, it later embraced the idea that actions or karma beyond the sacrifice affected the reincarnation of the individual soul.

3 Contemporary religious ferment

a) Samana groups

As in any major religious tradition, there is always a wide variety of teaching and practice. At the time of the Buddha, these variations were fairly small. Some people, however, rejected Brahmanism completely. Those who did this were known as **samanas**. They formed groups of wandering holy men or philosophers who were trying to find answers to ultimate questions. There are several examples of different types of Samanas, including Jains, Ajivakas, Materialists and Skeptics. A summary of their beliefs and practices will help gain some insight into the Buddha's cultural and religious environment.

What did the Samanas believe and how did they practise?
Samanas rejected Brahminism because they disliked the social elitism of the Brahmins and the idea of ritual sacrifice. They were similar to the wandering holy persons of modern-day India. Like them, they cut all family ties and were dependent upon the general public for their food. Samanas were usually **ascetic** and practised very advanced forms of meditation, having little sleep and very little food. It is often stated that Buddhism was originally a Samana movement, as the Buddha himself became a wandering holy man.

KEY WORDS

Brahman universal spirit or soul
Atman individual soul
Samsara cycle of existence: life, death and reincarnation or rebirth
Samana a group of wandering holy men or philosophers who were trying to find answers to ultimate questions
Ascetic living a very disciplined lifestyle

KEY IDEA

Brahminism
The religion is based on:
- ritual and sacrifice
- Brahman and atman
- karma
- meditation.

Samana movements:
- rejected Brahminism
- followed ascetic practices
- practised advanced meditation.

b) Jainism

Vardhamana the Mahavira or Great Hero was the first person to practise Jainism as an official philosophy and is often acknowledged as its founder.

TASK

Jainism is one extreme approach to non-violence. Jains even wear masks to avoid breathing in insects. Find out what else they do in the pursuit of absolute non-violence.

 KEY WORDS

Jiva Jain interpretation of, or replacement for, the idea of a soul
Yoga *literally* to unite or join; union; in Hinduism, a method for becoming one with the universal spirit referring to the atman and Brahman
Ahimsa non-violence
Niyati destiny

 KEY IDEAS

Jainism
- Believe in the jiva (life essence) instead of the atman (soul).
- Karma imprisons the jiva.
- Jiva is released through severe discipline and meditation.
- The aim is to get rid of the effects of karma.

Ajivakas
- Destiny, not our actions, controls our fate.
- Karma has no effect on an individual's path in life.

Jains wearing breathing masks

What did the Jains teach and how did they practise?

Jain teaching accepted reincarnation and the idea of samsara but disagreed with traditional views on escaping the cycle of samsara. Crucial to this difference was its notion of karma.

Instead of the atman or soul, Jains believed in the existence of a life-essence called **jiva**. This is like an internal spark, energy or essence that runs through all living and non-living matter. This jiva, however, is encased by karma that accumulates and leads to further reincarnation. The aim of the Jain practitioner is to free the jiva from the cycle of samsara in two ways:

- by following a very disciplined lifestyle involving **yoga** and very severe practices guided by the principle of **ahimsa** or non-violence towards any living being
- by wiping out any possible new karma, through a policy of non-action, and to wait for all previous karmic effects to take their course and die away.

c) Ajivakas

Makkhali Gosala was the famous leader associated with this Samana movement, although there are other leaders identified in the Buddhist writings.

What did the Ajivakas teach and how did they practise?

Gosala's major disagreement with other religious groups of the time was his outright rejection of the idea of karma. Instead, he replaced it with the idea of **niyati** or destiny. Every soul has its own, uniquely prescribed path that is already set out. Even the number of reincarnations has already been calculated. Therefore, the idea of karma becomes redundant.

In practice, the Ajivakas were similar to the Jains in that they also lived a life of strict discipline, even to the extreme of self-harming and starvation.

d) Materialists

The Buddhist writings identify two more influential groups that need to be considered briefly. The first of these were the Materialists.

What did the Materialists teach and how did they practise?
The Materialists, along with the other Samanas, rejected Brahminism. They did this not only because of dogmatic differences but because they regarded religious ritual as unscientific. Indeed, Materialists were **empiricists** and they rejected any ideas that were based upon non-empirical evidence that, they felt, could not be tested. These ideas included karma, reincarnation and the idea of a soul.

The main practice of a Materialist was to celebrate life, and, although this can be done in many ways, they were generally encouraged to follow a noble and moral path.

e) Skeptics

Another group of Samanas was the Skeptics or 'eel-wrigglers', as Peter Harvey describes them.

What did the Skeptics teach and how did they practise?
The Skeptics did not have any particular teaching or practice. Instead they constantly weighed things up and seemed reluctant to reach conclusions. Despite arguing against the views and theories of others they remained 'devil's advocates' at all times, without commitment to any particular position.

4 Siddhartha Gotama and Buddhist ideals – contemporary religious ferment

So how did the Buddha's teachings and practices fit into his immediate Indian context? There were common areas shared with all, common areas shared with some, some ideas that were rejected and even some ideas that were modified. There were also new ideas.

a) What the Buddha accepted

Samsara – the Buddha accepted the notion of an endless cycle of existences and also the possibility of **moksha**, which was escape from this cycle.

Meditation – in keeping with all religious traditions of the time, the Buddha taught that realisation of truth was through meditation. However, he did not feel that extreme physical meditation worked and he rejected the idea of a personal union with an absolute power.

Gods and goddesses – while the Buddha accepted the cosmology or theory of the Universe of the day, he felt that deities were still subject to samsara and therefore ignorant and in need of **nirvana** or **enlightenment**, which is ultimate wisdom. The concept of a supreme deity or creator God was not rejected outright, but it would be true to say that it was irrelevant to early Buddhism.

b) What the Buddha refined or modified

Reincarnation – the Buddha taught **rebirth** and not reincarnation. Reincarnation requires some kind of soul or entity that is constant but simply takes on a different form. The Buddha did not accept the existence of such an elusive entity but favoured a passing on of energies from one form to another.

KEY WORDS

Empiricism knowledge only comes through experience and testing
Moksha escape from the cycle of rebirth
Nirvana inexpressible enlightenment, impossible to put into words
Enlightenment ultimate wisdom
Rebirth the transfer of energies from one form to another; to the next incarnation at the point of death

KEY IDEAS

Materialists
● All knowledge and truth come through what we see and experience.
● Life is to be enjoyed.
Skeptics
All theories are to be challenged and none committed to.

EXAM TIP

It is important to be able to describe and explain the religious ideas at the time of the Buddha. *However*, it is even more important to be able to show how this influenced the Buddha. This would distinguish a level 4 answer that has 'good understanding' from a level 2 answer that 'focuses on the general topic' (see level descriptors, page 7).

KEY WORDS

Ineffable impossible to explain in words
Anatta not-self; the Buddhist idea that there is no metaphysical and permanently existing entity, such as a soul or self, within a person
Aryan invaders from the West of India referred to by their pale skin

TASK

Summarise, in table form, key points for the different religious groups at the time of the Buddha. Add an extra column and use it to compare and contrast the ideas.
Objective To ensure accuracy with religious ideas and the accurate use of correct terminology (a prerequisite for a level 5 response at AS)

❝ KEY QUOTE ❞

This was a developed urban culture. Mohenjo-daro and Harappa, separated by some 40 miles, were two of this civilisation's most important cities and housed some 40 000 inhabitants who enjoyed a high standard of living.

(Flood)

Karma – the concept of karma was refined or even redefined to include thoughts as well as actions. Karma became more precise and internalised, according to Gombrich.

Nirvana – the Buddha accepted that escape from the cycle of samsara was possible. However, the Buddha's concept of nirvana superseded this. Some have described the Buddhist notion of nirvana as truly **ineffable**, it was impossible to put into words.

c) What the Buddha rejected

Belief in the atman and Brahman, jiva and niyati, the idea that we all have a permanent, eternal entity within us, whether it be a force, power or soul, was firmly rejected by the Buddha.

d) What was new about the Buddha's teaching?

Instead of accepting the idea of a soul, the Buddha observed that things were **anatta** or not-self, and that we could not identify any one thing within ourselves that we could call 'me'. This, as we shall later see, has far-reaching implications for the rest of Buddhist teaching.

5 Challenges to the traditional caste system

In order to look at the traditional caste system it is important to understand its origins in both the Indus Valley Civilisation and the subsequent Aryan Invasion.

a) The influence of the Indus Valley Civilisation c3000–1500BCE

There is evidence of an advanced civilisation in the Indus Valley and Ganges basin, about 1000 years before the time of the Buddha. Two main cities, Mohenjo-daro and Harappa, which are famous archaeological discoveries of the last century, provide enough evidence to suggest the presence of a primitive water system, possibly including drainage and sewerage, and also baths, stone buildings and artefacts of religious significance. It is probable that these sites had a major influence on the surrounding areas, an impact that lasted through to the time of the Buddha (c480BCE) in terms of the continuity of religious practice, social structure and economy.

> **The civilisation seems to have come to an end a considerable time before the Aryan invasion; nevertheless, it is at least a possibility that some of the beliefs of these people lingered on in popular form, with elements eventually being absorbed into Hinduism alongside those inherited from the Vedas.**
>
> (Brockington)

b) The influence of the Aryan invasion

An invasion from the West began in around 1500BCE, just as the Indus Valley Civilisation was declining. The **Aryans**, as they were called, brought with them a society based heavily upon strict religious structures under the control of a priestly Brahmin group.

The religious writings of these invaders include the earliest of Hindu scriptures, the Vedas, and these are often associated with a class system that has, over the years, increased in complexity and developed into what is referred to as the jati (birth) or caste system in India today. Although it is now officially illegal to discriminate on grounds of caste or birth, at the time of the Buddha a basic caste system was in place.

Civilisation in the Indus Valley

Modern Hindus describe their **dharma** or faith in two ways:

- as the eternal way of life that is based on ethical principles such as truth and non-violence
- as a way of life based on social groupings and stages in life.

In Hinduism, dharma has several levels of meaning. It can represent the law. It is mostly understood as social duty, but also can be used generally to mean teaching. An individual's personal duty is to follow the family code of religious and social practice. It is determined by their social classification and also their birth or the caste to which the family belongs. The Buddha was part of this social system.

At the time of the Buddha, Indian society had inherited this ancient culture of social order but was undergoing major expansion and change. In the area of India where the Buddha taught, there were 16 regions or countries, each of which was a developing urban centre.

> **At the heart of these states appeared true urban centres where there had been none before. These swelling cities contained the kings' courts, and to the courts and cities were drawn the makings of an urban life: merchants and craftsmen with new skills, soldiers and labourers, conquered lords to render tribute, the displaced, the foreigners, the opportunists.**
>
> (Carrithers)

c) The caste system and challenges towards it

It is in the Hindu scripture known as the Rig-Veda that we find details of the caste system. Basically, the system comprises four social categories:

- Brahmin or priest
- Kshatriya or warrior
- Vaisya or business person, merchant, professional, skilled worker
- Shudra or labourer, unskilled.

The first three are deemed twice-born because they undergo a second spiritual rebirth when they take the sacred thread ceremony, one of the crucial rites of passage for a Hindu. The unskilled of society, however, are not twice-born and so cannot study the Vedas.

TASK

Civilisation in the Indus Valley demonstrated a high level of social organisation. Does it follow that their ideas about religion were also complex or highly structured? Try to find out more about the religious practices of the Indus Valley Civilisation.

 KEY WORD

Dharma social duty or the law or as a general term, teaching

 KEY IDEAS

Indus Valley Civilisation
There is:
- archaeological evidence of a highly advanced society
- evidence of religious and social organisation.

Aryan invasion
Important features include:
- the earliest writings, called the Vedas
- the idea of a caste system
- the role of the priest or Brahmin.

There were also many Indians who were outside the social system and these were known as outcastes or pariahs, translated as untouchables. These were people in a state of permanent spiritual pollution because of their birth and occupation. Gandhi renamed these people harijans, or the children of God, although today they prefer to call themselves dalits or the oppressed, rejecting Gandhi's label as they consider it to be patronising.

At the time of the Buddha, this system would have been both insular and exclusive and it would have been very difficult for people to change their circumstances in life. Gombrich explains the complementary roles of the highest two categories. Warriors were the rulers, responsible for good order in society. To maintain this order, sacrifices were necessary. These were performed by the priests but paid for by the warriors. Priests also depended on the rulers for their material support.

> **This pair of complementary roles, patron and functionary, became the model for a wide range of social arrangements in traditional India.**
>
> (Gombrich)

KEY QUOTE

Above all the question was, how were the Indians to understand themselves among these unprecedented forms of common life?

(Carrithers)

The Buddha himself is thought to have belonged to the ruling class of warriors, from the Sakya peoples who were based around the Kapilavatthu area of modern-day Nepal.

Although it is not clear exactly what the role and status of women were at the time of the Buddha, it is probable that women had fewer rights than men.

Even though stories about the Buddha often associated him with people from the higher castes, he clearly rejected the idea of a caste system. Stories such as that of Kisa (a woman who had lost her child) and Angulimala (a detestable bandit and murderer) show that the Buddha saw his teachings as challenging the validity of the boundaries established by society.

6 Conflict between the Kshatriya and the Brahmin castes

This social conflict in what had been established for years and the uncomfortable implications it brought with it meant that society in general was ripe for change and already questioning old traditions.

The Brahmins (priests) were at the top of this class system and led the people in the traditions of worship and social order. However, it was always the duty of the Kshatriya (warrior) class to fight for justice and protect the people in practical ways.

Over a period of time, and in the face of poverty, disease and neglect, the Kshatriyas challenged the authority and influence of the Brahmins. Uncomfortable tensions in the relationship between Brahmins and Kshatriyas emerged.

The Buddha, it is claimed, was himself from the Kshatriya class. During the time of the Buddha the tension between Brahmins and Kshatriyas was heightened. The Samana movement had brought a fresh challenge to Brahmins and there is evidence from Hindu writings that even kings were teaching the Brahmins' new religious ideas.

This tension reflected a struggle of minds, and it is no coincidence that the Buddha, as a Kshatriya, rejected the class system and the religious authority of the Brahmins.

> **However, the Sakyas considered themselves to have the effective rank of kings, nobles and warriors in respect of the wider civilisation, and indeed they probably did not recognise, as others did, the ceremonial precedence of Brahmins, priests of high rank.**
>
> (Carrithers)

In summary, the Buddha's response to his immediate environment reflected the changing nature of his times.

- He clearly accepted his status as a Kshatriya but also explored the ambiguous relationship of the Kshatriyas with Brahminism.
- As a result, he openly engaged with the changing religious climate of the day and experimented accordingly.
- He did reject the Vedic religion, the rigid social caste system and the prejudice and discrimination this created.
- His attitude towards women was radical, as was his open declaration of the right of everyone to explore religious freedom.
- He did, however, refine some social procedures, for example, the way to be a Samana.

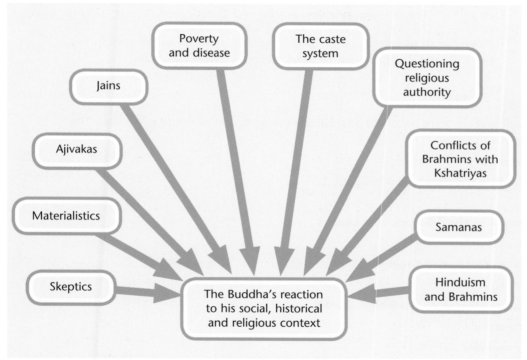

Summary diagram: Social, historical and religious background

KEY QUOTE

By ideology, of course, the Ksatriya (Kshatriya) ranks second, beneath the Brahmin. Yet he is the man with the real physical power, on whom even the Brahmin depends for his safety and physical welfare. The relations between Brahmin and ksatriya have always been somewhat ambiguous.

(Gombrich)

TASK

In pairs, identify 5–10 things the Buddha accepted, rejected or refined and record them as bullet lists. Present your lists to the rest of the group. Following discussion, add two or three more points to each list. Now look at the level 5 descriptor and see how your selections could be described as demonstrating 'understanding and engagement with the material' and 'accurate use of technical terms'. Then, individually, use your lists to prepare a summary that is 'well constructed and organised'.

Objective To differentiate accurately the Buddha's different responses to his immediate context, using collaborative learning and peer assessment (to aim for level 5)

EXAM TIP

Always point out the *variety* of religious ideas at the time of the Buddha. This demonstrates 'use of evidence and examples' (AO1 descriptor) and also builds up and will help any following 'analysis' (AO2 descriptor).

Reflection and assessment AO1

It is vital to bring together the information you have covered so far and recognise how it can be transformed into effective examination-style revision and answers. The best way to do this is to ask the question: 'How am I going to be assessed on my use of this information?'

The first way is through assessment objective 1 (AO1). For this you need to be able to 'select and clearly demonstrate the relevant knowledge and understanding through the use of evidence, examples and correct language and terminology'.

Try using the writing frame to answer the question:

Describe and explain the religious context in India at the time of the Buddha.

(25 marks)

Remember to match the correct teachings and practices to the appropriate groups. Relate these to what Buddha accepted, refined and rejected.

Writing frame

At the time of the Buddha there were a variety of religious ideas, traditions and practices. The most common form was …

The term Samana means …

A typical Samana group was the Jains, who believed …

The Jains practised …

Another influential group was the Ajivakas, who taught …

The Ajivakas practised …

There were also the Materialists, who taught …

Finally, the Skeptics believed …

The Buddha would have considered all the above views …

Some he accepted, for example …

Others he rejected, for example …

Some he changed or refined slightly, for example …

Remember to use correct technical language where appropriate. The distinctive beliefs would be demonstrated by showing how those of one specific group differed from other religious ideas and beliefs of other groups of the time.

As you work through the unit, you will find that the amount of support in these sections will gradually be reduced, in order to encourage you to gain independence and perfect your AO1 skills.

Suggestion for further application of skills

After completing the question, use the levels and AO descriptors to award marks out of 25. Identify strengths and areas for development in each answer. Then, as a group, collaborate to create an ideal answer that demonstrates a 'very high level of ability to select and deploy relevant information' and that is also 'well constructed and organised' (level 5 descriptor).

Part 2
Traditional accounts of the life of the Buddha

What am I required to study?

- Key events of, and experiences from, the Buddha's life

This means I am expected to know about:

- the four signs
- ascetic practices
- Buddhist enlightenment
- Buddhist teaching
- the nature of the Buddha's death.

The aim is to present key events of the life of the Buddha. There are many stories surrounding the Buddha's birth and upbringing. It is only necessary to consider these briefly in order to be able to establish a context for the key events to be studied.

Remember that your studies will include elements of the *two* basic assessment objectives of:

- Knowledge and Understanding (AO1)
- Evaluation (AO2).

See pages 7–8 in the Introduction to remind yourself of the key assessment objectives at AS level.

The evaluation material is set out in Part 3 of this topic (page 292) and can be studied either alongside the AO1 material, as you work through this topic, or as a discrete topic.

1 Birth of the Buddha

Paul Williams argues that the life story of the Buddha should be used as a teaching aid to help people to understand the central ideas of Buddhism. In other words, the Buddha is not as important in himself as the teachings that his life experiences demonstrate in relation to the **dhamma**. It is the central ideas of Buddhism, such as the status of the Buddha and aspects of his teachings, that are the focus of events from his life.

There are many versions of mythical occurrences associated with the birth of the Buddha. It is not necessary to explore such stories in detail. Suffice to say, all stories indicate that the Buddha was unique.

> ... from the commentary and legends we learn that ... at the time of his conception ten months earlier, Maya dreamed that a white elephant entered her womb.
>
> (Cush)

> **❝ KEY QUOTE ❞**
>
> It is only self-evidently appropriate to start the study of a religion with the life-story of its founder if we hold that the life-story of the founder is in some sense a crucial preliminary to understanding what follows.
>
> (Williams)

KEY WORD
Dhamma Buddhist teaching

KEY WORD

Pali Canon Buddhist scriptures

KEY QUOTE

His father provided him with the greatest comforts … Lacking nothing of the earthly joys of life, he lived amid song and dance, in luxury and pleasure, knowing nothing of sorrow.

(Piyadassi Thera)

EXAM TIP

Do not answer a question on the life of the Buddha by simply telling a story. Your answer should always select the key events, that is, the appropriate information relevant to the question. This demonstrates more personal understanding or 'ownership' of the knowledge. It is evidence of a 'good selection of material' (level 4 AO1).

KEY PEOPLE

Yasodhara Gotama's wife

Channa Gotama's charioteer

KEY IDEA

The four signs
● old age
● sickness
● death
● a wandering holy man

This is also suggested in the **Pali Canon**. The Buddha was born from her side, possibly indicating kammic purity, and this occurred beneath a tree.

> … the birth of Gotama under a tree fits the pattern of other key events in his life; attaining enlightenment under another tree, giving his first sermon in an animal park and dying between two trees. This suggests his liking for simple natural environments where he could be in harmony with all forms of life.
>
> (Harvey)

In addition, the baby immediately stood up and took seven paces, turned to all corners of the Universe and announced that he was the most enlightened being in the world and that he would have no more rebirths. In contrast, Ashvaghosha's work, the *Buddhacarita*, suggests that the Buddha's birth was more normal than this.

The Buddha's destiny is also a theme of the birth narratives and involves the relationship between holy men and the Kshatriya rulers. Seven holy men predicted that he would be a strong ruler, like his father. Another, called Asita, cried from happiness because he recognised him as the Buddha, and a final holy man, Kondanna, predicted that he would become a holy man and pursue the truth. The story continues that, to avoid this happening, the king had to ensure that the prince lived a life of absolute luxury that avoided any unpleasantness. In particular, four things were to be avoided.

2 The four signs

The four things to be avoided are known as the **four signs** or the four sights. In essence they are:

■ old age
■ sickness
■ death
■ a wandering holy man.

It was argued that, if the prince was kept away from these four things, then he would not waver from his path as future king and ruler. However, if the prince did encounter these signs, they would serve as a catalyst to stimulate a search for truth that would take Gotama on an alternative path as a wandering holy man.

Up until the age of 29, despite being surrounded by extraordinary levels of luxury and protection, Gotama's life was no more unusual than that of any other prince. He was married to **Yasodhara** at 16 and they lived within their palace grounds in relative calm.

The significant events that brought about change for Gotama, at the age of 29, involve excursions from the palace grounds with his charioteer, **Channa**.

The first sight was an old, weak man, bent over with age. The second sight was another man who had been ravaged by disease, existing as mere skin and bone with the very little strength in his body ebbing away. The third sight was one of grieving relatives carrying the corpse of their beloved on their shoulders in preparation for cremation.

The impact of such experiences was obviously heightened by the sheltered nature of the prince's life. It was his first understanding of the fact that he, like those he saw, was subject to the very same ravaging of time and nature and would ultimately die. This disturbed him and caused great anxiety. Why all this suffering?

Lastly, the sight that provoked the prince most deeply was a wandering holy man, walking calmly and contentedly in pursuit of truth and an answer to life's problems. This man was living a life of purity, in complete detachment from society. From where was his sense of peace derived?

On returning to the palace, and hearing the news that Yasodhara had just given birth to a son, **Rahula**, the prince felt even more tied by a new responsibility that bound him to his life as it was.

Despite his family situation and his rich inheritance, the prince immediately sought freedom. He renounced his birthright. Shedding his rich clothes and long hair, he took on the mantle of a wandering holy man, with a simple bowl for food offerings and a single robe, and the thoughts:

> **Verily, this world has fallen upon trouble – one is born, and grows old, and dies, and falls from one state, and springs up in another. And from the suffering, moreover, no one knows of any way of escape, even from decay and death. O, when shall a way of escape from this suffering be made known – from decay and death?**

(Eliade)

3 Ascetic practices

Gotama sought out two teachers, each renowned for their strict ascetic lifestyle and yogic practice.

The first was **Alara Kalama**, who trained Gotama in yoga. Soon Gotama had attained the same level of experience as his teacher: a state of nothingness. But this did not satisfy Gotama. He felt that desire, passion and attachments were not eradicated and that this method simply ignored them by taking an alternative route. Despite the fact that Kalama asked Gotama to become his teacher, Gotama moved on to find another way.

The second teacher was **Uddaka Ramaputta**. Similarly, mastery of Ramaputta's yoga led not to an awakening of truth or an enlightenment experience, but simply to a plane beyond nothingness referred to as neither perception nor non-perception. Such meditative states were later to become known as false states because they give an impression of awakening or enlightenment but are still far from it.

Whilst Gotama was experimenting with the two schools of yoga, the ascetic lifestyle began to take its toll. He had become so weak and thin that it is alleged that his backbone was visible through his stomach. At this point, after being revived with milk-rice by a woman called **Sujata**, Gotama decided to pursue an alternative lifestyle. Indeed, this was to be his last meal prior to enlightenment.

Carved rock image of meditating Buddha, from Sri Lanka

❝ KEY QUOTE ❞

To be a renouncer was a young man's, indeed a romantic's, aspiration, and from this point of view the Buddha was but one of many youths who left home, attracted by the challenge of the wandering life.

(Carrithers)

 KEY PEOPLE

Rahula Gotama's son
Alara Kalama Gotama's first yoga teacher
Uddaka Ramaputta Gotama's second yoga teacher
Sujata the woman who revived Gotama with milk-rice

TASK

Some statues of the Buddha show him touching the ground with one hand as he meditates. Find out why.

KEY PERSON

Mara was a god who used his divine status to tempt humans and keep them attached to the world.

KEY WORDS

Jhanas four absorptions or stages of meditation through which one passes to reach enlightenment
Nibbana enlightenment; the highest aspiration for all Buddhists
Meditative planes accessed through the fourth jhana, these are specific states of mind

4 The Buddha's enlightenment

Sitting beneath a Bodhi or Bo tree, in a state of deep meditation, Gotama contemplated the nature of existence, throughout the night. Traditional Buddhist writings have vivid accounts of his religious experience that night. All centre around the process of meditation through levels of insight known as **jhanas**, before explaining how Gotama then encountered the ultimate experience known as **nibbana** (Sanskrit: nirvana, see pages 316–18).

The first event was the temptation by the god, **Mara**, who challenged Gotama to abandon his quest. Earlier texts describe Mara encouraging Gotama to seek a more religious path of ceremony and good works in order to strengthen his karma. Gotama simply resisted and Mara vanished. Later texts give more detail, with Mara telling Gotama that no one could bear witness to his good works in previous lives and this one. But Gotama placed his hand to the ground and touched the Earth as a witness to his good works. This is often depicted in art and architecture as the Buddha sitting in a half-lotus (crossed-legged) meditation posture, with one hand in his lap and the other reaching out to touch the Earth as witness.

The second course of events was progression through the four jhanas meditative stages, also called absorptions. Each stage has a corresponding experience, which are:

First jhana – unbroken attention to the object of meditation, detached from the world and in a total state of calm

Second jhana – thoughts are discarded as detachment becomes more profound and a sense of joy: 'a state free from thought-conception and discursive thinking … which is born of concentration' (Nyanatiloka)

Third jhana – a state of equanimity, totally composed and with absolute attentiveness, but still clearly conscious

Fourth jhana – 'A state beyond pleasure and pain' (Nyanatiloka), indeed, beyond all sense of joy and thought construction, 'leaving a mind peaceful, tranquil, clear, a sharp tool ready to pierce into reality' (Cush).

There are also four other jhanas, sometimes referred to as numbers 5–8, but usually they are all grouped under the fourth and are listed as distinct stages within the fourth state. Generally speaking, it is the fourth jhana that tends to be seen as the most crucial stage.

The fourth jhana also involves access to **meditative planes** (Carrithers) usually associated with Hindu yoga. As seen earlier, Gotama had experienced these under his former teachers but was not satisfied. He felt that this was not the answer. At this stage of Gotama's experience, the fourth jhana gave him further access to three significant insights beyond any that he had experienced before.

- The first was the elevated insight into his many previous lives throughout time.
- After this, he obtained pure observational insight of the plight of other beings tied to the world of rebirth. He had an objective overview of how the world of existence functioned in terms of birth, death and rebirth throughout the Universe.
- Finally, he went through the enlightenment experience, gaining insight into true and perfect wisdom of how the barriers to spiritual truth can be destroyed.

Nibbana will be discussed later, but for now it can be understood as an experience that provided insight into the way things are in life but, more importantly, how to deal with them.

Gotama had now become the Buddha, the enlightened one or one endowed with wisdom. More accurately, he had achieved **samma-sambodhi**, or perfect enlightenment.

5 The Buddha's teaching

The Buddha's first sermon, known as *The turning of the wheel of truth*, was in the Deer Park of Isipatana. It can be found in the **Dhamma Cakka Pavattana** Sutta.

This sermon is dated approximately seven weeks after his enlightenment. It is the first record of his public teaching about his experience. It was also given directly to his five former ascetic companions with whom he had practised such an extreme lifestyle. Indeed, it is said that the Buddha was reluctant to share his new knowledge before meeting up with his former companions. However, it was his former ascetic companions who, amazed at his peaceful countenance, suggested that he break his silence and explain what he had discovered.

He rejected both the life of luxury and the life of extreme asceticism for a more moderate path, which became known as the **middle way**.

For our purposes, it will be enough simply to outline his basic teachings that resulted from his enlightenment experience, as recounted in the Dhamma Cakka Pavattana Sutta.

It is important to point out that the teachings given were not truths in the sense that they were to become doctrine and to be believed. They were truths more in the sense of evident observations of the world around him. It is interesting to see that a recent translation by Harvey refers to the truths as realities, to try to avoid such confusion.

In this way, Buddhism immediately adopts an empirical approach to life. The teachings are a practical tool to use in a personal way, to seek to follow the same path as the Buddha. The best way to explain this is: 'Test, and see for yourself.'

The Buddha outlines the following truths or observations in the Dhamma Cakka Pavattana Sutta.

The two extremes to avoid are:

1 a lifestyle that is driven by sensual pleasure

2 a lifestyle intent on extreme asceticism to the extent of self-mortification.

If a middle way between these two extremes is taken then it will lead to knowledge, peace and the ultimate awakening of nibbana.

The practical way to apply the middle path is by following eight principles, known as the **eight-fold path**: right view, right directed thought, right speech, right action, right livelihood, right effort, right mindfulness and right concentration (see page 342).

There are four concepts that underpin this.

1 The truth of life is that it is a painful experience and full of suffering (**dukkha** – see page 330). All aspects of life, no matter how pleasurable and attached to them we are, bring dukkha.

2 Craving (greed) and attachment are the cause of this painful experience.

KEY WORDS

Samma-sambodhi perfect enlightenment
Dhamma Cakka Pavattana turning of the wheel of dhamma
Middle way the balance between the extremes of asceticism and a life of luxury
Eight-fold path the ultimate teaching of Buddhism; the practical measures needed to become enlightened
Dukkha suffering or frustration, refer to the first Noble Truth

TASK

Design a flow chart to explain the process of the Buddha's enlightenment and surrounding events.
Objective To gain knowledge and understanding of the significance of the enlightenment experience for the Buddha and Buddhists, developing the 'use of evidence and examples' to 'demonstrate clearly relevant knowledge and understanding' (AO1).

3 The way to stop the suffering involved in life is to eliminate craving and attachment: 'the giving up and relinquishing of it, freedom from it, non-reliance on it.' (Harvey)

4 This is achieved by following the eight-fold path; suffering is eradicated and there is an experience of total freedom and enlightenment (nibbana).

These four principles are known as the **four Noble Truths**, the four Holy Truths or, as Harvey suggests, the four realities. In the Dhamma Cakka Pavattana Sutta, the Buddha continued to state how he had achieved the cessation of pain in his own life.

At this point, tradition holds that the holy beings from the heavens witnessed that the rediscovery of dhamma, the truth, in our world had been accomplished:

> **At Baranasi, in the Deer Park at Isipatana, the unsurpassed Wheel (of Vision) of the Basic Pattern (of things) has been set in motion by the Blessed One, which cannot be stopped by any renunciant or brahman or mara or brahma or by anyone in the world.**
>
> (Harvey)

After this experience, at which time he was 35 years old, the Buddha went on to deliver a ministry of teaching for a further 45 years. Thousands of people, from all walks of life, were converted to Buddhism, or the middle way, as it was known. His teachings and ministries can be found in the section of Buddhist scriptures known as the **Sutta Pitaka** (see below).

6 The nature of the Buddha's death

The most famous account of the Buddha's death can be found in the **Sutta Pitaka**, in a book called the Mahaparinibbana Sutta, belonging to the collection of writings from the **Digha Nikaya** 16. The account describes the last days of the Buddha before his **parinibbana**, when he passed over to nibbana. The Buddha died at the age of 80. We are interested in the nature of his death, rather than the events preceding it.

There are many theories concerning the specific cause of his death. First of all, it is argued that he predicted his own parinibbana three months earlier. The consensus is that the cause of death was an illness that developed after he ate some contaminated pork.

Returning to Williams' view that the life story of the Buddha should be read as a teaching aid, it is the way the Buddha coped with his death experience that is of benefit to Buddhist insights.

> **The Master's Parinibbana is, therefore, the one sorrowful event in the history of Buddhism that turns out in its true meaning, to be really the most blissful.**
>
> (Sister Vajira)

The **Maha-parinibbana Sutta** describes the Buddha's death as taking place while he was in a state of meditation. After this, there were several extraordinary natural events, different emotional and non-emotional responses from the company of followers, a typical Indian funeral with an extraordinary twist and the distribution of the Buddha's remains. Here is a brief summary of the nature of the Buddha's death.

- The Buddha accesses the fourth jhana and the associated meditative planes of infinite space, infinite consciousness, nothingness and the sphere of neither-perception nor non-perception.

KEY WORDS

Four Noble Truths the Buddha's teaching in its simplest form; the four teachings that explain the reality of our world
Sutta Pitaka the second section of the Pali Canon – Buddhist scriptures
Digha Nikaya section of the Sutta Pitaka
Parinibbana passing over into nibbana
Maha-parinibbana Sutta the story of the death of the Buddha

TASK

Design a timeline of the Buddha's life, focusing on the cause of the problem he faced, his reaction to the problem and how it was solved.
Objective To achieve knowledge and understanding of the significance of key events in the life of the Buddha, demonstrating 'selection and deployment of relevant material' (level 5)

- Ananda, the Buddha's devoted but unenlightened disciple, thinks that the Buddha has passed over at this stage. He is corrected by Anuruddha.
- The Buddha returns through the meditative planes and back through the jhanas to the first jhana, only to enter the process once again. When he reached the fourth jhana the second time he immediately achieved parinibbana, passing over into nibbana.
- At the moment of the Buddha's parinibbana there was thunder and an earthquake. Holy beings spoke out and there were speeches given by his followers.
- His followers exhibited two types of reaction. The first was emotional, with demonstrations of grief and acts of remorse. This was from the followers who were not yet free from the attachment of passion. The second, more noble response, was more calm and reflective, with observations that all things are impermanent and so how could it be otherwise? Needless to say, when the local townsfolk of Kusinara were informed, their response was also emotional.
- For six days people paid homage to the Buddha's body with dance, song, music, flower-garlands and perfumes.
- On the seventh day the Buddha's body was prepared for cremation. A procession took the body to the place of cremation.
- A traditional cremation began with a problem over lighting the pyre. It would only light when a respected disciple, Maha Kassapa, had paid respects at the feet of the Buddha and then it did so of its own accord.
- Only the flesh was burned and there was no evidence of ashes at all from his body. The Buddha's bones remained untouched by flame.

The remains of the Buddha were distributed into eight portions and allocated to seven Kshatriya clans and one Brahmin, each of whom built a monument, called a **stupa**, around it as a memorial. The urn itself formed another stupa, and finally the ashes, presumably from the clothes, were the final memorial. These stupas were early places of pilgrimage for Buddhists.

It is evident, then, that the events involved in the actual parinibbana of the Buddha may not be actual, factual accounts but may be more a reminder of who the person of the Buddha was and what he taught in life.

KEY WORD

Stupa monument built as a memorial to the Buddha and usually containing parts of his remains

EXAM TIP

When answering a question about the life of the Buddha, make sure that you focus on the area highlighted. Remember to pick out the key events and explain why they are important in relation to the Buddhist teachings. This ensures you focus on question rather than the general topic (level 2).

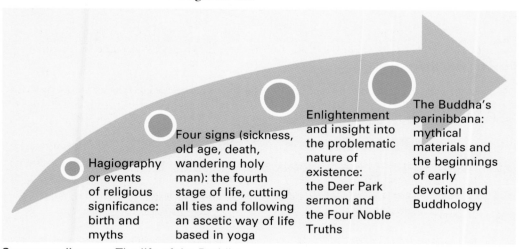

Hagiography or events of religious significance: birth and myths

Four signs (sickness, old age, death, wandering holy man): the fourth stage of life, cutting all ties and following an ascetic way of life based in yoga

Enlightenment and insight into the problematic nature of existence: the Deer Park sermon and the Four Noble Truths

The Buddha's parinibbana: mythical materials and the beginnings of early devotion and Buddhology

Summary diagram: The life of the Buddha

Reflection and assessment AO1

It is now time to channel the information you have considered in a more focused way. In order to do this, once again you need to ask yourself the question: 'How am I going to be assessed on my use of this information?'

Look back to page 7 in the Introduction to review the level descriptors for AO1. There is a description of the character and features for each level. The exam is marked with reference to levels.

Look at the following sample answer, which is a response to the question:

Explain how events in the Buddha's life demonstrate key Buddhist ideas.

(25 marks)

The comments around the response have been made by the examiner.

Quote is not needed as it has not been shown to be relevant to the question.

Through examining the basic understanding of the life of the Buddha it is possible to see how his life did influence his teachings: 'All texts generally agree on the basic story of the Buddha's earthly existence.' (Pye)

Good point, although more explanation of the middle way could be given.

This is because many of his experiences reflect his teachings and in particular the teaching of the 'Middle Way' are emphasised by discussing the Buddha as Gotama the prince and Gotama the ascetic. This is emphasised as it is a central doctrine in Buddhism and it would therefore seem

Explain how this served as a 'catalyst' by making the Buddha reflect upon suffering and impermanence.

logical. The Four Sights are also important as they not only act as a catalyst for Gotama's religious 'quest' but also raise the fundamental problem of suffering which the Buddha addresses and attempts to eradicate in his teachings.

It could be argued that the story of the life of the Buddha is only an effective teaching device as the events in his life deal with the principle teachings found in Buddhism and provide a reason why and how they were derived:

'I have conquered all; I know all; and my life is pure. I have left all, and I an free from craving. I myself found the way.' (Dhammapada v.353)

The story of the Buddha's life is important and useful as it encourages people from a variety of backgrounds to follow the Buddhist path, as the Buddha was a symbol of human

This conclusion does not follow from the above argument. The answer needs more examples of how his life reflects his teaching.

potential. However, when addressing the question as to what extent his life influenced his teachings, it would be difficult to assess as many would argue that the teachings were formed first so therefore should it be asked whether his teachings influenced his life story?

So what does it score?

This is where level descriptors are referred to and parts of essays are related to the levels.

In the exam the answer will be marked according to levels (see the Introduction, pages 7–8). There is certainly knowledge and understanding shown in this answer. The writer clearly has an understanding of the key events in the Buddha's life and some understanding of his teaching, so the answer is at least a level 2 (focus on the general topic).

However, it is not a well-organised account and it is limited in its explanation and selection of relevant material. For example, it does not explain any of the teachings of the middle way in any detail.

Despite this, there are some signs of understanding in how the answer actually relates the middle way to the Buddha's experience of life.

It does not qualify as a good attempt to address the question (level 4). However, there is some attempt to answer the question and it therefore scores a level 3 (satisfactory answer).

Suggestion for further application of skills

Use the points identified above to redraft this answer. Copy it to obtain a text version, then delete material as appropriate, expand on the points that are undeveloped and add in other possible points that could have been included. You can do this in pairs, groups or individually but it is important to discuss and compare possible answers. You could even start afresh, listing with points, then create a writing frame and complete the answer as a class.

This will help to improve a level 2 response and transform it into a level 4 or 5 response so that it demonstrates 'good understanding' (level 4) and a 'high level of ability to select and deploy relevant material' (level 5) through 'use of evidence, examples and correct language' (AO1).

TASK

Have a look at a recent piece of work you or another member of your group has completed. Refer to the OCR level descriptors and try doing your own comments analysis. Aim to make comments that focus on improvements towards level 4 and 5.

Objective To improve a piece of work and transform it into a level 4 or 5 response so that it demonstrates 'good understanding' (level 4) and a 'high level of ability to select and deploy relevant material' (level 5) through 'use of evidence, examples and correct language' (AO1)

Part 3

A critical analysis of the issues

What are the issues that I am expected to consider and to analyse critically?

- How the Buddha related to his immediate context
- How the Buddha reacted against society's influences
- Possible conclusions we can draw from this

1 How the Buddha related to his immediate social and religious background

The Buddha was certainly influenced by the social organisation and religious structure that had been established in previous eras and were still operating in his time. The Buddha worked his way through the traditional Indian four stages of life, was part of the social structure, defined by the caste system, as part of the privileged warrior or ruler class. He was familiar enough with Brahminic rites and rituals to be able to reject them in an informed manner.

The Buddha was a beneficiary of all that was best from the Indus Valley Civilisation and the Aryan culture that followed it. He had the benefit of a privileged life with a very rich culture. He did not have to work for a living and had leisure enough to pursue a life of contemplation.

As for the social organisation of his day, the Buddha was brought up as a typical Hindu. The idea of seeking one's own truth was becoming very much part of the religious and philosophical practice at the time. It was almost a social pastime. The Buddha's wealthy background protected him from the experience of poverty, disease and related aspects of human suffering.

The immediate poverty, disease and squalor of some of the less fortunate people around him would naturally have provoked thoughts about social justice and would have influenced his religious and philosophical thinking.

This brings us to the complex nature of the religious ideas at the time. Buddhism shares some common ideas with other contemporary religious traditions.

In general terms, we can see how the Buddha took a very familiar pathway of the time to investigate religious truths. He became an ascetic and cut off all family ties, as the fourth stage of Hindu tradition demands. He sought religious teachers of the day in order to learn advanced meditation practices. In all this there is nothing new.

When we consider such ideas as samsara (the process of living several lives, based on the principle of karma and the acceptance of several levels of existence involving deities) then, once again, we can see that there is much in common with other religious thinking of the time. This gives rise to several key questions.

? KEY QUESTIONS

- Was the Buddha simply a product of his religious, social and historical context?
- Was the Buddha really as radical in his views as some may think, or was he simply one of many similar thinkers of the time?
- How far did the Buddha's privileged upbringing and social position determine his eventual thirst for answers to the questions of life?

292

2 How the Buddha reacted against society's influences

We have looked at how the Buddha's teaching reflected the religious teaching of the time. However, there is another area to consider when assessing the originality of the Buddha's teaching. When we consider the way in which the Buddha reacted to his immediate background, we see him in a new light. We see that his teaching is distinct and often unique.

For example, although the Buddha was brought up within a rich historical heritage, he actually rejected this in favour of a society that was looking for change and new answers to old questions. Similarly, the ideal of the extreme practices of the wandering holy man and the stages of life became almost superfluous in his teaching and his establishment of the middle way. More obviously, the Buddha rejected the Vedic religious system in favour of a new, less rigid and more individualistic practice.

Despite being part of it, the Buddha rejected the caste system. He is often depicted in art as the teacher with an open hand. Also, his view of women was atypical and probably socially unacceptable.

As far as the Buddha's religious ideas are concerned, there was something original in anatta, or not-self, that can be found in no other tradition of the time. Additionally, as indicated earlier, the Buddha's originality was characterised by the way in which he refined or changed ideas such as karma and rebirth. The Buddha's practice of meditation was also very different. Again, this provokes key questions.

3 Possible conclusions

In addressing the key questions of how far the Buddha was a product of his environment, or to what extent the Buddha was a reactionary or even an original thinker, it is important to reflect upon the arguments previously discussed, to draw appropriate conclusions. You might accept none of those listed below, one of them, some or possibly all – and you may even have your own. However, what matters is the way in which you arrive at your conclusions. Use the arguments from the previous paragraphs to weigh up and balance your thoughts and provide evidence for your decision.

From the discussion above, here are some possible conclusions.

1 The Buddha shares some of the Indian ideas of the time. These were by no means exclusively Hindu in the usual understanding of the word. They were more typical of the Indic way of life. In this way, the Buddha may have been influenced by religious, social and historical factors but we should not in any way relate these to Hinduism in its strict form.

2 Alternatively, we could say that these common ideas are shared by, and are today identified with, popular Hinduism. In that case, we can clearly argue that the Buddha was influenced by both the history and ideas of Hinduism.

3 Buddhism is original because it not only displays many unique features, it is also very different in its interpretation of some key ideas.

4 The social and historical environment, the mixture of the extremes of pleasure and pain, social injustice and the failure to find a soul all served as a catalyst for the Buddha's response. This response was unique.

? KEY QUESTIONS

- **Is there anything unique about the Buddha's ideas?**
- **Was the religion established by the Buddha different from ideas at the time?**
- **Did the Buddha rebel against any of the social and historical conventions of the time?**
- **If the Buddha was original, which ideas show this?**

TASK

Make your own list of questions that you would like to ask about how the Buddha related to or reacted against his immediate historical, social and religious context.
Objective To encourage the use of questions in answers for AO2 and to provide information to use in 'sustaining an argument' (AO2)

5   The unique nature of Buddhism developed later, after the time of the Buddha. Based on the evidence given above, it would have been hard to recognise the Buddha and his teachings as original. The complexity of the ideas and the impact of a changing society make it impossible to distinguish between Buddhism and the ideas of the time.

TASK

Draw a table like this to show the Buddha's response to his background.

Factor	Buddha responded positively to	Buddha reacted against
Religious		
Social and historical		
Life events		
My conclusion		

Complete the table by putting the appropriate evidence from the text into the relevant boxes.

Objective To summarise the Buddha's response to his background, serving as a basis for evidence to include in the writing frame at the end of this chapter (AO1) and also to serve as information to use in 'sustaining an argument' (AO2)

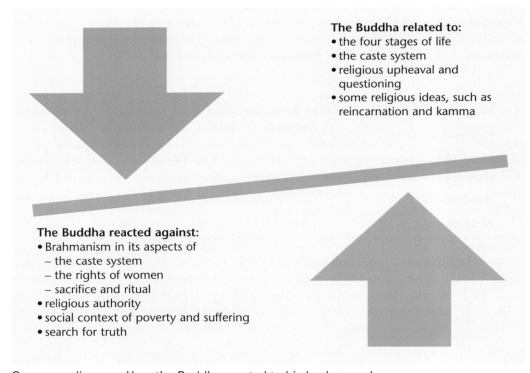

The Buddha related to:
• the four stages of life
• the caste system
• religious upheaval and questioning
• some religious ideas, such as reincarnation and kamma

The Buddha reacted against:
• Brahmanism in its aspects of
  – the caste system
  – the rights of women
  – sacrifice and ritual
• religious authority
• social context of poverty and suffering
• search for truth

Summary diagram: How the Buddha reacted to his background

EXAM TIP

Always point out how the Buddha both related to and reacted against his background. Include some key questions and make sure that you offer more than one possible conclusion. Then give your own, reasoned opinion, based upon what you have chosen to write about. Questions facilitate more than one point of view (AO2 Level 3 and above).

Reflection and assessment AO2

It is now time to channel the information you have considered in a more focused way. In order to do this, once again you need to ask yourself the question: 'How am I going to be assessed on my use of this information?'

The second way of being assessed is through assessment objective AO2. For this objective you need to be able to sustain a critical line of argument and justify a point of view.

Use the writing frame to answer the question:

Assess the view that the religious, social and historical context at the time of the Buddha had no influence upon his life and work. (10 marks)

As you work through each unit in this book, you will find that the amount of support in these sections will gradually be reduced, in order to encourage the development of your independence and the honing of your AO1 skills.

Writing frame

> The issue for debate here is ...
>
> There are different ways of looking at this and many key questions to ask, such as ...
>
> At the time of the Buddha, there were various religious ideas, traditions and practices. We need to look at how the Buddha reacted to these. For example, it can be argued that he was influenced by certain key ideas from his religious, social and historical context, such as ...
>
> However, he rejected some ideas outright, such as ...
>
> Despite this influence, another point of view would be that he introduced unique ideas and practices, such as ...
>
> In light of all this, it could be argued that ...
>
> Nevertheless, it is my view that ...
>
> and I base this argument on the following reasons ...

Although quite basic, this writing frame does focus on critical analysis. It is better to deal with three or four criticisms in some detail, than to compile a longer list with very brief comment. It is important also to make clear in what way your criticism challenges the argument or view.

Suggestion for further application of skills

After completing the question, use the levels and AO descriptors to award marks out of 10. Identify strengths and areas for development in each answer. Then, as a group, collaborate to create an ideal answer that demonstrates 'successful and clear analysis' (level 4) by 'using evidence to sustain an argument' (level 4). Discuss how this answer could be improved to show 'understanding and critical analysis of different view points' (level 5 descriptor).

EXAM TIP

Look at the levels and create a brief list of essential requirements in order to access a high level of response for an argument at AO2. For example, there needs to be a 'range of evidence' (level 5).

Part 1

How the Buddhist Sangha was established

What am I required to study?

■ How the Buddhist Sangha was established

This means I am expected to know about:

■ the development of Vinaya rules

■ the lifestyle of bhikkus and bhikkunis.

EXAM TIP

Always remember to point out the historical evidence for questions that focus on the development of Buddhism. How do we know of the early practices of the Sangha? What evidence do we have of the teachings of the Buddha? This will demonstrate 'relevant knowledge' and 'relevant information' (AO1 level descriptors).

KEY WORD

Sangha the Buddhist monastic community; Buddhist monks, nuns and lay people

This part of the topic covers the very early history of Buddhism during the period following the Buddha's death. It looks at how the first followers worked together to establish Buddhism as a religious tradition and how the teachings and practices of the Buddha were preserved. It would be helpful to write your notes under the headings listed above, under 'This means I need to know about', as it is from these areas that the exam questions will be derived.

Remember that your studies will include elements of the *two* basic assessment objectives of:

■ Knowledge and Understanding (AO1)

■ Evaluation (AO2).

See pages 7–8 in the Introduction to remind yourself of the key assessment objectives at AS level.

The evaluation material is set out in Part 3 of this topic (page 309) and can be studied either alongside the AO1 material, as you work through this topic, or as a discrete topic.

1 Introduction – the early history

During his lifetime, the Buddha established certain formal procedures for practising the path he taught. His followers, later to be named the **Sangha**, lived a very basic, although not too austere, lifestyle.

Although the Buddha travelled throughout the region of the Ganges basin during his ministry, there were periods of the year when travel was not practical. The rainy season was a period where the wanderers or samanas would take rest as a community, in one place, and focus on meditation. There were many wealthy people who donated land for this purpose.

During these periods a disciplined focus developed on the path that the Buddha had taught. This led to an environment specifically suited for intense spiritual development. In a sense, an ideal community was born and the donated lands became familiar refuges for this community to consolidate developments in their religious way of life.

The early history of Buddhism after the death of the Buddha (c400BCE), is unclear. There is little evidence from the period. The first detailed records come from Chinese scholars who visited India in the seventh century. Despite the wealth of textual sources about the life of the Buddha, there is very little about how Buddhism as a tradition expanded in India. There is, though, evidence of different schools of thought and splits that occurred among the Buddha's followers. We also have the formation of the Pali Canon – the Buddhist scriptures. How this all fits together has provoked discussion and research by many Buddhist scholars.

A study of the early period of the Sangha must begin with the assumption that they followed the principles established by the Buddha. Almost certainly, the samana element of wandering quickly disappeared, leaving a more static community known as the Sangha. It is important to consider two distinct aspects of its work.

Firstly, we must consider how the Sangha followed and developed the rules established by the Buddha. These were eventually written down and were known as the **Vinaya Pitaka**, the first section of the Buddhist scriptures, dealing with monastic discipline.

Secondly, and from this, it is possible to discern the lifestyle of the early Buddhist monks, the **bhikkhus**, and nuns, the **bhikkhunis**.

2 The development of Vinaya rules

Throughout the ministry of the Buddha, there were often points of misunderstanding or conflict among his followers. The Buddha's cousin, Devadatta, was a constant critic of the Buddha and often led splinter groups away from his following. This is not an unfamiliar practice in the samana tradition. Even the Buddha himself broke away from his teachers to form his own group. Most issues associated with early points of conflict and discussion were addressed by the Buddha personally.

It is no surprise, then, to see that after the death of the Buddha there was immediately dispute. From the description given in the Maha-parinibbana Sutta, the monk Subhadda was recorded to have said that, with the Buddha gone: 'now we shall be able to do as we wish, and what we do not wish, that we shall not do' (Vajira and Story).

It was in response to such attitudes as this that many of the early monks felt that there was a need to gather, with the purpose of consolidating the rules for practising the middle way. A set code of conduct for the Sangha could then be established. These gatherings are known in Buddhist history as the **councils**.

Buddhist monks

KEY WORDS

Vinaya Pitaka the first section of the Pali Canon

Vinaya discipline, rules of conduct

Bhikkhus Buddhist monks

Bhikkhunis Buddhist nuns

Councils gatherings to discuss matters of discipline and teaching held by the various monastic orders of the day (Sangha)

TASK

Look at the picture. What is there in this monastic setting that tells you that Buddhists are organised?

a) The three Buddhist councils

There were three very important councils in particular that influenced the course of early Buddhism. No doubt there were many such gatherings throughout this early period but these three are recognised as being the most significant.

i) The first council at Rajagaha

This was held about three months after the death of the Buddha. It lasted for about seven months and was held under the patronage of King Ajatasattu.

The purpose of the council was two-fold:

■ to establish the principles of practice for the Sangha, called the Vinaya, which was the discipline or code of conduct
■ to establish the teachings of the Buddha that had been transmitted orally.

The monk Kassapa, a central figure and well respected in Buddhist writings, was to oversee the Vinaya. Ananda, the Buddha's cousin and personal assistant, was to establish the teachings that the Buddha had given.

In respect to the Vinaya, there were several rules already established by the Buddha. He referred to some as minor rules but it is not clear what these were. Although Ananda proclaimed that the Buddha had told him that the minor rules could be abolished after his death, in the event he could not make a clear distinction between the major and minor rules. As a result, it was unanimously decided that all rules should be kept as they were at the time of the Buddha. It was also agreed that no new rules should be formulated.

Most scholars would accept that the basis of Vinaya rules was pretty much established at this time, although precisely what these rules were is unclear. There will always be debate about this council as different traditions have different versions of what exactly happened. As well, there is variant material to aid doctrinal understanding.

> **For this reason, the historicity of the First Council is debated by modern scholars, and will probably remain in doubt forever.**
>
> (Reat)

ii) The second council at Vesali

This occurred about 100 years later, in response to more serious internal conflict in the Sangha. There was dispute over how the rules were being applied, although not much is actually known about the nature of the dispute. Harvey suggests that this was because certain monks were lax about some procedures, one of which was financial. Reat describes Mahayana sources relating that a monk called Mahadeva accused the leading monks of the Sangha at that time of five counts of unenlightened behaviour. This naturally called into question the authenticity of their supposed supreme authority in the practice of the middle way.

Again, facts are sparse and accounts vary from tradition to tradition. There is further confusion over what actually happened at the second and the third councils.

Mahayana sources tend to suggest that the first major split occurred at the second council. Theravada sources suggest the official split between two groups happened at the third council (Harvey, Cush) but they also acknowledged the possibility that it could have occurred at Vesali. What happened, according to some scholars, was a simple disagreement over ten points of discipline and practice.

KEY IDEAS

● **First council Rajagaha**
● **Second council Vesali**
● **Third council Pataliputra**

Others, such as Bodhesako, suggest that the rift had clearly begun at the second council but that the split between two rival factions formally occurred shortly afterwards, at the third council. Harvey acknowledges the ten-point dispute at the second council but does not link it to the split between the Sthaviravadins and the Mahasanghikas that occurred at the third council.

However, it seems clear that the first major split in Buddhism, between the Sthaviravadins and the Mahasanghikas, occurred at either the second or the third council. It is generally believed that the Sthaviravadins wished strictly to follow the established rules and accused the Mahasanghikas of being lax in their application of these rules. In return, the Mahasanghikas accused the Sthaviravadins of trying to add even stricter rules to what the Buddha had established. The identity of the rules is not clear.

First council	Second council	Third council
Led by Kassappa and held in Rajagaha, it is believed to have established orally the discipline (for the first part of the Pali Canon) and the teachings of the Buddha (for the second part of the Pali Canon).	Issues of interpreting the Vinaya code were discussed and there was a disagreement between the Mahasanghikas and the Sthaviravadins.	The dispute over applying monastic rules continued and a split in the Sangha occurred, if it had not done so already at the second council, between the Mahasanghikas and the Sthaviravadins. Each went and practised in their separate ways.

Summary diagram: The three councils

iii) The third council at Pataliputra

This was very soon after the second council at Vesali; some suggest it was only 17 years later. It was held under the patronage of **King Asoka** and lasted nine months.

It is clear that the Theravada school was settled at this council and any undesirable elements were removed. Whether this was the actual split between Sthaviravadins and Mahasanghika is unknown. What is certain is that the split had happened by this time.

Overall, the three councils established what is now the basic Vinaya of the Theravada tradition. It is interesting to note, however, that the disputes and splits were very much in the mould of the Indian tradition and principles of the Buddha. No one tended to dispute particular teachings of the Buddha. In addition, splits in groups were never over belief. More pertinently, in the spirit of the Buddha's empirical path, the issues were always over how to put the Buddha's teaching into practice.

TASK

Do some further research about the three Buddhist councils at Rajagaha, Vesali and Pataliputta. Try to decide when the split between the Mahasanghikas and the Sthaviravadins actually happened, giving reasons for your decision.

Objective To become aware of the conflicting accounts about what actually happened here, and the lack of evidence that exists, and to gain knowledge and understanding of the nature of early conflicts within the Sangha; to fuel evidence and examples for both a demonstration of knowledge and understanding (AO1) and also to help sustain an argument (AO2)

EXAM TIP

Always remember to show that you understand the sections of the Vinaya in relation to what they contain. Avoid listing contents in your answer — be more selective. Explain how the different sections are linked to different audiences, with a focus on how to prevent a breach of discipline (patimokka) and not just with how to deal with such breaches by the Sangha as a whole (Khandhaka).

TASK

Find out more about the edicts of Asoka.

 KEY PROFILE: KING ASOKA

A Buddhist ruler who reigned in the Magadha region, he came to the throne in 268BCE and, after a dramatic conversion to Buddhism, became one of the greatest rulers of all time. He promoted Buddhism through social order and sent out missionaries to spread the religion.

King Asoka

KEY WORDS

Patimokka specific rules, traditionally 227, for Buddhist monks living in a monastery
Sutta Vibhanga the commentary on the Patimokka and the first part of the Vinaya Pitaka
Khandhaka the section of the Vinaya Pitaka that offers guidance on issues of organisation and discipline for the monastic life and the Sangha as a whole
Mahavagga the first section of the Khandhaka
Cullavagga the second section of the Khandhaka
Parivara the final section of the Vinaya Pitaka, which summarises all the Vinaya for teaching monks and setting examinations

b) The contents of the Vinaya

Traditionally, the contents of the Vinaya are the 227 **patimokka** or rules that deal with eight types of behaviour for monks and nuns. While they may appear negative, in terms of outlining how to deal with offences, the overall purpose of patimokka are positive and attempt to guide someone back to the right path.

The section of the Vinaya containing the patimokka is specifically directed towards the individual and is known as the **Sutta Vibhanga**. There is also an additional Bhikkhuni Vibhanga that deals with rules specifically directed towards nuns. Matters covered include:

- offences that require expulsion from the Sangha (sex, theft, murder and lying about spiritual achievements)
- rules that require either expiation or confession
- legal matters
- etiquette and general behaviour.

There are, however, two more important aspects of the Vinaya.

The second section is the **Khandhaka**, which deals with overall organisation of the Sangha. It is a document of rulings that apply to the collective Sangha and covers practical aspects of living as a community under the guidance of the Buddha's teachings. It is split into the **Mahavagga**, dealing with guidance on organisation, and the **Cullavagga**, covering procedures for matters associated with formal discipline. Issues covered include:

- admission to the Sangha
- reciting of the patimokka
- residence during the rainy season
- ceremony codes
- dress and diet codes
- sickness
- disagreements
- probation of monks and nuns
- settling legal matters
- accounts of the first and second councils.

The final section of the Vinaya is the **Parivara**. This is a summary and classification of all rules but is arranged so that it can be recited. It is often used for teaching or examination of Buddhist monks and nuns.

3 The lifestyle of bhikkhus and bhikkhunis

The impact of the various patimokka and the associated rulings in the Vinaya is that a monk or nun has a very simple lifestyle. The specific purpose of such a lifestyle is to develop that condition in life which most successfully promotes the path of Buddhism.

> **The purpose of the Vinaya rules was to provide ideal conditions for meditation and renunciation. They try to enforce a complete withdrawal from social life, a separation from its interests and worries, and the rupture of all ties with family or clan. At the same time the insistence on extreme simplicity and frugality was meant to ensure independence, while the giving up of home and all property was intended to foster non-attachment.**
>
> (Conze)

A few monks and nuns aspired to initiate the same procedures as the earlier Buddhist samanas by wandering, retreating only for the rainy season. Over time, however, the increasing donations of land and the growth in popularity of Buddhism led to the establishment of monasteries.

The rules of patimokka and the Khandhaka were followed within the monastic discipline.

Gombrich argues that the monastic life is the 'springboard' for higher, more spiritual attainment. The monastic life is designed to achieve victory over craving and the best way to begin is with a lifestyle that encourages one to be content with very little. It is the very spirit behind the rules that brings them to life and highlights their usefulness in aspiring to reach nibbana. Such a spirit can be seen in several themes of **sila**, or moral living, that run through the rules. Indeed, as discussed later, morality is the foundation for Buddhist meditation and is also one of three parts of the eight-fold path, comprising right speech, action and livelihood. It is to the details of this moral lifestyle that we now turn our attention.

a) Poverty

Conze and Gombrich both refer to the ideals of **poverty** within a monastic lifestyle. The state of poverty is symbolised by the few possessions a monk is allowed: robes, alms bowl, needle, Buddhist rosary beads, a razor, a belt, a staff and a filter to remove creatures from drinking water. Harvey suggest that, in practice, there are further additions such as sandals, a towel, extra work robes, a shoulder bag, umbrella, writing materials, books, a clock and picture of a teacher.

A monk must be homeless, or at least without a permanent shelter. In practice, this is often regarded as a state of mind rather than a pedantic rule. Effectively, a monk will not possess a home.

A monk's bowl is often inaccurately described as a **begging-bowl**. Monks do not beg; instead, they bless the gifts of food that people give. They are providing opportunity for others to make merit by, or giving, **dana** – which is the most significant ethical activity within Buddhism. Giving is the best example of not thinking of self, but of others.

Once again, it is important to remember the purpose of poverty; it is not adopted as a form of punishment, appeasement or a way of building character. The purpose is always to fight the drives of greed, hatred and delusion that cause attachment and suffering. Poverty in this sense is an aid to a better, more spiritually wholesome life.

❝ KEY QUOTE ❞

It (Vinaya) provides a complete way of life, a rule of conduct, for monks, nuns, novices; the general principles are never lost sight of, and they provide a means of generating a host of detailed, particular prescriptions.

(Gombrich)

KEY WORDS

Sila morality, moral living or moral virtue; one of the three aspects of the eight-fold path comprising right speech, action and livelihood

Poverty living a simple life with basic needs

Begging-bowl a bowl used *not* for begging but to allow people to offer food to the monks

Dana giving, the best example of selflessness

KEY IDEA

Monastic possessions: robes, alms bowl, needle, Buddhist rosary beads, a razor, a belt, a staff and a filter to remove creatures from drinking water. Extras, for practical reasons, may include: sandals, towel, extra work robes, a shoulder bag, umbrella, writing materials, books, a clock and picture of a teacher.

KEY WORDS

Chastity living a life free from human and emotional attachments
Inoffensiveness following the principle of non-harm to all living beings
Kamma (Pali) intentional actions, good or bad, bringing consequences and affecting this and future lives
Meditation the specific practice of concentration that the Buddha taught
Study (in Buddhism) to remember and preserve the Dhamma

b) Chastity

The tradition of **chastity** goes back to the fourth stage of a Hindu's life. It encourages total separation from family and dedication to an independent life in pursuit of truth. The Buddha himself entered this stage. Hindus who enter the fourth stage may make an effigy and perform a funeral, as a symbol that they have died and taken on a new life. This is often associated with taking a new name, common in many forms of Buddhism.

The idea of chastity is nothing to do with repression or a view of sex as in some way being contaminated with spiritual ills. It is similar to that of poverty; it is to help the practitioner to become detached from worldly attachments and commitments.

c) Inoffensiveness

The principle of **inoffensiveness** is not a new idea. As observed earlier, the Jains were extreme advocates of ahimsa – non-harm, non-violence. It is vital not to generate negative **kamma** (the Pali equivalent of the Sanskrit karma) by harming others. Moreover, it is also against one of the underlying principles of Buddhism, that of compassion. Because of this principle, many Buddhists are vegetarian. Although the Buddha was not, it is clear that he avoided meat if given the choice.

An important part of the ideal of inoffensiveness is intention. Although we cannot avoid some destruction of micro-creatures in daily life, it is important to minimise that damage. We are fully aware of the potential for this damage and should take care: 'to diminish the involuntary slaughter, for instance, by being careful about what we tread on when walking in the woods' (Conze).

d) Meditation and study

A major part of the life of a monk or nun is **meditation**, the practice of concentration taught by the Buddha. Learning how to meditate requires guidance in the traditions of Buddhism from the scriptures, which also need to be maintained, to preserve their teachings. Monks and nuns **study** scripture, aiming to match the spiritual practice and pursuit of nibbana with the intellectual understanding of how best to go about it. In the history of Buddhism, this balancing act has led to differences in opinion as to how much time should be given to each aspect, as discussed below. It is clear, though, that a healthy Buddhist lifestyle requires a fine balance between study and meditation.

TASK

Write a letter to someone who is going to join the Sangha. Include an explanation of what rules there are and also what possessions they must bring. Explain why there are such restrictions.
Objective To develop knowledge and understanding of the restrictions of monastic life and to give the reasons for such restrictions, giving clear 'evidence and examples' (AO1)

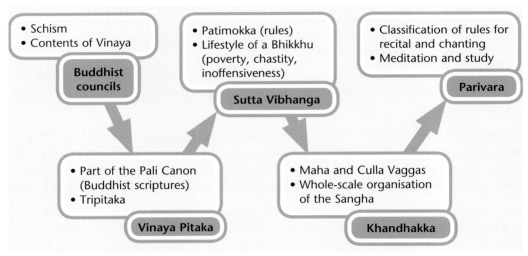

Summary diagram: Timeline of early Buddhism and schools

Reflection and assessment AO1

It is vital to bring together the information you have covered so far and recognise how it can be transformed into effective examination-style revision and answers. The best way to do this is to ask the question: 'How am I going to be assessed on my use of this information?'

Look back to page 7 in the Introduction to review the level descriptors for AO1. There is a description of the character and features for each level. The exam is marked with reference to levels.

Look at the following sample level 2 answer, which is a response to the question:

Describe the lifestyle of the early Buddhist monastic order.   (25 marks)

> The early Buddhist order was called the Sangha. They lived in a monastery and practised meditation all day. They were not allowed to have much although some monks were greedy and took extra gift for themselves. This caused a few arguments. Despite this there were many who were honest and tried to live a very basic lifestyle such as begging for their food and not having many possessions. They also were strict and followed set rules. If they broke the rules then they had to be disciplined. Some of the rules are very strict, like with food and such so it is hard to keep them. Generally, they were highly regarded by other people in society and kept themselves to themselves.

Suggestion for further application of skills

Look back at pages 297–301, to the discussion about the contents of the Vinaya and the description of how it was compiled. Read the text again, as a class. Without support of notes or text, try answering this question, allowing about 15 minutes:

Describe how the Vinaya was compiled and explain the nature of its contents.

(25 marks)

You should now have a basic answer to develop. In pairs or groups, share answers and select one for development. As before, identify ways in which you could improve this answer and complete your own comments analysis on it.

Now write your own answer to the same question, aiming at level 4–5.

TASK

What makes this a level 2 answer? Identify ways in which you could improve this answer.

Now write your own answer to the same question, aimed at level 4–5.

Objective To develop awareness of the characteristics of a good answer according to the level descriptors

---

EXAM TIP

Check for material that is irrelevant or material that is not explained. The answer should be organised in a sequential way so the reader follows a clear line of thought and development.

Part 2
Asoka and the early spread of Buddhism

What am I required to study?
- How Buddhism developed and spread with particular attention to Asoka's specific role in this

This means I am expected to know about:
- the early spread of Buddhism
- the role of Asoka in spreading Buddhism, fighting corruption in the Sangha and formalising the scriptures.

This part of the topic centres on King Asoka, a major figure in the history of Buddhism. He was the first truly Buddhist king in India. His impact on both the Sangha and his subjects, in terms of the establishment and spread of Buddhism, will be a focus for study. It would be helpful to write your notes under the headings listed above, under 'This means I need to know about', as it is from these areas that the exam questions will be derived.

Remember that your studies will include elements of the *two* basic assessment objectives of:

- Knowledge and Understanding (AO1)
- Evaluation (AO2).

See pages 7–8 in the Introduction to remind yourself of the key assessment objectives at AS level.

The evaluation material is set out in Part 3 of this topic (page 309) and can be studied either alongside the AO1 material, as you work through this topic, or as a discrete topic.

1 The early spread of Buddhism – a summary

- It was located mainly in the northern region of India, around the Ganges basin, the same region where the Buddha had travelled.
- The Sangha had grown in size and had become more static. Monastic Buddhism had developed as a result of donations of land from wealthy patrons. There is much evidence of this in the Buddhist scriptures.
- The evidence from the accounts of the councils (see page 299) leads us to believe that by the third council, at the very latest, the Vinaya and the basic Buddhist scriptures had some sort of formalisation.
- Under the patronage of kings, Buddhism had become popular as a state religion in many regions.
- Accounts of the crucial third council indicate that under the influence of King Asoka, the splits and arguments within the Sangha were sorted out.

EXAM TIP

When answering a question on the role of King Asoka, always make sure that you focus on the three areas outlined in the specification: 'spreading Buddhism, fighting corruption in the Sangha and formalising the scriptures'. Remember to link your answer to the third council.

Becasue of the lack of evidence, there is very little else we can assume. The scriptures were actually written down later. The earliest records indicate this was in the last century BCE, in Sri Lanka (Cush). All other evidence about what happened during the period running up to the third council comes from within the Pali Canon itself. It is from this council that we begin to gain more insight into the spread of Buddhism, based on further evidence associated with King Asoka.

2 The role of Asoka in spreading Buddhism

a) Introduction to King Asoka

In India, up until the 19th century, there was a legend about a great king who ruled with justice and sympathy a long time ago. Indian literature, such as the Asokavadana, tells of a prince who was a vicious warrior and murdered his brothers to ensure the throne. He was then converted to Buddhism and became one of the greatest rulers ever. The legend was similar to English folklore about Robin Hood and King Arthur.

However, in **1837** James Princep, a brilliant researcher who worked for the East India Company, successfully translated an inscription found on large stone pillar in Delhi. It included a series of **edicts** by a king referred to as **Piyadasi**, which means beloved of the gods. Between 1837 and **1915** more pillars were discovered, relating to the same king. Gradually, a picture emerged of a ruler similar to the one called Asoka of Indian legend. Scholars suggested there was a connection but it was not until 1915, when Asoka's name was found on an edict, that this was confirmed. The pillars, 32 in all, containing the works of Asoka, were found throughout India and also in Nepal, Pakistan and Afghanistan. Sadly, only ten pillars with inscriptions still survive.

He was born around **304BCE**, but there is dispute over the dates of Asoka's rule; however, it is generally agreed that he came to the throne around **270–268BCE**. Asoka would have been familiar with Buddhism, even as a ruthless king, and he is believed to have had an interest in Buddhism two years before his official conversion to it.

b) Asoka's turn to Buddhism

It is said that, after a particularly bloody campaign in Kalinga, where many lives were lost, Asoka became deeply remorseful. He was so horrified with the impact of war on society that he had a change of heart and turned to the non-violent principles of Buddhism.

From this point on (c262BCE), he not only began to practise Buddhism personally but became a **patron** of it. His edicts openly encourage all to follow the principles of Buddhist dhamma (teaching). But what exactly was this teaching that he encouraged?

First of all, Asoka understood dharma truly to mean righteousness that was more that just a specific set of teachings geared towards a spiritual goal. Examples of the application of this interpretation of dhamma are cited in the edicts and include:

- moral behaviour, essentially, non-violence towards all living beings
- responsible behaviour
- respecting elders
- helping the poor
- looking after the elderly and orphans
- giving to holy men
- treating employees and servants well.

KEY DATES

304BCE: Asoka born
270–268BCE: Asoka began to reign
CE**1837**: writings on ancient stone pillar in Delhi, India, translated by James Princep
CE**1915**: Asoka identified as the king mentioned in the writings on the stone pillars

KEY WORDS

Edicts public announcements
Piyadasi title given to Asoka, meaning beloved of the gods
Patron person who supports or sponsors

305

TASK

On small revision cards, design your own edicts with the key elements of Asoka's social reforms on them.
Objective To be able to provide 'evidence and examples' through reference to the various ways in which Asoka spread Buddhism throughout his kingdom (AO1)

> ## ❝ KEY QUOTE ❞
>
> **It (Dharma) is a bond, uniting people ... it is a fundamental insight, differently expressed in different cultures and religions, which serves as a basis for mutual understanding and peace.**
>
> **(Eliade)**

EXAM TIP

When answering a question about King Asoka's role in the development and spread of Buddhism, try to distinguish between his public role in society as a whole and his more personal quest of purifying the Sangha and sending out missions to other lands. Once again, this is a clear focus on the specification and avoids the 'general topic' (level 2 AO1).

Asoka applied this to himself, as a ruler, by:

- banning animal sacrifice
- establishing medical and veterinary services
- creating a state welfare system
- imposing a fair judicial system
- banning torture
- abolishing the death penalty
- becoming vegetarian
- tolerating all religions
- actively supporting holy men from different faiths (Brahmins, Jains and Ajivakas) and providing caves for ascetics
- giving up hunting
- building wells and reservoirs
- encouraging pilgrimage
- constructing stupas (memorial buildings).

All this information, which can be gleaned from his edicts, portrays a society grounded in religious harmony, peace and social order.

None of the above can be seen to be specifically Buddhist, or even affiliated to a specific religion. Some have questioned whether society was at all Buddhist under Asoka. It is important, therefore, to look at how Asoka reacted with the Sangha at the time.

Asokan edicts on part of an ancient pillar

3 The role of Asoka in fighting corruption in the Sangha

Evidence of Asoka's role in fighting corruption in the Sangha may be found in the accounts of the third council. Around the time of the council, elements of practice that were considered un-Buddhist had filtered into the Sangha.

In Part 1 of this topic, there is reference to undesirable characters and points of conflict. As mentioned previously, Harvey argues that the ten points of discipline usually associated with the internal conflict were not the reason for the split between the Sthaviravadins and the Mahasanghikas. Nevertheless, such points of dispute would certainly not have helped relations within the Sangha as a whole, and do indicate an existing underlying problem associated with financial and material matters.

In short, the Sangha had become more popular and was relying totally on gifts and offerings for survival. The more popular it became, the more was donated. Practices such as monks accepting money and gifts for themselves, rather than on behalf of the whole Sangha, were identified as the main cause of corruption. It was viewed that becoming self-oriented in the practice of the middle way was contrary to Buddhist teaching.

The temptation to join such a lucrative haven as the Sangha would have been very strong for those whose motives were less than sincere. Taken together with the patronage of the king, this way of life seemed to some to be a very attractive option.

Even with the ascetic ideal of indifference to worldly possessions, the respect earned from ordinary people further encouraged benefactors to give more to the monastery.

In line with his social understanding of dhamma, Asoka was keen to maintain the high standards of moral conduct. The idea of adding new rules in order to make the conditions within the Sangha more rigorous is also in line with the Asokan ideal.

There are records of Asoka, with the elder **Tissa Moggaliputta**, actively attempting to identify the non-Buddhist monks. There is also the possibility that the unscrupulous were then expelled, although there is still debate about this.

4 The role of Asoka in formalising the scriptures

From the evidence of the third council, it is clear that Asoka played a major role in establishing the Buddhist Vinaya and maintaining the Buddhist teachings.

It is argued by the Theravadin tradition that Asoka empowered Tissa Moggaliputta to organise the third council, at which the Buddhist scriptures were compiled and the last section of them, the Abhidhamma Pitaka, was completed.

Indirectly, his mission work had a major impact upon the whole history and survival of Buddhism and Theravada in particular. The mission to Sri Lanka, involving Asoka's own son, **Mahinda**, established Buddhism there, where it has remained a major force ever since. It is believed that the first written records of the Buddhist scriptures were created in Sri Lanka.

The empowering of Tissa Moggaliputta to oversee nine missions in c250BCE is also argued to have had some impact later on in history.

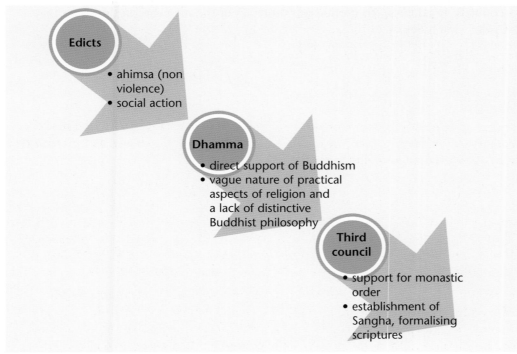

Summary diagram: Asoka

" KEY QUOTE "

Periodic claims that the Sangha has been infiltrated by men and women only interested in a comfortable life are all too plausible. The Sangha's tendency to luxurious living … has led again and again to demands for its purification.

(Gombrich)

TASK

Write an imaginary interview with Asoka, featuring questions about his public work and his private convictions.
Objective To be able to understand the different aspects of Asoka's work, both religious and social; again, this is a clear focus on the specification and avoids the 'general topic' (level 2, AO1)

 KEY PEOPLE

Tissa Moggaliputta one of the chief monks of Asoka's time who was entrusted with the missions to areas beyond Asoka's kingdom
Mahinda Asoka's son, who, according to legend, was involved with the mission in taking Buddhism to Sri Lanka

TASK

Write a message of tribute, fitting for Asoka's grave, that outlines his contributions to Buddhism.

Objective To develop an overall understanding of Asoka's contributions to the spread and development of Buddhism, demonstrating use of 'evidence and examples' (AO1)

TASK

Use these key points as a basis for a writing frame to answer the question:

Explain how Asoka helped in the spread of Buddhism. (25 marks)

Put the points in order and add two relevant quotes at suitable places.

Objective Exam practice

Reflection and assessment AO1

It is vital to bring together the information you have covered so far and recognise how it can be transformed into effective examination-style revision and answers. The best way to do this is to ask the question: 'How am I going to be assessed on my use of this information?'

Look back to page 7 in the Introduction to review the level descriptors for AO1. There is a description of the character and features for each level. The exam is marked with reference to levels.

Look at the key points, below, in answer to the question:

Explain how Asoka helped in the spread of Buddhism.   (25 marks)

You will need to refer to these points, which are not presented in any particular order, to complete the task.

- Missionary activity – Tissa Moggaliputta
- Role in the third council
- Asoka's edicts and what they contained
- How Asoka applied Buddhist principles to society – his achievements
- Assisting in disciplining and weeding out un-Buddhist monks
- His possible inspiration for Buddhist rulers today
- The impact of the mission to Sri Lanka – first written record of the Pali Canon

Suggestion for further application of skills

Design a summary diagram that demonstrates clearly the various links between Asoka's work and the establishment of Buddhism. As well as using ideas from this section, draw upon the information in Part 1, for example, about the Buddhist councils. In addition, try to find out more about the messages on the edicts that Asoka established.

Part 3

A critical analysis of the issues

What are the issues that I am expected to consider and to analyse critically?

■ How far the Vinaya helped develop and spread Buddhism

■ How far the role of King Asoka helped develop and spread Buddhism

■ Possible conclusions

1 How far the Vinaya helped develop and spread Buddhism

a) Ways in which the Vinaya may have helped

There is no doubt that the constant debate over the nature and content of the Vinaya helped to keep Buddhism stable and focused. The councils helped to provide clarity and form to the practice of Buddhism. There is also evidence within the Vinaya itself to indicate 'a great internal consistency' (Gombrich) and the only differences occur in minor details between varying lines of tradition and translation. This internal strength of the Vinaya itself has helped preserve the Buddhist tradition but has also forced it to reflect upon its practices and hence develop.

In addition, the monastic order, now embedded in society itself as opposed to being an assortment of wandering visitors, enabled the Vinaya code of conduct to become more familiar to all people within the immediate social context.

The location of monastic orders within societies promoted Buddhism, strengthened it and made it less susceptible to being usurped. The relationship between the Sangha and those who blessed it with gifts is clear evidence for this and helped to develop Buddhism.

b) Ways in which the Vinaya may have hindered

As already discussed, the restricted rules caused arguments; while dhamma was preserved throughout, there were divisions that brought about far-reaching changes. For example, it is often held that the Mahasanghikas were the forerunners of Mahayana Buddhism. Mahayana is so broad and vast that new writings, or even perhaps new dhammas, have been developed. The real point is that the work of the councils did not promote Buddhism to develop and spread in one particular form, but rather aided its fragmentation into several traditions. Whether this is considered to be development depends upon what Buddhism is considered to be about, but certainly it did lead to further spread.

There is, within the very fabric and nature of the Buddhist ideal, a lack of missionary zeal. Isolation and focus on meditation and study are the real priorities; Buddhism is reclusive in nature, as the monastic ideal testifies.

EXAM TIP

To 'sustain and justify an argument' a candidate has to put forward a view, explaining clearly what evidence supports it, while also being aware of how it links to the overall question and other arguments. This demonstrates a clear awareness of 'different views' and provides further development for an argument (AO2 level 4–5).

TASK

List the key problems that arose for the Sangha and consider how they overcame them. Judge them on a scale of 1 to 5, 1 being *overcoming them* and 5 being *causing real problems*.

Objective To approach an assessment of the effectiveness of the Vinaya in the spread and development of Buddhism (AO2)

KEY QUESTIONS

- Was the Vinaya code really a tool for developing and spreading Buddhism? Is it not simply a way of maintaining focus?
- How far were the practical guidelines of Vinaya useful for the monastic ideal?
- Were there any new challenges to which the Vinaya had to respond?
- Has the Vinaya code lasted the test of time and maintained its original identity?

TASK

Draw up three separate columns in your notes. Head the columns as follows.
1 Reasons why Asoka was a good Buddhist king
2 Reasons why Asoka was a good king
3 Reasons why Asoka could have been considered a weak king

List different reasons in the different columns.

Objective To be able to analyse critically the distinction between Buddhist principles and general principles and to present more than one point of view in an argument (level 3 and above, AO2)

2 How far the role of King Asoka helped develop and spread Buddhism

a) Ways in which Asoka may have helped

There were many ways in which Asoka actively promoted, helped to develop and also spread the Buddhist ideal. Firstly, he had the authority, the wealth and the ability to put measures into place that ensured Buddhist ideals were embedded into the fabric of society. We have seen this already in terms of the social reforms he established and the edicts he placed on stone pillars throughout his kingdom.

In addition to this, there is enough evidence to suggest that he played an active role in purifying the Sangha and maintaining the Buddhist traditions as they should have been. His involvement in the third council was also instrumental in clarifying the Vinaya.

By far the greatest influence of Asoka in developing and spreading Buddhism was the missionary activity that he commissioned. The presence of Theravada Buddhism in Sri Lanka is testimony to this success. It is also probable that the missions extended to, and established, Theravada Buddhism in lower Burma and Thailand. Despite questions over the historicity of Asoka's missions (all the evidence is in the Theravada chronicles), scholars generally accept that his influence here was profound.

Asoka's influence does not end here. Indeed, as a king, he has been a model ruler for others throughout history. Gombrich cites the various kings who have turned to the example of Asoka, including the ancient rulers of Sri Lanka, Burma, Thailand and possibly even China. Asoka has also been discussed by modern reformers such as Anagarika Dharmapala and D.C. Vijayavardhana, who referred to Asoka as 'the Lenin of Buddhism' (Gombrich).

b) Ways in which Asoka may have hindered

Despite all the positive contributions, some historians and Buddhist scholars have questioned whether Asoka was actually a Buddhist king. The focus of his edicts is mainly a social message. Also, Asoka was too tolerant towards other religions, actively supporting them.

It could be argued that, as a king, he did not embed Buddhism into Indian culture as much as he could have done. For example, he did not force people to convert.

Was Asoka's Buddhism truly Buddhist then? According to some scholars, it could have been observed as a weak application of Buddhist principles. The fact that Buddhism began to collapse in India so soon after Asoka, during the Hindu Gupta era (CE320–548), does support this.

Finally, the Buddhist dhamma that Asoka advocated was very similar to later Hindu principles and the Buddha was even assimilated into Hinduism as the ninth incarnation of the god Vishnu.

The Vinaya
• helped clarify dhamma
• promoted internal cohesion in the Sangha
• established the monastic setting
• formalised a code of conduct for religious practice

Asoka
• promoted the dhamma
• was a model Buddhist ruler, practising compassion and justice
• was involved directly with the Sangha

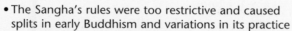

• The Sangha's rules were too restrictive and caused splits in early Buddhism and variations in its practice
• Asoka's Buddhism was only a social code and lacked distinctive Buddhist philosophy
• Buddhism disappeared from India soon after the end of Asoka's reign

Summary diagram: Evaluation of Vinaya, Asoka and the Sanga in promoting Buddhism

3 Possible conclusions

When assessing the impact of the Vinaya rules and the role of Asoka, it is important to reflect upon the arguments previously discussed and arrive at some appropriate conclusion. It may be that you accept none of these listed here, or just one of them, or you may have a different conclusion that is not listed. However, what is important is the way that you have arrived at your conclusion – the reasoning process.

From the preceding discussions, here are some possible conclusions you could draw.

1   The Vinaya and Asoka both firmly established the roots of Buddhism and ensured Buddhism could develop into a state religion and spread throughout India and beyond. Here the missionary work is crucial, enabling both Buddhism and the Vinaya to be both preserved and protected beyond India.

2   Asoka was not really a Buddhist king, simply a social reformer. Historians such as Basham and also Buddhist scholars such as Trevor Ling have suggested this.

He was, throughout his life, before and after his adherence to Buddhism, first and foremost a king; he did not give up the affairs of government for the affairs of some other, spiritual realm. He became a Buddhist because it seemed to him that to do so was to become a better king.

(Ling)

The public system associated with his rule could really have belonged to another religious ideology as it dealt mainly with morality, such was its vagueness. There is very little on nibbana or other key concepts of Buddhism.

3   Asoka's era was really the golden age of Buddhism. To argue that Asoka was only Buddhist in a superficial way, simply because his edicts have little of Buddhist theory in them, is 'foolish' (Gombrich). There is evidence of Asoka's more religious activities, such as pilgrimage, recommending specific Buddhist readings and also his influence within the Sangha.

Asoka is acting as the perfect Buddhist king who enables the Sangha to keep itself pure.

(Gombrich)

? KEY QUESTIONS

• What exactly was the Buddhism that Asoka promoted?
• What was the role of Asoka in purifying the Sangha?
• What evidence do we have that suggests Asoka did in fact spread Buddhism?
• How far does the influence of Asoka go through history?
• Was Asoka really a Buddhist king?
• If Asoka was a Buddhist, does it also mean that the kingdom he ruled had to be a Buddhist one?
• How long did Asoka's Buddhism last?

EXAM TIP

When preparing an answer for a question that involves AO2, critical analysis, try to divide it into the three sections, as in the text. Always use a plan to do this but keep it very brief. This helps you in memorising – but also in categorising – the material in your head for further development and analysis. These three sections broadly correspond to arguments for, against and reaching a conclusion. This again demonstrates that you have considered more than one point of view (levels 3–5 AO2).

4 Asoka's era was indeed a Buddhist success, but was merely tolerated by peoples of India who had no firm convictions. He was too tolerant of other faiths.

He himself honoured with gifts and attended to the affairs of Ajivakas, Jains and Brahmins as well as Buddhists.

(Ling)

The damnation of the caste system would have made Buddhism unpopular and it was soon to be at the forefront of social and religious life again.

As is often the case following a truly great leader, Asoka's heirs were unable to maintain his political legacy for long.

(Reat)

Reflection and assessment AO2

Earlier in this topic you considered the assessment objective AO1 focused on knowledge and understanding. The second way of being assessed is through assessment objective AO2. For this objective you need to be able to sustain a critical line of argument and justify a point of view.

Look back to page 8 in the Introduction to review the level descriptors for AO2. There is a description of the character and features for each level. The exam is marked with reference to levels.

Look at the following sample answer, which is a response to the question: 'Asoka did more harm than good for Buddhism's development.' Discuss.

(10 marks)

The remarks were made by an examiner.

> *No need to write down what you are going to do – just answer the question. The start is very poor and irrelevant.*

> *Good point but could suggest reasons why this is the case. This is not pursued but just left to move on to another point.*

> *This is not clear. Why were they vague? What are Buddhist principles for living?*

In answering this question I will look at the things that Asoka did in trying to develop Buddhism. Asoka was born in 304BCE and started his reign in 268BCE. He was converted to Buddhism because he felt bad about killing people in battle. Some people would argue that because Buddhism died out so soon after Asoka, that he did not really promote it enough. In fact, this is not the case when we look at what he did for the Sangha. He helped them to develop and spread Buddhism to Sri Lanka. Buddhism still exists there today. Although his rules about dharma were very vague he did really promote Buddhist principles of living. In conclusion, from the fact that Buddhism has spread and is still alive in Sri Lanka today it can be argued that this claim is clearly false.

> *This is not required. Context is important if it addresses the question. This does not.*

> *Good again, but he actually did much more than this. Evidence is required for his involvement in the Vinaya, etc.*

> *Conclusion drawn but on weak grounds.*

So what does it score?

In the exam the answer will be marked according to levels (see pages 7–8 in the Introduction). Certainly there is some basic reasoning. The candidate clearly has an understanding of the main debate and is aware that some consider Asoka as not really being specifically Buddhist. However, the initial claim is not really assessed. The problems posed by Asoka's social policies and his tolerance towards other religions are not explained, developed or discussed. There is a conclusion that does logically follow from what has been written, but why this is the case is not really explained.

This would score a top level 2 (an attempt to sustain an argument, views asserted but not successfully justified).

Suggestion for further application of skills

Read the section on pages 309–11 again, then decide how you would tackle this question:

'The establishment of the Vinaya helped to consolidate the central features of early Buddhist practice and helped in the spread of Buddhism.' Discuss.

(10 marks)

Consider some key questions and the possible conclusions. As a group, and building upon what you learned from the question above, try directly to create a plan for a higher level answer. Write this up under timed conditions and then compare answers. Finally, compare the standard of your answer with that of the response to the previous question. Are there any ways in which you can learn from one to develop the other further? In your group, discuss which is the best answer and explain why you think so.

TASK

Using this answer and the comments, write an answer that is at least level 4.

Objective To identify the weaknesses of a poor answer, to transform unsuccessful analysis and to identify 'asserted views' that differentiate a level 2 response from higher levels

Unit 4
Topic 3

Buddhism
Core concepts

Part 1

The Buddhist world view

What am I required to study?

■ Buddhist teachings about existence including the concepts of kamma, nibbana, samsara and rebirth

This means I am expected to know about:

■ specific teachings about kamma

■ specific teachings about nibbana

■ specific teachings about samsara and rebirth.

1 Introduction – the cycle of existence

This part of the topic covers some of the central concepts that form the basis of the Buddhist world view. The focus is on the teachings concerning life, death, rebirth and enlightenment. It would be helpful to write your notes under the headings listed above, under 'This means I need to know about', as it is from these areas that the exam questions will be derived.

Remember that your studies will include elements of the two basic assessment objectives of:

■ Knowledge and Understanding (AO1)
■ Evaluation (AO2).

See pages 7–8 in the Introduction to remind yourself of the key assessment objectives at AS level.

The evaluation material is set out in Part 3 of this topic (page 334) and can be studied either alongside the AO1 material, as you work through this topic, or as a discrete topic.

In Buddhism, the idea of life and death can be summarised in a process called the cycle of existence. The process of life and death is not linear. A person is born and lives a life, but upon death there is no sense of finality. Most western religions accept the final stage of judgement and reward or punishment by a creator God. There is no need for such an idea in Buddhism. Life simply changes form at death and continues with a new life.

This is rebirth (see page 277). Only when a person has followed the eight-fold path to become an **arhat**, a noble or worthy one, is there escape from rebirth; the state of parinibbana (passing over to nibbana) is achieved. Then the cycle of existence collapses. Central to this idea of cyclic existence, and the focus of this section, are several important concepts that need explaining: kamma, nibbana, samsara (page 275) and rebirth.

KEY WORD

Arhat one who has realised nibbana and is no longer to be reborn

2 Kamma

a) The concept of kamma

The most simplistic way to explain kamma (Sanskrit: karma) is by reference to what it literally means: action. Karma is the activity that humans carry out in the cycle of existence. Since everything in life is connected in some way, activities have consequences. The idea is simply that of cause and effect.

In an American sitcom, *My Name is Earl*, the main character is inspired by what he understands as a mystical force called karma. Earl's understanding of this is: 'Do good things and good things happen to you; do bad things and they return to haunt you.'

This is not dissimilar to an official Buddhist definition:

Good gets good. Evil gets evil. Like attracts like. This is the law of Kamma.

(Narada Thera)

Earl decides that, to benefit from karma, he has to work through a list of all the bad things that he has done in life. Thus, he will recreate a balance between the good and bad in his life. Once the good outweighs the bad, his quality of life, he reasons, will improve.

In reality, kamma is more complicated than this, but Earl's perception is a good starting point. A person does have ownership of their actions and this affects their future.

We ourselves are responsible for our own deeds, happiness and misery. We build our own hells. We create our own heavens. We are the architects of our own fate. In short we ourselves are our own kamma.

(Narada Thera)

Although kamma literally means action, the thought processes and intentions ultimately cause rebirth. The Buddha said: 'Intention, O monks, is what I call kamma.' Gombrich argues that the Buddha internalised the Indian concept of kamma, taking the idea of action and tracing it back to its cause. Everything, he deduced, begins with mind or mental formations.

b) Kammic formations and karmic consequences

Kamma is described as wholesome or unwholesome, fruitful or unfruitful, rather than as good or bad. The words good and bad tend to have more personal value judgements attached to them. An action is perceived as either beneficial – to oneself and to others – or not beneficial. But what determines the nature of the actions?

Nyanatiloka's *Buddhist Dictionary* identifies the three conditions for unwholesome kamma as lobha (greed), dosa (hatred) and moha (delusion); their opposites are the conditions for wholesome kamma. Greed, hatred and delusion are discussed later. However, the actual workings of kamma are impersonal, even though they may begin with a person and have personal motives.

The seriousness of an action is measured by its intention. This is different from the traditional Indian idea whereby the action itself is seen as kamma, for example, in Hinduism. Broadly, there are three types of intention that determine the seriousness of activities produced by kamma:

TASK

Try designing cards for a game of life, based on the concepts discussed in this section. They need to deal with kamma and rebirth specifically. Include practical examples of actions in life that reflect:

1 different intentions
2 different objectives
3 the three different causes
4 the ideas behind rebirth.

Objective To develop understanding of the complexities of Buddhist kamma and rebirth, demonstrating depth of understanding and engagement with the materials (AO1)

❝ **KEY QUOTES** ❞

Kamma, literally, means action; but, in its ultimate sense, it means the meritorious and demeritorious volition (Kusala Akusala Cetana). Kamma constitutes both good and evil.

(Narada Thera)

Action, correctly speaking denotes the wholesome and unwholesome volitions ... causing rebirth and shaping the destiny of beings.

(Nyanatiloka)

TASK

Use the three types of intention behind kamma to describe examples of typical actions, such as 'diminished responsibility' when someone reacts in anger. Be descriptive with your examples.

Objective To develop understanding of the idea that kamma is intention first and foremost, demonstrating depth of understanding and engagement with the materials (AO1)

KEY IDEAS

Summary of kamma
1 **Refers to activity.**
2 **Activities have consequences.**
3 **The consequences are either wholesome or unwholesome.**
4 **Activities begin with thought processes.**
5 **Intentions determine the seriousness in effect (wholesome or unwholesome) of activities.**
6 **Effects of activities may be immediate, short-term, long-term or even pass beyond death and into the next rebirth(s).**

KEY WORDS

Nirodha *literally* cessation or stopping; to stop (grasping); refer to the third Noble Truth
Tanha craving, grasping or attachment, the main cause of suffering; refer to the second Noble Truth

- spontaneous actions performed in a passionate state, with varying degrees of attachment and intensity
- planned actions, which are planned carefully over time
- actions that illustrate a lack of compunction (awareness and application of what is right or wrong).

Kamma determines all activities and has an impact upon rebirth. The effects of such actions can actually materialise during the current lifetime, the next birth or later births, depending on their impact.

c) Realms of rebirth

Each individual being is reborn into one of the following realms:

- devas or gods
- ashuras or semi-divine figures
- manushyas or humans
- tiryakas or animals
- pretas or hungry ghosts
- narakas or demons.

A variety of descriptions of such realms of existence can be found in Buddhist literature. It is important to note that:

- despite the gods being the highest realm, it is still a realm of ignorance, according to Buddhism
- the worst state of existence is in one of the hell realms, with the hungry ghosts or the demons
- the optimum realm for spiritual progress is the human realm.

In the popular Buddhist text, *The Questions of King Milinda*, the king asks a Buddhist monk to explain how karma ripens, both within life and beyond it.

Nagasena explains that kammic fruits must be passed on because the process of rebirth (see page 314) is continuous. Kamma is not a unit that attaches itself to a particular aspect of a person's being and remains there. Kamma is itself a continuous process of cause and effect, activating change and movement in a person's existence.

To illustrate this point, Nagasena offers the simile of a man who plants mango seeds. Someone who steals the fruit of the trees cannot be vindicated by using the excuse that the owner did not plant the fruit, only the seeds! Indeed, it is only because the owner planted the seeds that the mango fruit appears on the trees. Likewise, the actions of a person now determine what fruit will be borne in later life and beyond it.

3 Nibbana

a) The concept of nibbana

Nibbana constitutes the highest and ultimate goal of all Buddhist aspirations, i.e. absolute extinction of that life-affirming will, manifested as Greed, Hatred and Delusion ... the ultimate and absolute deliverance from all future rebirth, old age, disease and death, from all suffering and misery.

(Nyanatiloka)

The Buddha's teaching concerning his enlightenment was briefly considered in Topic 1. His enlightenment experience is often linked to the **nirodha**, the third Noble Truth (see page 288) the cessation of **tanha**, or grasping, which is the cause of suffering. Nirodha is the direct action taken to bring suffering to an end and thus bring peace and calm.

The end of tanha leads to nibbana, the ultimate goal of Buddhism. However, as Nagasena argues in *The Questions of King Milinda*, nirodha is only a cause for the realisation of nibbana and not for its achievement. Nirodha and nibbana are not the same. Nirodha is the opposite of the negative action that causes suffering. This eventually cultivates a state of mind conducive to the experience of nibbana.

Grasping or attachment, which causes suffering, is driven out by the three poisons, or the three fires (see page 325). Curbing or blowing out the fires leads to realisation of nibbana.

The experience of nibbana cannot be defined because it lies beyond the world of conditioned phenomena; it is therefore unconditioned or uncaused. Nibbana cannot be a place, like heaven, but it cannot be nothingness either.

b) What, then, is nibbana?

This question cannot be answered completely. Language is created for use within the conditioned world. Since nibbana is unconditioned, it is inappropriate to use words.

There is a very famous story to illustrate this, from Mahayana Buddhism. When the monk Vimilakirti is asked to describe and explain the ultimate truth, he responds with what is known as 'the thunderous silence of Vimilakirti'. This profound response was enough to express the ineffability of nibbana. Another Buddhist writing, the *Lankavatara Sutra*, compares the use of language in explaining nibbana to an elephant that gets stuck in mud.

However, words are necessary for explanation and yet the dilemma remains.

- If nibbana is described in positive terms then people will become attached to it.
- If nibbana is described in negative terms then people assume that it is a state of nothingness, which is a contradiction in itself.

Walpola Rahula offers various descriptions of both the positive and negative ways of depicting nibbana. The negative depictions are not always negative, since saying that nibbana is the extinction of thirst, or absence of desire, is not really a negative. In short, when attempting to describe nibbana, Buddhist texts do it in two ways: what nibbana is not, and what nibbana is like.

Nibbana is the absence of suffering, it is having no more attachment, it is not conditioned. It is the extinguishing of the flames that fuel our attachments. It is like freedom, a higher spiritual state, enlightenment or ultimate and perfect wisdom.

Harvey refers to nibbana as 'a radically transformed state of consciousness' and he disagrees with traditional Theravada Buddhism in terms of a precise definition for consciousness. Traditional Buddhism states that since nibbana is objectless then it cannot be a form of consciousness. This is because consciousness always has to have an object; otherwise it could not be aware of itself as consciousness. For Harvey, nibbana definitely is objectless consciousness.

c) The differences between nibbana and paranibbana

There are two types of nibbana: parinibbana, the one beyond life that the Buddha entered, and the experience of the arhat during life.

KEY IDEA

Nibbana encompasses concepts of enlightenment, absolute peace and pure bliss, literally means extinction or being blown out, from the Sanskrit verb **nibbati**, to extinguish.

TASK

The concept of nibbana is ineffable, which means it is difficult to describe in words. Create a series of illustrations that try to convey what this experience is. For example, the first could be a flame being extinguished.

Objective To become more familiar with the variety of analogies associated with nibbana, demonstrating good use of 'evidence and examples' (AO1)

EXAM TIP

Remember to explain fully each point that you make in an exam answer. Think carefully about each sentence and how it relates to the question and the previous sentence. Aim for at least three sentences to explain a point. For example, state what the teaching is and how it is understood, then give an example. This demonstrates 'understanding and engagement with the material' (level 5), 'good or successful selection of material' (level 3–4) and 'clearly relevant understanding' (AO1 descriptor).

The arhat that has realised nibbana during life still has to live out the earthly existence. The experience of the arhat is in no way inferior to parinibbana (nibbana beyond life). They are the same experience in different contexts.

d) Nibbana during life

The realisation of nibbana during life is the temporary stopping of all conditioned states. Nibbana during life is a state that excludes dukkha or suffering (page 287) and supersedes mind and body. It has no support and has no mental object. It is seen as sunnata or emptiness and is as indescribable as empty space. An arhat can drift in and out of nibbana during life.

Harvey describes nibbana during life as: 'a transcendent, timeless experience which totally destroys attachment, hatred and delusion … a state in which all the personality-factors and causal links "stop".'

The arhat has experienced the deathless and yet remains within the bounds of samsara and is still subject to dukkha. The impact of dukkha upon the arhat, however, is very different from normal human experience.

The arhat has destroyed the three fires of attachment (see page 325), has complete mental health and his actions no longer create kammic results. Pain is felt in physical terms and recognised as such; however, there is no anxiety over the fact that it is pain. The body may be disturbed, as it can bruise, but the mind remains unaffected, undisturbed and totally concentrated. The pain is not identified as 'mine'.

In *The Questions of King Milinda*, Nagasena responds to three key and practical questions concerning the experience of nibbana during life.

1. **Why care for the body once nibbana is realised?** The body is a vehicle for spiritual progression. Not to care for it would hinder progress. Nevertheless, this does not mean that there is sentimentality for the body. Just as anyone would treat a wound obtained in battle, the arhat will look after the body with a sense of detachment from it: 'so the recluses take care for the body as for a wound, without being attached to it'. Note that in this text, the recluse is the arhat.

2. **Does an arhat experience taste and pleasurable experience?** The arhat is someone without greed and is unattached. He can taste food without becoming attached to it, unlike the greedy person who experiences the taste but also develops an attachment to this taste. The difference between the arhat and a greedy person is the control of urges that cause attachment.

3. **Does the arhat feel pain?** An arhat has a developed mind and this is the reason why he feels no mental anguish over pain. The arhat's mind is 'well tamed … obedient and disciplined'. His thoughts are firmly tied to the 'post of contemplation … that remains steadfast and undisturbed'. Just as a tree trunk does not move in the strong wind, even though its branches shake, in the same way the mind of the arhat remains like the trunk, even though his body (branches) may be shaken.

Despite there being just two types of nibbana, there is one last observation to make.

Nibbana can sometimes be a glimpse experienced by others. Those disciples immediately below the stage of arhat (stream enterer, once-returner, non-returner) all have glimpses of the nibbanic object but no direct experience of nibbana – unlike the arhat. Harvey, in *The Selfless Mind*, describes this as: 'a state of high insight which has nibbana as its object is the "signless concentration", an advanced meditative state ... which is itself simply the best of all constructed states.'

e) Parinibbana

The problem with nibbana beyond life is that all questions about it hold inherent misconceptions (Rahula). For example, the many questions asked about the fate of an enlightened self include:

- Are 'you' enlightened?
- Will 'I' be enlightened?
- What will it feel like for 'me' when 'I' am enlightened?

As things are anatta (page 278) then such questions are illogical (see page 330). In the same way, the idea of nibbana beyond life as existing in some sense is another misconception. It is the middle way; it neither is nor is not. The Buddha saw such questions as time-wasting and a sidetrack from spiritual practice; as one Buddhist text observes: 'when all phenomena have been removed, all ways of describing have also been removed.'

This can be explained another way. For example, if we take D as being produced by the arising of A, B and C, it is also simultaneously the factor of causation for A. We have a cyclic, inter-dependent series of events. In simple terms, this relates to the acquisition of factors or attachments. It is the cycle of existence.

Nibbana is the eradication of factors of tanha (grasping) that cause attachment. If we remove D, then the cycle disintegrates because A, B and C are simultaneously removed.

What then remains to be identified as the cause? There is nothing that can be identified as a cause. Nor is there anything left over to describe in relation to these causes.

If a person lays down a path of stones, then each stone progressively causes the path. However, with the eight-fold path the stones are progressively being taken away as a person travels along the middle way. It is not possible to look back and identify a cause because no path remains. The Buddha often compared his teaching to a raft that takes a person across water. Once the far shore is reached, the raft has no more use and is discarded.

4 Samsara and rebirth

a) The concepts of samsara and rebirth

Samsara describes the cycle of life, death and rebirth. It is a Sanskrit word that literally means around and around or to and fro.

In essence, samsara describes the arising of mental and physical phenomena due to causes and conditions. This is known as **paticcasamuppada**, which literally means conditioned arising. Everything is either a cause or an effect. It is a similar idea to the workings of kamma. There are 12 causes and conditions, referred to as **nidanas** or links:

1 Ignorance	**5** Six senses	**9** Clinging
2 Mental formations	**6** Contact	**10** Becoming
3 Consciousness	**7** Feeling	**11** Birth
4 Mind and matter	**8** Craving	**12** Decay and death.

This image of the cycle of existence is famously portrayed as *The Tibetan Wheel of Life*, shown on the next page.

> **KEY QUOTE**
>
> It is an indispensable preliminary condition to grasp fully the truth of anatta ... without such an understanding, one will necessarily misconceive nibbana ... either as annihilation of an ego, or as an eternal state of existence into which an Ego or Self enters or with which it merges.
>
> (Nyanatiloka)

KEY WORDS

Paticcasamuppada *literally* conditioned arising or dependent origination, the Buddhist view of the 12-part causal chain of events that gives rise to existence
Nidanas the 12 links in the chain of conditioned arising

TASK

What are the pictures representing each of the twelve stages of causation that are depicted around the edge of the wheel? Try to find out. Can you think of any other appropriate images?

The Tibetan Wheel of Life

> **KEY QUOTE**
>
> This Buddhist doctrine of rebirth should be distinguished from the theory of reincarnation which implies the transmigration of a soul and its invariable material rebirth.
>
> (Narada Thera)

KEY WORDS

Punabhava rebirth
Khandhas the five factors that constitute a person
Anicca change or impermanence

> **KEY QUOTE**
>
> It is this doctrine of Kamma that can explain the problem of suffering, the mystery of so-called fate or predestination of other religions, and above all the inequality of mankind. Kamma and rebirth are accepted as axiomatic.
>
> (Narada Thera)

The word for rebirth in Buddhism is **punabhava**, which literally means re-becoming. This needs to be distinguished from reincarnation since the Buddha rejected the concept of a soul (see Topic 1).

A person simply comprises **khandhas**, a group of interacting mental and physical processes (see page 321) and is therefore physical matter, thoughts and feelings. There is no overall essence or permanent identity that is transferred from one life to the next. It is simply a collection of energies.

As rebirth is different from reincarnation, then an important question is raised. Can a person be the same beyond death or must they be different? This was raised by King Milinda to Nagasena.

The answer given is that the person is 'neither the same nor different'. King Milinda asks Nagasena for an illustration. Nagasena obliges by offering three comparisons:

- to picture an infant in comparison to an adult and consider whether he is exactly the same person
- to imagine a candle burning; it runs down but the light is continuous from one stage to the next
- to consider milk that changes into curds from butter and ghee but the ingredients and constituents remain the same.

Each of these experience change. It would not, however, be argued that the person, light or dairy product is completely different at any stage. There is always an element of continuity. So it is with rebirth.

Anicca, or change, is evident and paticcasamuppada is the cause. The nidanas, or links, constitute the chain of events. Together they make it into one continuous process. Rebirth, then, is just another aspect of this continuous process. In theory, it is no different from a person changing as they grow.

b) The role of kamma

It has already been established that a person's kamma, their actions or produced activities, can affect the future (see page 315). Kamma also works beyond life and determines the person's rebirth. Hence, kamma and rebirth are inextricably linked.

If this is the case, then what about personal moral responsibility? Would one not then in the next life be freed from the evil deeds committed in the past? If one is not the same person following rebirth then could one escape the effects of kammic law? Does a person begin a new rebirth with a fresh start? The answer is: 'Certainly not!'

c) The five khandas

There is quite a lot written about samsara, rebirth and kamma, all of which affect the individual.

The question remains: If a person is anatta (not-self) and has no permanent identity, then what is (s)he?

The Buddhist answer is that a person arises and functions according to the five groups (khandhas) of clinging (upadana).

These five groups (upadana khandhas) are:

- rupa (form) – basically the physical. This covers energy, action and all activities of an individual. It also refers to the non-extant matter surrounding us.
- vedana (feeling) – our reactions to the immediate environment. Reactions can be positive or negative. Reactions involve the senses and the emotions, which also include feelings of indifference or neutrality.
- sanna (perception) – the medium through which these feelings are actually interpreted or misinterpreted and given personal meaning. We tend to use language to give them labels, for example, cold, frightening, an old woman, a fierce dog.
- sankhara (mental formations) – a crucial group because it is the stage that initiates action. It determines how a person reacts to the experience that they encounter. For example, is this a happy experience? If so, how do I proceed?
- vinnana (consciousness) – seen to be the base of all our experience. It expresses itself in relation to sanna. It is not, however, an independent entity and is driven by the other four formations. In turn, vinnana also determines how the other four groups are formed in the first place. The fifth group is sometimes referred to as citta, meaning mind, awareness or consciousness. At this stage, an overall decision of action may be made.

Note that only the first group is actually concerned with the physical world. The remainder are all within the realms of the psyche. As Nyanatiloka writes: 'The moral quality of feeling, perception and consciousness is determined by the mental formations.' Therefore, as with kamma, it is mind that is the real initiator of action.

KEY IDEA

Rebirth

1 Each momentary consciousness of this ever-changing life process, on passing away, transmits its whole energy, all the detailed recorded impressions to its successor.

2 Every fresh consciousness consists of the potentialities of its predecessors together with something more.

3 There is therefore a continuous flow of consciousness without any interruption.

4 Here there is no identical being but there is an identity in process.
(Narada Thera)

" KEY QUOTE "

What is called individual existence is in reality nothing but a mere process of those mental and physical phenomena ... These five groups, however, neither singly nor collectively constitute any self-dependent real ego-Entity, or Personality (atta).

(Nyanatiloka)

d) Misunderstanding the khandhas

A very famous illustration of the five khandhas is seen in *The Questions of King Milinda*.

 KEY IDEA

In simple terms, we can compare this analysis to a biological description of action and reaction.

1 Bob is a Buddhist monk. Bob's hand (rupa) touches metal (rupa).

2 This does not feel (vedana) pleasant.

3 Bob says, 'Ah yes, this is extremely hot (sanna).'

4 'This unpleasantness is pain (sankharas) and causes me distress (sankharas).'

5 Driven by the other formations and their reaction to this experience, it is a sensible objective (vinnana) for Bob to move his hand.

KEY IDEAS

When Milinda and Nagasena first meet, Nagasena explains that, although he is called 'Nagasena', this is only a label and no more, since 'no person can be apprehended in reality'.

'Then Nagasena does not exist', reacts Milinda. 'A falsehood has been spoken' – even the term Nagasena is 'a mere sound', empty and meaningless.

This is the typical response to the Buddhist concept of the five khandhas. Milinda assumes that Nagasena is teaching that a person does not exist.

However, Nagasena did not say that he did not exist, rather, that 'no person can here be apprehended'. That is, the *person* that is identified as a physical substance underlying our existence is a fallacy. Strictly speaking, existence has to be defined and appreciated in terms other than those of permanent existing entities. That is, the idea of a 'Nagasena' or of what a *person* is needs analysing and carefully redefining.

Drawing upon Milinda's experience, Nagasena asks for a precise definition of the thing that Milinda refers to as a chariot. The King defines a chariot in terms of factors that cause this designation to arise, for example, 'a wheel' together with 'a cart'. These are all factors upon which the chariot is dependent for its existence. The chariot is therefore not a distinct entity in its own right: it is a composite of other physical factors. Just like Nagasena, the chariot has no real identity of its own. To describe a chariot, one has to use the components that make it and not the chariot itself. However, it would be foolish to deny the existence of the chariot.

In the same way, illustrates Nagasena: 'it is just so with me'. So, the terms Nagasena and chariot apply to processes rather than isolated products.

A Buddhist monk

TASK

What is a person? According to Buddhists, what are we made up of?

Nibbana (direct experience within samsara) and parinibbana (beyond samsara)

Paticcasamuppada (conditioned arising)

Anatta and the five khandhas

samsara

Kamma and the Buddhist path (morality, meditation and wisdom)

Life, death and rebirth

Summary diagram: Samsara

Reflection and assessment AO1

It is vital to bring together the information you have covered so far and recognise how it can be transformed into effective examination-style revision and answers. The best way to do this is to ask the question: 'How am I going to be assessed on this information?'

Look back to page 7 in the Introduction to review the level descriptors for AO1. In the examination you will be assessed by levels of response.

Below is an examination-style question about Buddhist responses to nibbana. Beneath it are three sets of bullet points under the headings 'basic', 'developed' and 'higher'. A basic answer relates to levels 1 and 2. The developed answer can score level 3 or possibly the lower requirements for level four. The higher level scores from level 4 up to the maximum.

Explain Buddhist teachings about nibbana.   (25 marks)

Basic	Developed	Higher
■ Ultimate truth or perfect enlightenment ■ May relate this to the life of the Buddha ■ Description of his enlightenment experience ■ May explain that it is difficult to describe	■ A clear discussion of the definition beyond enlightenment, for example, blowing out ■ Two types of nibbana ■ Examples of ways in which nibbana has been described ■ Problems associated with defining nibbana	■ A detailed discussion about how nibbana can be defined ■ Links to the teaching of nirodha ■ Misunderstandings about nibbana, for example, Nagasena's discussion about 'no cause' – nibbana is unconditioned ■ Problems in describing what nibbana is like and what it is not ■ The two types of nibbana with clear explanation of the experience of an arhat ■ Questions about parinibbana

Suggestion for further application of skills

Refer back to the two questions and notes on this page. For each of them, prepare a plan and then write up your answer under timed conditions.

Working as a group, grade the answer for each question. It would be beneficial to copy the best answers (one for each essay) and, still as a group, consider what makes them good. After this time of reflection, revisit your own work and redraft it to improve it.

TASK

Consider the following question:

Explain Buddhist teachings about kamma.   (25 marks)

Study the examples of responses that could be given for basic, developed and higher for the question about nibbana, opposite. As a group, add to this list. Now, in small groups, work out what could be included for basic, developed and higher for the question about kamma. You could swap ideas between groups, to finalise your notes, or each group could take the basic, developed and higher sections in turn and discuss your notes.

Objective To develop awareness of what will constitute a very good answer according to the level descriptors, by gradually building up a response

Part 2

The three threes (marks, poisons, refuges)

What am I required to study?

■ Buddhist teachings about the three poisons, the three refuges and the three marks

This means I am expected to know about:

■ specific teachings about the three poisons

■ specific teachings about the three refuges

■ specific teachings about the three marks of existence.

This part of the topic covers some of the most important concepts in Buddhism. The refuges are the collective focus of every Buddhist. The marks are the basic observations about the nature of the world in which humankind lives. Finally, the poisons describe the ways in which, through generating ignorance, a person is trapped in this world of suffering and prevented from liberation. Each of the concepts is a group of three. It would be helpful to write your notes under the headings listed above, under 'This means I need to know about', as it is from these areas that the exam questions will be derived.

See pages 7–8 in the Introduction to remind yourself of the key assessment objectives at AS level.

The evaluation material is set out in Part 3 of this topic (page 334) and can be studied either alongside the AO1 material, as you work through this topic, or as a discrete topic.

In Buddhist teaching there are many concepts that are grouped together and numbered. This technique illustrates the inter-relatedness of the teachings (see summary diagram, page 332). However, it also is a practical tool in aiding memory.

The original teachings of the Buddha were oral. The first evidence of written records of the dhamma is dated from the last century BCE. **Oral tradition** was the practice of collecting, ordering and passing on information by word of mouth. It was a very reliable way of transferring information. Grouping teachings together was also a very useful way to maintain accuracy. It is only with the rise of more widely available written records, advanced technology and new ways of recording data that the method of oral tradition is no longer common.

Although people may think that the risk of exaggeration, additions and inaccuracies is greater with this method, research demonstrates the process of oral tradition to be reliable. The brain is an extraordinary and amazing organ that can be trained to store and recollect a great deal of data. Training takes much practice; if the brain is not used

KEY WORD

Oral tradition the practice of collecting, ordering and passing on information by word of mouth in this way regularly the skill is not as effective. This is the reason why people today are less confident in oral methods of learning. The truth is that it can be very effective.

1 The three poisons or three fires – greed, hatred and delusion

a) The three poisons or three fires

These three concepts, the **kilesas**, have been referred to in several ways. Remember, concepts are translated from the original Pali (or Sanskrit) and so are translated differently by different scholars.

The most popular terms for the kilesas are poisons or fires; although there are many of these, three are seen to be the most important. They may also be called defilements.

It is argued that when a person is in a state of ignorance, it is the three fires of greed, hatred and delusion that are the driving forces within that individual's psyche that determine the course of their life and their attachment to the cycle of existence.

Each fire is an unwholesome quality in an individual. Although there are the defilements, the first three are the most important:

- **lobha** or greed
- **dosa** or hatred, aversion, anger
- **moha** or delusion

The other seven are conceit, speculative views, doubt, mental torpor, restlessness, shamelessness and lack of moral dread.

These three fires are fuelled by tanha, which is desire, craving or attachment. This is, itself, the most immediate cause of dukkha or suffering. Dukkha needs to be eliminated in order to aspire towards the realisation of nibbana.

Nibbana can be translated as blowing out or extinguishing. The fires of greed, hatred and delusion, along with the other fires, need to be extinguished. The path of morality, meditation and wisdom (the eight-fold path, see page 342) is the way to achieve this.

b) The role of the three poisons or three fires in keeping the wheel of samsara in motion

As mentioned earlier, it is tanha (attachment) that is the direct cause of suffering and the reason why, through ignorance, an individual remains within samsara, the cycle of existence.

The most famous image of the three fires is depicted in the Tibetan Wheel of Life (page 326).

The three fires are at the centre or hub of the wheel of samsara and are depicted as animals: a rooster or cockerel for greed, a snake for hatred and a pig for delusion.

In a state of ignorance, an individual's actions and intentions are determined by the fires. A basic way to understand this process is through kamma.

In the discussion of kamma (page 315), it was stated that activities are the result of intentions. These broadly correspond to intentions that are passionate, those that are clearly thought out and those that are totally ignorant of the reality of a situation. In a sense, it is these three types of intention that are behind kammic activity that relate to the fires.

KEY WORDS

Kilesas the poisons, fires or defilements: negative qualities that motivate a person and keep them attached to the cycle of existence
Lobha greed
Dosa hatred
Moha delusion

The centre of the hub of the Tibetan Wheel of Life

TASK

Write down some examples of situations in life where people react or are driven by the fires of greed, hatred and delusion. Try to use a reflection of your own experiences as a basis for this.
Objective To be able to demonstrate more ownership of the material and deeper understanding through reflection upon actual examples, using evidence and examples in demonstrating knowledge and understanding (AO1)

An activity that is performed in the heat of the moment may be related to the fire of hatred or anger. It is often said that there is a fine line between love and hate. In either case, it is clearly a passionate, emotive state that leads to attachment.

An activity that is thought out, that lies dormant and festers into further attachment can be related to the fire of greed. Greed is not just an immediate desire for gratification but also encompasses long-term desire, ambition and the need to satisfy the ego. It is the most immediate example of selfishness. Many actions are driven by this fire.

It is interesting to note that dana or giving, the opposite of greed and what Harvey calls 'the primary ethical activity', is seen to be the best example of selflessness.

Finally, the fire of delusion can be related to activities that are totally ignorant of how things are. Indeed, these can often be the most dangerous activities, for example, carried out by someone who cannot discern what is morally right or wrong. At the other end of the spectrum it can be as simple as superficial unawareness.

2 The three refuges: Buddha, dhamma, Sangha

a) The three refuges and their relative importance as a statement of faith, as a support for Buddhists and their mutual interdependence

KEY WORDS

Sarana refuge, of which there are three for a Buddhist: Buddha, dhamma and Sangha
Tiratana the three jewels, another term for the three refuges

Sarana is translated as refuge. However, this needs some consideration. Refuge is associated with a calm, safe environment, away from attack. In a sense, this is true. It is a place away from the unwholesome nature of the world in its entirety.

However, this understanding does not accentuate the positive side of refuge. For a Buddhist, the idea of a refuge relates to Buddha, dhamma and Sangha. It is not a place to hide away and cower from outside attacks. A refuge is a centre of excellence in spiritual terms. It is a place to gain strength, to be rebuilt and refreshed. It is a place to be purified and transformed. This latter understanding is by far the more accurate in terms of Buddhist practice.

The three refuges are also called **Tiratana** or the three jewels, such is their importance.

Tiratana – the three jewels or refuges, Buddha, dhamma and Sangha

TASK

The Buddha is represented as a figure of devotion, as one of the refuges. Why would it be incorrect to say that Buddhists worshipped the Buddha?

b) Buddha

The Buddha is seen as a teacher, the awakened or enlightened one. In Theravada, or traditional Buddhism, the Buddha is understood to be a human being and not a divine being. He is a figure whose words offer guidance and who is given respect for what he has achieved.

Buddhists pay devotion to, admire and respect the person of the Buddha, they do not worship him. The life of the Buddha is an example for others to follow. It is an example of how, from the human condition, enlightenment can be realised. The Buddha is a role model for inspiration.

The Buddha was special since he was unique in this world. He is **samma-sambuddhasa**, the perfectly self-enlightened one. The idea of rediscovery of the dhamma and self-enlightenment is what specifically makes one a Buddha.

The Buddha's life illustrates the fundamental teachings of Buddhism. For example:

- his discovery of a middle way between two extremes of living
- the insight provided by the four sights into the plight of the human condition
- the path away from suffering, the eight-fold path
- the diagnosis of the Four Noble Truths
- the way of mindfulness and meditation.

This can be related to the idea that the life story of the Buddha is not intended to be a factual, historical account, but more a **hagiography** or a religious or spiritual biography, to inform the followers of a particular path (see Topic 1 Part 2, page 283: Williams).

KEY WORDS

Samma-sambuddhasa **the perfectly self-enlightened one** Hagiography **a spiritual or religious biography**

c) Dhamma

The dhamma is the teaching of the Buddha, later to become the Pali Canon. It therefore can refer to the basic teachings as expounded in the Dhamma Cakka Pavattana Sutta or to the whole extent of the Buddhist traditional writings.

Much emphasis is given to practising the dhamma. Buddhism is empirical in nature and, in this sense, everyone has to work out their own path. The Buddha's emphasis was always on the scientific approach, or empiricism, testing for oneself.

The ultimate goal of taking refuge in the dhamma is always nibbana. The practical aspect of dhamma provides information on the process of meditation.

Dhamma is also a guide for moral living. In this sense, it is a guiding light for those lost in the cycle of existence.

For a Buddhist the aspect of refuge is in maintaining the dhamma both mentally and physically.

d) Sangha

The Sangha is the Buddhist community. The term is used in different ways but, in terms of refuge, it refers to the Buddhist community in its wider sense.

The purpose of the Sangha as a refuge is for training. This can take place either in a group or within a more formal setting, for example, a monastery.

The aim of the Sangha is to follow the path that the Buddha taught and to gain help and assistance from others. It is the gathering of like-minded people for encouragement, each with the common goal of nibbana.

There is a famous parable that the Buddha taught about an elephant that belonged to a king. The elephant was of exceptional character, calm and friendly. However, the king noticed the elephant's character changing. The elephant became irritable, prone to tempers and more difficult. Eventually the problem was identified. A group of criminals was meeting at the elephant's stable. The elephant was clearly picking up characteristics of the people it was spending time with. The criminals were removed and, in time, the elephant rediscovered its old character.

The idea of refuge in the Sangha can be compared to this. A person will develop characteristics from those people with whom they interact. The Sangha therefore is a place of positive, wholesome activity, with people who will help and not hinder spiritual progress.

e) The three refuges and how they might be applied in practice

In practice, the most famous application of the refuges is the chant that dutifully takes place as part of formal monastic procedure:

Buddham saranam gacchami
Dhammam saranam gacchami
Sangham saranam gacchami

Simply translated this means:

I go to the Buddha for refuge
I go to the dhamma for refuge
I go to the Sangha for refuge.

TASK

Design a diagram that links the three threes, explained in this section. Begin with the tiratana but remember that the links between the other two are not just with dhamma. Objective To develop ability to show the inter-relatedness of these teachings and demonstrate 'understanding and engagement with the material' (level 5)

It is a profession of faith. It is a crucial psychological reminder and focus for practice. It is seen as essential preparation mentally for meditation and walking the path that the Buddha taught.

Within Buddhism itself as a religion, there are variations within traditions as to how the words of the chant are both used and understood.

	Application
Buddha	Inspiration – as a figure of aspiration and encouragement Reverence – for the nature of his achievement or his unique status Respect – for the achievement of enlightenment Guidance – as an exemplary Buddhist role-model
Dhamma	Guidance – as advice about the Buddhist path Study – as an in-depth appreciation of teachings Information – as a source of knowledge about the Buddha and his teachings Practice – as a manual for the practical aspects
Sangha	Meditation – for practical learning and instruction Practice – for the communal aspect of learning alongside others Discussion – for analysis and debate Meeting – as encouragement, being in the presence of other like-minded individuals Formal training – for the monastic emphasis of Buddhism

3 The three marks of existence – anicca, anatta, dukkha

a) The relationship between the three marks of existence and their relative importance

The technical term for the three marks is **ti–lakkhana**. The term lakkhana can mean characteristics, signs, basic facts, realities, observations about, conclusions about and so on. There is a wide variety of interpretations.

b) Anicca

Anicca means impermanence. It is the idea that there is no one thing that stays the same. In the immediate world around us appearances can be deceptive. A table may appear to be static, a flower unchanged from one moment to the next. Analysed at a much deeper level it can be seen that the Universe is, in fact, in a constant state of movement.

Even the individual person is not the same as they were five years ago. This insight, for the Buddha, was a direct result of the first three sights of sickness, old age and death. Anicca is a law of the Universe and nothing can escape this fact.

Nibbana cannot be realised without a true understanding of the fact that things are impermanent. A true understanding of impermanence can be achieved only from direct meditative insight. Impermanence is not something to believe. Impermanence is not something to appreciate on an intellectual level. Impermanence is to be experienced through meditation.

There is only one thing that can be said to be not subject to change and that is nibbana. Nibbana is unconditioned, uncaused and is always the same. Nibbana, however, it can be debated, is not really a thing.

EXAM TIP

When discussing the Buddhist concepts try to follow the format given here.

1 Define the concept in literal terms.
2 Discuss how this is understood in different ways.
3 Relate the concept to other aspects of Buddhist teachings.
4 Use quotes only to illustrate a point you are explaining.
5 Indicate possible problems associated with this concept, including any misunderstandings that may arise.

This is a clear indication of a 'high level of ability to select and deploy relevant information' (level 5).

KEY WORD

Ti-lakkhana the three characteristics of existence

- Impermanence is a basic feature of all conditioned phenomena. (Nyanatiloka)
- Without deep insight into the impermanence and insubstantiality of all phenomena of existence there is no attainment of deliverance. (Nyanatiloka)

c) Anatta

Anatta is often translated as no soul or no self. The most beneficial translation for understanding the idea of anatta is not-self.

The Buddha, when he reflected upon himself through meditation, could not find any one thing that was unchanging within himself. There was no evidence of an underlying soul. There is no self in the sense Hindus or Christians would perceive. Instead, there are many things that combine to make us the people that we are.

The concept of anatta appears to be totally unique. Others have agreed with this and have argued that it is anatta that makes Buddhism unique among world religions.

Ajahn Chah, a renowned Thai Buddhist monk, compared human life to an ice cube that slowly melts away until nothing is left. However, this does not mean that a Buddhist would deny human existence.

The idea of anatta invites further investigation, through meditative insight, into whom or what a person actually is. In other words, it is like a rediscovery of the self.

Viewed in this way, anatta is very much a practical device, tool or vehicle for spiritual development. It is not at all a philosophical statement. When not-self is seen in abstract it loses its true perspective and value. If it were just a philosophical teaching or a theory then at face value it appears to be meaningless. It is only when, like anicca or impermanence, it is experienced that it actually becomes meaningful.

d) Dukkha

Dukkha is also the first of the Noble Truths (see page 288). It can be better translated as frustration. Narada Thera offers the literal rendering of dukkha as 'that which is difficult to endure': a compound of *du*, meaning difficult, and *kha*, to endure. Dukkha is often translated as suffering or ill, although this does not really convey the true breadth of its application to life.

Peter Harvey refers to it as 'frustration' or 'general unsatisfactoriness' with regard to life: 'suffering is inherent in the very fabric of life'.

Just as with anicca, the insight into dukkha comes from the Buddha's experience of the four sights. Along with anicca and anatta, it is a characteristic of being or existence.

Dukkha may be either physical or mental pain or suffering. However, dukkha is not limited to painful experiences. It is vital to understand that dukkha underpins the very nature of pleasurable experiences as well. This is because dukkha involves an inability to see that things are impermanent and not-self. A holiday may be a very enjoyable experience but awareness of the fact that it will soon end is *not* so enjoyable. The very nature of a holiday is temporary.

The best place to look for a more accurate understanding is in Nyanatiloka's *Buddhist Dictionary*: 'dukkha is not limited to painful experience ... but refers to the unsatisfactory nature and the general insecurity of all conditioned phenomena ... this includes also pleasurable experience.' Here, the idea of 'general insecurity' refers to the

" KEY QUOTE "

This is the central doctrine of Buddhism, without understanding of which a real knowledge of Buddhism is altogether impossible. It is the only really specific Buddhist doctrine, with which the entire structure of the Buddhist teaching stands or falls.

(Nyanatiloka)

other two marks of existence from which it cannot be divorced if we are to offer an accurate description.

Once again, it can be seen that:

The first truth does not deny the existence of pleasurable existence, as is sometimes wrongly assumed.

(Nyanatiloka)

Does this then make Buddhism pessimistic? No, it cannot be pessimistic, as the Buddha pointed out: 'This above all do I teach, suffering and the deliverance from suffering.'

Dukkha is any experience that does not recognise things as anicca and anatta. Objects, ideas and experiences that are seen as permanent and as existing in themselves lead to attachments. This inevitably invites a painful experience when these attachments are broken and they do not last.

On the whole, the relationship between the three marks of existence is one of necessity.

- Impermanence indicates that things are not-self and this gives cause to the possibility of suffering.
- Suffering is a condition whereby a person is unaware that things are impermanent and not-self.
- Things are not-self because they are impermanent. Therefore, the idea of a permanent attachment to a self or ego can only lead to suffering.

e) Whether belief in the three marks of existence is helpful or consistent with human experience

The Buddhist approach to the human experience parallels a scientific approach. It is not dogmatic. It is not based in belief but in thorough observation and testing. In this sense we might hope that it is helpful and consistent with what we know today of the human condition.

Indeed, there are strong parallels with the science of psychology. The writings of Susan Blackmore, a renowned psychologist and practising Buddhist, suggest the consistency of Buddhist analysis of the human experience with contemporary scientific thought.

Individually, each of the three marks has its strengths in helping people to understand the human experience.

A narrow interpretation of dukkha appears, at first, to be negative. However, when a broader interpretation and understanding is considered it is far more consistent with human experience of life. It involves not only negative experiences but positive ones as well. In short, it describes the ups and downs of human existence.

The idea of impermanence is sometimes difficult to harmonise with both religious and secular thinking. However, changes in scientific understanding about the nature of the Universe, for example, in the field of quantum physics, have made Buddhist thinking more helpful and consistent with what we can know about the human experience. Indeed, *The Tao of Physics*, written in 1975 by Fritjof Capra, an Indian physicist, first brought to international attention the parallels between scientific thought about the nature of the Universe and ancient Indian philosophy (including Buddhism).

> **" KEY QUOTE "**
>
> Birth is dukkha, ageing is dukkha, sickness is dukkha, death is dukkha; … association with what one dislikes is dukkha, separation from what one likes is dukkha, not to get what one wants is dukkha; in short, the five groups of grasping … are dukkha.
>
> (Dhamma Cakka Pavattana Sutta)

> **" KEY QUOTES "**
>
> It is from the fact of impermanence that, in most texts, the other two characteristics, suffering (dukkha) and not-self (anatta), are derived.
>
> (Nyanatiloka)
>
> It is because of the fact that things are impermanent that they are also dukkha: potentially painful and frustrating.
>
> (Harvey)

❝ KEY QUOTE ❞

While a metaphysical self is not accepted, a changing empirical 'self' is accepted … Reference to an empirical 'self' is simply a way of talking about the functioning personality-factors, not some reference to some hidden extra entity or structure.

(Harvey)

EXAM TIP

This section is full of new concepts. In revising, instead of just drawing up a glossary of key words try changing the material covered into a flow chart or spider diagram that links each aspect of the Buddhist concepts together. This shows an ability to present the inter-relatedness of the pillars and demonstrate 'understanding and engagement with the material' (level 5).

With anatta, the idea of not-self, there will always be conflict, although not necessarily with science. However, there are many scientists whose personal religious convictions hold fast to the idea of a soul. Of course, there is conflict between Buddhist and the other world faiths in the analysis of the human experience, but that is not be the focus of debate here.

It is in the very nature of the Buddhist philosophy that conflict about how things are can only be solved through doing something about it; the age-old response that originates with the Buddha himself would be: 'thoroughly observe, test and see for yourself.'

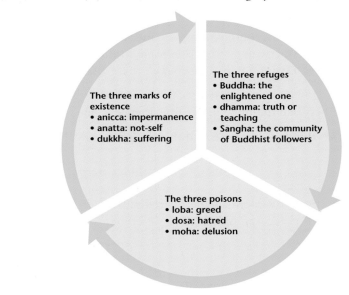

The three refuges
• Buddha: the enlightened one
• dhamma: truth or teaching
• Sangha: the community of Buddhist followers

The three marks of existence
• anicca: impermanence
• anatta: not-self
• dukkha: suffering

The three poisons
• loba: greed
• dosa: hatred
• moha: delusion

Summary diagram: The three threes

Reflection and assessment AO1

It is vital to bring together the information you have covered so far and recognise how it can be transformed into effective examination-style revision and answers. The best way to do this is to ask the question: 'How am I going to be assessed on this information?'

Read the following question and the answer that follows it.

Explain Buddhist teachings about the three characteristics of existence. (25 marks)

The remarks were made by an examiner.

Strength: Good awareness of a variety of translations of the basic concept. →

The three characteristics of existence are crucial teachings in Buddhism. The technical term for 'characteristic' is lakkhana. It can be translated as signs, marks or even basic facts.

The three characteristics of existence are really observations about life. In this sense, Buddhism is very scientific in its approach. The Buddha observed three things: everything is impermanent (anicca), there is not one thing that has a 'self' or 'soul' (anatta), and, life is suffering (dukkha).

Anicca teaches that everything in life has temporary existence. In addition, things are constantly moving and changing. Nyanatiloka writes: 'Impermanence is a basic feature of all conditioned phenomena'. That is, everything is caused by something else and so by nature this inherently involves change. There is, however, one 'thing' that is not anicca. This is nibbana because it is 'unconditioned'.

Development: This is not really justified. More depth is needed to explain why this assertion is made. In addition, is it a unique feature of Buddhism? →

Anatta means 'not-self'. When the Buddha meditated he could not find evidence of a soul. Instead, we are made up of a collection of physical and mental states. We call these states collectively 'a person' but really there is not a permanent person there.

Strength: Uses reference to scholar and also makes a direct link to another teaching. →

Dukkha literally means 'suffering' but this often leads to misunderstandings. Harvey refers to this term as more 'frustration'. It is directly linked to anicca because frustration is due to the fact that things are not permanent and do not last.

There are dangers with the three characteristics of existence in misunderstanding, especially anatta and dukkha. People think that they are negative.

Development: Could explain and relate these to each characteristic. →

Overall, the three characteristics of existence reflect the Buddha's experience of the first three sights. These served as a catalyst for his realisation that things were impermanent, not-self and full of suffering.

Suggestion for further application of skills

Now use what you have done to create the ideal mark scheme or plan for similar questions that might ask you to explain key ideas found in the three poisons and the three refuges. Using the principles developed in the above question and analysis exercise, try doing this under timed conditions. Then use the mark scheme to try some peer assessment. Mark each other's work, identifying strengths and areas for development.

TASK

Look at the sample answer to the question about the three characteristics of existence.

It is a very good answer but could still be improved. In groups, mark this answer by commenting on sticky notes and displaying them at the front of the classroom. In one colour, indicate the strong points. In a different colour, suggest ways in which this answer could be made perfect. You have been given four comments already to start you off.

Then, as a group, rewrite the answer so that it can score maximum marks according to the levels of response.

Objective To use critical analysis and application of the mark scheme to create a top-level answer

Part 3
A critical analysis of the issues

What are the issues that I am expected to consider and to analyse critically?

Ways in which concepts convey confusion and pessimism

Positive implications of the concepts (realism)

Possible conclusions

1 Ways in which the concepts may convey confusion and pessimism

The main concern about Buddhist concepts is that they can be confusing and tend to be pessimistic about the human condition and experience.

Kamma, for example, is a complex theory that is often misunderstood. In the sitcom, *My Name is Earl*, Earl understands it as a personal improvement programme from which he can benefit. In addition, there is also the issue of blame and punishment. Kamma becomes a vehicle of retribution as the situation becomes personal. Since Buddhism advocates anatta (not-self), this could not be further from the truth. Indeed, the ideas of guilt, blame and retribution are self-indulgence and therefore selfish. In direct contrast, the focus in Buddhism and in understanding the principles in operation behind kamma is one of selflessness.

Nibbana has always been shrouded in confusion. If it is something that is not there, then how can we verify it at all? As has been discussed earlier, the difficulty with nibbana is twofold. It is either too pessimistic when described, or it is too optimistic and conveys images of bliss, peace and heavenly notions that themselves become false attachments.

The ideas of samsara and rebirth can encourage a view of life as being like a game of *Snakes and ladders*. The object is to escape the cycle of rebirth but this is ironically very self-oriented. The idea of progress in Buddhism is not to move forward and accumulate merits, but rather to let go and eradicate the accumulation of unnecessary kamma. The character Earl makes a similar mistake.

The confusions and negative implications of the three characteristics of existence are a common stumbling block in understanding Buddhist concepts.

Dukkha is often viewed merely as a negative experience. Clarification is needed. There is a subtle difference between dukkha the concept and dukkha the experience. The concept of dukkha is always negative because it is a result of ignorance. The experience of dukkha is not necessarily negative.

There are similar negative connotations with anatta. Does this mean a person does not exist? Such understandings have been discussed. In the same way, impermanence

TASK

Think of some questions you would like to ask about each of the teachings. Is there anything that is not clear? What needs further explanation? Objective To develop awareness of areas in knowledge and understanding where there are 'gaps' to be filled; to aid self-reflection and development, creating 'clear analysis' expected for responses (level 4 and above)

? KEY QUESTIONS

- How can the system of kamma be verified?
- If nibbana cannot be described, then is it really worth making it a desirable goal?
- If the aim of life is to let go of attachments, then why should a person want to accumulate good kamma?
- Why is nibbana made a goal?
- Is Buddhism too pessimistic in its focus on life as suffering?
- Is there a difference between dukkha the concept and dukkha the experience?
- Is there really a difference between the idea of a soul and the idea of an empirical self?

is sometimes misapprehended as implying that change is immediately evident to the naked eye.

The three fires can easily be misunderstood to represent sins that a person should avoid, rather than as psychological drives that are inherent to being human and part of the cycle of existence. Such drives are not external vices but are internal states from which to be detached.

The three refuges are not, as some may understand, the Buddhist creed or statement of belief. It is the actual going to refuge that is the statement of faith or trust. Taking refuge is a state of mind, a determined approach to endeavour to follow the path of the Buddha. It is more like a series of vows with deep significance to the individual, not a profession of faith to some all-pervading deity. In essence, the tiratana are practical tools for spiritual development.

There is also the problem of language. Each Buddhist concept is translated from either Pali or Sanskrit. Different scholars translate such concepts in different ways. This can only add to the potential for misunderstanding, confusion and pessimism.

Overall, if Buddhist concepts are understood on a superficial level then they are only understood partially. In reality, one could argue that they are not really understood at all. On the contrary, when explored fully, Buddhist ideas are trying to avoid confusion and pessimism.

2 Positive implications of the concepts (realism)

It has often been a point of debate, by people who have studied Buddhism, whether or not it is too negative about human experience. Nothing could be further from the truth.

Granted that Buddhism's point of departure is with dukkha, the concept, as it stands, is negative. However, the Buddha began here in order to move away from the problem of dukkha. Whilst this movement is not towards a place of permanent positivism such as a heaven, it is a positive movement away from dukkha and negative experience.

Moreover, Buddhists would argue that the teachings of Buddhism are, in fact, realistic about life. They are neither positive nor negative, as such judgements are to do with perspective. The teachings are meant to be practical, geared towards dealing with the problem of dukkha.

In essence, the concepts within Buddhism equip a person to deal with life and cope with the situation within the cycle of existence. Such tools assist an understanding of the workings of kamma and how this relates to the cycle of samsara and rebirth. The concept of kamma is practical because it helps to make us aware of the complex nature of the immediate world. It draws attention to the root of activities and provides opportunity for people to reflect upon the appropriate mental states to develop.

In the same way, the concept of nibbana is not intended as a philosophical platform from which we can explore metaphysical issues.

It follows from this that it is not practical to describe the ultimate, perfect truth of nibbana. Nor is it beneficial to the Buddhist path to debate questions about such matters as the origins of the Universe or a creator God. Such issues, if not practical, are therefore not relevant.

TASK

Draw up lists of positives and negatives in relation to how the Buddhist teachings can be understood. Think about how the positives can address the negatives. Is there a solution?

Objective To reflect on the challenge to Buddhist ideas and how these are addressed by Buddhists, showing awareness of more than one point of view (essential for level 3 responses and above, AO2)

KEY QUESTIONS

- **How can the concept of dukkha be seen to be positive?**
- **Does a scientific approach to life really justify itself as being realistic?**
- **How helpful is the Buddhist analysis of kamma? What are its strengths?**
- **Why are the Buddhist concepts not really meant to be understood as concepts alone? What is the danger of making philosophical statements?**
- **Why are ultimate questions concerning the origin and nature of the Universe not relevant to Buddhism? How does the parable of the arrow help understanding of this?**
- **Is it really necessary to describe nibbana?**

Issues that *are* relevant to Buddhism and to Buddhist concepts are those that directly relate to solving the problem of dukkha. Pursuing a description of nibbana, or debating the existence of a supreme deity, would not be of any practical value in addressing the experience of dukkha. The experience of pain would still remain after such deliberations have been exhausted.

The most important task is to address dukkha. Once dukkha is eliminated, then other issues of a metaphysical nature may be explored. However, this invites the question, if dukkha is no more, is there a need for such other-worldly pursuits?

This practical, empirical approach is adopted for the many concepts discussed in this section. Essentially, the Buddhist concepts are collectively a practical tool for dealing with dukkha.

The best way to describe this view is by considering a parable from the Buddha himself.

> **It is as if a man had been wounded by an arrow thickly smeared with poison, and his friends, companions, relatives and kinsmen were to get a surgeon to heal him, and he were to say, 'I will not have this arrow pulled out, until I know by what man I was wounded ... of what family name the man is ... or, whether he is tall, or short ... or whether the bow with which I was wounded was a chapa or a kondanda ...'.**

> **(Eliade)**

The parable continues. Not until he knows what the bow and arrow were made from will he have it removed.

Obviously the reasoning of the wounded man described here is quite ludicrous. Likewise, according to Buddha, is debate about the origins and nature of the Universe.

> **Whether the view is held that the world is eternal, or that the world is not eternal, there is still rebirth, there is old age, there is death, and grief, lamentation, suffering, sorrow, and despair, the destruction of which even in this life I announce.**

In short, a religious life does not depend on speculation. Speculation is not useful.

3 Possible conclusions

When assessing the issues that arise from the role of and relationship between Buddhist concepts and their relevance to the human condition, it is important to reflect upon the arguments previously discussed and arrive at some appropriate conclusion. It may be that you accept none of these listed here, or just one of them, or you may have a different conclusion that is not listed. However, what is important is the way that you have arrived at your conclusion – the reasoning process.

From the preceding discussions, here are some possible conclusions you could draw.

1   Buddhist concepts are too superficial at a basic level and therefore too simplistic to be of any real practical benefit for the ordinary individual. Like the sitcom character Earl, there is always a danger of doing more harm than good. Basically, the concepts can be easily misunderstood.

EXAM TIP

Be careful when using quotes to assess critically. Always make sure that your quote relates to the argument that is presented. To make sure of this, always explain the relevance of the quote in your answer. This is the difference between 'not successful' (level 1–2) and 'successful' (level 3–5) analysis.

2   The great strength of Buddhist concepts is that they are practical at every level. The Buddha advocated the principle of a good teacher being able to deliver teachings that were realistic and achievable for a particular audience.

3   Buddhism is a very complex and advanced system; it is by nature very empirical and only the devoted few can fully appreciate its value.

4   Buddhism is too negative in its approach to human experience because it does not embrace dukkha as an essential part of what it means to be human. Surely an understanding of the nature of life in terms of dukkha brings a more balanced appreciation of life without the need for the pursuit of some higher goal such as nibbana?

5   Buddhism is practical. Whether or not the concepts cause confusion or are pessimistic at one level does not matter. The issue is whether or not the concepts can be applied. Until an individual has resolved this, there will be no answer.

EXAM TIP

Always make sure that you draw a conclusion from the arguments that you have put forward. This does not necessarily have to agree with any of your arguments. Your conclusion may be that questions are unanswered. You may even want to finish with further questions of your own in response to the debate. The argument has to be evident, clear and recognisable (see descriptors for level 3–5).

Negative aspects
Buddhist teachings convey confusion:
• the teachings surrounding nibbana, kamma are too complex
• rebirth is unrealistic
• teaching about not-self and focus on suffering is not really practical

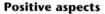

Positive aspects
Buddhist teachings:
• offer a realistic solution and focus on problem-solving
• have no need for divine assistance
• encourage personal development
• are empirical
• offer a personal path
• are optimistic
• aim at eradicating suffering and creating peacefulness

Summary diagram: The nature of Buddhist teachings

TASK

Look at the outline answer opposite.
Now add two or three more bullet points to indicate how a developed answer would deal with the question.
Now add further bullet points to develop this answer to indicate how a higher-level answer would deal with the question. Remember to keep the bullet points focused on the question.
Objective To develop awareness of what will constitute a very good answer by gradually building up a response that 'uses a range of evidence to sustain an argument' (level 5 descriptor)

Reflection and assessment AO2

It is vital to bring together the information you have covered so far and recognise how it can be transformed into effective examination-style revision and answers. The best way to do this is to ask the question: 'How am I going to be assessed on this information?'

Look back to page 8 in the Introduction to review the level descriptors for AO2. There is a description of the character and features for each level. The exam is marked with reference to levels.

Look at the following sample basic answer, which is a response to the question:

'Buddhism is too pessimistic and often misunderstood.' Discuss.   (10 marks)

The *basic* answer might deal with the question by:

- stating the basic problem of dukkha
- giving some basic information on anicca and anatta in relation to dukkha
- drawing a simple conclusion about whether dukkha is negative or not.

Suggestion for further application of skills

Now try this technique of building together a level 5 answer with a question such as:

- 'Buddhist teachings convey too much confusion.' Discuss.
- 'Buddhist teachings are realistic and positive.' Discuss.

Try making up a few questions about the teachings, based around this theme of their relative importance, clarity and helpfulness.

Buddhism

Part 1

Buddhist teachings about the Four Noble Truths and the practice of the Four-fold Sangha

What am I required to study?

■ Specific teachings of the Four Noble Truths and the specific practices associated with being a member of the Four-fold Sangha

This means I am expected to know about:

■ specific teachings found in the Four Noble Truths

■ specific practices of the Four-fold Sangha.

This part of the topic covers the foundations of the Buddha's teaching, namely, the Four Noble Truths. It also discusses their implications, by considering how Buddhists practise these truths. It would be helpful to write your notes under the headings listed above, under 'This means I need to know about', as it is from these areas that the exam questions will be derived.

Remember that your studies will include elements of the two basic assessment objectives of:

■ Knowledge and Understanding (AO1)
■ Evaluation (AO2).

See pages 7–8 in the Introduction to remind yourself of the key assessment objectives at AS level.

The evaluation material is set out in Part 3 of this topic (page 359) and can be studied either alongside the AO1 material, as you work through this topic, or as a discrete topic.

The Buddha and the early Sangha used numbers to summarise most teachings. The Buddha's teaching in its simplest form can be found within the Four Noble Truths, the Buddha's teaching in its simplest form. Truth has recently been reinterpreted as reality, which opens the way towards an empirical understanding of Buddhist teachings. The danger with the word truth is that in other religions it may refer to certainties that are not grounded in reality or experience, but in concepts that are more metaphysical in nature.

All of these truths or realities are inter-related; to consider each one individually, outside of its relationship to other teachings, can lead to misunderstanding. This is especially the case with dukkha or suffering.

> **EXAM TIP**
>
> The Buddha used numbers in his teaching. Try using numbers when you put together your revision notes, to help you remember key ideas. This can also work when preparing answers to questions.

1 The Four Noble Truths, dukkha, samudaya, nirodha and magga (the eight-fold path)

a) The significance of the teaching delivered in the Deer Park

The Buddha's first sermon was outlined in Topic 1, Part 2, of this unit. It dealt with the basic but central Buddhist teachings, called the Four Noble Truths. These have been mentioned several times already; now they will be analysed more closely.

According to the teachings contained in the first sermon, first of all the first truth, dukkha or suffering must be fully understood. Then the second truth, tanha or craving causing **samudaya**, the arising of dukkha, must be identified and recognised as something to be abandoned completely. The third truth, nirodha or prevention of craving, is to be applied. Finally, the fourth truth, **magga** or the eight-fold path (see page 287), which is the actualisation of nirodha, is to be cultivated so that nibbana may be realised.

This all sounds very technical but it is really quite straightforward. The Buddha has been compared to a physician. The Four Noble Truths are really a medical diagnosis and treatment of the disease of life.

1   The diagnosis of the problem: there is dukkha, or suffering.

2   The investigation of the cause: tanha, or craving, causes samudaya, or arising of suffering.

3   The statement of the solution: to stop and to prevent nirodha, or craving.

4   The application of a course of medicinal treatment in order to activate nirodha: to follow magga, the eight-fold path. This attacks the very root of craving. It treats the cause or arising of suffering and also prevents any further suffering.

b) The concepts and relative importance of the Four Noble Truths

Dukkha

Dukkha has already been discussed at length (see Topic 3, Part 2). It may be beneficial to review this discussion at this point but below is a simple summary, as a reminder.

■   Dukkha is often translated as suffering or ill, although this is not a satisfactory literal translation. Dukkha can be better translated as frustration.

■   The whole idea of dukkha comes from the Buddha's experience of the four sights. It is a characteristic of being or existence, along with anicca and anatta.

■   Dukkha can be both physical and mental pain or suffering. It can also involve pleasurable aspects of life.

■   The teaching about dukkha is only pessimistic when treated in isolation from the rest of the Buddha's teachings. Remember, the Buddha pointed out: 'This above all do I teach, suffering and the deliverance from suffering.'

Samudaya (or tanha)

Samudaya means arising, origin or cause immediately preceding. Tanha literally means craving or thirst but can also be referred to as attachment.

The arising of suffering relates to an analysis of the root cause of this arising. It is tanha that causes the arising of suffering. This is the second Noble Truth.

Thera describes tanha as: 'a powerful mental force latent in all'. According to Rahula: 'It (tanha) is not the first or the only cause of the arising of dukkha, but it is the most individual cause.'

KEY WORDS

Samudaya arising
Magga the eight-fold path

KEY IDEA

The Four Noble Truths

1   There is suffering (dukkha).
2   Craving (tanha) causes suffering to arise (samudaya).
3   Craving needs to be stopped (nirodha).
4   Following the eight-fold path will stop suffering.

❝ KEY QUOTE ❞

The truth of suffering is to be compared with a disease, the truth of the origin of suffering with the cause of the disease, the truth of extinction of suffering with the cure of the disease, the truth of the path with the medicine.

(Vis.M. XVI)

Harvey identifies both views and conceit as further causes of dukkha. Both of these are closely related to ignorance of anatta and are deeply rooted psychological drives that feed the ego.

The question remains, however: 'If tanha is the most immediate cause for dukkha, then what drives the need for tanha?'

The most common driving forces behind tanha are the three poisons or fires of lobha (greed), dosa (hatred) and moha (delusion), discussed in Topic 3, Part 2. These fires burn away and fuel the idea of, and desire for, a self.

These are all related to the cycle of existence in which is discovered a rationale for the whole human experience (see the nidanas, Topic 3, Part 1). Note here, however, that the initial reason for existence is driven by ignorance, or not being able to see things as they are in reality. It is therefore not until a person becomes wise, or is enlightened to the truth or reality of things, that the cause of suffering can be no more.

However, through ignorance of anatta, the attachment to material and non-material phenomena generates the experiences of suffering. The Dhamma Cakkapavattana Sutta describes three types of tanha: for sensual pleasures, for existence and non-existence.

Sensual pleasures are experiences that are initiated by interaction with the senses of sight, sound, smell, taste, touch and mental perceptions. Existence depends on the experiences that accumulate to create a desire for individuality, or the recognition of things as being 'me' or 'mine'. This can include protection of identity, further embellishment of the idea of self or even the idea of existence beyond death in the form of a self or soul. Non-existence is the other extreme; it is divorcing self from anything that is not a wholesome experience. The Jains and Ajivakas were over-enthusiastic in their pursuit of this type of tanha. The outcome can even include self-annihilation or suicide.

It is interesting to note that within these three types of tanha can be identified the extremes of pleasure and pain that the Buddha encountered during his life. It is no coincidence, then, that the eradication of tanha needs a middle way.

Nirodha

The idea of nirodha has already been discussed in association with nibbana (Topic 1, Part 2 and Topic 3, Part 1).

Nirodha literally means to cease. It refers to stopping tanha. Once tanha, or grasping, is stopped, peace and calm, known as nibbana, will follow.

However, although nirodha directly precedes it, it is not the cause of nibbana. Nibbana is unconditioned or uncaused. As discussed earlier (Topic 3, Part 1), nirodha is the eradication of negatives, which are forms of grasping, not an accumulation of positives that make up nibbana.

Just as the cause of suffering is linked to the nidanas and initiates the turning over of the whole cycle of existence, likewise, nirodha is the stage at which the wheel of life ceases to turn.

With the application of nirodha, ignorance is transformed and there is insight into reality. All states that result from conditioned arising are stopped. During life for the arhat, this means detachment from such states. Beyond life, in parinibbana, this is a permanent feature.

TASK

Use the medical diagnosis formula (problem, cause, solution, treatment) and apply it to the following problems: a migraine, an example of bullying, stress before an exam. Remember, the formula can treat the problem, but it also needs to be able to prevent. Objective To develop understanding of the Buddhist approach to life, demonstrating 'engagement with the material' to enhance understanding further (AO1)

EXAM TIP

Remember how the Buddhist teachings link together. One set often relates to, or helps to explain, another set. For example, the three poisons help to give a reason for the cause of suffering. Reading on, can you link any other Buddhist teachings to tanha? This takes your response beyond the 'general topic' (level 2 AO1).

KEY WORDS

Samma **right**
Ditthi **view**
Sankappa **thought**
Vaca **speech**
Kammanta **action**
Ajiva **livelihood**
Vayama **effort**
Sati **mindfulness**

66 **KEY QUOTES** 99

**The stopping
of becoming is
nirvana (nibbana).
It is called nirvana
(nibbana) because
of the getting rid of
craving.**

(Samyutta–Nikaya)

**This is the real,
this is the excellent,
namely the calm
of all the impulses,
the casting out
of all 'basis', the
extinction of craving,
dispassion, stopping,
Nirvana (nibbana).**

(Anguttara–Nikaya)

KEY IDEAS

The eight-fold path
● Right view
● Right thought
● Right speech
● Right action
● Right livelihood
● Right effort
● Right mindfulness
● Right concentration

Ariya magga

Ariya means either noble or worthy, whereas magga means path. Since there are eight aspects to this path, it is know as the Noble Eight-fold Path.

A symbol of Buddhism is the eight-spoked wheel. It represents the eight teachings of the Buddha that bring insight into reality. These teachings prevent and stop the worries and frustrations within life, ultimately bringing calm and peace of mind.

Each teaching begins with **samma** or right. Samma describes a correct, appropriate or effective method. The Buddha demonstrated the right path.

The eight-fold path is as follows:

1   **Samma ditthi**, or right view, is when a person is aware of the reality of life. The Buddha described this as: 'the understanding of suffering, of the origin of suffering, of the extinction of suffering, and of the path leading to the extinction of suffering.' (Thera). It is, however, more than this. It involves a deeper appreciation of the wider implications of these realities in association with other Buddhist teachings such as the three characteristics of being, conditioned arising and the khandhas.

2   **Samma sankappa** (right thought or intention) is when a person thinks only pure, wholesome and positive thoughts. It is a quality of consciousness that is unimpeded by obstructions. There is a direct link here to kamma, in that intentions generate actions. Such thoughts or intentions are purely selfless, devoid of attachment and full of compassion.

3   **Samma vaca** (right speech) involves truth and polite speech. It discourages lying or exaggerating and also cruelty to others through language. It is very broad, including the idea that at times it is right to be silent. On the positive side, it promotes purposeful, meaningful speech, conducive to spiritual development.

4   **Samma kammanta** (right action) means that a person will not harm others in any way by violence or theft. This extends to a general awareness of others and encourages dana or giving as a demonstration of selflessness. Sexual misconduct is to be avoided. In summary, right action promotes a good, moral life that initiates honourable, peaceful and beneficial conduct for others and oneself.

5   **Samma ajiva** (right livelihood) means making a living that benefits others and that does not involve any harm. This also relates to a range of Buddhist teachings. In essence, five livelihoods are identified as specifically inauspicious: trading in poisons, human beings, intoxicating substances, weapons and flesh.

6   **Samma vayama** (right effort) means a person is determined to avoid unwholesome or evil things. It is linked to the second part of the path, in that this discipline is required to avoid the arising of unwholesome or unskilful states of mind. This enables both stimulation and cultivation of pure, wholesome states of mind. The discipline underlined here is reinforced by moral precepts and a monastic lifestyle.

7   **Samma sati** (right mindfulness) means to be fully aware of one's motives and reasons for doing something. According to Saddhatissa, this refers to 'gradually extending one's awareness until every action, thought and word is performed in the full light of consciousness.' In meditation, the foundations from which mindfulness is seen to operate include form, feelings and mental constructions.

8 **Samma samadhi** (right concentration) means focusing the mind in meditation. It is complete detachment from the unwholesome states and an immersion into the four jhanas or absorptions of meditation. It is the ideal standard set by the Buddha, the middle way between extremes. It is a higher state of awareness and understanding. The monastic life nurtures this and concentration refers directly to Buddhist meditation.

c) The division of the eight-fold path into sila, prajna and dhyana

The eight-fold path is usually divided into three groupings:

- sila or morality
- **prajna** or wisdom
- **dhyana** (or sometimes samadhi) or meditation.

There is some inconsistency in the order in which the three aspects are presented, in relation to the listing of the eight-fold path. Texts generally speak of: 'morality, meditation and wisdom'.

Morality, as the first mentioned, reinforces the traditional Indian ideal that, in order to practise any form of yoga or meditation, one needs to be of moral character. Indeed, moral character, as can be seen from an analysis of the eight-fold path, is outward evidence of inner spiritual development.

The eight-fold path is not chronologically progressive. The numbering and groupings are merely practical ways of preserving dhamma. In practice, all elements of the path are cultivated together.

Wisdom
- right view
- right thought

Morality
- right speech
- right action
- right livelihood

Meditation
- right effort
- right mindfulness
- right concentration

The eight-fold path divided into three sections

d) The use of the Four Noble Truths

The Four Noble Truths are essentially a medicinal course and remedy to life. This is how they are applied. They are practical tools for realising nibbana.

The Four Noble Truths are not doctrines upon which to reflect, to deliberate over or debate in great depth and at great length. They are a simple plan of action or things to apply to life.

In this sense they are used for training, especially the eight-fold path. They are used to facilitate detachment from tanha and eradicate dukkha.

TASK

Look at the aspects of the eight-fold path. For each, provide a practical example or situation from life to which it applies. Then try to explain this situation, using references to other Buddhist teachings. Objective To demonstrate how Buddhist teachings are inter-related and to help to make these connections through use of 'evidence and examples' (AO1)

 KEY WORDS

Samadhi meditation or concentration
Prajna wisdom
Dhyana meditation or meditative trance

66 ▌ KEY QUOTE ▐ 99

That the sequence of the items of the path does not conform to the order of these three categories of practice highlights an understanding of the spiritual life that sees all three aspects of practice as … interdependent and relevant to each and every stage.

(Gethin)

Once again, the parable of the raft (page 319) applies.

> **Monks, I will teach you dhamma – the Parable of the Raft – for crossing over, not for retaining. Listen to it, attend carefully, and I will speak.**
>
> **(Majjhima–Nikaya)**

The purpose of The Four Noble Truths, the dhamma, is to travel beyond the 'sea of samsara' to the further shore of nibbana. Once nibbana has been realised or, in terms of the parable – the shore has been reached, it would be foolish to carry the raft (dhamma) any further. The purpose of the raft is to carry, not to be carried.

The journey upon the raft is what is cultivated in monastic conditions as part of the Sangha. This alone is its purpose.

2 The Four-fold Sangha

a) The vinaya rules

The origin and development of the vinaya rules were discussed in Topic 2, Part 1, where its content was analysed. There was a broad description of the lifestyle of monks and nuns within a monastic setting. It may be useful to review this here. Below is a very brief summary.

- The Vinaya Pitaka contains all codes for monastic procedure.
- The Vinaya is divided into two sections:
  - the first, Sutta Vibhanga, is a commentary on the pattimokka (individual rules)
  - the second, Khandhaka, deals with communal rules.
- Monks and nuns have limited possessions and endeavour to follow a life of poverty, chastity and inoffensiveness.
- The underlying principles of the vinaya are to preserve, through study and teaching, and practise, through meditation, the dhamma.

So how does this impact upon daily life in a monastery? In practice, a typical day in a Theravada monastery would involve rising at around 4.30am.

4.30am	Study or meditation
6.30am	Alms-round
7.00am	Breakfast
8.00am	Communal chanting
9.00am	Teaching and instruction
10.30am	Main meal
11.30am	Rest period
1.30pm	Further instruction or ordinations
5.00pm	Refreshments (drinks only)
5.30pm	Chores or personal free time
7.00pm	Communal chanting
8.00pm	Evening administration, study, further chanting or meditation

TASK

Find out why the alms round is an important feature of monastic life for both monks and lay-people.

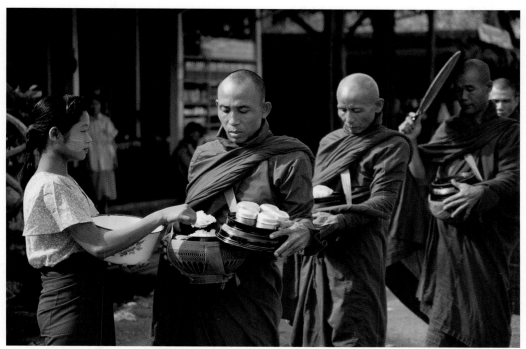

Monks meditating or practising dana (giving)

b) The Four-fold Sangha

The four-fold Sangha comprises the different categories of members within the Buddhist community. At its simplest, it includes:

1 bhikkhus or monks

2 bhikkhunis or nuns

3 upasakas or lay-men

4 upasikas or lay-women.

Other than gender, the more complicated issues are what precisely differentiates between a monk and lay-person, and the varying degrees of status within each category.

c) The relative status of bhikkhus and bhikkhunis

In order to become ordained as a monk or nun, a Buddhist must complete two stages.

The first is a process called renouncing, in keeping with the Indian tradition of the fourth stage of life. At this point the intention is clearly to become an **anagarika** or homeless one, going forth (**pabbajja**) in search of truth.

In the early history of Buddhism, many anagarikas were accepted by the Buddha without formal ordination ceremony. Over time a second, more formal procedure was introduced. This is the official **upasampada** or ordination.

Today, at the first stage of renouncing, the Buddhist becomes a **samanera** or novice; in Theravada these may be recognised by their white robes. The minimum age for this is seven years, although, technically, it is defined as the point at which a child is old enough to scare crows away.

KEY WORDS

Anagarika **homeless one**
Pabbajja **going forth**
Upasampada **ordination**
Samanera **novice, trainee monk or nun**

345

KEY WORD

Sima monastic
boundary

❝ **KEY QUOTE** ❞

**It is the senior monk
who is to preside
at the patimokkha
ceremony and
generally has
precedence in
ecclesiastical affairs.
Nuns, on the other
hand, were subject
not only to their
own hierarchy of
seniority, but also to
monks … any nun,
no matter how long
ordained, ranked
below the most
junior monk.**

(Gombrich)

TASK

**Write a diary for a
typical day from the
perspective of a monk.
Describe how you
joined the monastery
and also how it is run.**
Objective To develop
understanding of a
typical Buddhist day
and the procedures
of social etiquette
within a monastery,
demonstrating 'accurate
knowledge' and 'good
selection of material'
(level 4 and above,
AO1)

The status of bhikkhu, and the right to wear the orange or brown robe, is achieved through the ordination ceremony. Usually, this is at around the age of 20 and takes place within a **sima** or monastic boundary. At least five ordained bhikkhus must be present to authenticate it.

Throughout both stages, the traditional Indian relationship between teacher and pupil is vital. A novice is usually given a mentor or preceptor as a guide. This role is taken very seriously.

The Buddha discouraged the idea of disrobing, or relinquishing the status of monk. However, in places such as Thailand there is an option of temporary ordination for young men. Those monks who have disrobed, for one reason or another, are not very well regarded.

Within a monastery there is a definite hierarchy, based purely upon age and gender, although age is based upon the point of ordination, not birth. Junior monks bow to senior monks. Nuns bow to any monks, no matter how junior to them they may be. However, status is considered a mere formality and part of respectful interaction; it is not an indication of worth. Indeed, this would be contrary to Buddhist purposes of cultivating selflessness.

d) The variations between forest- and village-dwelling bhikkhus

Throughout the history of Buddhist monasticism there has been a clear intention to maintain Buddhist traditions. The ideal for a monk is that he spends much of his day in meditation. This is balanced by a healthy mix of study of the dhamma and application of formal vinaya procedures.

Geographically, the monastery is sited outside a village or town. It is a place of refuge, isolated from society. The needs of the monastery are met by donations from the laity, the local village and by wealthy patrons. Money is handled by volunteers, as are administrative matters; these volunteers are usually from the laity. Villagers work the land and offer produce as alms, instead of rent. It is an idyllic existence, enabling those within the monastery to follow Buddhist practices.

However, as Buddhism develops as a religion and former indigenous practices and traditions are abandoned, quite naturally a vacuum is created. Who is there to meet the more practical needs of the villagers? Education, moral guidance, disputes, ceremonies and rites of passage all form part of a given culture. Before the advent of Buddhism, such needs were usually met by religious people.

In time, then, the village monasteries evolved into more practical sociological establishments. Monks would perform death rites and weddings, offer guidance and advice, and instruct in the more practical and moral aspects of dhamma. They would settle disputes and lead on matters of social concern. Medicine and astrology, although not advocated by the Buddha, could only be practised by the literate. All this took them away from the ideal and thus created tension.

The dilemma was between preservation and practice of dhamma. Spending time in meditation and in isolation reduced interaction with the laity, other monks and time for ensuring Buddhist traditions were being preserved. Time spent administering to the wider needs of society reduced time for meditation and the true purpose of monastic life.

Thus, from about the sixth century CE, a distinction evolved between those monks wishing to spend more time in meditation and those who considered preservation of the dhamma and serving the needs of the community took priority. The **arannikas** or forest-dwellers, as they came to be called, preferred more isolated locations, away from dense population. Their aim was **vipassana dhura**, to follow their duty to gain insight and to focus on practising meditation or studying dhamma. The **vannavasins** or **gamavasins**, the village-dwellers, tended to reside in monasteries close to the villages, spending less time in meditation than their counterparts and more time in **gantha dhura** or book duty, which was study and preservation of the dhamma. This necessarily involved more interaction with the laity.

The forest-dweller practice tended to fade with time but in the last century there has been a surge of forest monasteries in Thailand and Sri Lanka. Historically, Sri Lanka has a tendency for village-dwellers and Thailand for forest-dwellers. As Gethin indicates, this does not mean, however, that forest-dwellers are more austere in discipline.

Indeed, he cites an example whereby a forest monk is considerably less austere than a village monk. Instead, the real distinction is not how easy a path may be but rather how best to follow the path of Buddhism.

A Buddhist monastery

KEY WORDS

Arannika forest monk
Vipassana dhura insight, duty or meditation
Vannavasin village monk
Gamavasin another term for village monk
Gantha dhura book duty or study

TASK

Why do you think that a Buddhist monastery is usually separated from a village but, at the same time, placed on high ground for all to see?

e) The relationship between the monastic Sangha and the laity

The relationship between the monastic Sangha and the lay community has always been one of interdependence.

The monastery serves the community (see above) and, in return, the laity forms the economic base of monasticism through alms, land donations, labour and service within the monastery.

At times, the balance needed to be redressed. For example, in the history of Sri Lanka the king has periodically reclaimed land from the Sangha.

In general, however, the relationship has been a happy one of willing and mutual interdependence.

f) The difficulties in following vinaya rules

Gethin identifies four main areas that underlie the vinaya as it works in practice.

The first is a concern for unity and cohesiveness within the Sangha. When applied, the rules mean that daily life can be focused, communal and have a common goal.

The second concern is this common goal: to provide an environment that promotes spiritual development.

❝ KEY QUOTE ❞

The relations between the Sangha and their lay supporters were conceived as reciprocal generosity: the Sangha gave the dhamma, the laity gave material support, rather disparagingly termed 'raw flesh'.

(Gombrich)

347

" **KEY QUOTE** **"**

It is possible, I think, to identify four particular concerns in the Buddhist monastic rule as set out in Vinaya:
1 the unity and cohesion of the Sangha,
2 the spiritual life,
3 the dependence of the Sangha upon the wider community, and
4 the appearance of the Sangha in the eyes of that community.

(Gethin)

KEY WORDS

Precept rule of personal conduct, or doctrine that is taught
Pancasila the five moral precepts

The third concern is intended to protect this spiritual life from being tainted by the outside world; it is the issue of how the Sangha relates to the wider community.

Finally, the rules are there to maintain trust between the monastic order and the wider community on which it depends. It is important for the monastic community to be seen in the correct light. This has been a concern throughout the history of the Sangha. The rules aim to maintain a delicate balance between the life of a renouncer and meeting the physical and spiritual needs of all concerned.

Obviously, all the above vary depending upon culture and how far Buddhism has had to be adapted. As seen from the early history of the Sangha, there have been times when some removal of less than sincere individuals has occurred.

In addition, there is the issue of modernism and reform movements. Debates still surround the extent to which the vinaya must be adhered to.

g) The ethical principles and practices for monks and lay people

The major ethical principles for a Buddhist beyond the vinaya can be found in the **precepts** or rules of personal conduct. These precepts are not commandments but serve as vows and form a very powerful and personal vehicle of spiritual motivation. These vows are taken and adhered to in practice. Unlike commandments or rules, they can be adapted to different levels of commitment.

For a lay Buddhist there are the **pancasila**, which are five moral precepts. Each embodies a personal vow to abstain from negative action that is contrary to Buddhist principles.

All Buddhists undertake to refrain from:

1 harming living beings

2 stealing

3 misconduct of the sense-pleasures (sexual)

4 lying or false speech

5 using intoxicants.

For a monk and nun there are five more.

They undertake to refrain from:

6 eating after midday

7 dancing, singing, music and shows

8 garlands, scents, cosmetics and adornments

9 luxurious beds

10 accepting gold and silver.

The benefits of the precepts in guiding a person through life on the path of Buddhism are self-evident.

In the morality section of the eight-fold path there is complete parity and correlation with other Buddhist teachings, such as kamma. As Harvey remarks: 'behaving ethically reduces dukkha and increases happiness for oneself and others.'

Anicca – impermanence or flux
…evident because of Pratityasamutpada or paticcasamuppada – conditioned arising or dependent origination

[1] Dukkha – suffering or frustration
…evident because of
[2] Samudaya tanha – the arising of thirst or craving

Anatta – not-self
…evident because of
Upadana khandha – the groups of grasping or clinging:
rupa – form
vedana – feeling
sanna – perception
sankhara – mental formations
vinnana – consciousness

12 nidanas or links
(ignorance, mental formations, consciousness, mind and matter, six senses, contact, feeling, craving, clinging, becoming, birth, decay and death)

…evident because of the three mind-defiling kilesa or defilements:
• lobha – greed
• dosa – hatred
• moha – delusion

[3] Nirodha – cessation
…evident because of the state of nibbana/ nirvana – extinguishing or blowing out, also known as enlightenment, coolness, bliss, peace, thusness, emptiness, freedom from desire, unborn, unoriginated, deathless

[4] Ariya magga – the noble eight-fold path, the way to a realisation of nibbana by:

(Wisdom)	samma ditthi	right view
	samma sankappa	right thought
(Morality)	samma vaca	right speech
	samma kammanta	right bodily action
	samma ajiva	right livelihood
(Meditation or concentration)	samma vayama	right effort
	samma sati	right mindfulness
	samma samadhi	right concentration

Summary diagram: Buddhist teachings

Reflection and assessment AO1

It is vital to bring together the information you have covered so far and recognise how it can be transformed into effective examination-style revision and answers. The best way to do this is to ask the question: 'How am I going to be assessed on this information?'

Look back to page 7 in the Introduction to review the level descriptors for AO1. There is a description of the character and features for each level. The exam is marked with reference to levels. Then read the following question and complete the task.

Explain Buddhist teachings about the Four Noble Truths.   (25 marks)

Suggestion for further application of skills

Read through the question and task above, then do the same for this question:

Explain how the Buddhist Sangha practises the principles of Buddhism.

Remember that the focus is on the features of practice in the Sangha. Refer back to the section on pages 344–8, which deals with significant aspects that are relevant to this question. In your plans, as well as being descriptive, you should indicate how the teachings of Buddhism are reflected in the practices.

> **TASK**
>
> **From what you have learnt so far about levels of response, make a list of points for a developed-level answer. Improve this further for a higher-level answer. Then create writing frames and fully drafted answers.**
>
> **Objective** Gradually to build up and improve on an answer in relation to the level descriptors displaying a very high level of ability to select and deploy relevant information (level 5)

Part 2

Key attitudes towards the Buddha and the possibility of enlightenment

What am I required to study?

- Key attitudes towards the Buddha and the possibility of enlightenment

This means I am expected to know about:

- key differences between the possibility of enlightenment in Theravada and Mahayana Buddhism
- different attitudes towards the Buddha
- the Buddha and the Trikaya doctrine in Mahayana Buddhism.

This part of the topic covers the different ways of aspiring to enlightenment in both Theravada and Mahayana Buddhism, through a consideration of the paths of the arhat and bodhisattva. This naturally leads into a consideration of the ways in which the Buddha is viewed across these traditions. It would be helpful to write your notes under the headings listed above, under 'This means I need to know about', as it is from these areas that the exam questions will be derived.

Remember that your studies will include elements of the *two* basic assessment objectives of:

- Knowledge and Understanding (AO1)
- Evaluation (AO2).

See pages 7–8 in the Introduction to remind yourself of the key assessment objectives at AS level.

The evaluation material is set out in Part 3 of this topic (page 359) and can be studied either alongside the AO1 material, as you work through this topic, or as a discrete topic.

1 Introduction: the Rise of Mahayana Buddhism

The early history of the Sangha was discussed in Topic 2, Part 1. Part of the development of Buddhism inevitably involved disagreements about practice. This led to splits in the Sangha. As Buddhism spread, further splits occurred. Eventually, a new and distinct form of Buddhism emerged, the earliest evidence for which dates from around the end of the first century CE.

This new form of Buddhism is known as **Mahayana** or the Greater vehicle and encompasses all types of Buddhism different from Theravada. Earlier scholarship has linked this type of Buddhism to the Mahasanghikas (see Topic 2, Part 1). More recent scholarship has suggested that Mahayana originated with different forest-dwelling monks. Whatever its origins, this new type of Buddhism is characterised by new ideas.

There are too many of these new ideas to list them here but, in general, Mahayana is characterised by:

- emphasis on the **bodhisattva** path instead of the path of the arhat
- a new and extended **Buddhology**, comprising ideas about the person and nature of the Buddha, that saw the Buddha as more of a glorious being, playing down his historical side
- new **sutras** or writings, claiming to be utterances from the still extant Buddha
- a focus on **karuna** or compassion, to balance prajna or wisdom
- devotional groups focusing on heavenly Bodhisattvas
- the idea that merit could be passed on or turned over – **parivarta** – from heavenly beings to devotees
- a more balanced view about the potential of the laity for spiritual development
- deeper insight into the Buddha's original teachings such as the **sunyata** or emptiness of all phenomena
- the idea that **tathagatagarbha**, the Buddha nature, lays dormant within each individual and provides the potential for Buddhahood.

Taken together, these new ideas suggested a new level of truth. Indeed, the Mahayana is seen as the second turning of the dhamma wheel, bringing new insight into the Buddha's original teachings.

It was argued that the Buddha taught through **upaya kausalya** or skilful means. He delivered truths in ways that related directly to the spiritual capacity of his immediate audience. The original teachings were appropriate for the day. These were conventional truths that were now to be superseded by deeper, more insightful or ultimate truths. This was **prajna paramita** or perfect wisdom. This made Mahayana the truly 'greater vehicle'.

This section covers the first two of these new ideas: the different paths to enlightenment and new ideas about the nature and person of the Buddha (Buddhology).

Note: Apart from arhat and words associated with the arhat path, other terms are Sanskrit, not Pali.

2 The arhat and bodhisattva paths

a) The relative importance of the arhat and bodhisattva paths in Theravada and Mahayana Buddhism

In Theravada Buddhism the ultimate spiritual status is one of the arhat or worthy one. An arhat is one who has aspired to nibbana during this life and will enter parinibbana upon death.

In Mahayana Buddhism, the ultimate spiritual status is one of Buddhahood. However, it is the way of the bodhisattva, the being whose essence is wisdom or, as Snelling calls it, the spiritual hero, that is held as the route to Buddhahood.

KEY WORDS

Mahayana greater vehicle, the term given to the types of Buddhism different from Theravada
Bodhisattva a being whose essence is intelligence
Buddhology issues surrounding the nature, person and status of the Buddha
Sutras Mahayana writings or scriptures
Karuna compassion; sometimes interpreted as the idea that concern for others demonstrates selflessness
Parivarta turning over, referring to passing on merit earned
Sunyata emptiness of all phenomena
Tathagatagarbha Buddha nature, the inherent ability to become a Buddha
Upaya kausalya skilful means
Prajna paramita perfect wisdom

EXAM TIP

When revising, use different coloured pens to compare and contrast points between Theravada and Mahayana views about the Buddha.

TASK

On a piece of plain A4 paper, draw two parallel paths. Label one 'bodhisattva' and the other 'arhat'. As you go through this section, add key points about the different paths, using different colours. Then, on a piece of lined A4 paper, draw out any comparisons or contrasts between the two paths. Objectives To devise an outline of the two paths and develop an understanding of their similarities and differences, showing 'accurate knowledge and good understanding' (level 4, AO1)

TASK

Look at the picture of the bodhisattva Avalokitesvara. Find out what his name means. How does the meaning of his name fit in with the ideal of the bodhisattva path?

KEY WORDS

Sotapanna stream-enterer
Sakadagami once-returner
Anagama non-returner

Arhat and bodhisattva are the standards to which Theravada and Mahayana Buddhists respectively aspire. There is some debate as to the status of each when they are considered together.

In general, a bodhisattva would claim to be more compassionate, and a superior being, due to the length and complexity of the path taken. In return, the arhat would claim to be equally compassionate, despite being more introverted and concerned with personal spiritual development rather than that of countless other beings. The bodhisattva path is neither mentioned nor recommended as superior to, or as an alternative to, the path of the arhat. There is also no record in Theravada scriptures of a disciple stating this as the goal.

The arhat and the bodhisattva each take different routes to achieve their aims. The path for the bodhisattva is much longer and more complex to understand. The bodhisattva aims to return to the world of samsara whereas the arhat aims to escape from it and reach the state of parinibbana. Despite this, ultimately their goal is the same in that they both wish to eliminate suffering.

The bodhisattva Avalokitesvara

b) Key aspects of each path (including the stages and perfections of the bodhisattva path)

The path of the arhat

In Theravada Buddhism, the way to enlightenment is through the eight-fold path. This takes a long time to cultivate. Some do not aspire to nibbana during this life. It may take several lives to perfect. However, as discussed earlier, those that do realise nibbana are the arhats or worthy ones.

The nature of an arhat and the nibbanic experience during life was discussed in Topic 3, Part 1. However, there are four different stages to be realised on the way to becoming an arhat, namely:

- **sotapanna**, the stream-enterer
- **sakadagami**, the once-returner
- **anagama**, the non-returner
- arhat, the worthy one.

All of these are close to full and complete enlightenment; they have experienced what Buddhism calls dhamma vision. The arhat enters parinibbana at death. The non-returner will not be reborn in human form but gain enlightenment in a higher realm. The once-returner will achieve arhat status in the next life. Finally, the stream-enterer will gain enlightenment in less than seven rebirths.

In Theravada Buddhism the path of the arhat is a solitary one. Despite being in an environment surrounded by other like-minded practitioners, the Theravada Buddhist has to depend on individual effort. This path has sometimes been called the way of the **pratyeka Buddha**, the solitary or lonely Buddha.

The path of the bodhisattva

Although everyone has the tathagatagarbha, which is the inherent ability to become a Buddha, it is in need of stimulation in order to begin the bodhisattva path. This awakening or stimulation affects the **bodhicitta**, which is the intelligent consciousness.

According to Mahayanists, the bodhicitta is essentially a blend of compassion and wisdom. It is the purest essence of existence, an expression of the ultimate truth of perfect wisdom. Suzuki amplifies this to: 'intelligence-heart that is supreme and most perfect'.

There are four causes of the awakening of the bodhicitta:

- thinking about the Buddha
- reflecting on the faults of material existence
- considering the misery and suffering of beings to arouse the compassion of the bodhisattvas
- reflecting on the virtue of the **Tathagata**, another term for the Buddha – or emptiness.

Once the bodhicitta is aroused, the bodhisattva will proceed to undertake **pranidhana** or personal vows. Vasubandhu lists ten vows common to all bodhisattvas. They generally include the desires for merit, knowledge, enlightenment, to be close to all Buddhas and a desire for supramundane powers. However, these are wished for not just for themselves but to be shared with all other beings.

The undertaking of vows is important as it is seen as a powerful, independent, psychological force for that individual. The vows also involve other beings. If the vow is broken this would lead to greater demerit, not only for the individual but for others as well. However, describing them as vows is perhaps putting it too strongly as, in reality, they are wishes or aspirations to succeed along the path.

The most famous vow is that in which the bodhisattva makes an ultimate expression of compassion and selflessness. This promise makes the individual a true bodhisattva. Within it is a vow to aspire to enlightenment but only to enter into full and complete enlightenment when all other beings have become enlightened. Therefore, at the point of enlightenment, the bodhisattva will make the ultimate sacrifice and return to the world of samsara to help other beings.

> **Would that, by causing the wheel of immaculate dharma to revolve, all sentient beings in the ten quarters of the Universe who may listen to my teachings or hear my name, be freed from all passions and awaken in them the bodhicitta.**

> **Would that I all the time accompany and protect all sentient beings and remove for them things which are not beneficial to them and give them innumerable blessings, and also that through the sacrifice of my body, life and possessions I embrace all creatures and thereby practise the Right Doctrine.**

(Vasubandhu, translated in Suzuki)

KEY WORDS

Pratyeka Buddha solitary or lonely Buddha (with reference to an arhat)
Bodhicitta intelligent consciousness
Tathagata *literally* thus gone one or one who is gone thus, another term for the Buddha
Pranidhana vows of a bodhisattva

❝ KEY QUOTES ❞

One on the path to perfect Buddhahood, whose task is to compassionately help beings while maturing his or her own wisdom.
(Harvey on bodhisattva)

Would that all the merits I have accumulated in the past as well as in the present be distributed among all sentient beings and make them all aspire after supreme knowledge.
(Bodhisattva vow)

The Bodhisattva-path begins with the arising of the bodhicitta, the aspiration to strive for Buddhahood for its own sake, and for the sake of helping suffering beings.
(Harvey)

KEY WORDS

Bhumi stage of the
bodhisattva path
Paramita perfection
Ksanti patience
Virya vigour
Jnana knowledge

" **KEY QUOTES** "

The bodhicitta
is present in the
hearts of all sentient
beings. Only in
Buddhas it is fully
awakened and active
with its immaculate
virility, while in
ordinary mortals
it is dormant and
miserably crippled
by its unenlightened
intercourse with the
world of sensuality.

(Suzuki)

... love is the essence
of the Bodhicitta.
The Bodhicitta is
the highest essence.
Therefore, all
Bodhisattvas find
their *raison d'être* of
existence in this great
loving heart ... One
who understands
this heart becomes
emancipated from
the dualistic view of
birth and death and
performs such acts as
are beneficial both to
oneself and others.

(Nagarjuna)

The bodhisattva must first go through a series of ten **bhumis** or stages, each with a parallel **paramita** (perfection). These are:

1 Delight and joy
At this stage the perfection of dana or giving is generated for the benefit of others. Merit accumulated is to be invested in the future aspiration of Buddhahood for the bodhisattva and others.

2 Purity
At this stage all actions are spontaneously pure and sila (moral virtue) is perfected. Heavenly Buddhas are visualised in meditations.

3 Brightness
Ksanti is perfected at this stage, through meditation on compassion. Patience helps the bodhisattva to persist in fathoming the profound dhamma.

4 Inflammation
Here the purifying bodhi is said to consume all remains of ignorance and **virya** is perfected. It is at this stage that a practitioner can become ordained and follow the seven categories of virtues. The seventh category is the eight-fold path.

5 Very difficult to conquer
Insight is highly advanced and dhyana (meditative trance) is perfected; 'the Bodhisattva has developed an intellectual power to penetrate deep into the system of existence.' (Suzuki).

6 Showing one's face
Prajna (wisdom) is perfected and the bodhisattva has an ability to see into the very fabric of existence and identify its true nature as being empty of essence. While experiencing this, the bodhisattva also reflects upon the plight of other beings trapped in samsara. It is at this crucial stage that the bodhisattva, now equal to an arhat, makes the decision to return to samsara for the sake of other beings.

7 Going far away
At this stage upaya kausalya or skilful means are applied and the bodhisattva is able to project into different worlds to help and teach others. He tirelessly practises the ten virtues of perfection.

8 Immovable
At this stage, the bodhisattva becomes able to choose the place of rebirth.

A bodhisattva cannot fall away from this stage, which is when all desire and aspiration for Buddhahood are removed from the consciousness.
The conscious striving that distinguished all his former course has now given way to a state of spontaneous activity, of saintly innocence, and of divine playfulness. He wills and it is done. He aspires and it is actualised.

(Suzuki)

9 Good intelligence
The bodhisattva acquires four complete and comprehensive knowledges: the nature of things as empty, their individual characteristics as subject to rebirth, their indestructible nature beyond duality and their eternal order and intrinsic value.

10 Clouds of dharma
Now **jnana** is complete. The bodhisattva is surrounded by lesser bodhisattvas and Buddhas offer blessings in preparation for final Buddhahood.

2 Attitudes to the Buddha

a) Differing attitudes to the Buddha in Theravada and Mahayana Buddhism and the status of the Buddha

In Theravada Buddhism there is generally a rational view of the Buddha. He was human, the **samma-sambuddha** or self-enlightened one. He is revered for his wisdom and for the role model he provides.

Theravadins take literally his command: 'work out your own salvation with diligence'; they are to take refuge in the dhamma and test it for themselves. There is no dependence upon the Buddha as a vehicle for salvation or enlightenment. Gombrich refers to Theravada as a **soteriology**; it is a personal religious quest, with no god-figure.

Despite this, the human-ness of the Buddha does not mean that **supramundane** powers were not possible. Indeed, we only have to draw upon the Theravada scriptures to see a teacher with some remarkable abilities. Some put these incidents, such as the birth narratives, down to legend and dispense with them. Others may explain them in terms of the Buddhist **abhinnas**, supernatural powers developed through high states of meditation.

Mahayana Buddhism overtly plays down the historical aspects of the Buddha. As Suzuki writes: 'the Buddha in the Mahayana scriptures is not an ordinary human being walking in a sensuous world.' Mahayana Buddhism emphasises the transcendent aspect of Buddha in all his glory. The Buddha was not just human but also has heavenly manifestations and ultimate expressions.

In line with this, the idea about the three bodies of the Buddha developed.

b) The trikaya doctrine

The trikaya doctrine is the idea that there are three manifestations, planes of existence or modes of perception from which the Buddha operates.

In Mahayana Buddhism there is a multitude of Universes. Each Universe has its own Buddha. This Buddha resides in this **Buddha ksetra** (Buddha field) or personal Universe. Gotama Buddha resides in this Universe. Another example of a Universe is in Pure Land Buddhism where Amida Buddha, or Amitabha, resides to welcome those that wish to be reborn there. There are, of course, many more examples.

Each Buddha, then, has **trikaya** or three bodies of expression.

Nirmanakaya or transformation body

Nirmanakaya is a kind of semi-physical body in which a Buddha appears in samsara. Although this body appears to be both physical and subject to the laws of samsara, it has been generated by the Buddha specifically for the purpose of reintroducing dhamma to the world.

> Thus while it may appear that a Buddha takes birth as an individual being like the rest of us, in truth he does not. What we ordinarily see here on Earth, as it were, is merely a body created by the Buddha, a nirmana-kaya.
>
> (Gethin)

As the Buddha has completed the Bodhisattva path he has developed the power to transform and appear to beings in different realms. Nirmanakaya can be viewed to be an expression of this.

KEY WORDS

Samma-sambuddha self-enlightened one
Soteriology a personal religious quest
Supramundane paranormal or extraordinary powers accessed through advanced meditation
Abhinnas supramundane powers or supernatural powers
Buddha ksetra Buddha field or Universe
Trikaya three bodies
Nirmanakaya transformation body

KEY IDEA

Abhinnas are extraordinary or supernatural powers. There are six, comprising magic, a divine ear, mind-reading, remembering former lives, divine sight and the extinction of all evils, although some traditions have more.

KEY WORDS

Sambhogakaya
enjoyment body
Dharmakaya ultimate
body of truth

Sambhogakaya or enjoyment body

Sambhogakaya is a body for the heavenly realms. In this form the Buddha appears to bodhisattvas in his Buddha ksetra, the Buddha Universe. In itself, the sambhogakaya is an image of enlightenment – not enlightenment but it is as close to it as is possible.

Dharmakaya or dharma body

Dharmakaya is the ultimate body that is beyond existence. It is also beyond all dualities and conceptions. It neither exists nor does not exist. It is ultimate truth and reality.

> 66 **KEY QUOTE** 99

One of the most remarkable differences between ... Hinayana and the Mahayana Buddhist literature, is the manner of introducing the characters ... In the former, sermons are delivered by the Buddha as a rule in such a natural and plain language as to make the reader feel the presence of the teacher ... while in the latter ... we have a mysterious, transcendent figure ... surrounded and worshipped by beings of all kinds ...

(Suzuki)

 KEY IDEA

The first two bodies are temporal existences whereas the third is the ultimate body. The former two bodies, as are all beings, are partial manifestations of the ultimate dharma body.

Though they are conceived as three, they are in fact all the manifestations of one Dharmakaya.

(Suzuki)

The Buddha in his sambhogakaya surrounded by bodhisattvas

TASK

Find some examples of different Buddhas and bodhisattvas. Create a brief character profile for each one.
Objective To develop understanding of the complexity of the Buddhology within Mahayana Buddhism, demonstrating good understanding through the use of examples (AO1)

KEY IDEA

Pure Land Buddhism

Within the Mahayana tradition, there is a form of Buddhism known as Pure Land Buddhism. Its origins can be traced back to China and were as early as the second century CE. It is based upon writings known as the Sukhavativyuha Sutras or the Pure Land Sutras. At this time, China was ravaged by war, famine, disease and poverty, a social context that meant, for many, there was little hope in life. This, combined with the difficult and advanced meditative practices promoted by Buddhism, made even a religious escape seem impossible. Thus, to many the idea of a heavenly new world or Sukhavati, translated as Pure Land, into which people could be born after death was immediately attractive. This Pure Land is inhabited by Amitabha Buddha who would offer help to all those who called upon his name and would enable them to achieve rebirth there.

In its original form in China, it not only offered hope when it was needed, it also encouraged the pursuit of the Buddhist path in conjunction with Amitabha's help. As this form of Buddhism developed, there was more emphasis on Amitabha and his help for those in this world of suffering. When it spread as far as Japan, in the twelfth century, this aspect emerged even more. In Jodo Shin Shu, or Japanese Pure Land Buddhism, the view is that salvation and the opportunity to enter Pure Land have nothing to do with the follower's own power but are completely dependent on the power of Amida (Amitabha) Buddha. A follower who calls upon his name to be saved demonstrates the purest form of anatta or not-self by abandoning any idea of self or self-achievement and surrendering completely to the power of Amida Buddha. It has been suggested by some that the practical, empirical path of Buddhism has, in this form of Pure Land, been replaced by a religion of faith in a supernatural Buddha who offers salvation.

Summary diagram: Theravada and Mahayana

You will now be close to revision. Try arranging a study group with friends to help you all revise. Use tips and techniques for peer learning that you have developed here.

TASK

Use the information you have learnt so far about levels of response, writing frames, mark schemes and essay plans for this task.

1 Work in groups of four.
2 For each question, use bullet point lists to plan levelled responses. Use a different sheet of paper for each question.
3 Now each person should take the points for one question and write up the answer.
4 Swap the answers and use the level descriptors to mark and comment on the work.
5 Return the work and each use the suggestions made to improve and develop the answer.

Objective: Collaborative learning and peer assessment for examination focus

Reflection and assessment AO1

It is vital to bring together the information you have covered so far and recognise how it can be transformed into effective examination-style revision and answers. The best way to do this is to ask the question: 'How am I going to be assessed on this information?'

At this point it is essential to remind yourself of the different tasks you have done so far.

After revisiting the tasks, look back to page 7 in the Introduction to review the level descriptors for AO1. There is a description of the character and features for each level. The exam is marked with reference to levels.

You will need these level descriptors to complete the next task.

Read through the following questions carefully and then work through the task. You may need extended time for this but it will be worth it.

Questions

1 Explain the different ways to enlightenment in Buddhism, with reference to the arhat and the bodhisattva.

2 Describe the various stages and perfections found in the bodhisattva path.

3 Explain the different views about the status of the Buddha found within Theravada and Mahayana Buddhism.

4 Explain what Mahayana Buddhism means by the trikaya doctrine.

Suggestion for further application of skills

In your revision sessions, use this approach as a basis for revisiting the other topics. This not only applies to specific focuses on questions but can also be used as a way of creating some good-quality summaries that demonstrate the skills relevant to AO1.

Part 3

A critical analysis of the issues

What are the issues that I am expected to consider and to analyse critically?

- The practicality of Buddhism
- The identity and status of the Buddha
- Possible conclusions

EXAM TIP

If you have formed a study group, use a session to write down questions that you would like clarifying or discussing, and share them.

1 The practicality of Buddhism

a) Ways in which the teachings are practical

The place to begin is with the nature of what the Buddha taught. In essence, his teachings are practical. They are not intended to be beyond reach, although it is clear that discipline is required.

Within the Four-fold Sangha there are different degrees of practicality. Not everyone takes on the ten precepts before they are ordained. There is no pressure to progress. Progression is through personal discipline and striving.

Each individual is encouraged to take on only what they can cope with. A great strength of the Sangha is that everyone operates at their own level.

The support among individuals and the teaching and training also help to make Buddhism a practical path to follow.

Similar points can be made about Mahayana Buddhism. Much emphasis is given to the role of devotion to bodhisattvas. Indeed, a person can earn merit by paying devotion.

In the case of Pure Land Buddhism the ultimate expression of anatta, or letting go, is to put one's faith totally into Amitabha Buddha in order to generate enough merit to be reborn in his Pure Land or Sukhavati Universe. Here is guaranteed enlightenment.

In Mahayana Buddhism the emphasis upon the laity is also a great strength and makes it a very practical path for the ordinary person to follow. This makes it very appealing to anyone who is new to the Buddhist path. It is also an application of skilful means, gradually to nurture an individual at their own spiritual pace.

b) Ways in which the teachings are not practical

Within Theravada Buddhism, the status of arhat is very difficult to achieve and can take many rebirths. Indeed, the arhat path is very restrictive and limited only to monks and nuns.

Many people will therefore be satisfied with gaining a better rebirth through moral virtue. It could thus be argued that the difficult nature of the Buddhist path can actually

❓KEY QUESTIONS

- Is the Buddhist path really that difficult?
- In Theravada Buddhism, does the monastic emphasis isolate the lay Buddhist?
- Is devotion in Mahayana Buddhism truly a Buddhist practice?
- Does the difficult nature of the Buddhist path challenge or deter people from testing it out?

TASK

Make a list of further questions you would like to ask about this topic. Try to find answers from your teacher or from personal research.
Objectives Pursuing lines of enquiry to demonstrate an independent and questioning approach to critical analysis essential for AO2; the use of questions also facilitates different lines of argument and more than one point of view (level 3 and above, AO2)

put people off striving to achieve the highest goal. Indeed, is not nibbana the ultimate purpose of Buddhism?

In addition, it could be argued that people will shy away from the challenge that Buddhism presents and reside in the safety of the knowledge that they can have a better chance next rebirth. To be satisfied with their current situation is not really what the Buddha taught.

The same criticism can be put forward regarding the bodhisattva path in Mahayana Buddhism. This path is so immense and complex that surely humans are only ever starters on the path.

The overall complexities involved with Mahayana Buddhism raise the question as to whether the teachings extend far beyond what is necessary when compared to Theravada.

Is it possible that with branches such as Pure Land and the idea of faith in Buddhas and bodhisattvas that Buddhism is not recognisable any more?

2 Diversity of views concerning the identity and status of the Buddha

a) Theravada views about the Buddha

There are clear differences within the Theravada tradition concerning the identity and status of the Buddha. This can be gleaned from Theravada texts themselves. In the Maha-parinibbana Sutta, the Buddha is depicted at times as a rational teacher who does not draw attention to himself but points only to the dhamma. At other times he is clearly a being that can demonstrate supramundane powers and who is almost worshipped beyond death. Scholars such as Walpola Rahula would take a rationalist approach to Buddhism and dispense with any real focus on the super-human side to the Buddha. Dhamma is the focus for attention and practice of it a priority.

There is also the question about the differences of understanding and perception between a lay Buddhist and an ordained and well-informed Buddhist. Even in Theravada, the flexibility over the varying degrees of development means that there may be different interpretations of what the idea of Buddha as refuge may mean to different individuals.

b) Mahayana views about the Buddha

The Mahayana cosmology is both complex and far-reaching in the nature of its imagery. The idea of different Buddhas and bodhisattvas, the range of Universes and the different ways of achieving enlightenment all indicate a very superstitious view of the Buddha.

The trikaya illustrates the supramundane character of the Buddha, even in nirmana kaya. The sambhoga kaya only adds to the view that the Buddha is almost god-like.

In addition, different branches of Mahayana have different practices and Buddhas. For example, Pure Land Buddhism and the saviour Amitabha Buddha have already been discussed.

The visualisation practices aspired to in Mahayana meditations are seen as aids to the ultimate truth. However, it could be argued that there is a risk that those who are not at such an advanced level may identify them as realities to be believed in and held on to.

Is the Buddhist view about the Buddha really one of worship or one of aspiration?

3 Possible conclusions

When assessing the issues that arise from the relationship between teachings and practices and attitudes towards Buddhism, it is important to reflect upon the arguments previously discussed and arrive at some appropriate conclusion. It may be that you accept none of these listed here, or just one of them, or you may have a different conclusion that is not listed. However, what is important is the way that you have arrived at your conclusion – the reasoning process.

From the preceding discussions, here are some possible conclusions you could draw.

1   The status of Buddha is incidental. The image of the Buddha is a tool for practice only. Whether he is supramundane or just a teacher does not matter as long as the issue does not detract from the practical path of following his dhamma.

2   The status of Buddha can reflect development of religion and the impact of cultures it encounters. In this sense it is only natural that variety occurs and this variety only enhances and helps people strive towards nibbana–nirvana.

3   It is unnecessary to compare the bodhisattva and the arhat. Both share the same ultimate aim. Indeed, the bodhisattva path incorporates that of the arhat. It does not really matter how they reach this goal.

4   The status of Buddha in Mahayana diverges from the original Buddhist principles. Theravada, the original form, maintains the sober teachings of the Buddha. If the simple practices of Theravada worked for the Buddha then why complicate matters with further developments?

5   The bodhisattva ideal is deliberately unreal. It is a vehicle to express compassion towards all and to drive and motivate the individual in the correct way. In this it is following directly the approach of the Buddha, enabling all who wish to access the Buddhist path as opposed to restricting it to the few.

6   The path of the arhat is deliberately restrictive. Not all can aspire to the goal of nibbana during this life. To open up the possibility of enlightenment to those that are still bound by worldly commitments is at best misleading. The Buddha taught the discipline of monasticism. It is the best environment for spiritual progress.

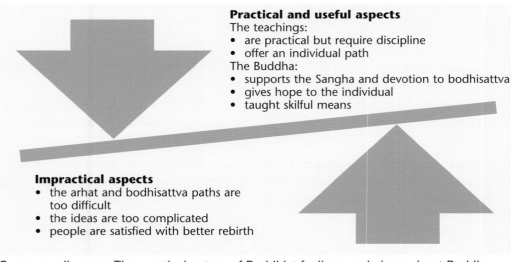

Practical and useful aspects
The teachings:
• are practical but require discipline
• offer an individual path
The Buddha:
• supports the Sangha and devotion to bodhisattva
• gives hope to the individual
• taught skilful means

Impractical aspects
• the arhat and bodhisattva paths are too difficult
• the ideas are too complicated
• people are satisfied with better rebirth

Summary diagram: The practical nature of Buddhist feelings and views about Buddha

KEY QUESTIONS

• Is there a consistent view of the exact nature of the Buddha in Theravada Buddhism?
• Is the idea of faith in Buddhas and bodhisattvas really a Buddhist ideal?
• Does it really matter who the Buddha was? Surely it is dhamma that should be the guiding light?
• Does the Mahayana cosmology make Buddhism more similar to the Indian religious views superseded by the Buddha through nibbana?
• Does the Buddha become more divine in Mahayana Buddhism?

EXAM TIP

Always refer back to the question in your answers, demonstrating that you 'comprehend the demand of the question' (level 5, AO2).

TASK

Make a list of the strengths and weaknesses of both the path taken by the arahat and the bodhisattva path. It may be helpful to discuss this as a group first.
Objective To produce an evaluation of the diversity of views and practices within Buddhism, evaluating different views (essential for success, AO2)

TASK

Use these key points as a basis for a writing frame to answer the question:

'The bodhisattva path is greater than that path taken by the arhat.' Discuss.   (10 marks)

Remember to add relevant quotes and questions at suitable places.

Objective To build an argument that uses a 'range of evidence to sustain an argument' (AO2 level 5)

Reflection and assessment AO2

It is vital to bring together the information you have covered so far and recognise how it can be transformed into effective examination-style revision and answers. The best way to do this is to ask the question: 'How am I going to be assessed on this information?'

Look back to page 8 in the Introduction to review the level descriptors for AO2. There is a description of the character and features for each level. The exam is marked with reference to levels.

Look at the key points, below, in answer to the question:

'The bodhisattva path is greater than that path taken by the arhat.' Discuss.

(10 marks)

You will need to refer to these points, which are not presented in any particular order, to complete the task.

- For an arhat it is personal spiritual progression.
- A bodhisattva puts off the escape from samsara to help others.
- The bodhisattva appears more compassionate and selfless than the arhat.
- The Theravadin tradition would argue that the arhat practises selflessness.
- The arhat's aim is progression through the traditional teachings.
- The bodhisattva's aim is to help countless other beings to search for and aspire to enlightenment before themselves.
- The path of a bodhisattva is much longer and could be argued to be more challenging.

The list is deliberately basic. At this stage you should be able to recognise that it contains the general issues but does not have the detail for development. You will need to add this.

Suggestion for further application of skills

You will now be focusing on revision skills and, more importantly, past questions. Now you have developed your skills in essay preparation to this stage, return to other topics of critical analysis (Part 3 in each topic in this unit) and consider some key questions. Aim to build up some responses to these key questions.

Glossary

A posteriori from, or after, experience

A priori prior to, without reference to, experience

Abhinnas supramundane powers or supernatural powers

Absolutist an ethical system involving rules that are to be followed by all people at all times, in all circumstances; the idea that actions are right or wrong, devoid of the context

Act utilitarianism a form of utilitarianism in which people are to act in the way that will produce the best actual overall consequences

Ahimsa non-violence

Ajiva livelihood

Allegory narrative in which objects, persons and actions are equated with meanings that lie outside the narrative itself

Anagama non-returner

Anagarika homeless one

Analogy a comparison of two or more things to show how they are similar

Analytic existential propositions propositions that are about existence and are analytic, having the property that no new information is added

Analytic statements statements of which the truth value is determined by the definition of their concepts

Anatta not-self; the Buddhist idea that there is no metaphysical and permanently existing entity, such as a soul or self, within a person

Anicca change or impermanence

Apocalyptic a type of literature with a narrative framework, containing certain features such as obscure symbolism and mysterious revelations; often, but not always, about the end times

Apologetic concerned with defensive arguments, particularly in Christianity

Apostolic Age the time of the twelve apostles, from the time of Jesus' death and resurrection to the Fall of Jerusalem in CE70; the period is detailed, in part, in the book of the Acts of the Apostles

Applied ethics debates that arise in discussion of ethical issues

Aramaic a semitic language, spoken by Jesus, that is closely related to Hebrew and gradually replaced it amongst the Jews

Arannika forest monk

Argument a set of statements such that one of them (the conclusion) is supported or implied by the others (the premises)

Arhat one who has realised nibbana and is no longer to be reborn

Aristotelian of, or relating to, Aristotle

Aryan invaders from the West of India referred to by their pale skin

Ascetic living a very disciplined lifestyle

Atman individual soul

Atonement the reconciliation of human beings with God through the sacrificial death of Christ

Attribute a property, quality or feature belonging to a person or thing

Begging-bowl a bowl used *not* for begging but to allow people to offer food to the monks

Beneficial order a regular arrangement that produces an advantage or assistance

Bhikkhu Buddhist monk

Bhikkhuni Buddhist nun

Bhumi stage of the bodhisattva path

Big-Bang theory the theory of an expanding Universe that began as an infinitely dense and hot medium at some finite time in the past; the initial instant is called the Big Bang

Birth the point at which the child is separated from the mother and becomes a separate entity

Blastocyst a group of multiplying cells

Bodhi the wisdom by which one attains enlightenment

Bodhicitta intelligent consciousness

Bodhisattva a being whose essence is intelligence

Brahman universal spirit or soul

Brahmin priest

Brahminism religion based upon priestly rituals and sacrifices

Buddha enlightened one; one who possesses insight into ultimate and perfect wisdom

Buddha ksetra Buddha field or Universe

Buddhology issues surrounding the nature, person and status of the Buddha

Categorical imperative an unconditional moral law that applies to all rational beings and is independent of any personal motive or desire (For Kant, *the* categorical imperative was the principle that one should act on a maxim only if one can will that it becomes a universal law.)

Chastity living a life free from human and emotional attachments

Church tradition writings and oral traditions passed down and accepted by the Church

Classical theism the belief in a personal deity, creator of everything that exists and who is distinct from that creation

Cloning acquiring a group of genetically identical cells from a single cell; making identical copies of a gene

Codex in the form of a book where the pages are bound together, as against a scroll

Codex Sinaiticus a fourth-century manuscript housed in the British Museum; contains part of the Old Testament and the complete New Testament in Greek

Codex Vaticanus the most famous manuscript, in the possession of the Vatican library, believed to be fourth century; thought to be the oldest and most complete copy of the Greek Bible in existence

Concentration employment of all one's powers or attention

Conclusion a statement that purports to be drawn from a set of premises

Consciousness awareness of self

Consequentialism another name for teleological ethics

Contingent that which need not be, that which could have been different; something that has dependency

Contingent being a being that either in fact exists, but might not have, or that does not in fact exist, but might have.

Continuity occurs at the first point at which potential life is recognisable

Cosmology the scientific study of the origin and nature of the Universe

Councils gatherings to discuss matters of discipline and teaching held by the various monastic orders of the day (Sangha)

Counter-argument an argument that sets out to refute another argument

Covenant God bestows his favour on the people

Cullavagga the second section of the Khandhaka

Dana giving, the best example of selflessness

Darwinism the theory of natural selection to account for changes in nature

Day of Atonement also known as Yom Kippur, the most solemn of the Jewish festivals where the theme is repentance (Leviticus 23: 26–32)

Deduction a process of reasoning by which the conclusion is shown to follow necessarily from the premises

Deontological focusing on the rightness or wrongness of actions themselves, rather than the rightness or wrongness of the consequences

Deontological ethics any ethical system that is concerned with the act itself rather than the consequences of the act

Dhamma Buddhist teaching

Dhamma Cakka Pavattana turning of the wheel of dhamma

Dharma social duty or the law or as a general term, teaching

Dharmakaya ultimate body of truth

Dhyana meditation or meditative trance

Digha Nikaya section of the Sutta Pitaka

Disinterested having no stake in something

Ditthi view

Divine command theory a system of ideas or commandments given by a supreme being

Divine law God's law mediated through special revelation; the Bible and the Church

Doctors of the law mostly Pharisees, more associated with giving teaching through speaking rather than written opinions

Doctrine of double effect even if a good act has bad consequences, it is still right to do it

Dosa hatred

Double effect even if a good act has bad

consequences, then it is still right to do it

Doublets sayings that occur twice in Matthew and twice in Luke, seeming to support the existence of Q since, in both gospels, one of the sayings could be from Mark and one could be from Q

Dukkha suffering or frustration, refer to the first Noble Truth

Early Church an ambiguous term used to denote the Church at its inception or through its development in the first five years

Edicts public announcements

Eight-fold path the ultimate teaching of Buddhism; the practical measures needed to become enlightened

Embryo an animal in the early stage of development before birth; in humans, the embryo stage is the first three months after conception

Empirical based on evidence and experience

Empiricism knowledge only comes through experience and testing

Empiricist a person who takes the view that the dominant foundation of knowledge is experience

Enhancement gene therapy attempts to make an already functional person better than they are

Enlightenment ultimate wisdom

Ensoulment the point when the soul enters the body

Epistemic distance God is

hidden and so this allows human beings to choose freely

Epistemology a branch of philosophy concerned with the nature, sources and limits of knowledge

Eschatology a study of the last things and final events; often linked to the arrival of the Messianic Age

Eternal law order in the mind of God

Ethical and religious pacifism belief that war cannot be condoned on any grounds

Ethics a theory or system of moral values

Eucharist an alternative name for the celebration of the Last Supper, from the Greek word for thanksgiving

Eudaimonia a contented state of being happy, healthy and prosperous

Eugenics the belief that information about heredity can be used to improve the human race

Euthanasia the ending of one person's life by another, usually to relieve suffering

Ex nihilo Latin, meaning out of nothing; God did not use any previously existing materials when he created the Universe

Fallacy unsound reasoning

Fetus the unborn baby from the end of the eighth week after conception (when the major structures have formed) until birth

Form an abstract property or quality, that which makes something what it is; it is not just an idea, but exists independently in a different mode of existence (Plato's *Theory of Forms* is also called the *Theory of Ideas or Ideals*)

Form of the Good that which is responsible for whatever is right and valuable in anything

Four Noble Truths the Buddha's teaching in its simplest form; the four teachings that explain the reality of our world

Fruitful description of actions that will yield positive results

Gamavasin another term for village monk

Gantha dhura book duty or study

Garden of Gethsemane *literally* garden of the oil press, the quiet garden area at the foot of the Mount of Olives where Jesus prayed after the Last Supper

Genetic engineering the artificial introduction of changes to the genes in a cell

Genocide mass killing, unlawful mass murder; the intentional destruction or eradication of an entire racial, political, cultural or religious group

Germ cells reproductive cells; the egg and sperm cells

Germ line the line or sequence of germ cells that have genetic material that maybe passed to a child

God's goodness all that God is and does is worthy of approval

God's omnipresence there is nowhere free from God's presence

God's omniscience God knows all things, actual and possible

Good news literal meaning of gospel

Good will the highest form of good, not concerned with consequences or self-interest

Gospel of Thomas found in 1945 in Egypt and thought to date back to 200CE, it contains 114 sayings attributed to Jesus

Grace a state of sanctification by God

Great commission the last recorded personal instruction given by Jesus to his disciples, emphasising mission work, evangelism, and baptism

Hagiography a spiritual or religious biography

Hedonic calculus a method of calculating the degree or amount of pleasure that a specific action is likely to cause

Hedonism an ethical theory that defines what is right in terms of pleasure

Henotheism the worship of one god as the special god of one's tribe or clan

Hierarchy arranged in a graded order

Hiri shame, reflecting the idea of self-responsibility and encouraging self-respect

Holy Communion an alternative name for the celebration of the Last Supper

Holy of Holies the inner sanctuary of the Temple, only the High Priest could enter and then only on the Day of Atonement

Hypothetical imperative a moral command that is conditional on personal motive or desire

Immaterial that which is not formed of matter

Impermanence the idea that the universe is in an unstable state of flux

Induction a process of reasoning that draws a general conclusion from specific instances

Ineffable impossible to explain in words

Inoffensiveness following the principle of non-harm to all living beings

Jataka sutras narrating the birth stories of the Buddha in past lives, and effects related to the past and the present lives

Jhanas four absorptions or stages of meditation through which one passes to reach enlightenment

Jiva the Jain interpretation of, or replacement for, the idea of a soul

Jnana knowledge

Jus ad bellum a set of criteria to be consulted before engaging in war, in order to determine whether entering into war is justifiable

Jus in bello law stating acceptable practices while engaged in war, such as the Geneva Conventions

Jus post bello suggested rules about justice after a war, including peace treaties, reconstruction, war crimes trials and war reparations

Just war a specific concept of how warfare might be justified, typically in accordance with a particular situation or scenario

Kamma (Pali) intentional actions, good or bad, bringing consequences and affecting this and future lives

Kammanta action

Karma (sanskit) *see* kamma

Karuna compassion; sometimes interpreted as the idea that concern for others demonstrates selflessness

Khandhaka the section of the Vinaya Pitaka that offers guidance on issues of organisation and discipline for the monastic life and the Sangha as a whole

Khandhas the five factors that constitute a person

Kilesas the poisons, fires or defilements: negative qualities that motivate a person and keep them attached to the cycle of existence

Ksanti patience

Latinisms Latin words that have been transliterated into Greek characters; generally refers to transcribing words written in one alphabet or writing system into another

Levites members of the tribe of Levi, responsible for many of the duties in the Temple

Liturgy a particular order or form of public service prescribed by a Church

Lobha greed

Logic a branch of philosophy that is concerned with the process of reasoning

Logos fundamental principle

Lord's Supper an alternative name for the celebration of Eucharist

Magga the eight-fold path

Maha-parinibbana Sutta the story of the death of the Buddha

Mahavagga the first section of the Khandhaka

Mahayana greater vehicle, the term given to the types of Buddhism different from Theravada

Mass from the Latin *missa*, meaning dismissal, a word used in the final sentence of the service celebrating the Last Supper

Matter that of which something is made

Maxim a general rule or principle governing the action of a rational person

Medical abortion by means of the abortion pill

Medical futility a situation in which treatment achieves no positive medical results, or is against the patient's best interests

Meditation the specific practice of concentration that the Buddha taught

Meditative planes accessed through the fourth jhana, these are specific states of mind

Messiah in Jewish tradition, a future Jewish king from the line of David, who will rule the Jewish people during the Messianic Age; the Messiah is associated with events of the end times

Messianic banquet a celebration when the Messiah brings in the Kingdom of God

Metaphysics literally after physics; Aristotle's book, *Metaphysics*, examines the question: 'What is being?', seeking to explain the ultimate nature of being

Middle way the balance between the extremes of asceticism and a life of luxury

Minuscules early texts were all written in capital letters; manuscripts

written in lower-case letters that went below base line (minuscules) appeared later

Modal relating to the form of a thing, for example, necessary, possible

Moha delusion

Moksha escape from the cycle of rebirth

Monotheism the belief or doctrine that there is only one god

Moral relating to human behaviour and what ought and ought not to be done

Morality the application of an ethical theory to produce appropriate conduct; conformity to moral principles

Natural law an ethical system based on the view that humans have a set of natural inclinations that, if followed, will lead to the perfection of our being

Natural theology establishing truths about God through human reason rather than revelation

Naturalistic fallacy when moral judgements are confused with factual judgements; an error in reasoning to conclude how the world ought to be from observing how the world actually is, goodness is not a property of nature

Necessary being a being that, if it exists, cannot *not* exist, whose non-existence would be a self-contradiction (This is its sense in the ontological argument. It can also be used in the causal sense, of a being who is required as an explanation.)

Nibbana enlightenment; the highest aspiration for all Buddhists

Nidanas the 12 links in the chain of conditioned arising

Nirmanakaya transformation body

Nirodha *literally* cessation or stopping; to stop (grasping); refer to the third Noble Truth

Nirvana inexpressible enlightenment, impossible to put into words

Niyati destiny

Objective external to the mind, real or true regardless of subject and their point of view

Ontology a branch of metaphysics dealing with the nature of being; the study of being, or what is

Oral law law passed down, by word of mouth

Oral period the period when the stories and sayings were passed around only by word of mouth; the period of verbal transmission, before the words were written down

Oral tradition the practice of collecting, ordering and passing on information by word of mouth

Ottappa complete awareness of intentions and motives behind moral actions

Pabbajja going forth

Pacifism the doctrine that all violence is unjustifiable; opposition to war or violence as a means of settling disputes

Pali Canon Buddhist scriptures

Pancasila the five moral precepts

Panna wisdom

Pantheism the idea that the whole of the Universe is identical to God or is, in

some way, an expression of his nature

Paramita perfection

Parinibbana passing over into nibbana

Parivara the final section of the Vinaya Pitaka, which summarises all the Vinaya for teaching monks and setting examinations

Parivarta turning over, referring to passing on merit earned

Passion narrative the description of the events leading up to the death of Jesus

Passover a Jewish festival commemorating the liberation of the Israelites from Egypt

Paticcasamuppada *literally* conditioned arising or dependent origination, the Buddhist view of the 12-part causal chain of events that gives rise to existence

Patimokka specific rules, traditionally 227, for Buddhist monks living in a monastery

Patron person who supports or sponsors

Persistent vegetative state (PVS) a state in which body processes are maintained but the brain is functioning only at its lowest automatic levels

Petrine of or relating to Peter

Phenomenal composed of or relating to things that occupy space and can be perceived by the senses

Piyadasi title given to Asoka, meaning beloved of the gods

Platonic relating to Plato or his teachings

Platonism the teachings of Plato and his followers

Possible world anything that can be conceived of, or is logically consistent

Potential the possibility, at conception, of becoming a human person

Poverty living a simple life with basic needs

Prajna wisdom

Prajna paramita perfect wisdom

Pranidhana vows of a bodhisattva

Pratyeka Buddha solitary or lonely Buddha (with reference to an arhat)

Precept rule of personal conduct, or doctrine that is taught

Preference utilitarianism an ethical theory that sees actions as right when they allow the greatest number to live according to their own preferences, even if those preferences are not those that will make them experience the most pleasure

Premise a statement that forms part of an argument from which a conclusion is drawn

Prime Mover the self-moved being that causes all motion

Principle of utility an action is right if it maximises happiness

Pro-choice supporting women's rights to have abortions

Pro-life against abortion

Punabhava rebirth

Q source of common sayings

Qua A Latin word meaning 'as relating to'

Quelle (Q) the material common to Matthew and Luke, but not found in Mark, consisting mostly of sayings

Quickening traditionally, when the child is first felt to move inside the mother

Rabbi from the Hebrew meaning great in knowledge, refers to a Jewish religious teacher

Rabbinic relating to the rabbis

Real predicate something that adds to our concept of the subject

Rebirth the transfer of energies from one form to another; to the next incarnation at the point of death

Relational factors different interpretations of the same words or terms, depending on the viewpoint of the observer

Relativist an ethical system that has no fixed rules but each action depends on the situation

Reproductive cloning the cloning of an embryo for transplantation into a uterus with the intention of producing offspring genetically identical to the donor

Right (in Ethics) doing what is morally acceptable

Rule utilitarianism a form of utilitarianism in which general rules rather than acts are assessed for utility

Sabbath the seventh day of creation when God rested; in Judaism, it is observed from sundown on Friday until sundown on Saturday

Sadhu an itinerant holy man

Sakadagami once-returner

Samadhi meditation or concentration

Samana a group of wandering holy men or philosophers who were trying to find answers to ultimate questions

Samanera novice, trainee monk or nun

Sambhogakaya enjoyment body

Samma right

Samma-sambodhi perfect enlightenment

Samma-sambuddha self-enlightened one

Samma-sambuddhasa the perfectly self-enlightened one

Samsara cycle of existence: life, death and reincarnation or rebirth

Samudaya arising

Sanctity of life the belief that life is sacred or holy, given by God

Sangha the Buddhist monastic community; Buddhist monks, nuns and lay people

Sanhedrin a Jewish judicial body who ruled mostly over religious issues

Sankappa thought

Sarana refuge, of which there are three for a Buddhist: Buddha, dhamma and Sangha

Sati mindfulness

Scribes the interpreters, preservers and teachers of the law; scribes of the Pharisees (Mark 2: 16) may have been Pharisees who were learned in law

Selflessness the idea that there is not a permanent essence within a person as all is impermanent

Shema the first word of Deuteronomy 6: 4

Sila morality, moral living or moral virtue; one of the three aspects of the eight-fold path comprising right speech, action and livelihood

Sima monastic boundary

Situationist individual circumstances rather than sets of rules determine the outcome of any ethical dilemma

Sitz im leben literally life situation; the Early Church used particular material to meet particular needs and situations within their community, often taking the material out of its original context; refers to these possible Early Church circumstances

Skilful description of intelligent or wise actions

Skilful means the application of wisdom so that kammic benefits are maximised

Somatic cell any cell in the body that is not a sperm or egg cell

Sotapanna stream-enterer

Soteriology a personal religious quest

Source non-specific term that does not make clear whether it is written or oral; in contrast, a document is a written source

Source criticism the attempted identification of the sources of documents

Study (in Buddhism) to remember and preserve the Dhamma

Stupa monument built as a memorial to the Buddha and usually containing parts of his remains

Subjective having its source within the mind; a particular point of view, dependent on the subject

Suffering the idea that life involves dissatisfaction

Summum bonum the highest good; the supreme good from which all others derive; the ultimate end or goal to which human beings ought to aspire; comprises both virtue and happiness

Sunyata emptiness of all phenomena

Supramundane paranormal or extraordinary powers accessed through advanced meditation

Surgical abortion abortion by means of the suction method

Surrogacy one woman carrying a baby for another woman who cannot do so herself

Sutras Mahayana writings or scriptures

Sutta Pitaka the second section of the Pali Canon – Buddhist scriptures

Sutta Vibhanga the commentary on the Patimokka and the first part of the Vinaya Pitaka

Symbolism the use of one thing to represent another, generally important ideas or beliefs

Synagogue place of meeting for prayer and reading the Torah

Synoptic *literally* seeing together, identifying similarities between the first three gospels set out in parallel

Synoptic gospels the first three gospels: Matthew, Mark and Luke

Synthetic statements statements of which the truth value cannot be determined by the definition of their concepts

Talmud a record of rabbinic discussions about Jewish law, ethics, customs and history

Tanakh a word formed from the initial letters of the three parts that make up the Hebrew Bible (Torah/Nevi'im/Ketuvim) as a collective term for what Christians call the Old Testament

Tanha craving, grasping or attachment, the main cause of suffering; refer to the second Noble Truth

Tathagata *literally* thus gone one or one who is gone thus, another term for the Buddha

Tathagatagarbha Buddha nature, the inherent ability to become a Buddha

Teleological explanation by reference to end, goal or purpose

Teleological ethics any ethical system that is concerned with consequences of actions

Teleology the study of the Universe in terms of ends or final causes

Theodicy a justification of the righteousness of God, given the existence of evil

Therapeutic cloning cloning an embryo for the purpose of deriving stem cells for therapeutic uses

Theravada *literally* the way of the elders, it focuses on the devotion to and support of the sangha as the primary source of teaching and example

Ti-lakkhana the three characteristics of existence

Tiratana the three jewels, another term for the three refuges

Torah usually refers to the first five books (the law books) of the Hebrew Bible

Tosefta *literally* supplement, a supplement to the oral law in Judaism

Transcendent having existence outside the Universe

Transmigration the passing over of one consciousness stream into another

Transubstantiation idea that the bread and wine change in substance but not in outward appearance

Trikaya three bodies

Truth value whether a statement is actually true or false

Upasampada ordination

Upaya kausalya skilful means

Utilitarian ethical doctrine that the moral worth of an action is solely determined by its contribution to overall utility

Utilitarianism an ethical theory that maintains that an action is right if it produces the greatest balance of good over evil; morality of actions is therefore based on consequences for human happiness

Vaca speech

Valid a logically correct argument

Value judgement an assessment that reveals more about the values of the person making it than about the reality of what is assessed

Vannavasin village monk

Vayama effort

Viability the ability to grow and develop into an adult, especially the ability of the child to exist without dependence on the mother

Vinaya discipline, rules of conduct

Vinaya Pitaka the first section of the Pali Canon

Vipassana dhura insight,

duty or meditation

Virya vigour

Vows personal undertakings rather than rules

Weapons of mass destruction weapons capable of killing enormous numbers of people

Wholesome description of positive and beneficial actions

Wisdom ability to apply knowledge and experience critically

Wrong (in Ethics) failing to do what you should do

Yoga *literally* to unite or join; union; in Hinduism, a method for becoming one with the Universal spirit, referring to the atman and Brahman

Zygote a cell formed by the union of a male sex cell (a sperm) and a female sex cell (an ovum), which develops into the embryo according to information encoded in its genetic material